The Secret Ceremonies

The Secret Ceremonies

Critical Essays on Arthur Machen

Edited by Mark Valentine and Timothy J. Jarvis

Hippocampus Press
New York

The Secret Ceremonies: Critical Essays on Arthur Machen
Copyright © 2019 by Hippocampus Press

All works are © 2019 by their respective creators and used by permission.
Selection and editorial matter © 2019 by Mark Valentine and Timothy J. Jarvis.

Published by Hippocampus Press
P.O. Box 641, New York, NY 10156.
www.hippocampuspress.com

All rights reserved.
No part of this work may be reproduced in any form or by any means without the written permission of the publisher.

Cover illustration by Nicholas Day (1935).
Frontispiece photograph by E. O. Hoppé, provided by Mark Valentine.
Cover design by Daniel V. Sauer, dansauerdesign.com.
Hippocampus Press logo designed by Anastasia Damianakos.

First Edition
1 3 5 7 9 8 6 4 2

ISBN 978-1-61498-245-6 trade paperback
ISBN 978-1-61498-261-6 ebook

Contents

Introduction 7
    MARK VALENTINE

I. Biography and Bibliography 13
    Arthur Machen: The Evils of Materialism 15
        S. T. JOSHI
    Arthur Machen: The Pagan—His Work and His Personality 27
        GEOFFREY H. WELLS
    Arthur Machen: A Novelist of Ecstasy and Sin 31
        VINCENT STARRETT
    About My Books 41
        ARTHUR MACHEN
    The City, the Vision, and Arthur Machen 61
        GODFREY BRANGHAM

II. Aestheticism and Decadence 73
    The Book in Yellow: How Dorian Inspired Lucian 75
        ROGER DOBSON
    A Yellow Creeper 81
        ARTHUR RICKETT
    Arthur Machen and Decadence: The Flower-Tunicked Priest of
       New Grub Street 85
        JAMES MACHIN
    New Arabian Frights: Unholy Trinities and the Masks of Helen 101
        ROGER DOBSON
    A Glow in the Sky: Some Observations on Machen's Style 117
        JON PREECE
    The Secret and the Secrets: A Look at Machen's *Hieroglyphics* 129
        JOHN HOWARD

III. Mysticism, Magic, and Paganism 137
    Arthur Machen's Panic Fears: Western Esotericism and the Irruption
       of Negative Epistemology 139
        MARCO PASI

A Fit Symbol for His Meaning: Arthur Machen and the Inexpressible ... 161
    KAREN JOAN KOHOUTEK
The Revenge of Vulcan 171
    G. J. COOLING
Perfume of the Trellised Vine 173
    RON WEIGHELL
Of Sacred Groves and Ancient Mysteries: Parallel Themes in the
    Writings of Arthur Machen and John Buchan 181
    PETER BELL
Beyond the Veil of Reality: Mysticism in Arthur Machen's "The White
    People" 199
    EMILY FOSTER
Sanctity Plus Sorcery: The Curious Christianity of Arthur Machen 209
    IAIN SMITH
"The Abyss of All Being": "The Great God Pan" and the Death of
    Metaphysics 221
    GEOFFREY REITER
Arthur Machen and King Arthur, Sovereigns of Dream: A Personal
    Interpretation 239
    DONALD SIDNEY-FRYER

IV. Myths and Wonders 331
The Impossible History: Machen's "A Fragment of Life" 333
    JOHN HOWARD
Three Great Hoaxes of the War 345
    ALEISTER CROWLEY
The Canning Enigma: Some Observations on Arthur Machen's
    The Canning Wonder 351
    JEREMY CANTWELL
"All Manner of Mysteries": Encounters with the Numinous in
    The Cosy Room and Other Stories 359
    JAMES MACHIN
Some Thoughts on "N" 367
    THOMAS KENT MILLER
"It Is Getting Very Late & Dark": Machen's Last Fiction 381
    MARK VALENTINE

Bibliography 391
Acknowledgments 397
Index 401

Introduction

Mark Valentine

There were, indeed, many Arthur Machens. The one I found first was the youthful dreamer living near "that noble, fallen Caerleon-on-Usk," his home town in Gwent, and imaging himself back among the white walls and fountain-haunted gardens of the Roman city (FOT 8). In the semi-autobiographical *The Hill of Dreams* (1907), I read with burning joy of a boy trying to begin the adventure of literature and to perfect a sort of spiritual alchemy, in which the things of the senses are transmuted to a mystical exaltation. Soon after, I found in "The Great God Pan" (1894) and other tales, the maker of dark myths, the 'Nineties bohemian who shocked the prudish with his tales of mad doctors, lascivious *femmes fatales*, and glimpses of the abyss.

Then there was the man-about-town, exploring with vast curiosity the by-ways of the great city and assuring us, in *The Three Impostors* (1895) and elsewhere, that the mysteries may be found in the meanest quarters, and in the turn and the chance we least expect. Soon there was also the aesthete and decadent who composed some of the most exquisite prose-poems ever written, in his *Ornaments of Jade* (written in the 1890s but not published in book form until 1924), rife with half-stifled eroticism and the drift of incense in the high roads of London. What, too, of the literary hermit, that votary of De Quincey and Pickwick, who proclaimed, in *Hieroglyphics* (1902), that ecstasy was the touchstone of true literature?

Later still, in *The Secret Glory* (1922), there was the scholar searching out legends of the Holy Grail, hinting at vessels kept in secret cupboards in lonely Welsh farmhouses, and tracing the idea of a lost Mass of the early Celtic church; and the Grail was seen in glory also in a little Welsh harbour town in *The Great Return* (1915). Then there was the married man and respectable journalist mulling over the war news as he sat on his pew in church, mingling it with his medieval imagination and creating, in "The Bowmen," a national myth that men and women came to believe was true. I do not overlook either the splendid essayist, the master of the digression, who in *Dog and Duck* (1924) gave the world with all due solemnity the history of that recondite bowling game, with its quaint terms and customs.

And I found, to my surprise at first, that there were other readers who, relishing all these, still said they were not the best of Machen, which must be found in his memoirs, *Far Off Things* (1922), *Things Near and Far* (1923), and that strange Persian carpet of a book, *The London Adventure* (1924). There, they said, is the essence of him, in his evocations of the deep lanes of old Monmouthshire, the ancient white farmhouses alone in the hills, the primeval stones, and the stile where he would lean to give the postman his latest manuscript. And I soon came to understand that view of the matter, while never quite yielding the prime of place I gave to his two great spiritual romances, *The Hill of Dreams* and *The Secret Glory*.

Even these do not bring us to the end of the many Machens. There was the young man, alone in a garret in London, subsisting on dry bread, green tea, and dark tobacco, who catalogued occult books, studying, as he said, "that inclination of the human mind which may be a survival from the rites of the black swamp and the cave or—an anticipation of a wisdom and knowledge that are to come, transcending all the science of our day" (*TNF* 17). Then there was the strolling player who went on the stage at the age of forty and "wrote his own part in Shakespeare" (*SL* 251), as he jocularly remarked, for he was allowed to devise authentic magical incantations for his part as the conjurer Bolingbroke in *Henry VI, Part 2*. And when he was rich in years, if never in gold, here was the venerable man of letters, patient mentor to so many younger writers and votaries, who delighted in his company for the sake of his sonorous voice, his treasury of piquant tales, his relish for the simple pleasures of the table, the tankard, and the tobacco bowl, and most of all his faithful, unwavering allegiance to the Mysteries.

This is to say nothing, of course, of the lost tales: the pages and chapters torn up in the days when Machen was working to perfect his own style and to write the Great Romance; the yarns he wrote for the *Unicorn*, a 'Nineties journal that proved to be almost as mythical as its title, and which included one in which a suburban clerk becomes a werewolf at night; the romance of the maze, and of the dance, and of the vine, outlined in *The London Adventure*, but never devised; and the book for which he solemnly reserved the title *The Dark Lantern and the Mask*, saying that it would be his last treatise, *libellus vere mysticus* (always that fondness for Latin tags), which he would write "when the turmoil has died down, when the clouds have cleared for the sunset, and the apparition of the evening star, as I sit by a western shore awaiting the boat of Avalon" (*FOT* 106). These pleasant works we shall find only upon the yew-wood shelves of the celestial library, if ever we find our way there. They shall be robed in scarlet and purple like the sunsets of the western lands and adorned with gilded blazons, and their pages, white as apple-blossom from the cider orchards of Gwent, will be printed in ink as black as the boughs of the trees of Wentwood in winter.

Arthur Machen's writing has always inspired both ardent advocates and determined opponents. In the 1890s, Oscar Wilde, Jerome K. Jerome, and Sir Arthur Conan Doyle admired his work, but the majority of critics were hostile, and he was often seen as part of the Decadent movement of the "Yellow 'Nineties." Machen later compiled *Precious Balms* (1924) devoted entirely to the vituperation he had received during these years. The *Manchester Guardian*, for example, called *The Great God Pan and The Inmost Light* "the most acutely and intentionally disagreeable" book it had seen in English: a blunder, said Machen, as it was "a valuable free advertisement" (xiii). Other reviews were equally pungent: the *Observer* said, "one shakes with laughter rather than with dread"; and the slangy *Sketch* claimed that "his bogles don't scare" (xiii). There were, in fact, more positive notices, but the hostile reception was the more typical.

In the Edwardian period, he was warmly praised by the poet John Masefield and by the Worcestershire novelists Francis and Eric Brett Young, and his landmark collection *The House of Souls* (1906) brought him acclaim, but he still met strong antipathy. The Modernist magazine the *New Age*, edited by A. R. Orage, carried out from 1911 to 1916 a five-year campaign of sniping and sneering against him, calling him "this cackling old gander of Carmelite Street"[1] (the headquarters of the *Evening News*, the newspaper for which he then worked). During the First World War, his story "The Bowmen," which gave rise to the legend of the Angels of Mons, brought him a measure of fame, but he was widely reproached for claiming (truthfully) that the story was his alone: people wanted to believe it was true. Several pamphlets, and numerous sermons, inveighed against him for casting doubt on the authenticity of the visions supposed to have been witnessed by troops in the trenches. This moved the poet and magician Aleister Crowley to come to his defense, in an essay reprinted here.

---

1. A. R. Orage, *New Age* 12, No. 7 (19 December 1912): 156.

It was only in the 1920s that an American-led boom at last garnered him the praise and respect he deserved. Champions such as Vincent Starrett, Carl Van Vechten, Robert Hillyer, James Branch Cabell, and Paul Jordan-Smith celebrated him in essays and by word of mouth, and soon a minor cult was created. His books were reprinted across the Atlantic, new work was commissioned, and book collectors sought out his titles avidly. He also began to be appreciated as a general man of letters, and his lyrical autobiographies and collections of essays appeared.

Though this surge of interest dwindled a little in the 1930s, he found a new crusader in the poet and bibliophile John Gawsworth, who wrote the first biography of him (though it was not to be published until 2005) and persuaded publishers to bring out both old and new work by Machen. In the 1940s, in semi-retirement in Amersham, Buckinghamshire, with his wife, Purefoy, he became the center of a new circle of young admirers, including Colin Summerford and the authors Frank Baker, Edwin Greenwood, Norah Hoult, Morchard Bishop (the pen-name of Oliver Stonor), and Sylvia Townsend Warner (Machen's niece by marriage). He also achieved a substantial readership for the first time with a Penguin paperback of some of his stories, even if they were not his best (*Holy Terrors*, 1946).

After his death in 1947, his reputation was maintained mainly by a strong selection of his stories, *Tales of Horror and the Supernatural*, edited by Philip Van Doren Stern (1949), and by a new edition of his first two books of memoirs, as *The Autobiography of Arthur Machen* (1951), edited and introduced by Morchard Bishop. His centenary in 1963 was marked by a selection of appreciative essays compiled by the Carmelite friar and literary figure Fr. Brocard Sewell, by a BBC radio program, and by the first substantial biography, *Arthur Machen: A Short Account of His Life and Work* by Aidan Reynolds and William Charlton. American critic Wesley D. Sweetser provided the first full critical study the following year (*Arthur Machen*, 1964), and in 1965 the definitive bibliography appeared, compiled by Adrian Goldstone and Sweetser, an extremely thorough survey and a model in its field. All Machen readers and scholars are indebted to this landmark work.

Some of Machen's work was caught up in the counter-culture of the 1960s and the new zest for the fantastic in literature, and some of his books and stories in this vein found paperback publication for the first time. However, there was a decided lull in the next two decades, so that by the time I discovered his books, in the late 1970s, I was convinced I must be one of the few people who appreciated his work. Virtually all his books went out of print, he could not be found in most literary reference books, and he was once again the preserve of a few *cognoscenti*.

Gradually, this neglect began to be addressed, and in the last twenty years a new enthusiasm and appreciation has arisen. It would be fair to say that critical and creative responses to his work are now wider and richer than ever before. Not just in literature, but in music, film, and the visual arts, Arthur Machen is now celebrated for the beauty and strangeness of his visions. It remains the case, however, that his work still calls for proper study: there is the critical neglect of more than a century to put right. In this volume, we seek to offer a selection that will make a contribution to that task. As these demonstrate, both Machen's major and lesser-known works reward close attention.

The first section provides important contextual information about Machen's life and works. S. T. Joshi provides a judicious summary of Machen's writing and philosophy. We reprint two essays that give a clear impression of how Machen was regarded in the 1920s, when his books began to emerge from the shadows. As part of this new interest, the bookseller Henry Danielson published the first bibliography of his work, and Machen provided a fascinating, often rueful, commentary on each of his books, which is both helpful for understanding how they each came about and an attractive example of his later style. Though he grew up in Gwent, the Welsh/English border county, Machen left there at the age of eighteen and seldom returned: he spent by far the greater part of his adult life in London, which he came to regard as the map of a great mystery. He spent many hours exploring its obscure back-streets, by-ways, and squares, and Godfrey Brangham's essay explains the significance of the city in his work.

In the second section, we offer contributions concerned with Machen's role as a figure of the 1890s and a participant in the Decadent movement. His first two important books, *The Great God Pan* and *The Three Impostors*, were both issued by the modish publisher John Lane, in its Keynotes series, a touchstone for the 'Nineties style, and had covers designed by Aubrey Beardsley, the *enfant terrible* of the period. Machen himself admitted his books benefited from the noise of the 'Nineties but claimed he was not really part of the *fin-de-siècle* ambience. However, as the essays here show, this is not quite the full picture. Included is a contemporary pastiche, "A Yellow Creeper" by Arthur Rickett, which certainly places him as quintessential to the time.

Though these 'Nineties books were written under the influence of the macabre work of Poe and Stevenson, Machen soon saw that he had to perfect his own style, and he devoted many anguished hours to the task. At the same time he yearned to convey "awe" not "awfulness": the spiritual intensity he felt in certain landscapes. Though it is for his darker tales that he is often most remembered, the greater part of Machen's fiction is actually devoted to the mystical and numinous. In the third section, we present discussions of several different aspects of this quest, exploring Machen's interest in ritual magic, occultism, classical mythology, the sublime, and his own individual and particular form of Christianity.

In his later work, Machen never lost his deep interest in folklore and popular customs, eccentric characters and curious historical episodes. He both wrote about them directly in his journalism and in collections of essays, and made use of them in his fiction, often inventing motifs and incidents that seem quite as authentic as the genuine article. In the final section, we show how these continued to inform his work right up until his last writing. Whether it is the remembrance of the ancient armigerous families of his home county, the study of a strange disappearance, the furor about "the Angels," or the possibility of other worlds alongside our own, we find in these pieces that Machen remained, as he had ever been, a grand master of the mysterious.

Abbreviations

CF *Collected Fiction* (New York: Hippocampus Press, 2019), 3 volumes
FOT *Far Off Things* (London: Martin Secker, 1922)
H   *Hieroglyphics* (London: Grant Richards, 1902)
SL *Selected Letters* (Wellingborough, UK: Aquarian, 1988)
TNF *Things Near and Far* (London: Martin Secker, 1923)

I. Biography and Bibliography

Arthur Machen: The Evils of Materialism

S. T. Joshi

Arthur Machen's own life is perhaps his greatest creation; for it is exactly the life we might expect a poet and a visionary to have lived. Born in 1863 in the village of Caerleon-on-Usk in Wales (the site, two millennia earlier, of the Roman town of Isca Silurum and the base of the Second Augustan Legion), Machen was fascinated since youth by the Roman antiquities in his region as well as the rural Welsh countryside. He attended Hereford Cathedral School, but in 1880 he failed an examination for the Royal College of Surgeons; he felt he had no option but to go to London to look for work, where he hoped that his ardent enthusiasm for books might land him some literary work.

But only poverty and loneliness were his portion. Dragging out a meagre existence as a translator (his translation of the *Heptameron* of Marguerite de Navarre [1886] long remained standard, as did his later translation of Casanova's memoirs [1894]), tutor, and cataloguer, he knew at first hand the spiritual isolation that his alter ego, Lucian Taylor, would depict so poignantly in *The Hill of Dreams* (1907). In his first autobiography, *Far Off Things* (1922), he speaks of this period with a wistfulness that scarcely conceals his anguish. Although Machen published a few works during this period—*The Anatomy of Tobacco* (1884), an owlishly learned disquisition on various types of tobacco; the picaresque novel *The Chronicle of Clemendy* (1886)—they were commercially unsuccessful and are today not highly regarded.

But the death of Machen's father in 1887 suddenly gave him, for the next fourteen years, the economic independence he required to write whatever he chose, without thought of markets or sales. And yet, one of his first works of fiction of this period—"The Great God Pan" (1890)—created a sensation, especially when it appeared in book form in 1894. It shocked the moral guardians of an enfeebled Victorian culture as the diseased outpourings of a decadent mind; but the reviewers who condemned it as sexually offensive could not know that Machen shared the very inhibitions he seemed to be defying. This tale—as well as the infinitely superior "The White People" (1899)—succeeds largely because Machen himself, as a rigidly orthodox Anglo-Catholic, crystallised his horror of aberrant sexuality by giving it a supernatural dimension.

In "The Great God Pan" we are asked to believe that a scientific experiment performed upon a young woman of seventeen results in her "seeing" the Great God Pan; she instantly loses her mind and becomes an idiot. Some years thereafter a strange woman named Helen Vaughan plagues London society, causing a rash of suicides and destroying the lives of several prominent men about town. In the end we learn that Helen is in fact the daughter of the young woman, born nine months after the fateful experiment.

Without so much as hinting it, Machen has conveyed to astute readers that the young woman had done more than merely "see" Pan; she had been (somehow) impregnated by the great god of Nature. (This is the point of the Latin inscription at the end of the second section: "And a devil was made incarnate. And a human being was produced.") But the way in which Machen portrays Pan—and, by extension, Nature itself—is interesting, especially in contrast to his great contemporary Algernon Blackwood, a pantheist for whom Nature was pure, uncorrupt, and unadulterated by the pollution of human civilisation. Machen takes a precisely opposite view. For him, the life-principle itself was inherently horrific, and can be made acceptable only by the rigid repression of civilised society. This is why Helen Vaughan's activities cause the greatest disturbance among the refined aristocrats of London. The scientist, Raymond, confesses toward the end that "I broke open the door of the house of life"—in other words, that he has broken down the barriers that separate human life from all other life on the earth (CF 1.267). But the result is only horror; and Helen Vaughan's death-throes—whereby she transmogrifies "from woman to man, from man to beast, and from beast to worse than beast"—convey Machen's own horror of untamed, uncontrolled, uncivilised life (CF 1.268).

Throughout the novella Machen hints at illicit sex in a way that to us seems coy but to his original readers would have appeared suggestive to the point of obscenity. The young Helen is once seen in the company of a "strange naked man" (no doubt Pan himself, perhaps in his traditional guise as a man with the legs of a goat) (CF 1.227). Another young woman, Rachel, is found weeping and "half undressed" in her room: clearly she has been raped by Pan (CF 1.229). Mercifully, she dies shortly thereafter. Helen herself, a young woman in London, is said to be guilty of "nameless infamies"—no doubt of a sexual nature (CF 1.258). All this would have titillated Machen's Victorian audience, and indeed did so.

All this makes Machen sound like the Erica Jong of his day, but this reaction was only to have been expected in the final decade of Queen Victoria's reign. H. P. Lovecraft, although at one point heaping scorn on Machen's horror of sex—"The filth and perversion which to Machen's obsoletely orthodox mind meant profound defiances of the universe's foundations, mean to us only a rather prosaic and unfortunate species of organic maladjustment—no more frightful, and no more interesting, than a headache, a fit of colic, or an ulcer on the big toe" (letter to Bernard Austin Dwyer, early 1932; *Letters to Maurice W. Moe and Others* 471)—was himself highly reserved and puritanical in matters of sex, so it is no surprise that he adapted Machen's notion of a "god" impregnating a mortal in his own tale, "The Dunwich Horror" (1928).

Another scientific experiment is at the focus of "The Inmost Light," written in 1892 and first published in 1894. Here we find that a doctor has persuaded his own wife to allow him to extract her soul and place it in a gem—the "inmost light" in that gem *is* her soul. The result is that the woman continues to live, but presents—like Helen Vaughan—a visage of mingled beauty and horror. One man who sees her in a window thinks of her as a "satyr" (CF 1.306). To one of Machen's conventional religiosity, a person without a (Christian) soul can only appear as a figure of pagan antiquity.

"The Shining Pyramid" (1895), aside from continuing the adventures of Mr. Dyson, the pseudo-detective who was introduced to us in "The Inmost Light," is one of Machen's first expositions of what might be called his "Little People mythology." Although it features a spectacularly potent scene in which the stunted, primitive denizens of Britain—now dwelling in caves, having been driven out by successive waves of fully human peoples—perform a hideous ritual around a pyramid of fire, "The Shining Pyramid" is perhaps too much of a detective story to be fully effective as a weird tale. But the "Little People mythology" is of some interest in itself. In the essay "Folklore and Legends of the North" (*Literature*, 24 September 1898), Machen makes it clear that he himself believed in the former existence of just such a race of creatures as he depicts in these stories:

> Of recent years abundant proof has been given that a short, non-Aryan race once dwelt beneath ground, in hillocks, throughout Europe, their raths have been explored, and the weird old tales of green hills all lighted up at night have received confirmation. Much in the old legends may be explained by a reference to this primitive race. The stories of changelings, and captive

women, become clear on the supposition that the "fairies" occasionally raided the houses of the invaders. (CF 1.517)

This was written more than two decades before the publication of Margaret A. Murray's *The Witch-Cult in Western Europe* (1921), which gave a momentary stamp of approval to the thesis. But Machen knew that the really adventuresome aspect of his theory—or, rather, the radical extension of it which he made for fictional purposes—was that "the people still lived in hidden caverns in wild and lonely lands," something he maintained was "wildly improbable" ("On Re-reading *The Three Impostors* and the Wonder Story" [CF 1.538]).

But behind all this speculative anthropology is the symbolism of the Little People. They are horrible and loathsome, to be sure, but they have at least one advantage over modern human beings: they have retained that primal sacrament (perverted, of course, by bestiality and violence) which links them with the Beyond. There is something of awe mingled with the horror experienced by the narrators when they witness the "pyramid of fire" summoned by the Little People in "The Shining Pyramid," and this signals the truth uttered by the protagonist of "The White People": "Sorcery and sanctity ... these are the only realities. Each is an ecstasy, a withdrawal from the common life" (CF 2.185).

Probably Machen's most sustained weird work is *The Three Impostors*, published in 1895. Also poorly received, it was criticised for being excessively imitative of Robert Louis Stevenson. It is commonly believed that the model for the novel—both in its episodic structure and in its flippant and jaunty style—is Stevenson's *The New Arabian Nights* (1882); but the true model is that novel's sequel, *The Dynamiter* (1885), written by Stevenson in conjunction with his wife, Fanny van de Grift Stevenson. Machen ultimately acknowledged this criticism, and for the next two years he worked with difficulty, even agony, to hammer out his own style; the result is that luminous novel of aesthetic sincerity, *The Hill of Dreams*.

What is *The Three Impostors*? On the surface, it appears to be a random collection of episodes strung together with the flimsiest kind of narrative thread. One episode—"Novel of the Iron Maid"—had in fact been written and published in 1890, and for copyright reasons it and its introductory segment ("The Decorative Imagination") do not appear in many American editions of the novel. Other episodes—notably the celebrated "Novel of the Black Seal" and "Novel of the White Powder"—have been abstracted from the narrative fabric and reprinted as self-standing stories. This occurred on several occasions during Machen's lifetime, and he appears to have registered no great complaint; but Machen was scarcely in a position to do so, as the period between 1901 and 1932 (when he received a Civil List pension of £100 a year) was of considerable poverty for him, and he could ill afford to pass up any revenue his writings yielded.

Both the title of *The Three Impostors* and its subtitle ("or, The Transmutations"—frequently omitted from reprints) may provide the clue to the interpretation of the novel. Who are the "three impostors" of the title? Who can they be but the two men and a woman we encounter in the prologue, who have at last captured and perhaps killed the "young man with spectacles" they have evidently been pursuing? For it is they who, under a series of guises, tell the various "novels" (from the French *nouvelle*, or tale, especially one of a romantic or fantastic character) scattered throughout the work. Their sole audience is a pair of friends, Mr. Dyson and Charles Phillipps, who wage an ongoing philosophical battle on the nature of reality and the nature of fiction, and it becomes gradually clear that the tales spun by the "three impostors" may be entirely fictitious, being instead somewhat laborious contrivances meant to dupe Dyson and Phillipps into leading them to the spectacled young man.

Toward the end it begins to dawn upon the two gentlemen that the stories they are hearing are perhaps not entirely reliable; Dyson finally resolves to "abjure all Milesian and Arabian methods of entertainment"—a reference to the Milesian tale (the Greek version of the tall tale) and, of course, to the *Arabian Nights* (CF 1.439). This connects with a theme that runs throughout *The Three Impostors* and Machen's work as a whole—the fantastic nature of the metropolis of London. "A Fragment of Life" (1904), a pensive novella on the borderline of the weird, conveys this conception poignantly: "London seemed a city of the Arabian Nights, and its labyrinths of streets an enchanted maze; its long avenues of lighted lamps were as starry systems, and its immensity became for him an image of the endless universe" (CF 2.290).

But what purpose could Machen have in seemingly dynamiting the seriousness and power of the episodes in *The Three Impostors* by putting them in the mouths of dubious characters? There may be no clear answer to this question, but perhaps some clues can be provided by considering Machen's general philosophy. I hesitate to call his view of the world a philosophy, for really it was a set of dogmatic prejudices that changed little through the whole of his long life; but at its essence was a violent hostility and resentment at what he perceived to be the growing secularism and "scientism" of the modern world.

To Machen, the religious mystic, the triumphs of nineteenth-century science were anything but victories; instead, it seemed to him that science was coming to rule all aspects of life, even those aspects—the spiritual life and its corollary, art—where it had no place.

In *The Three Impostors*, Phillipps clearly espouses the hard-headed scientific scepticism Machen wishes to combat. It is no surprise that the woman who calls herself Miss Lally tells him the "Novel of the Black Seal"; for in this story it is Professor Gregg who embodies what Machen believes to be the genuinely scientific attitude of open-mindedness to unusual phenomena: "Life, believe me, is no simple thing, no mass of grey matter and congeries of veins and muscles to be laid naked by the surgeon's knife; man is the secret which I am about to explore, and before I can discover him I must cross over weltering seas indeed, and oceans and the mists of many thousand years" (CF 1.369–70). Indeed, it seems quite likely that Miss Lally tells Phillipps this story only in order to overcome his innate scepticism; for Phillipps "required a marvel to be neatly draped in the robes of Science before he would give it any credit" (CF 1.357).

Perhaps the subtitle of *The Three Impostors* provides a further clue. Exactly what transmutations are in question? To be sure, on a superficial level the various "novels" and other episodes transmute scenery, as we flit from the suburbs of London ("Novel of the Iron Maid," "Novel of the White Powder") to the wilds of the American West ("Novel of the Dark Valley") to the "wild, domed hills" of Wales ("Novel of the Black Seal"). Miss Lally casually notes that "I looked out of my window and saw the whole landscape transmuted before me" (CF 1.375). But the reference here is merely to topography; elsewhere there are much more profound transmutations going on. When Professor Gregg finally decodes the cryptic black seal that appears to confirm his theory of the "Little People," he states with awed solemnity: "I read the key of the awful transmutation of the hills" (CF 1.398). Here it is not landscape but Gregg's entire outlook on life that has been transmuted. The "Novel of the White Powder" confirms this view. Miss Leicester, who tells the tale (and who is presumably identical to the Miss Lally of the earlier narrative), speaks offhandedly of "the transmutation of my brother's character" after he begins taking the strange drug from a careless apothecary's shop (CF 1.425). But what really happens to the hapless student is the transmutation of his very being, physically and morally, leading a doctor to write harriedly, "my old conception of the universe has been swept away" (CF 1.435). This is the ultimate transmutation.

That doctor, in effect, gives voice to Machen's own view of the world:

"The whole universe . . . is a tremendous sacrament; a mystic, ineffable force and energy, veiled by an outward form of matter; and man, and the sun and the other stars, and the flower of the grass, and the crystal in the test-tube, are each and every one as spiritual, as material, and subject to an inner working" (CF 1.435). It was this view that Machen was determined to convey to his audience over a lifetime of writing.

The final years of Machen's "great decade" of fiction writing produced several of the works for which Machen is known today. Even excluding the marginally weird novel *The Hill of Dreams* (written in 1895-97 but not published until 1907), we are faced with such works as "The Red Hand" (1897), the prose poems collected in *Ornaments in Jade* (1924), "The White People" (the second-greatest horror tale ever written, according to Lovecraft, next to Algernon Blackwood's "The Willows"), and the unclassifiable novella "A Fragment of Life." Had Machen written nothing else, these works alone would be sufficient to grant him a place in weird literature—or in literature as a whole.

"The Red Hand" (written in 1895) is a pendant to *The Three Impostors*, revivfing the two central figures in that novel, Phillipps and Dyson, as they continue their intellectual dispute over the nature of reality while becoming involved in what proves to be an exceptionally clever supernatural detective story. Dyson, the mystic (hence the stand-in for Machen), evokes a "theory of improbability" to account for the remarkable series of coincidences that leads him to the solution of the case (CF 1.478); but this is less interesting than the overall philosophical thrust of the tale, in which Machen utilises the tools of rationalism (specifically, the forensic analysis of evidence in regard to the murder at the heart of the case) to undermine rationalism and thereby to "prove" to his satisfaction that the matter can only be accounted for by appealing to the supernatural—in this case, the continued existence of "little people."

Of the prose-poems in *Ornaments in Jade* it is difficult to speak in detail. These delicate vignettes may in some sense be pendants to *The Hill of Dreams*—not in terms of plot, but in terms of style and substance. Comparable only to those of Clark Ashton Smith as the finest in English, they complete Machen's transformation from clever imitator to independent artist. If there is any dominant theme that unites them, it is the constant contrast between mundane modernity and the hoary past—a past that is simultaneously terrifying in its primitivism and awesome in its suggestions of intimate, symbolic connexions with the essence of life and Nature. However brutalised modern people are by the dominant materialism of the age, their sense of spirituality can well up in spite of themselves in the practice of ancient rituals.

As for "The White People," in a sense it returns to the theme of "The Great God Pan" (1890) in its emphasis on illicit sex. For Machen, the orthodox Anglo-Catholic, sexual aberrations represented a kind of violation of the entire fabric of the universe. This is the substance of the remarks by Ambrose at the beginning of the tale, especially his comment that sin is "the attempt to penetrate into another and higher sphere in a *forbidden* [my italics] manner" and "the effort to gain the ecstasy and knowledge that pertain alone to angels" (CF 2.188). This story—in which a young girl unwittingly reveals in her diary her inculcation into a witch-cult and, evidently, her impregnation by some nameless entity—transmogrifies illicit sex into a cosmic sin that will either lift us up into the ranks of the angels or plunge us down into the company of demons. And yet, Machen's exposition of the details of the matter (especially the sexual element) are so indirect that many readers have been puzzled as to the exact nature of the scenario. One such reader was the young J. Vernon Shea, who asked his friend H. P. Lovecraft to elucidate the tale. Lovecraft did so, concluding: "On account of a sympathetic action like that described in the prologue, the now-adolescent child—though without contact with any creative element—became pregnant with a Horror, to whose birth (knowing what she did of dark tradition) she could not look forward without a stark frenzy far beyond the fear of mere disgrace. Thus she killed herself" (letter to J. Vernon Shea, 9 December 1931; *Letters to J. Vernon Shea* 82). In the absence of contrary evidence, this interpretation must be accepted. Machen's single sentence at the end ("She had poisoned herself—in time") is the only clue this repressed Victorian writer can provide to the sexual anomalies of the situation (CF 2.220).

And yet, Lovecraft was manifestly inspired not by the mechanics of the plot of "The White People," but by its magnificent allusiveness and subtlety. The diary in which the girl tells of her initiation into the witch-cult is a masterstroke: we know what is happening, but she in her naïveté does not. And those chilling hints of nameless rituals that the girl provides ("I must not write down ... the way to make the Aklo letters, or the Chian language, or the great beautiful Circles, nor the Mao Games, nor the chief songs") carries hints of hideous *suggestion* that are the more potent for their being so ill-defined (CF 2.193).

"A Fragment of Life" is an altogether different proposition. If this short novel is only on the very edge of the weird, it deserves far wider recognition as one of Machen's most finished works. The exquisitely gradual way in which the stolid bourgeois couple, Edward and Mary Darnell, slowly awaken to their sense of wonder and abandon London for their native Wales is one of Machen's great literary accomplishments. Amidst all the mundane details of the small-scale social life of the Darnells, we receive hints that their love of beauty has not been entirely destroyed, as it has for so many who live too fully in the modern world. Machen delivers an unanswerable criticism of the narrowing of vision that such a life engenders: "So, day after day, he lived in the grey phantasmal world, akin to death, that has, somehow, with most of us, made good its claim to be called life" (CF 2.243). And yet, something so simple as birdsong heard by Edward ("That night was the night I thought I heard the nightingale . . . and the sky was such a wonderful deep blue") provides an anticipation of the coming change (CF 2.239). Mary, too, although seemingly more hard-headedly practical than Edward, senses the alteration in her being ("one would have almost said that they were the eyes of one who longed and half expected to be initiated into the mysteries, who knew not what great wonder was to be revealed") (CF 2.254). The entire novel is a kind of instantiation of the critical theories in Machen's idiosyncratic treatise, *Hieroglyphics: A Note upon Ecstasy in Literature* (1902), in which he criticised such writers as Jane Austen and George Eliot for being too closely tied to mundane reality and failing to include that modicum of "ecstasy" which ought, in Machen's eyes, to inform all literature. We may well believe that Machen was insufficiently attuned to the "ecstasy" that is in fact present in the work of the social realists he disdains, but we can hardly gainsay that he himself has flawlessly embodied his own principles in "A Fragment of Life."

After writing this novel (which was itself worked on sporadically over five years, 1899–1904), Machen appeared to lose focus as far as fiction writing was concerned. In 1907 he wrote the curious novel *The Secret Glory* (a satire on the British school system that was not published until 1922), but that was the extent of his creative output between 1904 and 1914. With his inheritance gone, Machen was forced to produce mountains of journalism; the book publications of his fiction—specifically *The House of Souls* (1906) and *The Hill of Dreams* (1907)—brought him fleeting attention, but not much in the way of income. It was only in 1914 that he resumed fiction writing—but he did so in a peculiar way.

Machen had, since 1910, been serving on the staff of one of the leading newspapers in London, the *Evening News*, as reporter and columnist. At least two of the four stories that comprised *The Bowmen and Other Legends of the War* (1915)—"The Bowmen" (29 September 1914) and "The Soldiers' Rest" (20 October 1914)—appeared in the *Evening News*. The well-known story of how "The Bowmen"—a tale about the ghosts of mediaeval British soldiers who come to the aid of a beleaguered British unit at the battle of Mons in late August 1914—came to be regarded as a real occurrence, with angels rescuing the soldiers and supposedly first-hand accounts by the soldiers themselves testifying to the miracle—need not be discussed in detail; Machen himself recounts the matter in the introduction to *The Bowmen and Other Legends of the War*. His repeated protestations that the story was entirely a product of his imagination went for naught; the outbreak of the European war—which had commenced less than two months prior to the publication of "The Bowmen"—was so traumatic that the emergence of such legendry was inevitable. Machen himself alludes to Kipling's "The Lost Legion" as a central literary influence on the tale, although other literary sources reaching back to Herodotus' *Histories* have recently been postulated. But what is more significant is Machen's own attempt to pull off a kind of hoax with "The Bowmen." The mere fact that it was published in a newspaper—even though newspapers at this time published more fiction than they do now—and the fact that it was written with the plain-spoken sobriety expected of factual articles, suggest that Machen is not wholly blameless in the subsequent furore caused by his little tale.

Much the same could be said for "The Great Return," which also appeared in the *Evening News* (21 October–16 November 1915) and was subsequently published in book form by a religious publisher, the Faith Press. Here Machen seeks no more than to present, in the most orthodox repertorial manner, a series of curious incidents in Wales that, to his mind, suggest the actual rediscovery of the Holy Grail. Once again, as in "The Red Hand," although in a somewhat cruder way, Machen seeks to use the tools of rationalism to undermine rationalism: here the outwardly sceptical newspaper reporter—who is none other than Machen himself, with no attempt made to establish a distance between author and persona—becomes gradually convinced of the reality of the phenomena described. Machen is content to present a scenario whereby something miraculous might have happened: this is sufficient for his current purpose of attacking the godless materialism of his age.

The European war was obviously a highly disturbing event to Machen. Already alienated from his time by his religious mysticism, so much in contrast with the prevailing scientific rationalism of the later nineteenth century, he found his own faith shaken by a war in which Christians were killing other Christians with great gusto. Toward the end of the conflict he wrote a series of sophistical articles attempting to justify the ways of God to man; they were collected as *War and the Christian Faith* (1918). But Machen's work of fiction revolving around the war is of course *The Terror* (1917), a short novel that has inspired a host of imitations of its basic plot—animals turning against human beings.

The Terror reveals several features characteristic of Machen's later fiction. The first, perhaps, is frank autobiography. Not only does the first-person narrative voice seem to be Machen himself, but he plays upon his own role as a journalist and reporter—something we will find again in the later tale "Out of the Picture" (1936). Indeed, it is not insignificant that The Terror was also first published as a serialisation in the Evening News (16-31 October 1916), under the title "The Great Terror." Is Machen attempting to pass off the narrative as a "true" story? To be sure, there is no deliberate intent to deceive; but the circumstantiality of his account, and its generally reportorial tone, make one wonder whether Machen is hoping to convey a deeper truth—the truth that the brief, fitful, and ultimately temporary "revolution" of the animals against humanity's reign over the earth is a signal that human morals are collapsing as a result of the hideous and unprecedented warfare that had broken out two years earlier.

Machen wrote relatively few actual works of fiction in the 1920s, aside from a few stories for anthologies edited by Cynthia Asquith. In the 1930s he resumed somewhat greater productivity in fiction-writing and published two late collections, The Cosy Room and The Children of the Pool, in 1936. The former volume contains stories written over a wide period, but the latter is an original collection of previously unpublished tales. They are, however, a sadly uneven mix, and some stories—such as "N," "The Exalted Omega," and "The Tree of Life"—are among his poorest work. But Machen could on occasion still wield the magic that makes his earlier works so shuddersomely memorable. In particular, "Out of the Picture" and "Change" seem to be among the final instalments of the "Little People mythology"; it is possible that "The Bright Boy" also belongs to this cycle.

Then there is The Green Round (1933), a short novel later reprinted by Arkham House. But this insubstantial account of a man who goes to a quiet resort in Wales, only to be plagued by a strange, stunted being whom others can see but he cannot, is a disappointment in more ways than one. It is, really, a novella or even a short story stretched out to novel length, and its thinness of inspiration, verbosity, and failure to come to a satisfying conclusion must condemn it as a false start. Machen himself dismissed The Terror as a "shilling shocker," but that short novel stands leagues higher than the only other novel-length work of the supernatural that emerged from his pen.

In a career that spanned more than six decades, Arthur Machen produced some of the most evocative weird fiction in all literary history. Written with impeccably mellifluous prose, infused with a powerful mystical vision, and imbued with a wonder and terror that their author felt with every fibre of his being, his novels and tales will survive when works of far greater technical accomplishment fall by the wayside. Flawed as some of them are by certain crotchets—especially a furious hostility to science and secularism—that disfigure Machen's own philosophy, they are nonetheless as effective as they are because they echo the sincere beliefs of their author, whose eternal quest to preserve the mystery of the universe in an age of materialism is one to which we can all respond.

Works Cited

Lovecraft, H. P. *Letters to J. Vernon Shea, Carl F. Strauch, and Lee McBride White.* Ed. S. T. Joshi and David E. Schultz. New York: Hippocampus Press, 2016.

———. *Letters to Maurice W. Moe and Others.* Ed. David E. Schultz and S. T. Joshi. New York: Hippocampus Press, 2018.

Arthur Machen: The Pagan—
His Work and His Personality

Geoffrey H. Wells

Arthur Machen is a somewhat unusual figure in the modern world of letters; an artist in words who is yet, as a literary man, something of an amateur. He is a writer who cannot "work to order." Conscientious to an extraordinary degree, finding the act of composition a thing of intense labour, he is driven on by the creative impulse to the expression of one conception of life through one process which he defines as being "to invent a story which would recreate those vague impressions of wonder and awe and mystery that I myself had received from the form and shape of the land of my boyhood and youth." He states definitely that these impressions have been the sole source of his inspiration, and adds that "he who has any traffic with the affairs of the imagination has found out all the wisdom that he will ever know, in this life at all events, by the age of eighteen or thereabouts." In Mr. Machen's case at least this is true. His best novels are those which follow frankly, if with a certain dramatization and heightening of effect, the development of his youthful mind, while his autobiography of those *Far-Off Things* is undoubtedly the most enduring of all his works.

The Celtic Strain in Him

Essential to an understanding of Mr. Machen is a realization of the Celtic strain in him. He was born in 1863 in "that noble, fallen Caerleon-on-Usk" on the border of South Wales, the only child of a country clergyman, the vicar of Llanddewi. There seems an almost eighteenth-century air about this rectory with its haphazard library of old volumes, situated in serene isolation from Newport to the south and the mining valleys to the north, isolation which even today has scarcely been broken. It was an "enchanted land" to the lonely boy, its woods and fields, sombre in the shadow of Twyn Barlwm, "that mystic tumulus"; of Mynydd Maen; of the other peaks which stretched away right to the "pointed summit of the Holy Mountain by Abergavenny." Such names as these, and others as Caerwent, Llanddewi, Wentwood, sing through the pages of his books like the incantations that they must have been to him then. For Gwent is a magic land, haunted by memories of the past, and most magic of all is Caerleon, "once the golden Isca of the Roman legions ... golden forever and immortal in the romances of King Arthur and the Graal." And the border-Welsh are a strange and silent people.

Solitude, Woods, and Wonder

In summer weather he roamed the woods and mountain slopes, but when the rain and cold of winter nights kept him at home he relived in his mind the old romances of Cervantes and Rabelais and *The Arabian Nights*. When he was seventeen he left Hereford Cathedral School, where he had been for six years, more lonely there than ever at the home to which he returned. "Solitude and woods, and deep lanes and wonder; these were the chief elements of my life." That summer, in 1880, he made his first visit to London, where he was to suffer still greater loneliness and hunger and cold and disappointment. From that time on his sojourns in Gwent were only temporary and occasional.

The literary career of Arthur Machen is clearly divided into two periods. First the twenty years from 1880 to 1900, during which he wrote everything printed up to 1907, with the exception of the short and unimportant *Dr Stiggins* (1906), but including *The Secret Glory* (1922). There follows a gap of fifteen apparently uncreative years, with the exception noted, until the publication of *The Bowmen* in 1915. Since then six new volumes have appeared.

He Finds His Sphere

The earliest work can be passed over very quickly. The notable items are *The Anatomy of Tobacco* (1884), *The Chronicle of Clemendy* (1888), and the translations of the *Heptameron* (1886), *Le Moyen de Parvenir* of Beroalde de Verville (1890), and *The Memoirs of Jacques Casanova* (1894). All the above had been completed before 1890, when Arthur Machen realized that his true subject was not Touraine of old days but the Wales and England which he knew, his true rôle was not to be "an English Rabelais" but simply—himself! The first products of this realization were the well-known *Great God Pan and The Inmost Light* (1894), and these were followed in the next few years by the individual, though somewhat similarly treated tales of *The Three Impostors*, *The White People*, *The Red Hand* and *A Fragment of Life*, all of which, with the first two, are now published in one volume as *The House of Souls* (1907).

The Shadows That Hide

Each of these stories is an attempt to tear aside "the shadows that hide the real world from our eyes," to lift the veil of appearances and to reveal the "eternal, inner realities." Through them all runs that suggestion of incantation of names strange and wonderful, names savouring of magic—a little too often, perhaps, of black magic. In fact it must be reckoned their greatest fault that the awe the writer tries to convey is too often confused with mere awfulness. One feels that if *this* is the reality behind the "transitory, external surfaces" a veil is hardly sufficient protection; one would prefer a fireproof curtain! But in the best books of this period there is more than that. *The Hill of Dreams* (written in 1896), "a *Robinson Crusoe* of the mind," is one of the most "decadent" books ever written; certainly it contains the most terrible scene Arthur Machen has ever painted, and the ecstasy of the end is passionate and evil. Yet in the earlier passages of the story, in the visions which come to the young man on the hills of Gwent, there are moments of real wonder and beauty. Incidentally it, like all the author's work, in greater or lesser degree, is a masterpiece of beautiful prose. *The Secret Glory*, written immediately after *The Hill of Dreams*, is a clearer and sweeter story, and the wild visions are crystallised here in the "veiled and splendid" cup of the Graal. There are passages in both books which attain a startling profundity of ecstatic revelation.

Serene and Calm

The stories of the second period are more serene, but except in the case of *The Great Return* (1915), "a little book of mine which no one has heard of," his peculiar power seems weakened until one comes to the two volumes of autobiography. Then, reading *Far Off Things* (1922) and *Things Near and Far* (1923), one begins to wonder whether an even deeper revelation is not attained by the simplicity of these books. Here is no "Bacchic fury, unveiled and unashamed," but a quieter spirit which speaks to the soul with a truth beyond that of words alone.

All Arthur Machen's work is a statement of his unswerving attitude to life. As a boy, he realized that "we live and move in a world of profound and ineffable mystery," before the vision of which he stood awe-struck and worshipping. And that mystery, he knew, could never be solved by reason. Only when moved by "ecstasy, the infallible instrument," can man peer beyond the barrier and comprehend something of the glory and terror that are about him. It is this belief which has led him to state the case he does so brilliantly and logically in his one book of literary criticism, *Hieroglyphics*. Here he claims definitely as the highest literature that which moves one to ecstasy. "*Vanity Fair* is information, while *Pickwick* is Truth; the one tells you a number of facts about Becky Sharp and other people, while the other symbolizes certain eternal and essential elements in human nature by means of incidents."

All Existence a Hieroglyph

The title *Hieroglyphics* is not specifically discussed in the volume itself, but it is a good Machen title, as near to a statement of his philosophy as anyone could get in one word. For to him all life, all existence, is but a hieroglyph, symbol of a hidden glory; and all art is but the flickering candle of the human soul, stumbling in the black void of "transitory, external surfaces." "He dreamed in fire; he has worked in clay," Arthur Machen writes of the boy he was, and indeed he views all the seeming actuality of this world as but the expression in clay of a secret reality of splendid flame. Again and again he has striven to rend the veil and convey to us something of his vision, and here and there, at precious moments, he has succeeded. But ultimately he accepts the hieroglyph: "at the last, what do we know?"

Only this: that "reality is always above actuality"; that "all things, from the most abstract to the most concrete, are involved in this mystery"; and that "no mere making of the external shape will be our art; no veracious document will be our truth; but to us, initiated, the Symbol will be offered and we shall take the Sign and adore, beneath the outward and perhaps unlovely accidents, the very Presence and eternal indwelling of God."

Arthur Machen:
A Novelist of Ecstasy and Sin

Vincent Starrett

Some thirty odd years ago a young man of twenty-two, the son of a Welsh clergyman, fresh from school and with his head full of a curiously occult mediaevalism, privately acquired from yellowed palimpsests and dog-eared volumes of black letter, wrote a classic. More, he had it published. Only one review copy was sent out; that was to *Le Livre,* of Paris. It fell into the hands of Octave Uzanne, who instantly ordered Rabelais and Boccaccio to "shove over" on the immortal seats and make room by their side for the author. The book was "The Chronicle of Clemendy"; the author, Arthur Machen.

Three years ago, about, not long after the great war first shook the world, a London evening newspaper published inconspicuously a purely fictional account of a supposed incident of the British retreat from Mons. It described the miraculous intervention of the English archers of Agincourt at a time when the British were sore pressed by the German hordes. Immediately, churchmen, spiritualists, and a host of others, seized upon it as an authentic record and the miracle as an omen. In the hysteria that followed, Arthur Machen, its author, found himself a talked-of man, because he wrote to the papers denying that the narrative was factual. Later, when his little volume, "The Bowmen and Other Legends of the War," appeared in print, it met with an extraordinary and rather impertinent success.

But what had Machen been doing all those long years between 1885 and 1914?

In a day of haphazard fiction and rodomontade criticism, the advent of a master workman is likely to be unheralded, if, indeed, he is fortunate enough to find a publisher to put him between covers. Mr. Machen is not a newcomer, however, as we have seen; no immediate success with a "best seller" furnishes an incentive for a complimentary notice. He is an unknown, in spite of "Clemendy," in spite of "The Bowmen," in spite of everything. For thirty years he has been writing English prose, a period ample for the making of a dozen reputations of the ordinary kind, and in that time he has produced just ten books. In thirty years Harold Bindloss and Rex Beach will have written one-hundred-and-ten books and sold the moving picture rights of them all.

Of course, it is exactly because he does not write books of the ordinary kind that Arthur Machen's reputation as a writer was not made long ago. His apotheosis will begin after his death. The insectial fame of the "popular" novelist is immediate; it is born at dawn and dies at sunset. The enduring fame of the artist too often is born at sunset, but it is immortal.

More than Hawthorne or Tolstoy, Machen is a novelist of the soul. He writes of a strange borderland, lying somewhere between Dreams and Death, peopled with shades, beings, spirits, ghosts, men, women, souls—what shall we call them?—the very notion of whom stops vaguely just short of thought. He writes of the life Satyr-ic. For him Pan is not dead; his votaries still whirl through woodland windings to the mad pipe that was Syrinx, and carouse fiercely in enchanted forest grottoes (hidden somewhere, perhaps, in the fourth dimension!). His meddling with the crucibles of science is appalling in its daring, its magnificence, and its horror. Even the greater works of fictional psychology—"Dr. Jekyll and Mr. Hyde," if you like—shrink before his astounding inferences and suggestions.

It is his theory that the fearful and shocking rites of the Bacchic cultus survive in this disillusioned age; that Panic lechery and wickedness did not cease with the Agony, as Mrs. Browning and others would have us believe.

Of Hawthorne, Arthur Symons wrote: "He is haunted by what is obscure, dangerous, and on the confines of good and evil." Machen crosses those perilous frontiers. He all but lifts the veil; himself, indeed, passes beyond it. But the curtain drops behind him and we, hesitating to follow, see only dimly the phantasmagoria beyond; the ecstasies of vague shapes with a shining about them, on the one hand; on the other the writhings of animate gargoyles. And we experience, I think, a distinct sense of gratitude toward this terrible guide for that we are permitted no closer view of the mysteries that seem to him so clear.

We glimpse his secrets in transfiguring flashes from afar, as Launcelot viewed the San Graal, and, like that tarnished knight, we quest vainly a tangible solution, half in apprehension, always in glamour. But it is like Galahad we must seek the eternal mysteries that obsess Arthur Machen. There is no solution but in absolution, for it is the mysteries of life and death of which he writes, and of life-in-death and death-in-life. This with particular reference to Machen's two most important books, "The House of Souls" and "The Hill of

Dreams," in which he reaches his greatest stature as a novelist of the soul.

There are those who will call him a novelist of Sin, quibbling about a definition. With these I have no quarrel; the characterizations are synonymous. His books exhale all evil and all corruption; yet they are as pure as the fabled waters of that crystal spring De Leon sought. They are pervaded by an ever-present, intoxicating sense of sin, ravishingly beautiful, furiously Pagan, frantically lovely; but Machen is a finer and truer mystic than the two-penny occultists who guide modern spiritualistic thought. If we are to subscribe to his curious philosophy, to be discussed later, we must believe that there is no paradox in this.

But something of what we are getting at is explained in his own pages, in this opening paragraph from his story, "The White People," in "The House of Souls": "'Sorcery and sanctity,' said Ambrose, "these are the only realities. Each is an ecstasy, a withdrawal from the common life'" [CF 2.185]. And, a little later, in this: "'There is something profoundly unnatural about sin" the essence of which "really is in the taking of heaven by storm'" [CF 2.188].

One gathers from a general vagueness on the subject that sin is not popular in these times. There are, of course, new sins and advanced sins and higher sins, all of which are intensely interesting. The chief puzzle to the lay mind is why they should bear these names, since they are usually neither new, advanced and high, nor particularly sinful. I am speaking of sin as an offense against the nature of things, and of evil in the soul, which has very little to do with the sins of the statute book. Sin, according to the same Ambrose I have quoted, is conceivable in the talking of animals. If a chair should walk across a room, that would be sinful, or if a tree sat down with us to afternoon tea. The savage who worships a conjurer is a far finer moralist than the civilised who suspects him—and I use the name moralist for one who has an appreciation of sin.

This is not the sin of the legal code. *Ambrose* I conceive to be Arthur Machen. There are only two realities; sorcery and sanctity—sin and sainthood—and each is an ecstasy. Arthur Machen's is the former.

Perhaps his most remarkable story—certainly I think his most terrible story, is "The Great God Pan," at first published separately with "The Inmost Light"; now occurring in "The House of Souls." It is the story of an experiment upon a girl, as a result of which, for a moment, she is permitted a sight of the Great God, beyond the veil, with shocking consequences. Yet it is told with exquisite reticence and grace, and with a plausibility that is as extraordinary as it is immoral. Here is the conclusion of that story:

"What I said Mary would see, she saw, but I forgot that no human eyes could look on such a vision with impunity. And I forgot, as I have just said, that when the house of life is thus thrown open, there may enter in that for which we have no name, and human flesh may become the veil of a horror one dare not express.... The blackened face, the hideous form upon the bed, changing and melting before your eyes from woman to man, from man to beast, and from beast to worse than beast, all the strange horror that you witnessed, surprises me but little. What you say the doctor you sent for saw and shuddered at, I noticed long ago; I knew what I had done the moment the child was born, and when it was five years old I surprised it, not once or twice, but several times, with a playmate, you may guess of what kind.... And now Helen is with her companions." [CF 1.268]

There is the very quintessence of horror in the unutterable suggestion of such passages. As for "The Hill of Dreams," I have found its reading one of the most desolate and appalling experiences in literature. Reading it, himself, years after publication, its author decided that it was a "depressing book." That is undoubtedly true, but spiritually as well as technically it marks to date the topmost pinnacle of his tormented genius. It reaches heights so rarefied that breathing literally becomes painful. To the casual reader this sounds absurd; hyperbolical if not hypocritical rant; but in a day when a majority of critics find it difficult to restrain themselves in speaking of Harold Bell Wright, and place Jeffery Farnol beside Fielding and Thackeray, one cannot go far wrong in indulging a few enthusiasms for so genuine an artist as Arthur Machen.

Of the reviewers into whose hands fell this remarkable book, in the year of its publication, 1907, only one appears to have valued it at its real worth—the editor of *The Academy*, who, carried away by the tale and its telling, turned out a bit of critical prose which might have been lifted from the book, itself. "There is something sinister in the beauty of Mr. Machen's book," he wrote. "It is like some strangely shaped orchid, the colour of which is fierce and terrible, and its perfume is haunting to suffocation by reason of its intolerable sweetness. The cruelty of the book is more savage than any of the cruelty which the book describes. Lucian shuddered at the boys who were deliberately hanging an ungainly puppy; he had thrashed the little ruffian who kicked the sick cat, before he wrapped himself away from the contact of such infamy in the shelter of his own imaginings. For in "The Hill of Dreams" you seem to be shown a lovely, sensitive boy who has fashioned himself a white palace of beauty in his own mind. He has had time only to realize its full beauty when disease lays its cold touch upon him, and gathers him into her grasp, until he lies decaying and horrible, seeing his own decay and seeing that his decay makes the white palace foul. The boys did not chant songs as they looped the string round the neck of the uncouth puppy. Mr. Machen fashions prose out of the writhings of Lucian, who is dear to him: and his prose has the rhythmic beat of some dreadful Oriental instrument, insistent, monotonous, haunting; and still the soft tone of one careful flute sounds on, and keeps the nerves alive to the slow and growing pain of the rhythmic beat. Lucian in ecstasy of worship for the young girl whose lips have given him a new life, pressed his body against sharp thorns until the white flesh of his body was red with drops of blood. That, too, is the spirit of the book. It is like some dreadful liturgy of self-inflicted pain, set to measured music: and the cadence of that music becomes intolerable by its suave phrasing and perfect modulation. The last long chapter with its recurring themes is a masterpiece of prose, and in its way unique."

After that, there would seem to be no need for further comment on "The Hill of Dreams." But there is—there is!

Quite as important as what Mr. Machen says is his manner of saying it. He possesses an English prose style which in its mystical suggestion and beauty is unlike any other I have encountered. There is ecstasy in his pages. Joris-Karl Huysmans in a really good translation suggests Machen better, perhaps, than another; both are debtors to Baudelaire.[1]

The "ecstasy" one finds in Machen's work (of which more anon) is due in no small degree to his beautiful English "style"—an abominable word. But Machen is no mere word-juggler. His vocabulary, while astonishing and extensive, is not affectedly so. Yet his sentences move to sonorous, half-submerged rhythms, swooning with pagan color and redolent of sacerdotal incense. What is the secret of this graceful English method? It is this: he achieves his striking results and effects through his noteworthy gift of selection and arrangement. I had reached this conclusion, I think, before I encountered a passage from "The Hill of Dreams," which clinched it:

> "Language, he understood, was chiefly important for the beauty of its sounds, by its possession of words resonant, glorious to the ear, by its capacity, when exquisitely arranged, of suggesting wonderful and indefinable impressions,

---

1. I have let this last assertion stand as part of the original article, although Mr. Machen writes me that I am in error. "I never read a line of Baudelaire," he says, "but I have read deeply in Poe, who, I believe, derives largely from Baudelaire." Of course, it is the other way 'round, Baudelaire derives from Poe, but my own assumption is rendered clear.–V. S.

perhaps more ravishing and further removed from the domain of strict thought than the impressions excited by music itself. Here lay hidden the secret of suggestion, the art of causing sensation by the use of words." [CF 2.83-84]

Was it ever better expressed? He defines his method and exhibits its results at the same time. And dipping almost at random into the same volume, here is a further example of the method:

"Slowly and timidly he began to untie his boots, fumbling with the laces, and glancing all the while on every side at the ugly, misshapen trees that hedged the lawn. Not a branch was straight, not one was free, but all were interlaced and grew one about another; and just above ground, where the cankered stems joined the protuberant roots, there were forms that imitated the human shape, and faces and twining limbs that amazed him. Green mosses were hair, and tresses were stark in grey lichen; a twisted root swelled into a limb; in the hollows of the rooted bark he saw the masks of men. . . . As he gazed across the turf and into the thicket, the sunshine seemed really to become green, and the contrast between the bright glow poured on the lawn and the black shadows of the brake made an odd flickering light in which all the grotesque postures of stem and root began to stir; the wood was alive. The turf beneath him heaved and sunk as with the deep swell of the sea. . . ." [CF 2.18-19]

And:

"He could imagine a man who was able to live in one sense while he pleased; to whom, for example, every impression of touch, taste, hearing, or seeing should be translated into odor; who at the desired kiss should be ravished with the scent of dark violets, to whom music should be the perfume of a rose garden at dawn." [CF 2.77-78]

This is not prose at all, but poetry, and poetry of a high order. And it is from such beautiful manipulation of words, phrases, and rhythms that Machen attains his most clairvoyant and arresting effects in the realms of horror, dread, and terror; from the strange gesturings of trees, the glow of furnace-like clouds, the somber beauty of brooding fields, and valleys all too still, the mystery of lovely women, and all the terror of life and nature seen with the understanding eye.

So much for Arthur Machen as a novelist. It is a fascinating subject, but it is also an extensive one, and the curious, tenuous quality of his work may lead one into indiscretions.

The peculiar philosophy of Arthur Machen is set down in "Hieroglyphics" and in "Dr. Stiggins: His Views and Principles." The first chapter of the latter work is a scathing satire on certain foibles and idiosyncracies of the American people—such as lynching, vote-buying, and food-adulteration—but as it is, on the whole, a polemical volume which, by the nature of the subjects it treats, can have less permanent interest than the author's other work, it may be put to one side; although as a specimen of Machen's impeccable prose it must not be ignored.

In "Hieroglyphics" he returns to those ecstasies mentioned in "The White People" and gives us further definitions. The word ecstasy is merely a symbol; it has many synonyms. It means rapture, adoration, a withdrawal from common life, the other things. "Who can furnish a precise definition of the indefinable? They (the "other things") are sometimes in the song of a bird, sometimes in the whirl of a London street, sometimes hidden under a great, lonely hill. Some of us seek them with most hope and the fullest assurance in the sacring of the mass, others receive tidings through the sound of music, in the colour of a picture, in the shining form of a statue, in the meditation of eternal truth."

"Hieroglyphics" is Arthur Machen's theory of literature, brilliantly exposited by that "cyclical mode of discoursing" that was affected by Coleridge. In it he promulgates the admirable doctrine that fine literature must be, in effect, an allegory and not the careful history of particular persons. He seeks a mark of division which is to separate fine literature from mere literature, and finds the solution in the one word ecstasy (or, if you prefer, beauty, wonder, awe, mystery, sense of the unknown, desire for the unknown), with this conclusion: "If ecstasy be present, then I say there is fine literature, if it be absent, then, in spite of all the cleverness, all the talents, all the workmanship and observation and dexterity you may show me, then, I think, we have a product (possibly a very interesting one) which is not fine literature."

Following this reasoning, by an astonishing sequence of arguments, he proceeds to the bold experiment of proving "Pickwick" possessed of ecstasy, and "Vanity Fair" lacking it. The case is an extreme one, he admits, deliberately chosen to expound his theory to the nth. degree. The analytical key to the test is found in the differentiation between art and artifice, a nice problem in such extreme instances as Poe's "Dupin" stories and Stevenson's "Dr. Jekyll and Mr. Hyde," as Mr. Machen points out. By this ingenious method the "Odyssey," "Oedipus," "Morte d'Arthur," "Kubla Khan," "Don Quixote," and "Rabelais" immediately are proven fine literature; a host of other esteemed works merely, if you like, good literature.

"Pantagruel" by a more delicate application of the test becomes a finer work than "Don Quixote," and in the exposition of this dictum we come upon one of the mountain peaks of Machen's amazing philosophy.

He begins the discussion with a jest about the enormous capacity for strong drink exhibited by *Mr. Pickwick* and his friends, and reminds us that it was the god of wine in whose honor Sophocles wrote his dramas and choral songs, who was worshipped and invoked at the Dionysiaca; and that all the drama arose from the celebration of the Bacchic mysteries. He goes on to the "Gargantua" and "Pantagruel," which reek of wine as Dickens does of brandy and water.

The Rabelaisian history begins: "*Grandgousier estoit bon raillard enson temps, aimant a boire net,*" and ends with the Oracle of the Holy Bottle, with the word "*Trinch . . . un mot panomphee, celebre et entendu de toutes nations, et nous signifie, beuvez.*" "And I refer you," continues Machen, "to the allocution of Bacbuc, the priestess of the Bottle, at large. 'By wine,' she says, 'is man made divine,' and I may say that if you have not got the key to these Rabelaisian riddles, much of the value—the highest value—of the book is lost to you."

Seeking the meaning of this Bacchic cultus, this apparent glorification of drunkenness in all lands and in all times, from Ancient Greece through Renascent France to Victorian England, by peoples and persons not themselves given to excess, he finds it again in the word ecstasy.

> "We are to conclude that both the ancient people and the modern writers recognised ecstasy as the supreme gift and state of man, and that they chose the Vine and the juice of the Vine, as the most beautiful and significant symbol of that Power which withdraws a man from the common life and the common consciousness, and taking him from the dust of earth, sets him in high places, in the eternal world of ideas . . . Let us never forget that the essence of the book ("Pantagruel") is in its splendid celebration of ecstasy, under the figure of the vine." [H 110-11, 113]

At this point Mr. Machen places the "key" in our hands and declines further to reveal his secrets. In *Mr. Pickwick's* overdose of milk punch we are to find, ultimately, "a clue to the labyrinth of mystic theology."

By his own test we are enabled to place Arthur Machen's greatest works on the shelf with "Don Quixote" and "Pantagruel"; by his own test we find the ecstasy of which he speaks in his own pages, under the symbol of the Vine, and under figures even more beautiful and terrible. For minor consideration he finds in Rabelais another symbolism of ecstasy:

> "the shape of gauloiserie, of gross, exuberant gaiety, expressing itself by outrageous tales, outrageous words, by a very cataract of obscenity, if you

please, if only you will notice how the obscenity of Rabelais transcends the obscenity of common life; his grossness is poured out in a sort of mad torrent, in a frenzy, a very passion of the unspeakable." [H 115]

In Cervantes he finds the greater deftness, the finer artifice, but he believes the conception of Rabelais the higher because it is the more remote. *Pantagruel's* "more than frankness, its ebullition of grossness . . . is either the merest lunacy, or else it is sublime." And the paragraph that succeeds this one in the book, perhaps it is part of the same paragraph, sums up this astonishing philosophy with a conclusion calculated to shock the Puritanic. Thus:

"don't you perceive that when a certain depth has been passed you begin to ascend into the heights? The Persian poet expresses the most transcendental secrets of the Divine Love by the grossest phrases of the carnal love; so Rabelais soars above the common life, above the streets and the gutter, by going far lower than the streets and the gutter: he brings before you the highest by positing that which is lower than the lowest, and if you have the prepared, initiated mind, a Rabelaisian 'list' is the best preface to the angelic song. (!) All this may strike you as extreme paradox, but it has the disadvantage of being true, and perhaps you may assure yourself of its truth by recollecting the converse proposition that it is when one is absorbed in the highest emotions that the most degrading images will intrude themselves." [H 118-19]

And so on. . . . The sense of the futility almost of attempting to explain Machen becomes more pronounced as I progress. You will have to read him. You will find his books (if you are fortunate) in a murky corner of some obscure second-hand bookshop.

Arthur Machen was born in Wales in 1863. He is married and has two children. That is an astonishing thought, after reading "The Inmost Light." It is surprising indeed to learn that he was *born*. He is High Church, "with no particular respect for the Archbishop of Canterbury," and necessarily subconsciously Catholic, as must be all those "lonely, awful souls" who write ecstasy across the world. He hates puritanism with a sturdier hatred than inspires Chesterton; for a brilliant exposition of this aversion I commend readers to his mocking introduction to "The House of Souls." That work, "The Hill of Dreams," and "Hieroglyphics" were written between 1890 and 1900, after which their author turned strolling player and alternated for a time between the smartest theatres in London and the shabbiest music halls in London's East End. For the last six years or so he has been a descriptive writer on the London *Evening News*.

His works not before mentioned comprise a translation (the best) of the "Heptameron"; "Fantastic Tales," a collection of mediaeval whimsies, partly translated and partly original and altogether Rabelaisian and delightful; "The Terror," a "shilling shocker" (his own characterization), but a finer work withal than most of the "literature" of the day, and "The Great Return," an extraordinary short tale which may find place some day in another such collection as "The House of Souls."

I have mentioned "The Chronicle of Clemendy," calling it a classic, and something further should be said about that astonishing book. It is the Welsh "Heptameron," a chronicle of amorous intrigue, joyous drunkenness, and knightly endeavor second to none in the brief muster of the world's greatest classics. In it there is the veritable flavour of mediaeval record. Somewhat less outspoken than Balzac in his "Droll Stories," and less verbose than Boccaccio, Machen proves himself the peer of either in gay, irresponsible, diverting, unflagging invention, while his diction is lovelier than that of any of his forerunners, including the nameless authors of those rich Arabian tapestries which were the parent tales of all mediaeval and modern facetiae.

The day is coming when a number of serious charges will be laid against us who live in this generation, and some severe questions asked, and the fact that we will be dead, most of us, when the future fires its broadside, has nothing at all to do with the case.

We are going to be asked, *post-mortem,* why we allowed Ambrose Bierce to vanish from our midst, unnoticed and unsought, after ignoring him shamefully throughout his career; why Stephen Crane, after a few flamboyant reviews, was so quickly forgotten at death; why Richard Middleton was permitted to swallow his poison at Brussels; why W. C. Morrow and Walter Blackburn Harte were in our day known only to the initiated, discriminating few; their fine, golden books merely rare "items" for the collector. Among other things, posterity is going to demand of us why, when the opportunity was ours, we did not open our hearts to Arthur Machen and name him among the very great.

About My Books

Arthur Machen

Eleusinia: 1881

This is a horrible production. The only defence is that it was written when I was seventeen, just after I had left school. That being the case, it is a pity that there is a mistake in the Greek epigraph: "muomenos" should be "muoumenos." I wished to have this epigraph in Greek characters, but Mr Jones, the stationer, bookseller and printer of Broad Street, said that Greek type would be extra. 100 copies were printed of this small pamphlet.

It is a "poem." So far as I recollect, it was done by the process of turning the article "Eleusinia" in *Smith's Classical Dictionary* into verse, some of it blank, some rhymed, all of it bad.

"H.C.S." stands for "Hereford Cathedral School."

The Anatomy of Tobacco: 1884

In 1883, aged twenty, I was up in London, trying to make a living. At first I tried the "editorial" department of Messrs Marcus Ward, educational publishers. I got tired at the end of a month and left. Then I taught a family of small children, getting, if I remember, twenty-five shillings a week for doing so. I lived on dry bread, green tea and tobacco, and saved money. I inhabited one room of a house in Clarendon Road, Bayswater. It measured, I should say, ten feet by six. There was no fireplace in it, so in winter I sat in my greatcoat and made the best of the gas-jet. I was almost without a friend in London, so life on the whole was rather lonely.

However, I read everything I could get hold of, and somehow I got hold of a book of scholastic logic, a science I had never studied before. I found it entrancing, and thus out of tobacco and logic, the two chief solaces of my loneliness, I made a book, *The Anatomy of Tobacco*, and in the occupation of making it found a third and most powerful relief. And *The Anatomy* had this further merit, that it put a final stop to my writing of bad verse.

It was published by an odd accident. I was always a dabbler in the occult sciences, and had been re-reading Hargrave Jennings's *The Rosicrucians*, a farrago of captivating nonsense. Reading also in Herodotus, I found there an account of certain Egyptian mysteries, and I saw a point that Jennings might have made in his mad argument and wrote to him about it. He gave my address to his publisher, George Redway, and Redway sent me his publication list, which contained some books dealing with tobacco; and thus I was moved to send the MS. of *The Anatomy* to Redway.

The Heptameron: 1886

At the end of 1884 I was back in the country again, with nothing particular to do. The publisher of *The Anatomy of Tobacco*, Redway, found me an occupation. He asked me to make a new translation of the Heptameron, and I did so. I had been reading a good deal of seventeenth-century prose, and I did my best to make my version a seventeenth-century one.

A graceful book, but, as it strikes me now, a little faded. The Heptameron always reminds me of some embroidered, silken dress that has lain in a dark chest for many long years. It is still beautiful; but the embroidered roses have grown somewhat dim.

Collectors who want the "right" edition should see that there is a frontispiece portrait of Margaret of Navarre and eight etchings by Léopold Flameng.

Don Quijote de la Mancha: 1887

This is an advertisement. Redway, besides publishing new books, sold secondhand ones. These were kept in a garret over Vizetelly's publishing office in Catherine Street. A street now runs over the place where the house stood. Here, during the summer of the year '85, I was occupied in cataloguing these books, and chiefly in writing notes under the titles. They dealt principally with the occult sciences, and a rather elaborate catalogue was issued, called *The Literature of Occultism and Archaeology*. Later, in 1887, it struck me that a parody of the famous chapter in *Don Quixote* relating to the examination of the Knight's library by the Curate and the Barber would make an amusing advertisement of the occult library of Catherine Street; and so I wrote the "chapter" aforesaid.

It was in this Catherine Street garret, by the way, that I heard old Vizetelly telling Redway about a book he had just published—I choose to forget the name of the book. This was the scrap of conversation:

"He—the author—came here the other day and said: 'You ought to have sold more copies; people are talking of nothing else.' 'You are talking of nothing else, you mean': that was my answer."

The Fortunate Lovers: 1887

This was designed to be a "drawing-room" edition of the Heptameron. Miss Robinson selected a certain number of the more polite tales, and wrote an elaborate and very tiresome preface, concerned chiefly with the identification of the characters who tell the various stories. It is wonderful how the academic mind contrives to get hold of the wrong end of every stick that it handles! Who cares now who "Hircan" was in the real life of 1510? As Miss Rebecca West said so sagely of the great Swinburne-Watts-Dunton debate of a few years ago: "Anyhow, they are all dead, and it doesn't matter!"

Miss Robinson on the Heptameron somewhat reminds me of a Mr Tilley, of the University of Cambridge, on Rabelais. He wrote a book which made it quite clear, let us say, that Rabelais was not born at Chinon, but at a village near Chinon; and that his father was a lawyer, not an apothecary. In fact, he made everything quite clear, saving this: that Rabelais wrote perhaps *the* most amazing book that was ever written. *That* fact was left in infinite, uttermost obscurity.

The Chronicle of Clemendy: 1888

I thought of this book and began to write it in the summer of 1885. Its origins were: a great delight in Balzac's *Contes Drolatiques*, in Rabelais the unsearchable, and in my own country, Gwent. I was quite fixed that I must write a book combining, so far as I could, all these delights; but, unfortunately, I could not find out for my life what this book was to be about; the very shape and form of it were dark to me. But, looking back, and remembering faintly the nights when I lay awake thinking of it in the 10 × 6 room in Clarendon Road, I believe it was to be "a great Romance." But, somehow, this romance would in no wise get going. There was to be a voyage in it—because there is the Voyage to the Oracle of the Holy Bottle in Rabelais—but whither that voyage, and in search of what?—these problems were never solved. I wrote the first chapter. It was so bad that it would kill me now; but one is tough at twenty-two. All of this period of effort that survives into the printed book is the "Epistle Dedicatory" and the "Epilogue." I like them both still, after thirty-six years. I even venture to commend the latter to the notice of young gentlemen "commencing authors"; I maintain it puts a certain situation very delicately. The situation was this: in a few days—I had every reason to expect—I should find myself without a roof over my head or a crust of bread in my belly. However, things changed for the better, and I went home again to the country, and thought a little more about the book.

Somehow, in the winter of '85–'86, it got a shape of some sort. It became a volume of tales of the medieval pattern. I did it as well as I could, and finished it in August 1886.

Thesaurus Incantatus: 1888

The fantastic tale of "The Enchanted Treasure" is an exercise in a somewhat rare literary *genre:* the occult extravaganza. I believe that *The Chemical Marriage of Christian Rosycross* (early seventeenth century) is in this kind, though some Rosicrucians take it seriously. My effort arose from various occult readings of the ancient sort, and, largely, from the study of Beroalde de Verville's *Moyen de Parvenir*.

I only know of one perfect copy of the Large Paper edition; it is in the possession of my friend, Mr Harry Spurr. There is another L.P. copy, which is, or was, in the possession of my friend, Mr Vincent Starrett, of Chicago. It is "imperfect," owing to the methods of a young collector, a relative of mine, who found it in a cupboard, and thought it would be amusing to tear out a page or two. So I sent what remained of the copy across the Atlantic, for safety's sake.

The Way to Attain: 1889

A very curious story. The Dryden Press, Long Acre, undertook to print the complete translation of *Le Moyen de Parvenir*. Some dispute arose—I forget on what matter—and the printing went no further. I "modified" my version, and gave it the title of *Fantastic Tales*. I cannot account for the existence of the fragmentary copies of *The Way to Attain*. If I ever had the clue, I have lost it.

Fantastic Tales: 1890

As may have been observed, I had Rabelais a little on the brain in the late 'eighties and early 'nineties. Consequently, when I came across an early edition of Béroalde de Verville's *Moyen de Parvenir* I fell an easy prey. I only wonder that I did not insist on translating *Les Caquetis de l'Accouchée* and *Le Printemps d'Yver*. Anyhow, I gaily undertook the task of rendering this monster of a book, *Le Moyen de Parvenir*, into English. It was "twelve months' hard."

The book is said to be the only one which begins with the word "For." I wish that this were its worst peculiarity. But it is one of the most shapeless things ever compounded by the human brain. I am like the man in *Rudder Grange*, who, speaking of German literature, said he didn't know how it was done or what it was for. The author was the son of a famous Calvinist and Renaissance scholar, Matthieu Beroalde. The son abjured his father's Calvinism, called himself Beroalde de Verville, and became a priest and a canon of Tours Cathedral. His book, if it can be analysed at all, which is more than doubtful, is a collection of discourses, in dialogue form, on Reformation politics, on the correct idiom of the French language, on some unknown subject which has been conjectured to be Alchemy—on anything which came into the head of this crazy canon. Interspersed in this mixture are many tales, some pointless, a few amusing, a few of some folk-lore value, and not a few both dull and disgusting. The lantern may be the lantern of Rabelais, but the candle has guttered and fatted away into darkness and the wick stinks abominably. And, worst of all, the book is full of feeble and strained puns, which have little point in the original French, and worse than no point at all in my rendering of them.

Yet, I must say that the *Moyen de Parvenir* is a curious book.

The Great God Pan: 1894

I have written the whole story of this book as a preface to the latest edition of it, published in 1916 by Messrs Simpkin, Marshall.

It was one of the early "Keynotes Series," and in this form went into two editions. It was included in the collection called *The House of Souls* published by Grant Richards. It was reissued separately by Grant Richards in 1913. It was translated into French by my friend P. J. Toulet (1901), and reissued by Simpkin, Marshall in 1916 with an introduction by me telling the whole story from the literary point of view. In this I have quoted the reviews at some length. They are exquisite, but not so exquisite as the remark of a literary agent whom I met one day in Fleet Street. He looked at me impressively, morally, disapprovingly, and said:

"Do you know, I was having tea with some ladies at Hampstead the other day, and their opinion seemed to be that such a book as *The Great God Pan* should never have been written."

The Memoirs of Jacques Casanova: 1894

I made this translation in 1888-89. For one reason or another it was not issued till 1894.

I began my version in the middle of the fourth or fifth volume, and when I had come to an end, my employer handed me three little quartos—translations of the early part of Casanova made by a German who knew English well, but not well enough. The task of correcting his queer prose was infinitely tedious. These volumes had been printed in Germany; I think at Wurtemberg.

Casanova has always puzzled me. On the face of it, he reads as a liar of the worst—or best and most sumptuous—kind. He wanders all over Europe and cannot cross the street without meeting "the famous this" or "the infamous that." When he is staying in London he goes out for a ride and gets thrown from his horse, opposite the park gates of "the notorious Duchess of Kingston." By one means or another he meets the whole European society of the pre-revolutionary period. It seems unlikely; but the best French critics say it is all true! "Casanova est un véridique," as Octave Uzanne wrote to me.

Yet he has been tested at one point and found wanting. He occupied, as he says, a furnished house in Pall Mall, paying twenty guineas a week for it. He put an odd advertisement for a housekeeper in the paper, and he quotes an editorial comment in the *St James's Chronicle* on this advertisement. The files of the paper have been searched. There is no such comment to be found.

On the other hand, he is perfectly correct in saying that "La Charpillon" lived with her family in Denmark Street, Soho. She was afterwards the mistress of Jack Wilkes, whom she humbugged almost as badly as she humbugged Casanova.

The Three Impostors: 1895

The title of this book has a curious history. *De Tribus Impostoribus* was a book much talked of by the learned in the seventeenth century. As far as I can remember, quoting without book, Browne of the *Religio Medici* speaks of that "villain and secretary of hell that wrote the miscreant piece of *The Three Impostors.*" But it is doubtful whether such a book were ever in existence—in print at any rate. Afterwards, such a book was forged; just as the German occultists, not being able to get into communication with the mythical Rosicrucian Society of the Andrea pamphlets, invented a society, several societies, which they declared to be the genuine article. Indeed, this forging business went on and spread to England, so that in the 'eighties of the last century an imposing Rosicrucian Order, laying claim to high antiquity, was invented and "put on the market" with such ingenuity that the refinements and intricacies of the process remain obscure to this day.

So, perhaps, with the tract, *De Tribus Impostoribus*—the three impostors, by the way, were Christ, Moses and Mahomet. Perhaps there never was such a book, perhaps such a book did exist in manuscript, was seen by a few and talked about by many. Anyhow, I liked the sound of the title, and noted it in '85, and indicated in my notebook the sort of book—a picaresque romance—I should like to write under that head; and so had the title waiting for me in the spring of 1895.

The book itself, my *Three Impostors*? An imitation, I regret to say, of Stevenson's *Dynamiter* and *New Arabian Nights*. I have always wished I were Shaw; for then I should speak of the "Stevensonian Anschaung"; as it is, I must say that I imitated this "Arabian" manner of Stevenson's as well as I could. As for the matter, the vital spring of the best stories in the book, that is my own. I speak with timidity, knowing something of the hidden and mingled and secret founts of "notions" and plots; but I do not think that anybody before had written anything like the tales of "The Black Seal," or, "The White Powder." The hypothesis on which the former story is based is, of course, not my own: it is that the Fairies, the Little People, were, in fact, the dark, dwarfish, Pre-Celtic inhabitants of Britain. But the supposition that these people still dwell under the hills, that they are horribly evil, and that they are something more or something less—than human: all this I must put down to my own account. The general hypothesis of "The White Powder" is obtained, very distantly, from Payne Knight; the special *machina*, the magical division of personality, is, to the best of my belief, my own.

It gave me great pleasure, by the way, to murder, under singular circumstances of ingenious atrocity, a former employer of mine—see the chapter headed, "Strange Occurrence in Clerkenwell." This was Edward Walford, who compiled Peerages and such stuff.

But he told one good story. He was calling on his publishers, Chatto and Windus. One of the partners had a great dog, a mastiff, or St Bernard. As Mr Walford mounted the stairs to the publishers' parlour, this dog barked furiously.

"It's all right," said Mr Chatto—or Mr Windus—"you needn't be afraid of the dog, Mr Walford."

"No," said Mr Walford, "I'm not afraid of him. It isn't the dog I'm afraid of when I call on a publisher."

And this reminds me of a little incident in the history of *The Three Impostors*. I sent the MS. to Messrs Heinemann towards the close of 1894. Early in 1895 I received a very warming letter from the firm, praising the book highly, and begging me to call. I called, and saw Mr Pawling. He was more enthusiastic than the letter. He read me glowing extracts from the reader's report, uttered phrases such as "better than Stevenson's best"—I was not fool enough even in '95 to believe that—and spoke of liberal royalties, of large sums in advance on account of those royalties. He also expressed a hope that my future books might come the way of Messrs Heinemann.

Rare indeed! In three weeks' time I received the MS. of *The Three Impostors* with a bare, brief formula from Messrs Heinemann declining its publication. There was no word of explanation, no attempt at any sort of apology.

Is there any little manual written for the benefit of these publisher people called *Common Decency Without Tears?*

Hieroglyphics: 1902

I remember well how I got the proof-sheets of *Hieroglyphics*. I was at Margate, playing the Professor in the three-act comedy, *The Varsity Belle*. Such are the mutations of things. Let me give a fragment of the dialogue of the farce, to reconstitute the scene. I quote, let it be said, from distant memory.

> *The Old Actor:* "When your brother died, he left behind him a rare and sparkling jewel."
> *The Professor:* "Indeed! I didn't know that he left anything that sparkled—except his glass eye!"

Hieroglyphics owes its origin to the fact that during the year '98 I was on the staff of *Literature*, a paper published by *The Times*. I had to review books, and to find reasons for my liking and disliking, my appreciation and depreciation. I had to ask myself, "What is romance? Is the *Prisoner of Zenda*, for example, romantic?" And this question became fused into the larger question: "What is literature?"

The book, *Hieroglyphics*, is an attempt to answer this larger question. A partner in one of the most eminent publishing firms of London assured me the other day that "it had influenced the whole standpoint of English literary criticism."

Which is very soothing, as Mr Pecksniff remarked. I am quite ashamed to mention, after this, that I have not received one single farthing for the book from 1902 even until now. However, the work had its use. It irritated serious people. Mr Walkley, the dramatic critic of *The Times*, the man who knows Greek, didn't like it at all. He began his notice:

"I do not know whether Mr Arthur Machen is to be described as an actor who amuses his leisure by writing books or as an author who fills up his evenings by appearing on the stage. He was a member of the Benson Company, and is now to be seen in a small part in *Paulo and Francesca*. He wrote some years ago a clever, disagreeable book, *The Great God Pan*."

And I fared ill with another critic on the Rationalist side, Sir A. T. Quiller Couch.

But, on the other hand, the pious liked me still less. The *Pilot*, an extinct Anglo-Catholic weekly paper began:

"The device by which vendors of patent wares tempt curiosity by giving them some curious name is hardly worthy of imitation in a man of letters, and we admire neither Mr Machen's title nor," etc. etc.

A pleasant story of Sir A. T. Quiller Couch lingers in my memory. The distinguished author was producing a play at The Haymarket—*The Mayor of Troy*, I think it was called. In the exercise of my unhappy business of journalist I had to pester Couch for an "interview," which he gave me with great good temper. A day or two later I met Lyall Swete, who was playing in the piece. I mentioned my interview with his author.

"Ah," said Swete. "I was talking to Couch. He said: 'Swete, how do you think I spent yesterday? In being interviewed by journalists! Do you know, I feel as if I were covered with slime!'"

And the well graced actor made eloquent gesture with mouth and arms, as if he would indicate how Sir A. T. Quiller Couch loathed the contact of the reptile press, and would fain cleanse his little hands of defilement.

I tell this true, sad story in order that my fellow journalists, who are sometimes puffed up, may know how good men regard them.

The second edition of *Hieroglyphics*, published by Secker, has for frontispiece a photograph of myself. It seems to express great gloom, righteousness and austerity. What it really expresses are my sentiments during the process of "sitting."

"Oh Lord!" I was saying to myself, "why should I waste my time being photographed at Baron's court this blessed Sunday, when I might be drinking my absinthe at the Yorkshire Stingo?"

Dr Stiggins: 1906

This is a volume of controversial theology. There are good things in it for those who like controversy, and also many weary pages. It was written in a hurry—30,000 words in a fortnight—was badly printed on bad paper, was barely noticed by the Press (two reviews, I think), and fell stone dead on publication. Oddly enough, second-hand copies now fetch 25/-. It is an attempt to amplify the Preface I wrote to *The House of Souls* at the request of the publisher.

The House of Souls: 1906

This is a collection of stories, containing: "A Fragment of Life," "The White People," "The Great God Pan," "The Inmost Light," "The Three Impostors" and "The Red Hand." The "Pan" and the "Impostors" I have already discussed.

"A Fragment of Life" has an oddish history. It was begun in May or June 1899, when I had just finished *Hieroglyphics*. Its origins are queer and incredible. I had gone for a walk with a friend one bleak Sunday afternoon in the March of that year in a favourite region of mine, which I have always regarded as sacred to grey Sunday afternoons and gloomy, bitter weather: Islington, Canonbury and the parts thereto adjacent. We inclined to the right, and came, I think, to the Ball's Pond Road—where Mr Perch lived—and dropped somehow, down into Hackney, via Dalston?—Thence by tram back to Bloomsbury, for I lived then in Gray's Inn.

Well, in a long street in the Ball's Pond region or in Dalston, I noted the houses built exactly in the same fashion, each with steps up to the hall door, each with a "breakfast-room," half beneath the level of the black front garden, each breakfast-room displaying the table laid for Sunday tea. Then in the tram a little family party got in, no doubt on their way to spend the evening with friends. A colourless, mildly whiskered man, and a foolish-looking young woman, his wife, in her foolish black satin Sunday dress, holding the simple baby on her knee, and I thought, glancing at them: "These, silly as they look, limited as they doubtless are, these two also have been initiated in the everlasting mysteries and have partaken of the great secrets, and have known what is concealed under the barley in the sacred basket of the holy procession of Eleusis."

That, then—Sunday tea-tables and Sunday people—was the fount of what became "A Fragment of Life": the formless impression which comes before any plot or designed succession of circumstances. Behind it was also a tale which I wrote and printed in some weekly paper which I have forgotten, which is forgotten, called "The Resurrection of the Dead." This told how a small London clerk, living in some small, raw suburb, suddenly realised that he was the last descendant of an ancient house of Welsh squires, who had lived for a thousand years between the river and the wood, in a wonderful country.

"The White People" is a fragment—not of life, but of a story. This was to have been something quite long and elaborate and magnificent; it was planned, like *Hieroglyphics*, just after I had left *Literature*. Indeed, I think that the strongest literary impulse that I have ever received arose from the joy and relief that I experienced on being rid of the detestable office life. I daresay that all offices are tiresome places, but an office in any way concerned with literature or writing is a mere stultification factory.

So, released from the web of tiresome nonsense that they wove on *Literature*, I set about real writing with a will. *Hieroglyphics* went well enough, but the tale was too much for me. "The White People" is but a broken fragment of it. It was first printed in a magazine called *Horlick's*. This was run by my old friend A. E. Waite, the distinguished writer on all topics of occult and mystic interest. He was manager at the time to Horlick's Malted Milk, and he contrived to persuade Horlick, in a manner obscure to me, which I feel sure must have implied the exercise of occult powers of a high kind, that the firm would be benefited by the publication of a magazine devoted to the mysteries. And so, in addition to Waite's wonderful and enchanting and illuminating essays on "The Holy Grail," *Horlick's* gave hospitality to "A Fragment of Life," *The Hill of Dreams*—under its first title, *The Garden of Avallaunius* and "The White People." I do not know that the sale of the Malted Milk was unfavourably affected.

"The White People," a single stone instead of a whole house, was naturally a disappointment. But it contains some of the most curious work that I have ever done, or ever will do. It goes, if I may say so, into very strange psychological regions.

"The Great God Pan" and "The Three Impostors" have been already annotated. But, by the way, I may note that "The Inmost Light," which was originally published with the "Pan," was written to one of the few commissions I have received in my literary lifetime. In the early 'nineties I was writing, oddly enough, stories of "society" for various papers, including *The World*, then still a power. I fancy that it must have been someone connected with *The World*, or *Life*, or one of those forgotten journals, who mentioned my name to the late Miss Braddon. Miss Braddon was getting out some sort of an annual, and she wrote to me asking for a tale. I wrote "The Inmost Light" for Miss Braddon. Miss Braddon refused it with lightning speed; and so no harm was done.

The last tale in *The House of Souls* is "The Red Hand," a highly ingenious and quite inferior piece of work. It was written in 1895—I did not know my way about very well in those days—for an American short story competition. Naturally—I decline to explain the exact force of the word "naturally"—it did not win any sort of prize. But, I don't know why, I sent it to Messrs Chapman, and it appeared in a ghostly Christmas number of *Chapman's Magazine*.

The Hill of Dreams: 1907

The Hill of Dreams was originally called *The Garden of Avallaunius*, a more distinctive title, but abandoned in view of the probability that "the trade" would call it "Avall-ay-yoonius"—if they called for it at all. The word, an invention of my own, has its little history. There was a Roman-British name, Vallaunius. This I conjectured to be, more properly, Avallaunius, the man of Avalon, I know not whether this derivation be well founded or no.

But the book itself. I have already said that *The Three Impostors*, so far as the style—rather, the manner—goes, was a crib from Stevenson. I perceived this, with some assistance from reviewers, in 1896, the year in which *The Three Impostors* was published. It was borne in on me that I must smash this borrowed manner to bits and build up another manner, which should be more worthy of being called a style, an expression of individuality. It was hideous work, doing this; almost like the learning of a new language. I had become fluent in the Stevensonian vein; now, I found, I was halting, uncertain, harsh, tautological. Nothing flowed easily, naturally; it was as if, accustomed to work in wax, one had suddenly to beat shape out of rock or stubborn metal. The MS. of the first chapter is an appalling mass of corrections and interlineations. But it was done at last, somehow.

So much for the manner; the matter I got from a hint of Mr Whibley's. It was, if I remember, in an introduction to *Tristram Shandy* that he described that work as being a picaresque of the soul, or of the mind. The phrase struck me, and I said to myself: "I will write a *Robinson Crusoe* of the soul; the story of a man who is not lonely because he is on a desert island and has nobody to speak to, but lonely in the midst of millions, because of his mental isolation, because there is a great gulf fixed spiritually between him and all whom he encounters." That was the first thought from which *The Hill of Dreams* proceeded.

Then, add to this the thought of the country in which I was born and bred, which counts for a great deal, directly or indirectly, in all my books; add the Roman associations of my native town, Caerleon-on-Usk, "Isca Silurum"; add the pains of literature, semi-starvation and loneliness which I had actually experienced in a pretty sharp degree; add a profound contempt for the popular book and the popular criticism of the day: and you have a fair analysis of the "motives" of *The Hill of Dreams*.

The pains of literature: of these I should have been able to write eloquently, since I experienced them to the uttermost in writing this very book. I began to think of it and to plan it in the autumn of 1895; it was not finished till the spring of 1897. First of all, there was the difficulty of the new manner, which broke away utterly from the Stevensonian cadence; and then the greater difficulty of carrying out the general scheme into detail. The first chapter was achieved: what story should the second tell? For three weeks I sat down, night after night, with the clean pile of paper. Sometimes I wrote three lines, sometimes three folios; and every night I found it hopeless; I knew that I was not on the right road.

The thought of the second chapter came at last, and things went on pretty smoothly till the end of the fourth. Then another break in the continuity. I went off on the wrong track, into a kind of elaborate philosophical dissertation. It is true that I discovered Buddhism by the way—the doctrine of the ego as an illusion—but this had been done two thousand five hundred years before, and, anyhow, it was not to the purpose of the book. I went floundering on, getting deeper and deeper in the marsh, and when I at last knew that I had lost my way utterly, I was for some time in despair of ever finding it again. There was a horrible struggle before I could get on the comparatively firm land of the fifth chapter; and that land was none too firm. Six followed easily when five had been done; then a grim fight that lasted for many months—followings of false tracks, endeavourings to write chapters that could not be written, brain-wrackings to desperation. The end seemed impossible; but the seventh chapter and the end were found and done somehow. And a pile of manuscript, at least a foot high, had accumulated. All of it unusable, all of it the wreckage of false starts and worse continuations: a monument of the folly of conscientious labour.

It had been a long battle. I lived in Gray's Inn in those days, and every afternoon I used to take out my old bulldog, Juggernaut, and the thought and problem of my book for a walk of half an hour or so, sometimes along the Clerkenwell Road past St John's Gate, with its memory of the great saint of literature, sometimes up Rosebery Avenue to Sadler's Wells. These are both hideous places, desolate regions of the grey world; but I reverence them to this day, remembering all that I endured in them; remembering the hopeless effort and agony of perfection. There is a small Italian restaurant on the right-hand side of Rosebery Avenue; it is there still as it was in '95, '96, '97, and I am glad, and trust that it flourishes. I have never been inside, but the name "P. Puncia," still brings to me the thrills, the agonies, *sudores, angores, dolores* that went to the making of *The Hill of Dreams*.

Still, all hard and honest work has its reward at last. A new publisher, Grant Richards, had written to me to ask for the right of my next manuscript. I sent him the finished book; and in return had a long letter, almost a fatherly and affectionate letter–though I had only met the gentleman once–urging me for the sake of my own reputation, never to publish this dull, futile, unhappy failure.

Then I tried Methuen. They sent me a long letter too, all on quarto paper. It was full of good advice. I tried the Unicorn Press, I think it was called that, and the Unicorn–who eventually turned into a Wine Merchant–wrote me perhaps the kindest letter of all. In fact, everybody was very kind, and ready to give up valuable time to the task of advising me on large quarto notepaper of excellent quality. It took Grant Richards ten years to change his mind and publish the book.

The Bowmen: 1915

I have told the whole story of *The Bowmen* so fully in the Preface to the book that there is little or nothing left to be said. The sale, I believe, was a very large one, but, for reasons into which I need not enter, the book was not highly remunerative to me. However, it is always a satisfaction to feel that one has put a little money into the pockets of good men. *The Bowmen* and the other tales in the volume originally appeared in *The Evening News*.

The Great Return: 1915

In the autumn of 1915, after the great success of *The Bowmen*, my friend Mr Burgess, a well-known authority on Plain Chant, and also, at that time, the Manager of the Faith Press, asked me to give him "something" running to 10,000 words or thereabouts. I warned him, once in conversation on the westernmost corner of the northern pavement of the Strand, and once in a letter, not to do it. My reasons were, firstly, that the firm he represented was not widely known in secular circles, and secondly, that I did not think they would care to spend very much money on advertisement. Both these reasons I kept to myself, but, as I say, I urged Mr Burgess to desist from his plan, which included, I may add, a very liberal fee to myself.

I am inclined to think that this case of an author trying to warn off a publisher is unique. The only parallel I can remember is afforded by the life of the poet Collins. Collins, it is said, wished to make up to the publisher the loss incurred on publishing his poems, and, as Leslie Stephen observes, it may not be irrelevant to note that soon afterwards Collins's mind began to show signs of giving way. However, the book, *The Great Return*, was written, and after a serial issue in *The Evening News*, was published by the Faith Press. I believe that it did very badly indeed. I know that a few months ago, wanting a copy, I went to the firm's offices in Buckingham Street and asked for *The Great Return*—"author's terms," I added, showing my card.

"Really," said the gentleman who waited on me, "I can't have the heart to charge you anything at all for it, Mr Machen." And he indicated a huge and dusty mound of *Great Returns*—the very phrase will be ominous in trade ears—lying in a cupboard. There were hardly any reviews. There was one little gem in *The Times Literary Supplement*. The story, I may say, relates to certain extraordinary manifestations of the Holy Grail in the western part of Wales, these manifestations or appearances or hallucinations—call them what you will—being not altogether in accord with the accepted Grail legend as presented in Tennyson's *Idyll*, and, indeed, showing traces of older sources than Malory. Well, the Literary Supplementer observed, firstly, that it was nonsense to be romancing about The Grail at all, since it had been proved to be merely a Feeding Vessel of pagan-Irish origin. This remark displayed a sumptuous ignorance of one of the greatest problems and greatest complexes in literature that has never, I suppose, been equalled.

But he made up for this in his second criticism. He protested against the Grail being manifested, as in my story, to quite common people, such as farmers and grocers. And I admit that it *was* low. But the Order of the British Empire was not in existence when the book was written. If it ever goes into a new edition—which seems unlikely—I shall certainly make all the characters O.B.E.'s. They will thus be more worthy to behold

> ... the Holy Grail
> All pall'd in crimson samite, and around
> Great angels, awful shapes, and wings and eyes.

The Terror: 1917

A "shilling shocker." It was also issued in America by the firm of McBride. They sold the first serial American right to some magazine, the *Century*, if I remember, and the *Century* cut down the 40,000 words or so into 10,000 words or so with a skill that was really remarkable. Needless to say, my permission was not asked. Some one sent me the magazine, and I saw my story in miniature, but, in the agreeable American idiom, I "had not a cough coming." If the *Century* had been so pleased, it could have cut down the tale to 1,000 words, and I should have had nothing to say.

This story appeared serially in *The Evening News*.

War and the Christian Faith: 1918

A series of Essays, written at the suggestion of Mr Alfred Turner, then Acting-Editor of *The Evening News*. The Essays appeared in that journal, and afterwards in book form.

The Secret Glory: 1922

The humble have many treasures; and one of the greatest of these is the gift of vision. I do not mean by this the vision of the higher kind, or the sight of those things which it is not lawful to utter, nor even that lower gift which enables the palmist and the astrologer to do some very astounding things every now and again. The vision I speak of has nothing to do with this or that; and yet we poor folk certainly are enabled to see the secrets of many hearts, and this *ex opere operato*; from the very fact of our humble condition. I have been in my day both a strolling player and a newspaper reporter. Neither occupation, I fear, is held in very high esteem, and thus from both careers I have been enabled to gather certain very choice observations. For example, soon after I joined the reporting staff of the London *Evening News*, I was sent to interview an old actor acquaintance, on his commencing manager. I often used to meet him in places of theatrical resort when I was playing at the St James's Theatre in 1901–1904. He was always very pleasant, and he invariably told me of his great quarrel with George Alexander. I forget what the quarrel was about, but I know it contained the brisk incident of Alexander suddenly popping out of his brougham in Bond Street, and shaking his fist in the face of the astonished player who was sauntering harmless on the pavement of that pleasant western thoroughfare, thinking no evil. Well, I had listened to this tale so often that I felt that it was almost a link between us, and years afterwards when the interview with the new manager was "assigned" to me I was pleased at the opportunity of renewing an old acquaintance. He received me with cold civility and observed: "You will of course understand that the last thing I want is vulgar puffery."

And it was as a reporter that I was once the guest of Keble College, Oxford.

And then the stage has its opportunities of a similar kind. Once on a time I was strolling in "Pastorals," that kind of theatrical entertainment which is given in the open air—unless it comes on to rain, and then the company and some of the audience adjourn to the town hall or the village schoolroom, where two geraniums in pots and one aspidistra in the same, artistically arranged on the platform, represent, with a technique that is quite Chinese, "these woods" of the Forest of Arden, declared in the text to be more free from peril than the envious court. Well, in the course of one of these old pastoral tours, my management, Messrs Garnet Holme and Harcourt Williams, had secured a "cert." That is, we were to give our show at a fixed fee from a gentleman who was entertaining all friends round Stow-on-the-Wold at a garden party. The gentleman lived in a noble fifteenth-century house in that noble old village. He was waiting for us at his arched doorway; waiting eagerly. Not exactly out of the spirit of antique hospitality: but, to warn the players to go up by the back stairs. As we went up he called another and a still more stringent warning after us: we were by no means to use any of the hot water from his bath-room tap. I am sorry to say that Henry Herbert—now a "star" in America, I believe—at once had a hot bath, not because he wanted such a thing, but because his was a spirit that revolted against all the forms and circumstances of oppression. Hungry and thirsty we came to that house after a long railway journey, hungry and thirsty we left it in the evening, though the tea spoons were clinking in the saucers, though the ice chimed musically in the big jugs of claret cup, though there must have been an abundance of broken victuals; bread and butter and cake, which would be either thrown away or given to the pigs. I believe the gentleman was a retired potter of the Five Towns.

Then there was another occasion, like but yet unlike to the Adventure of Stow-on-the-Wold. Again, we were a company of Pastoral Players, again the management had got a "cert." But this time our host was the late Duke of Norfolk, not a retired potter. Well, need I say more? the Duke treated us poor vagabonds as if we had all been dukes and duchesses, with the kindest hospitality and the most genial friendliness.

So much in explanation of the gift of vision which is vouchsafed to the poor and humble; and now for that particular application of the doctrine which serves as comment to *The Secret Glory*. Those who have read that tale are aware that it shows a certain lack of enthusiasm for the *ethos* of our great public schools. Well, in 1904, my old master, the Admirable Sir Frank Benson, was touring some of the big public schools with a representation that had been at his heart for many years. This was the Æschylean Trilogy: the *Agamemnon*, the *Libation Bearers* and the *Furies*. The first school to be visited was Harrow. Of course, the whole affair had been arranged with the school authorities; the performance was given in the school Speech Room; and, I suppose, Harrow School was in a sense the host, and we, of the Benson Company, were the school guests.

In the Greek classics we read that guests and strangers are the children of God. But I believe that for many years the study of the classics has declined in our schools. It has been pointed out by weighty authorities that Homer and Virgil do not lead to eminence in that form of swindling the public which is called "business" and more nobly still "big business." I am willing to suppose that young Harrow as long ago as 1904 had realised this, and was devoting its attention to more up to date studies: the manufacture of stinks and shocks and the careful and daily perusal of the *Daily Mail*. This curriculum, perhaps, fails to deal with the treatment due to guests, especially to guests of a humble kind. At any rate, the Benson Company was escorted up Harrow High Street—the street that goes up "the Hill" that makes your heart thrill when you think of the day when you came so strange and shy—by gangs of boys who were lavish of such courtesies as are usually bestowed on procurers and prostitutes. Some of the girls of the Company had their back hair pulled; the manly English schoolboys wanted to find out whether it were real: insults and offensiveness of every sort were rained on all.

At this time, there was a show on the Halls, a sort of Glee Party, called *Somebody's Eton Boys*. I was telling a friend the story of our reception at Harrow. He spoke of the "Eton Boys," and suggested that we ought to run an opposition show, to be called *Wood's Harrow Boys*—Dr Wood was then headmaster of Harrow.

"If," he said, meditatively, "if there were any reason to suppose that we could find in the worst slums of London a gang of hooligans offensive enough to be able to play the Boys." Thus, it will be noted, the poor strollers, by reason of their low estate, were given a vision of the heart of "the Hill" which would never be vouchsafed to the Prince of Wales.

So much for the *ethos* of the Great Public Schools, as it is dealt with in *The Secret Glory*. Another point in that work relates to the tributes which schoolmasters bestow on one another. I depict them as writing highly offensive folly concerning their colleagues. Not long ago, a few days, in fact, after the publication of *The Secret Glory*, I read a review of *Edmond Warre*, a life of a late Eton headmaster. Here is the sort of thing that Dr Warre's colleagues wrote of him.

I distinctly feared Warre's accession. I feared the dominance of athletics, his own autocratic ways, his strict adherence to the routine of what I thought a narrow and dry "scholasticism." The change came, and never was a more delightful surprise—it was like a fresh wind from the sea blowing into the place.

Another:

I like to think that Warre regarded the school as a great army on the march, the pace of which must necessarily be kept uniform.

The Lower Master:

Warre's visits to schoolroom were tremendous, there is no other word for it. The door flew open and in he swept. The boys sprang up with palpitating hearts, and the master looked suddenly bewildered. Yet there was nothing to fear; the awe was that naturally felt in the presence of majesty.

Another one, on his *Boots!*

They were not ungainly nor policemanlike boots, but only the Head could have wielded them—and "wield" is the only verb that fits the case ... he seemed hardly mortal in his bigness.

Yet another, on his Voice, which Vibrated:

This vibration had an effect on one's spine like that of the fiddles in the overture to *Tristan*.

So here was a Head—very likely the poor man in real fact was as harmless and as decent a pedagogue as ever took the Sixth in Sophocles—who was like a fresh wind from the sea, who thought that every one of his thousand scholars must learn their lessons at the same rate, just as an army must march at the same pace, who gave the boys a well-known functional disease of the heart by opening a door, bewildered the masters—no great feat, it would seem—wielded boots that none else of men could wield—cf. Bow of Odysseus—was of ordinary height but seemed hardly mortal in his bigness, and had a voice like fiddles!

I give it up! I tried in *The Secret Glory* to parody the sort of rot that schoolmasters write about each other; but I find that my attempt was useless. These Eton masters on their late Head read like an extravagant parody of my parodies.

What can such fellows as these teach—save cant?

There was once (1830-1840) a Berkshire Tory Squire, an old Winchester boy named Hughes, who wrote a letter of grave rebuke to a son at Rugby. The son, a præposter, was accused of having allowed an Italian image-man to be "ragged" by the boys. And the father, who seems to have belonged to that interesting though extinct species called "Christian Gentleman," wrote—I quote from memory—

> Do you not know that it is the special privilege of a gentleman to protect the poor; and that he who despises the poor despises the ordinance of god in making them so?

Ah, if old Mr Hughes—he was the father of the author of *Tom Brown's Schooldays*—could have seen the Harrovians hounding their guests, the play actors and play-actresses, through Harrow street!

The Confessions of a Literary Man: 1915

This opus has never been published in book form. It appeared, serially, in *The Evening News* in March-June, 1915. It is a magic book. It has the singular quality of making strong publishers turn pale at the mere thought of issuing it. It may not be irrelevant to remark—I have used the phrase before in these notes—that it is a favourite of mine.

It is a book that I was "going to write" for many years. I used to think of it on February nights, when high winds blew and sounded in the chimney, reminding me of the mountain winds that blew about my old home at Llanddewi, at the top of the long hill from Caerleon. It is seldom that one hears the great winds in London, and the noise and rumour of them at night always brings back to me the thought of the old days and the old ways; dark winter woods, dead fires, dead faces: the mountain in the west, the forest in the east, and a wild land between them. I was always going to write this book— and I never should have written it, if Alfred Turner, then editor of *The Evening News,* had not given me the order to write it for his paper. For that office of his, in spite of the publishers' pale faces, I am profoundly grateful to him.

The puzzle to me is, how he knew that the book was there.

So far I had written, when *The Confessions* was actually accepted by Martin Secker. But I changed the title. I knew that the mere mention of such words as "literary," "literature," will send the reading public rushing away in mad panic, as they rush away when somebody raises the cry "Fire!" at the theatre. So the printed book is called *Far Off Things*. I have dedicated it to Alfred Turner with very deep gratitude.

The City, the Vision, and Arthur Machen

Godfrey Brangham

If the doors of perception were cleansed everything would appear to man as it is, infinite. For man has closed himself up, till he sees all things thro' narrow chinks of his cavern.—William Blake, *The Marriage of Heaven and Hell* (154)

The science of the great city; the physiology of London; literally and metaphysically the greatest subject that the mind of man can conceive.—Arthur Machen, "The Inmost Light" (CF 1.303)

The late Victorian period appears to have emerged from an earlier more stable, self-assured, and self-congratulatory era. In London's moneyed West End there lay beneath an apparent film of respectability a seething cauldron of self-indulgence, whose mix included sexual licence, a proclivity for all things occult, secret societies, and countless other risqué enjoyments. By way of contrast the cauldron's ingredients that bubbled and steamed in the east of the city consisted of scouring poverty, prostitution, crime, anarchy, slums, and mass unemployment; all producing a recipe for a City of Sin. Those "sins" in the more affluent areas being rather more subtle than the overt nature of those in the East End.

Indeed, the East End could well have been viewed as existing as another country compared with its affluent neighbour. Its alleyways were often so narrow that the toppling upper stories of the houses on either side were almost touching. Life was a struggle, death by starvation, illness, or even suicide was common, whilst for many alcohol brought temporary relief from the rigours of their existence.

However, segmented between these two extremes lies North London, a region having little in common with either the riches of the West or the degradation and grinding poverty of the East. This was a relatively poor, lower-middle-class area where employment was still menial, but brought in a regular if small weekly wage. It was the ingrained nature of many of the districts of North London, such as Barnsbury, Clerkenwell, Pentonville, and the outer reaches of Islington, that was eventually to become the substrata of many of Arthur Machen's short stories. It was as if he developed an almost filial relationship with his surroundings as he delved deeper and deeper into its "undergrowth." As J. P. Hogan commented in his book *Hair under a Hat* (1949): "Machen was one of the last to have seen the Tyger burning bright in the forests of Bloomsbury and Barnsbury (35)."

But we have digressed, for the young Machen is still mooning around his beloved lanes in Gwent, though the Siren call of London is now beginning to echo in and about the walls of the old rectory at Llanddewi Fach. A further enticement was his eagerness to read the London newspapers, and to this end he regularly visited the bookstall at Pontypool Road Station to acquire them. Yet the phantom fragrance of those years were to remain with him throughout his long life.

The Neophyte

The great Metropolis—surrogate mother to so many artists, composers, and writers, all following their dreams and aspirations, some cresting the wave and finding fame and sometimes fortune, others floundering and lost beneath the unforgiving swirl of the city. In retrospect Arthur Machen neither crested nor floundered; he became a survivor, though the recipe for success (or even failure) remains a mystery. Momentary popularity rarely metamorphoses into lasting renown. Such writers as Edgar Wallace, Nevil Shute, and John Galsworthy were the kings of their day, their latest books avidly acquired by the public: they are now mostly out of print and out of mind.

It was in London that Machen spent most of his creative life frequently writing about his sojourns through the sullen and less desirable areas of the city. These experiences did indeed become intrinsic to many of his supernatural stories. However, the subjective nature of the influences that become the determinant factors in guiding people towards their destiny is almost impossible to quantify. Machen himself in the first volume of his autobiography *Far Off Things* (1922) intimates quite strongly that it was without doubt the idyllic childhood he spent at the remote rectory in the valley of the Soar. Here he wandered though lanes and fields, over domed hills, entered dark woods, and through innocent eyes visualised the Roman occupation of the nearby village of Caerleon-on-Usk. This sensitive, lonely young boy no doubt imbibed many sensations, both of wonder and during his nocturnal excursions, terror. As "Alain" (Émile-Auguste Chartier) commented: "There is little but the sublime to help us through the ordinary in life" (291).

Yet it must be acknowledged that life's journey will add modifying experiences to embellish those already acquired, so each day, each month, each year will alter (often insidiously) our perceptions of the world around us. There is little doubt that Machen's long association with London added layer upon layer to this foundation, which as we shall see is reflected in much of his work. An early example would be the cataloguing of occult literature he undertook in 1885 for the publisher George Redway, a task that no doubt greatly influenced the genre he was to choose as a writer. Thus his time at Llanddewi Fach might well have been the catalyst for those tales that are actually grounded in the city, and certainly there is a grain of truth in the following sentiment expressed by Sherlock Holmes in the "The Adventure of the Copper Beeches": "It is my belief, Watson, founded upon my experience, that the lowest and vilest alleys in London do not present a more dreadful record of sin than does the smiling and beautiful countryside."

Machen arrived in London for the first time in 1881, eventually finding lodgings at 23 Clarendon Road, Notting Hill, where he occupied a tiny room at the top of the building. It was there that he encountered the paradox of being in a city of many millions and yet finding himself quite alone. In *Things Near and Far* (1923) he was to write: "'Alone in London' has become a phrase, it is a title associated, I think, with some flaring melodrama; but the reality is a deadly thing" (*TNF* 15).

However, his determination to become a writer in some ways benefited from this isolation, allowing him to concentrate solely on his intended profession. Indeed, it must be admitted that those in the creative fields, whether composers, artists, or authors, exhibit a certain level of selfishness which is perhaps incumbent upon their trade, so the position Machen found himself in might well have provided the impetus needed at that crucial moment in his career. The pulse of his passion for his chosen profession without doubt visibly quickened now that he was an inhabitant of the metropolis.

Exploration is of course the natural inclination of anyone new to a city, but Machen first saw London as a place of infinite life and gaiety, especially the Strand, Regent Street, Piccadilly, and Bond Street with their glittering lamps, theatres, and multitudes of shops. They conjure up many disparate images, where frock-coated men alight from hansom cabs, offering a gloved hand to bustle-clad ladies of fashion. However, as time went on and he began to explore the less salubrious districts of North London he realised that these famous landmarks represented only a tiny part of the city as they vividly contrasted with fog-bound yellowing alleyways, vague squares, staring houses, sinister footsteps, blurred outlines of cloth-capped men wearing single-buttoned frayed jackets that he now witnessed. It may well be that his haunts changed due to an alteration in his circumstances, for by late 1882 he was rapidly approaching penury; poverty ostracising him from the brighter side of London. There is little doubt that Robert Louis Stevenson's *New Arabian Nights* (1882) became his "bible" as, to his great joy, he encountered through his wanderings perpetual surprises and discoveries. However, there is an intriguing disagreement over how he viewed the latter scenes. In *The Life of Arthur Machen* (2005), John Gawsworth writes about Machen's attempt in his short story "The Inmost Light" (1894) to express his loathing of these raw suburbs of London. Yet I suspect that the opposite was true, for in his autobiographical *Things Near and Far* Machen offers the following:

> Sometimes I took a friend with me on my journeys, but not often. The secret of it all was hidden from them.... On one grey day that I remember I had personally conducted a man on a most interesting exploration of the obscurer by-ways of Islington. He grew silent as the streets grew greyer and the squares dimmer and the remoteness of the whole region from any conceivable London that he knew filtered through his soul.... But this London that was a grey wilderness, these streets that went to the beyond and beyond, these squares which nobody that my friend could ever have known could ever inhabit: it was all too much for him.... So, of course, I never took him to Barnsbury. (*TNF* 63-64)

The words *secret* and *interesting* indicate a totally different viewpoint from that expressed by Gawsworth. Machen's world vision was on a different level altogether; I suspect that Gawsworth was really stating his own reaction to those environs. Perhaps to understand this *intrigue*, the experiments carried out by Aldous Huxley with the drug mescaline in the 1950s are of note. His paper *The Doors of Perception* describes the effects he underwent and his explanation of them. One of the most striking changes he experienced under the drug's influence was a heightened awareness, especially in his immediate surroundings where simple colours and shades were no longer homogeneous. This led to the conjecture that there is a baseline for visual experience, yet some individuals have, under certain circumstances, innate elevated perceptions. Thus Machen's excursions through "the beyond and beyond" yielded to him alternative or altered viewpoints: in his case a natural phenomenon rather than drug induced. In *Things Near and Far* he once more emphasises this: "And it is utterly true that he who cannot find wonder, mystery, awe, the sense of a new world and an undiscovered realm in the places by the Gray's Inn

Road will never find those secrets elsewhere" (*TNF* 59).

Machen was gradually becoming a connoisseur of the hidden by-ways of the city, and in *The London Adventure* (1924) he adopted a Sherlockian pose where he gives a detailed review of the inhabitants of an obscure street lying in the borderland between Camden Town and Holloway. Following the master detective's methods he deduces from the rows of modest houses that the occupants are also on modest wages. Each household would have a maid for domestic duties, a "boy" who would blacken the shoes, and if a pony and trap were kept then again their welfare would fall to him. He further describes their range of daily meals, depending on whether the master was retired or not, concluding that it was a very small life.

The Flâneur

> ". . . an entire civilisation lies just outside the pale of common thought . . . such life is different from any yet imagined . . . I see as clearly as the noonday that this is not all . . ."–Richard Jefferies (53)

Machen's observations of daily life in the city, its kaleidoscope of human behaviour, the pedantic daily life of office workers, the splendour of the Strand, the colourless back streets, each and every scene was assimilated into his personal encyclopaedia. However, in order to be able to read and write about the city—that is, to use the city as a text—one must be part of it, form a symbiotic relationship with it, come in from the outside. Yet after the exhilaration of his excursions he was forced each evening to return to his tiny room, to gaslit gloom, to cold and to isolation. It was Baudelaire who offered the following description of such a person residing in his native Paris: "For the perfect flâneur, for the passionate spectator, it is immense joy to set up house in the heart of the multitude, amid the ebb and flow of movement, in the midst of the fugitive and the infinite" (9).

How curiously similar is the following narrative by Machen in "The Encounter on the Pavement" from *The Three Impostors* (1895), where, strolling along Oxford Street, Mr Dyson "enjoyed in all its rare flavours the sensation that he was hard at work. His observation of mankind, the traffic, and the shop windows tickled his faculties with an exquisite bouquet" (*CF* 1.338).

Although the flâneur can be viewed mainly as a detached spectator, Machen takes it further by his obvious engagement with his subject. Just as, in *The Three Impostors*, Dyson is swept along by the unfolding events, so the spectator also becomes one of the players. We find that the actuality of London becomes the all-important setting for Machen's struggles as a writer. His *flâneurie* is the melting pot for the themes he uses either to create horror or less frequently wonder, so it is interesting to note that in many of his tales the starting points for both horror and revelation are the same. There is an initial normality which slowly, but inevitably, either descends into the pit or rises into a new transcendental realisation. Within this framework he seeks to elucidate the indescribable, the mystery that lies beneath the surface.

After he and A. E. Waite met in the 1880s and became the closest of friends, Machen often took him as a companion on his pilgrimages through North London. It can be conjectured that their very conversations must have added a certain hue to Machen's viewpoint. In *The Grande Trouvaille* (1923) we find them idly strolling up a hill in Pentonville, their intended goal to search out the school that Poe mentions in "William Wilson" (1839). Machen explains that they had often set out with this intention but were easily diverted from their quest. Waite certainly believed that somewhere amongst these dingy neighbourhoods lay the "Holy Grail," unnoticed, unrecognised, and waiting to be found. Machen had "the absorbing desire of going the other way. The other way? That is the secret" (n.p.).

In its entirety *The Grande Trouvaille*, a mere pamphlet, gives a microcosm, a flavour of those walks they undertook in late nineteenth-century London. It was some years later that he wrote about the transmutation he witnessed in Pentonville, where on an autumnal day its dusty, dreary appearance with its foreboding house fronts were of a sudden "all glowing purple with rich bunches of ripe grapes. Dionysius crowned and triumphing on the sad mount of Pentonville; the southern Latin vine glade and flourishing *in sicco* . . ." ("The Joy of London" 82).

This ability to convert his impressions onto the page is of course not merely a mechanical process. Machen's genius lies within his prose, the rhythm of the line, the accentuation or diminution of words or sentences. He was fully aware of this, as is shown in the following extract where he is attempting to write at the rectory when all others have retired for the night. It is one of the most brilliant expositions of the writer's task:

> To win the secret of words, to make a phrase that would murmur of summer and the bee, to summon the wind into a sentence, to conjure the odour of the night into the surge and fall and harmony of a line; this was the tale of the long evenings, of the candle flame white upon the paper and the eager pen. (CF 2.136)

This was echoed many years later by Carl Van Vechten in his novel *Peter Whiffle* (1922):

> Now Peter, as he sat on the bench beside me began to speak of Arthur Machen: The most wonderful man writing English today and nobody knows him! His material is handled with the most consummate art; arrangement, reserve, repose, the perfect word, are never lacking from his work.... (196)

Another element of Machen's London was his love of old buildings and styles. His savouring of eighteenth-century and early Victorian establishments is aligned with his intense dislike for change; in his philosophy modernity was notably equated with evil conspirators. Gerald Cumberland in *Written in Friendship* (1923) offers an interesting comment when he was first introduced to Machen in one of the "journalists'" taverns: "I looked at him now with curiosity, feeling that he belonged to the age of Johnson, Boswell, Reynolds, Garrick and Goldsmith. He was out of place, and, in spite of the fact that he was drinking beer from a tankard, he did not 'fit'" (121).

An oft-mentioned lament of Machen was the loss of so many of these inns, taverns, and coffee-houses. He conjures up, in high prose, appealing descriptions of them: warm dark rooms, low-beamed ceilings, wood fires with brasses reflecting their glow, green curtains, solid oak tables, snugs, and of course choice meats and ales. This yearning for past glories might well have been engendered by an overactive imagination, yet it does yield a pleasing aroma of other times. His love of ale, quality ale, was shared by his many friends and companions, none more so than Christopher Wilson, one-time musical director of the Benson Shakespearean Company. The following extract from a letter sent by Wilson to Machen is illustrative of this:

> I think you will be glad to hear that I have at last taken to strong ale, which I drink in season and out of season, as Juggins should bear me witness. I can hardly get it strong enough. Bass's "Barley Wine" is my chief support. But at Hoddendon (when I visit) there is a tavern where you may get the most curious strong ale I have ever tasted. You shall certainly taste of it. (Unpublished letter)

Machen's drinking and eating haunts were catalogued by R. B. Russell in his booklet *The Anatomy of Taverns*, where he lists nearly twenty such sites. Machen had an extraordinary capacity for alcohol, for although sometimes described as rosy-cheeked and merry he was never known to be actually drunk. In *Peterley Harvest* (1960) the author, David Peterley, recalls drinking with Machen before finding himself the next morning in a strange bedroom in a strange hotel, with no memory of what had happened (139–44).

In the pantheon of literature the 1890s has been accorded its own particular niche. The age of "yellow bookery," scandal, and effete consumptive writers has created an indelible mood, that of the *fin-de-siècle*. Yet Machen always seemed to be apart from it: as Gerald Cumberland says, he did not fit. True, his novella "The Great God Pan" with its erotic undertones caused quite a stir amongst both critics and the reading public, but despite this he forged his own individual path. From our perspective the reviews of the time appear to border on the ludicrous, for a puritanical ethos pervades many of them, as can be witnessed from the selection below:

> This book is gruesome, ghastly, and dull. The majority of readers will turn from it in utter disgust.—*Lady's Pictorial* (*Precious Balms* 12)

> The wild absurdity of all of this really makes comment superfluous. It is an incoherent nightmare of sex and the supposed horrible mysteries behind it.—*Westminster Gazette* (*Precious Balms* 10)

Despite this apparent glorification of sex and evil machinations, together with the stir caused by its Keynotes publication, Machen was still not "in the circle" of the 1890s entourage. The well-known image of pale, languid young men, dying for their art, never applied to him. In fact he was a strong, sturdy man with equally strong and trenchant views.

His knowledge of London was by now almost encyclopaedic; few people, even London-born, could have had a deeper understanding of the city, especially on the subject of its history, its bygone age. This knowledge of the city would become the leitmotif of many of his short stories. However, he continued to fulminate against the changes that were happening all around him. Modern houses, each identical and built in straight lines, raised his ire, whilst the replacement of the old equipages with their high-stepping, high-spirited horses by snarling, choking motorcars was to him insufferable.

By the next decade Machen was a married man with a young family, so a stable income was needed and he became a Fleet Street journalist. His walks around the city were now "reported"; at the same time, his ornate prose was reconstructed in order to survive the editor's "red" pencil.

The extraordinary influence that London exerted on Machen can only be explained by the fact that he became a devoted *reader* of the city. He haunted its endless mazes and, as he once wrote, its protoplasmic streets, especially in the bleaker, more run-down areas. For him it was the soul of the city, for only then could horror or wonder be created from it. I have cited a small selection of his fiction to illustrate this duality, for Machen's characters stand on the borders between two worlds: sometimes they are led to enchantment, sometimes to Stygian depths.

Revelation

The grim endless streets, grey forgotten squares, and ugly terraced houses he knew so well are fully realised in the construct of his stories. The key lies in how *he* viewed them; they hold a secret, hidden but seen by him. Their façades are just that—merely façades. There is an innate rhythm to many of his tales which gradually and subtly builds to a crescendo. In these stories the *veil* is not torn asunder but gently parted; our glimpses beyond are benign in nature, revealing scenes of wonder and often fulfilment.

This is especially true in his story "The Holy Things" (1924) where he employs these gradations more directly than in many of his other stories. The hero, for we may call him that, wears hopelessness, depression like a sealed suit of armour. Nothing appeals to him, success with a novel is a mere trick, his life has become grounded in boredom and monotony.

After aimlessly strolling through unnoticed streets and squares he eventually finds himself in the vast sweep of Holborn High Street. Here the perpetual noise from the hansom cabs grates upon him; there is a pastille seller, children ringing their bicycle bells, an organ player, all viewed within his sullen stare, his consciousness. Then the veil is slowly lifted, the entire scene is transformed, Holborn High Street becomes magically transmuted into the great arch of a cathedral, he has seen beyond the *veil*.

"A Fragment of Life" (1904) has a similar if more subtle theme where we meet the Darnells, newly married and still retaining a touching air of innocence and mutual shyness. Initially Machen emphasises the repetitive and dull nature of the lives that have been assigned to them by their social positions. Firstly the husband's daily routine of leaving for the office each morning and duly returning each evening. Then there is the question of how they should spend a £10 gift from an aunt—a mundane problem which appears to occupy much of their free time.

We can equate this picture of grey monotonous routine with the equally grey monotonous outreaches of Machen's North London. Yet it is there that he sees hidden wonder beneath its visible appearance. He now introduces this element into their lives, as Darnell is constantly disturbed by dreams, dreams of another life, another world.

It is in the ambiguously titled story "N" that Machen embraces two of his favourite themes, the ecstatic vision and the commonplace, together with his love of old inns and taverns. We find three elderly men, Perrott, Arnold, and Harliss, ensconced in such an inn; there they are reflecting with some sadness on the old days, and the old ways, each recounting a particular aspect of the city until in their conversations they venture north of the Gray's Inn Road: "'And here,' said Arnold, 'we have left the known world behind us.'"

The atmosphere is warm and cosy, and as they relax in front of a roaring fire and drink from a bowl of heavily spiced punch, their ruminations begin to revolve around a house whose window overlooks the mysterious Canon's Park in Stoke Newington. Ostensibly it is a view of undistinguished terraced rows with an adjacent piece of insignificant grassland. It seems that on glancing through this window for a second time the "park" is transformed into a wonderland: "Before me, in place of the familiar structures, there was disclosed a panorama of unearthly, of astounding beauty" (CF 3.334).

Three people—a cousin of Perrott's up from the West Country, a frightened young curate who noted it in a book half a century before, and a young man who was lodging in the house after escaping from the local asylum—all experienced this phenomenon. The mix of reality and illusion is typical of Machen and again shows the imprint of his steady tread through the outer districts of London. The question he asks, of course, is, which is reality and which is illusion?

The Undiscover'd Country

The iconic biblical phrase *Thou Shalt Not* is endemic to these tales, as retribution is surely at hand. Here the countenance of London no longer smiles, there are deeps and hollows; it is the place of nightmares. Machen's surveillance of the city now passes behind the stucco frontages into those who inhabit them and their unfrequented streets and alleyways. The seal of wonder has now faded away as scales from one's eyes. We are in the land of horror and the supernatural. Journeys between London and his beloved Gwent are a common theme; *The Hill of Dreams* (1907) sees Lucian go eastwards to the city, whereas in "Novel of the Black Seal" (1895), and "The Shining Pyramid" (1895) London is abandoned for the West.

"The Red Hand" (1895) is a bravura piece. Machen employs his full descriptive powers as we meet his erstwhile "detectives," Dyson and Phillipps, as they set off for an evening stroll through North London. Their journey is wonderfully illuminated by Machen's rhythmic array of adjectives and phrases: "flaring causeway," the distant "roll of the traffic," "deserted squares," "faded respectability," "the eye," "the quarter seemed all amorphous," "blind passages [. . .] heavy with silence" (CF 1.462, 463).

In the Machen canon this story is in many ways atypical in that he gives, through Dyson's investigations, an apparently benign elucidation of the mystery, yet in the final denouement horror raises its head in triumph. It ranks easily alongside the solutions found in the stories of Sherlock Holmes.

Dyson, the self-styled man of letters, appears yet again in "The Inmost Light" (1894), still the investigator but this time expounding his theories with another close friend, Charles Salisbury. This story is built on a series of coincidences, their improbability melting under Machen's astute penmanship. A medical man, Dr. Black, practices in an obscure area of the city, but his real interest lies in the occult, and night after night he carries out secret experiments. These eventually lead him to the ultimate sin, whereby he involves his wife in his perversity. The climax is reached when he withdraws her soul, leaving her as a desiccated creature from hell, a Satyr. Dyson in his walks through the area catches a terrifying glimpse of her at an upstairs window. Black eventually reports his wife's death, although the post-mortem shows her brain to be "not human." Throughout, Salisbury is sceptical. By a series of encounters Dyson manages to secure a notebook of the now deceased Black. Here he details the entire tragedy.

In this story Machen projects Dyson as a man open to the mysteries of London, whilst Salisbury is cast as a believer in the solidity of the world, the man of science. It is Salisbury who becomes the more disturbed as he tries to hold on to reality with both hands. With his scepticism in abeyance, he stumbles back into the welcoming light of everyday existence.

The Chase of the Phrase

It was in 1929, in the evening of his life, that Machen finally left London and retired to Amersham; the old days and old ways were over. Yet within their wake he left a treasure house of unforgettable stories. To escape from solitude, from isolation, Arthur Machen had embraced the city. It was the provider. His *secret*, a word he revered, lay in his ability to transcribe onto the page its colours and moods, sometimes light and sometimes dark. His ornate style of prose captures our attention, sometimes forcibly, at other times subliminally. The coalescing of his vision of London into many of his works only partly explains his pre-eminence as an author of such fiction. Machen's daughter recalled the infinite pains he took over his writings in his later years, discarding script after script as he sought the right word or phrase to kindle beauty on the page. Within the framework of the plots he devised, Machen achieved a high level of musicality, a level that few other authors ever managed to attain. The city and his vision of it produced literature that has endured the passage of time. Given the rarefied atmosphere of the landscape he inhabited throughout his life, it is perhaps fitting to end with an acute if plaintive observation made by one of his admirers, the poet John Betjeman: "If only one could see through the eyes of Arthur Machen."

Works Cited

"Alain" [i.e., Chartier, Émile-Auguste]. *Préliminaires à l'esthétique*. Paris: Gallimard, 1939.

Baudelaire, Charles. *The Painter of Modern Life and Other Essays*. Tr. and ed. Jonathan Mayne. London: Phaidon Press, 1964.

Blake, William. *The Complete Writings of William Blake*. Ed. Geoffrey Keynes. London: Nonesuch Press, 1958.

Cumberland, Gerald. *Written in Friendship*. London: Grant Richards, 1923.

Doyle, Sir Arthur Conan. "The Adventure of the Copper Beeches." In *The Adventures of Sherlock Holmes*. London: George Newnes, 1892.

Hogan, J. P. *Hair under A Hat*. London: Chaterson, 1949.

Huxley, Aldous. *The Doors of Perception*. London: Chatto & Windus, 1954.

Jefferies, Richard. *The Story of My Heart: My Autobiography*. London: Longmans, Green, 1883.

Machen, Arthur. *The Grande Trouvaille*. London: First Edition Bookshop, 1923.

———. "The Joy of London" (*Evening News*, 27 January and 14 February 1914). In *The Secret of the Sangraal*. Horam, UK: Tartarus Press, 1995. 81–90.

———. *Precious Balms*. London: Spurr & Swift, 1924.

Peterley, David. *Peterley Harvest*. Ed. Richard Pennington. London: Hutchinson, 1960.

Russell, R. B. *The Anatomy of Taverns*. Hunters Bar, UK: Tartarus Press, rev. ed. 1990.

Van Vechten, Carl. *Peter Whiffle: His Life and Works*. New York: Alfred A. Knopf, 1922.

II. Aestheticism and Decadence

The Book in Yellow:
How Dorian Inspired Lucian

Roger Dobson

It is irresistible to speculate on how Machen's literary history might have developed had not Oscar Wilde's fatal attraction to youth—his "feasting with panthers"—landed him in the dock of the Old Bailey in 1895. For in the backlash that erupted against the "artists in sin" and aesthetic perversity, Wilde's fall undoubtedly blighted Machen's career. As Machen wrote in *Things Near and Far* (1923) of the commercial failure of *The Three Impostors* (1895), "some ugly scandals in the summer of '95" made people impatient with unhealthy reading material (*TNF* 115). Rejected by London publishers, the manuscripts of *The Hill of Dreams* (1907) and *Ornaments in Jade* (1924) languished for years in his Japanese bureau. Had they been published during the period in which they were written, Machen's literary career may not have suffered the break it did around the turn of the century, when he temporarily abandoned literature to take to the stage, and then entered journalism. Had the Wilde scandal never occurred, perhaps he would have had his works printed in the era in which they were written and managed to embed himself more firmly in the public consciousness. He might have persevered with that "broken fragment" (some fragment!) "The White People" (1904), mourned by him as "a single stone instead of a whole house" ("About My Books" 53). The story may have been the "Great Romance" he always dreamed of writing, and it is possible we may have had more masterpieces from him. Perhaps *The Secret Glory* (1922) would have been a greater work, with its disparate elements more integrated.

Even a slight degree of recognition might have saved Machen from throwing in his lot with the *Evening News*; and so a subsidiary question arises. Had "The Bowmen" (1914) never been written, would the Angels of Mons mythology have arisen? Who can say with certainty? All such questions are imponderables. What happened happened, and presumably it was fated so. Amy's death in 1899 may have discouraged Machen from continuing with literature even had the Wilde scandal never occurred. He told P.-J. Toulet at this period that he had given up writing for acting.

One of the ironic aspects of *The Hill of Dreams* is that Machen began it, or began planning it, in the autumn of 1895, only months after Wilde's fall. To undertake such a sensuous, overtly decadent work in such a climate could be regarded as foolhardy, but Machen always walked his own lonely road. He wrote what he felt compelled to write, without thought of commercial markets.

Regarded from the perspective of the events of 1895, Wilde, the "High Priest of the Decadents," can be viewed as Machen's *bête noire*; but, other than the passage in *Things Near and Far*, did Machen ever refer to the effect the scandal had on his career elsewhere in print? One can imagine other authors never letting their readers forget that such a tragedy had occurred. Yet had it not been for Oscar Fingal O'Flahertie Wills Wilde we might never have had *The Hill of Dreams*—or at least the book may have been radically different, and who would have it so?

Machen admitted that *The Picture of Dorian Gray* (1890) influenced *The Hill of Dreams*. He wrote to Munson Havens on New Year's Day 1925, "I read the tale & was a good deal impressed by it; though I did not think then & do not think now that it was a masterpiece" (*A Few Letters* 29). Machen saw the story when it appeared in the July 1890 issue of *Lippincott's Monthly Magazine*. The book edition followed in April 1891. An unspecified reference in the novel prompted Machen to send Wilde a copy of his recently issued *Fantastic Tales* (1890), his translation of Béroalde de Verville's *Moyen de Parvenir*, and the two met and dined at the Florence, the Italian restaurant alluded to in *Dorian Gray* (Chapter 6). Dyson and Salisbury dine here at the beginning of "The Inmost Light." The Florence also appears in "The Great God Pan" and is referred to as "Azario's," after the proprietor, in "The Lost Club." The second time they met, Wilde showed Machen the famous preface written for the book edition of *Dorian Gray*, the series of aphorisms, "half serious, half jocular," which included the statements "All art is quite useless," and "There is no such thing as a moral or an immoral book" (Wilde 168, 167). Critics have pointed out that Dorian is corrupted by a book, but Wilde argued that in art every truth had its antithesis. As Blake wrote, "There is a place where Contrarieties are equally True" (518).

In Oliver Stonor's "The Table-Talk of Arthur Machen" Machen said of the influences on the Roman episodes in *The Hill of Dreams*: "Suppose you put down amongst its origins a certain chapter in *Dorian Gray*—which derived, by the way, from Huysmans." So which part of *Dorian Gray* contains the seed of inspiration for Chapter 4 of *The Hill of Dreams?* In Chapter 10 of *Dorian Gray* the untitled "yellow book" sent to him by Lord Henry Wotton, which exerts such an evil influence on Dorian, is described:

> It was a novel without a plot, and with only one character, being, indeed, simply a psychological study of a certain young Parisian, who spent his life trying to realize in the nineteenth century all the passions and modes of thought that belonged to every century except his own, and to sum up, as it were, in himself the various moods through which the world-spirit had ever passed, loving for their mere artificiality those renunciations that men have unwisely called virtue, as much as those natural rebellions that wise men still call sin. The style in which it was written was that curious jewelled style, vivid and obscure at once, full of *argot* and of archaisms, of technical expressions and of elaborate paraphrases, that characterizes the work of some of the finest artists of the French school of *Symbolistes*. (Wilde 274)

In one sense this plotless novel is Joris-Karl Huysmans's Bible of decadence *À Rebours* (1884), and in another sense it is not *À Rebours* at all, but an imaginary work inspired by Huysmans's book. Huysmans died, aged fifty-nine, in May 1907, a few months after *The Hill of Dreams* was published. His book proved to be a huge influence on the Decadent movement. Matthew Sturgis in his biography *Aubrey Beardsley* (1998) speculates on whether the Beardsley drawing room/studio at Cambridge Street, Pimlico, was painted orange in Francophile homage to the colour scheme preferred by Huysmans's protagonist.

But as certain chapters are described in *Dorian Gray* it becomes apparent that the yellow book cannot be *À Rebours*. Wilde's young Parisian is portrayed as having a decayed beauty, whereas in the opening to *À Rebours* Huysmans describes the Duc Jean des Esseintes as atavistically resembling a strange, sly forebear; he is frail, hollow-cheeked, anaemic, and the product of inbreeding. He has never been handsome. Wilde's character dreads mirrors, polished metal surfaces, and still water, since they would reveal his lost looks: an echo with Dorian who has his ageing portrait hidden away in the playroom of his innocent childhood. Des Esseintes has no such fear of mirrors, though the idea may have originated with Huysmans quoting, in Chapter XIV, from Mallarmé's poem "Hérodiade" when Herodias mourns over her reflection in a mirror.

Des Esseintes buries himself among gems, old books, Latin folios, perfumes, and strange plants. Dorian similarly devotes himself to collecting and studying perfumes, jewels, embroideries, tapestries, and ecclesiastical vestments. When writing the first version of *Dorian Gray* for *Lippincott's Monthly* Wilde gave the poisonous book in yellow a title and an author, *Le Secret de*

Raoul by Catulle Sarrazin, but later deleted these specifics, leading casual readers to assume that the book referred to was *À Rebours*. It was after all *À Rebours* that was cited by the prosecution during Wilde's trial. The great Huysmans scholar and translator Robert Baldick does not, for example, draw the distinction between *À Rebours* and the imaginary work in the introduction to his translation published as *Against Nature* (1959). Wilde's biographer Richard Ellmann calls the invented book "the pseudo-*À Rebours*." A curious real-life parallel exists: when Wilde was arrested at the Cadogan Hotel in April 1895 he carried to the waiting carriage outside a yellow book, an unknown French novel, beneath his arm. This was misreported in the press as *The Yellow Book*, published by John Lane at The Bodley Head. John Betjeman has immortalized the myth in his poem about Wilde's arrest: "He rose, and he put down *The Yellow Book*" (18).

How does all this relate to *The Hill of Dreams*? In Chapter 11 Dorian reflects that "the whole of history was merely the record of his own life, not as he had lived it in act and circumstance, but as his imagination had created it for him, as it had been in his brain and in his passions." He imagines himself experiencing the lives of people from antiquity and the Renaissance. Wilde colourfully evokes a number of decadent daydreams:

> The hero of the wonderful novel that had so influenced his life had himself known this curious fancy. In the seventh chapter he tells how, crowned with laurel, lest lightning might strike him, he had sat, as Tiberius, in a garden at Capri, reading the shameful books of Elephantis, while dwarfs and peacocks strutted round him and the flute-player mocked the swinger of the censer; and, as Caligula, had caroused with the green-shirted jockeys in their stables, and supped in an ivory manger with a jewel-frontleted horse; and, as Domitian, had wandered through a corridor lined with marble mirrors, looking round with haggard eyes for the reflection of the dagger that was to end his days, and sick with that ennui, that terrible *tædium vitæ*, that comes on those to whom life denies nothing; and had peered through a clear emerald at the red shambles of the Circus, and then, in a litter of pearl and purple drawn by silver-shod mules, been carried through the Street of Pomegranates to a House of Gold, and heard men cry on Nero Cæsar as he passed by and, as Elagabalus, had painted his face with colours, and plied the distaff among the women, and brought the Moon from Carthage, and given her in mystic marriage to the Sun. (Wilde 289)

It is not a vast leap from this to Lucian Taylor conjuring up the lost Roman world of Isca Silurum and dwelling there as Avallaunius in his splendid garden of delights. Did the "mystic marriage" allusion inspire Lucian's fantasy of being summoned to the dark sabbat with his flame-haired streetwalker mistress, when the nightmares of Gwent and London are intermingled in phantasmagorical delirium? Though of course Machen's imagination, weirder than Wilde's, was rich enough not to require any such stimulus.

Yet, as Lord Henry Wotton says, "Nothing is ever quite true" (Wilde 236). It may be that Machen had a different passage in mind, and readers of *Dorian Gray* might care to suggest other influences. It is perfectly feasible that all the above is a coincidence. More than five years passed between Dorian's début in print and Machen beginning *The Hill of Dreams*. Because Dorian's identification with the ancient world is not a vital part of the story, it is possible that Machen may have entirely forgotten this sub-plot. The influence of *Dorian Gray* may lie in Lucian's amoral, and very Wildean, detachment from notions of good and evil while he resides in the garden of Avallaunius. Lucian dismisses as absurd the insistence on ethics as "the chief interest of the human pageant" (CF 2.85). As one of Wilde's more tiresome maxims has it, "Any preoccupation with ideas of what is right and wrong in conduct shows an arrested intellectual development." In Wilde's novel, "Dorian Gray had been poisoned by a book. There were moments when he looked on evil simply as a mode through which he could realize his conception of the beautiful" (290). Similarly, "Lucian saw a coloured and complex life displayed before him, and he sat enraptured at the spectacle, not concerned to know whether actions were good or bad, but content if they were curious." In *Arthur Machen* (1964), Wesley D. Sweetser ascribes this philosophy to the author, since Machen was famously opposed to moral didacticism in art—consider his original "Note" to *The House of Souls*—but surely Machen is dispassionately depicting Lucian's state of mind here. He is not necessarily endorsing his hero's decadent phase. Consider the lustful Roman beauty in Chapter 4 who sends her slave to die in the arena after she has seduced him; and, in Chapter 6, after startling the woman in the mist, Lucian yearns for "some dark place where they might celebrate and make the marriage of the Sabbath, with such rites as he had dared to imagine" (CF 2.114). Do these sentiments win Machen's approval? Hardly; but to condemn them would be to state the obvious and fall into the didactic trap.

There may be another minor influence from a Wilde story on one of Machen's works from the 'Nineties. Readers might care to hunt for it. One can perhaps detect the influence of Wildean paradox in Mr. Dyson's observation on Edgar Russell to "Miss Leicester" in *The Three Impostors* that "no Carthusian monk can emulate the cloistral seclusion in which a realistic novelist loves to shroud himself. It is his way of observing human nature" (CF 1.422).

Anyone who has read or leafed through *Marius the Epicurean* (1885) by Wilde's master Walter Pater—hailed as "the golden book of English prose" by George Moore—may find elements possibly relating to *The Hill of Dreams*. Although Machen confessed himself bored by Pater, Glen Cavaliero (*The Supernatural and English Fiction*, 1995) has detected "Paterian echoes" in the last chapter of *The Hill of Dreams*. Lucian's namesake, the classical writer, makes an appearance in *Marius*. Had Lucian gone to Oxford, for "B.N.C."— Brasenose College—to knock all the "nonsense" from his head, as his father forlornly hoped, he would doubtless have encountered the university's "saint of sensation," a fellow of Brasenose. Despite his eventual tragedy, readers can only be grateful that Lucian opted instead for "the city of the unending murmuring streets" (CF 2.89).

Works Cited

Betjeman, John. *Collected Poems*. Ed. Earl of Birkenhead. London: John Murray, 1958.

Blake, William. *The Complete Writings of William Blake*. Ed. Geoffrey Keynes. London: Nonesuch Press, 1958.

Machen, Arthur. "About My Books." In Henry Danielson. *Arthur Machen: A Bibliography*. London: Henry Danielson, 1923.

———. *A Few Letters*. 1932. Wirral: Aylesford Press, 1993.

Stonor, Oliver. "The Table Talk of Arthur Machen." Unpublished.

Wilde, Oscar. *The Complete Works of Oscar Wilde, Volume 3: The Picture of Dorian Gray: The 1890 and 1891 Texts*. Ed. Joseph Bristow. Oxford: Oxford University Press, 2005.

A Yellow Creeper

Arthur Rickett

(Dedicated to the Author of
"The Great God Pan" and "The Inmost Light.")

The Doctor poured a green fluid into a phial containing red fluid: then he poured, very carefully, something black into the mixture, and held up, as the result of the foregoing process, a clear, limpid, crystal-like fluid.

"How do you manage that?" said the friend.

"I don't quite know," replied the Doctor, thoughtfully. "You see, I proceed by an intuitive process, shutting my eyes and taking the first bottle that comes. Great experiments defy the arbitrary rules of scientific formulae. You, my friend, shall share this great discovery with me."

"Shall I?" said the friend, without enthusiasm. He was only an ordinary man, and connected discoveries with Government duty.

"Certainly," asserted the Doctor. "Here, smell this mixture; it has an exquisite aroma."

"Hum—well—rather peculiar, isn't it?" said the friend, sniffing doubtfully at the crystal fluid. "Rather reminds me of the decayed remains of Hawthorne and Edgar Allan Poe."

"Bah!" snapped the Doctor, "I ought to have remembered that the nostril of the unimaginative man is lacking in delicate appreciation."

Pastiche as a Compliment

"I always had an unreasonable dislike of anything mouldering," sighed the ordinary friend, "but I may improve in course of time."

The Doctor put down the phial and took up a glass rod. "You'll excuse my putting out the light."

"Where was Moses—" commenced the ordinary friend to cheer himself up, but a scowl from the other quenched him.

A faint phosphorescent gleam came from the crystal fluid.

"You doubtless know," observed the scientist, with gusto, "that the chemical constituent R_2OT_3 reacts on its agent $P_4IFF_5LE_6$ so as to re-combine and deposit a neutral acid-alkaline—"

"Excuse me," said the ordinary friend, modestly, "but I only took a Poll degree."

"Dear me, how unfortunate!" deprecated the Doctor; "the Natural Science Tripos made me the man I am. The practical papers aroused in me a passion for experiment which will make me a nuisance to every one for the rest of my life. However, I will omit the scientific explanation. Watch me. I take this glass in my right hand and the globules in my left—"

The mind of the ordinary friend began to wander. His memory reverted to childhood's days, and to the annual conjurer at Christmas parties. Then he fell into a troubled sleep, with his head resting on a large bottle of ammonia.

"Wake up!" cried the Doctor, "you will miss the experiment."

"Oh, why did I take lork and pobster—I mean pork and lobster," gasped the friend, awaking with a start; "I will be a porktotaller after this."

"It is not matter that is affecting you, but spirit," commenced the Doctor. The friend looked indignant, but the other went on. "What I mean is, you are approaching the gurgling mysteries, that dwell in cheap books. Man alive! However can you pass Smith's bookstall without shrinking appalled in large-nosed, white-eared, terror from the hideosities that abound there? How can you do it?"

"Answers to be received by the first post on Monday, written on a post-card," murmured the very ordinary friend. His mind was wandering.

The Doctor gave him up, and returning to his phial, dropped a small quantity of the fluid on a young bluebottle lost in meditation on a plate. For one moment the bluebottle paused stupefied; then it lubricated its legs together with violence, gave a fearful buzz of despair, and turned into an old blowfly. Only for a second. It rapidly became a red-bottle ("Best Scotch"), then an alligator, a scarecrow, a Beardsley poster, and finally dissolved into nothing. All this was viewed by the light of a lucifer.

"This is the dreadful secret of personality," remarked the Doctor. "Thus does the spirit triumph over matter, and disregarding the petty limitations of sense—Blast! . . . !!!"—for the lucifer had burnt down to his fingers.

The ordinary friend got off a 'bus ten years later, and nearly knocked down a man who was getting in.

"You, Jim! How changed you are!"

"Aye," said Jim, with a haggard look (he always said "aye" when he felt unwell. It was more impressive than "yes"). Then seizing the other by the arm, he conveyed him into a "Bodega," feverishly drank off some raw spirit, and muttered, "Excuse my incoherence—married life failure—collect curios—just purchased collection of flies—amongst them bluebottle."

"It's portrait—it's portrait," said the ordinary friend, excitedly.

"Here," said Jim, producing a *carte de visite*. "It has come between me and my wife. Yesterday I saw an alligator in the drawing-room. Last night my wife saw a bottle of Scotch whiskey in my study."

"This is indeed a blue story," said the ordinary friend, "but I know that bluebottle, it comes from the Doctor's laboratory. Kill it, Jim—kill it!"

"I am an anti-vivisectionist," exclaimed Jim, and rushed out, leaving the ordinary friend to pay for the drinks.

I, Doctor Bunkum, have been asked to recount what I saw. My knowledge of the English language is but slight, owing to the excessive attention given in early manhood to the classical subjects in the Little-Go. But I will do my best. When I was called in, the temperature of the room was 212° degrees Fahr., and a green twilight suffused everything. I am a stolid man, but my pulse beat 599 to the minute; yet I retained my self control.

The thing was buzzing fiercely after a dissipated course of fly-papers. I felt its pulse, and gave it a bottle of influenza mixture. It rapidly grew worse; it resembled a saneless, painless, brainless lump of blue jelly. Neither male nor female, animal, vegetable or mineral. Then it began to dissolve. I have been at the Dissolution of Parliament, but never have I—!! yet words fail!! I crept under a copy of the *Westminster Gazette*, and waited for the finale. No, excuse me, I did not wait, I hurried out, wrote down my impressions for the Public, and then made my will. When these pages are being read, I shall probably be either dead or living!!

Arthur Machen and Decadence: The Flower-Tunicked Priest of New Grub Street

James Machin

As with many writers who first came to public attention in the 1890s, Arthur Machen's name has become inextricably linked with "Decadence." This is perhaps an inevitability when the word has become "for the English [...] simply shorthand for the 1890s itself" (Fletcher and Bradbury 7). In a piece written for the Christmas 1936 edition of the *Radio Times*, Holbrook Jackson (1874-1948) took pains to disentangle the decade from Decadence, and *vice versa*:

> George Moore, A. E. Housman, W. B. Yeats, H. G. Wells, Israel Zangwill, Joseph Conrad, George Gissing, Arthur Machen, Alice Maynell, Bernard Shaw, and Rudyard Kipling [...] all of whom belonged to the decade but not to what is called decadence. All the originality of the decade was not decadent any more than all that was called decadent was disastrous. (5)

However, and despite Machen's own protestations,[1] other commentators have unequivocally claimed him as a Decadent writer, even an exemplary one. The fact that his work was published by John Lane, under whose imprint the *Yellow Book* and the Keynotes series of novels also appeared, was enough to deem him guilty of Decadence by association by at least some of his contemporaries (see below). By the time of Machen's American renaissance in the 1920s, a more positive representation of Machen's alleged Decadence emerged:

---

1. Machen begins his introduction to the 1916 edition of *The Great God Pan* by asserting that the book only accidentally "profitted by the noise that the movement was making" and that "it stands, not for the ferment of the 'nineties, but for the visions that a little boy saw in the late 'sixties and early 'seventies" (CF 1.523).

After spending almost 40 years writing in obscurity [...] Machen was dispiritedly employed as a journalist on the London *Evening News* when a number of American authors hailed him as a an unsung genius. [...] His new-found followers, exalted by his transcendental philosophy and his accomplished prose, lauded Machen with such ornate titles as "a novelist of ecstasy and sin" and "the flower-tunicked priest of nightmare." (Dobson 5-6)

Machen's *The Hill of Dreams*, published in 1907 but completed in 1897, has been described as not only "one of the most Decadent novels of the period" (MacLeod 159) but also "the most decadent novel in all of English literature" (Hughes, Punter, and Smith 413). The question remains, then: was Machen a Decadent or was he not?

What Is Decadence?

Before attempting to delineate Machen's relationship with Decadence, it will be necessary to discuss briefly the word—at once so resonant and vague—itself. It originated in the Latin *cadere* ("to fall"), in the early eighteenth century. Montesquieu used the term *décadence* to discuss the collapse of the Roman Empire and "the simultaneous rotting of its cultural life and its military might" (Stableford 6). By the *fin de siècle*, both implications of the word proved useful to account for avant-garde cultural productions seen to epitomize a perceived late-historical moment—or modernity itself—and many of the anxieties precipitated thereby. As far as literature was concerned, Paul Bourget was one of the first to use the term critically, in his discussion of the work of Baudelaire. Bourget was "one of the most prestigious contemporary critics to dignify Decadent art with serious consideration and tentative approval" and provided the "first formal 'explanation' of what the writers of the Decadent Movement were doing, and why it was culturally significant" (Stableford 64). The French influence (of, for example, Gautier, Zola, and Huysmans as well as Baudelaire) on British letters at the end of the nineteenth century—cautioned against by Tennyson as "Art with poisonous honey stol'n from France"—was part and parcel of a progressive artistic animus looking to escape the stifling conformity and moral didacticism of the popular fiction of the time.

Even if the manifestations of this influence varied widely, there was at least a common sympathy between many of the avant-garde writers and artists who, informed by what Holbrook Jackson described as the many "isms" of the age (not only Walter Pater's and Oscar Wilde's Aestheticism, but Impressionism, Naturalism, Realism, Symbolism, and so on), "gracefully accepted the pejorative label thrust on them by higher journalism and the progressive critique" (Fletcher and Bradbury 9). And pejorative it was: almost immediately upon entering the consciousness of the British public upon the publication of Wilde's *The Picture of Dorian Gray* in the July 1890 edition of *Lippincott's Monthly Magazine*, the word assumed connotations of Francophile immorality and of writing that was distasteful in its alleged desire to shock and incompetent in its execution (MacLeod 5).

The *Pall Mall Gazette*, for example, lambasted Eric, Count Stenbock's poetry collection *The Shadow of Death* (1894) as "an elaborate and screaming parody of that latterday literary abortion, the youthful *decadent*," citing its "slipshod versification, the maudlin sentiment, the affected preciousness, the sham mysticism and sham aestheticism, the ridiculous medley of Neo-Paganism and Neo-Catholicism, Verlaine and Vulgate—all the nauseating characteristics of the type" ("Reviews" 4). This review was published only a year after Arthur Symons had, with some enduring success, attempted to define and legitimize this new cultural turn in his essay "The Decadent Movement in Literature"—before ultimately opting to distance himself from the term by retitling the revision for the 1899 book version of the essay *The Symbolist Movement in Literature*. The flowering of British Decadence is usually understood to have been cut short, brutally, by the trial of Oscar Wilde in 1895—or "the disaster" as Machen referred to it (Machen, *Arthur Machen and Montgomery Evans* 18)—which precipitated a backlash against perceived immorality in culture and the frantic purging of publishing houses of all the representatives of the movement, now considered a commercial liability rather than an asset.

Since its first appearance in the consciousness of the reading public, therefore, British Decadence has been as much caricatured as celebrated. Moreover, its "representative figures have been mythologized in many a memoir and literary history as doomed souls, whose histrionics and excesses resulted in a pretentious and overwrought literary output" (MacLeod ix). Kirsten MacLeod has argued in detail that the prevailing "myths" of British Decadence have led to its serious misrepresentation: "the myth of the 'tragic generation,' the myth of Decadence as high art, and the myths of Decadents as bohemians and aristocratic dandies" (7). That these myths are still prevalent is evidenced by A. N. Wilson's treatment of Decadence and Machen in *The Victorians* (2002). He discusses the movement as an almost exclusively aristocratic, high-art phenomenon, and contrastingly and with some condescension positions Machen as a hapless outsider: "it is no accident that Arthur Machen [...] should have flourished at the same time as Mr Pooter" (553). Machen is presented as a middle-class aspirational Decadent; a suburbanite dreaming up louche and exotic fantasies amusingly at odds with his shabby-gentile anonymity—a serious distortion that I address in detail below.

Buying into the prevailing myths of Decadence identified by MacLeod makes such clumsy glosses inevitable. In this instance the misreading is considerably conflated by Wilson's obvious lack of acquaintance with Machen's biography, which results in his account ignoring, among several other things, Machen's shared background—as a middle-class son of a clergyman—with many of the "tragic generation"; his initial commercial success; and his acquaintance and friendship with many of the leading literary figures of the time, including Wilde, Jerome K. Jerome, George Egerton, and W. B. Yeats. These misrepresentations aside, however, there are other complications to negotiate if one is to convincingly position Machen as a Decadent writer.

The Inadvertent Decadent

Several convergent factors resulted in a publishing boom in the closing decades of the nineteenth century: the newly literate population resulting from the Education Act of 1870; the "growth in numbers of teachers as training colleges and universities expanded to meet the new educational demands" (Keating 143); and the steady repeal of various publishing taxes from the mid-century onward which saw production costs fall, cover prices drop, and circulations and profits increase exponentially. This combination of circumstances increased potential publishing revenues and removed obstacles from fulfilling the clamour of demand from the newly expanded reading public. Traditionally, fiction had been produced and consumed in the form of the serial (with each part issued monthly) and the Victorian "three-decker," the latter form too expensive for outright purchase by the average middle-class reader. This gave monopolizing lending libraries like Mudie's and W. H. Smith a disproportionate influence and control over what type of literature was deemed fit for public consumption. No longer in thrall to these often religiously motivated censors, the new periodical and one-volume book market allowed far greater (though certainly not untrammelled) freedom to experiment, both stylistically and with challenging or risqué subject matter.

In response, many writers experimented with and shifted authorial identity according to the promise of commercial success or artistic status, sometimes attaining both at once or at different times. Peter McDonald has analysed in detail the career of Arnold Bennett, who felt free to produce works of both belletrist naturalism and formulaic populism according to his mood and his bank balance, although not without attracting criticism from his more purist peers. The expansion in demand for fiction did not translate unambiguously into a sellers' market, however. Less popular writers, or those establishing careers in the 1890s, would often struggle to strike the right tone, find their voice, and balance commerce with artistry, a process vividly and starkly portrayed in George Gissing's *New Grub Street* (1891).

Machen began his career in the late 1880s at this same, often unforgiving, coal face of writing and publishing, struggling for several years translating, cataloguing, engaging in temporary clerical work, and producing loss-making pastiches and pseudo-medieval romances. Inadvertently encouraged by Oscar Wilde, he turned his pen to producing short stories for the vibrant periodical market (Gawsworth 101). Paul March-Russell says of the short story that it is a "neologism [signifying] a redefinition of literature towards the end of the nineteenth century; how it is produced, received and consumed" (1). Reflecting on "English Literature in 1893," the *Athenaeum* observed that there "has been a distinctly new growth in the short story," adding that "with two or three exceptions, all the best fiction of the year has been in the form of short stories" ("English Literature in 1893" 17-18). The American critic Brander Matthews's "dissemination of Poe's theory" in the *Saturday Review* in 1884—to the effect that "a *true* Short-story differs from the Novel chiefly in its *essential* unity of impression"—was as influential to periodical editors as much as individual writers (March-Russell 35).

It is then perhaps hardly surprising that the subsequent literary culture found a ready place for short fiction that—like Machen's—aspired to Poe in its content, as well as its form. Moreover, one could speculate that, courtesy of this received wisdom, a piece of fiction exhibiting a Poe influence might axiomatically be assumed to be of some worth: Poe's influence on the literature of the period, therefore, had a more direct and pragmatic route than via Baudelaire and French Decadence. Machen's alleged Decadence was arguably a manifestation of a shared inheritance of Poe rather than a direct one imbibed from the heady cup of French Symbolism. That the latter assumption is incorrect is indicated by a footnote in Vincent Starrett's essay on Machen, *Arthur Machen: A Novelist of Ecstasy and Sin* (1918), in which Starrett retracts the assertion made within the text of a Baudelarian influence on Machen's writing, having been corrected by Machen himself: "Mr. Machen writes me that I am in error. 'I never read a line of Baudelaire,' he says, 'but I have read deeply in Poe,' from whom (Machen goes on to say) he believes Baudelaire largely derives" (19). Machen regarded Poe as no less than "one of the most important figures in the whole history of the fine art of letters" (Machen, "Poe the Enchanter" 55).

Similarly, Robert Louis Stevenson had done much to pioneer the English short story. "A Lodging for the Night," originally published in *Temple Bar* in 1877, is regarded as the first British example of the "new" style of short story ("clearly and consciously [. . .] impressionistic") established in American letters by Poe (Canby 322). This tale was later included in the *New Arabian Nights*, which together with its sequel *More New Arabian Nights: The Dynamiter* (1885) had a profound impact on Machen's writing of this period, widely discussed and acknowledged by critics as well as the author himself (see Trotter, for example). In his study of popular fiction magazines of the period, Mike Ashley follows Roger Lancelyn Green's lead in crediting Stevenson with almost singlehandedly ushering in what Green styles the "age of the Story Tellers," the period of proliferation of serial titles catering to a middlebrow family audience and providing them with "romances and adventure stories in an ever thickening stream" (1–3). However, and like Poe, the "Francophile" Stevenson was also claimed by the Decadents as one of their own, on both sides of the Channel (Canby 323). For example, the French symbolist Marcel Schwob translated not only Wilde into French but Stevenson also, and was an ardent enough admirer of the latter to undertake a "pilgrimage" to Samoa in homage to his literary hero (White 3–5).

Taking his lead from both Poe and Stevenson, Machen soon established a reputation with his two contributions to the Keynotes series, *The Great God Pan* (1894) and *The Three Impostors* (1895). Gissing in fact anticipates Machen's impact with "The Great God Pan" in a passage in *New Grub Street* when, in an attempt to ensure some commercial success for struggling literary "artist" Reardon, the careerist and practical Milvain suggests a suitably sensationalist title for Reardon's next project:

> "How would this do: 'The Weird Sisters'? Devilish good, eh? Suggests all sorts of things, both to the vulgar and the educated. Nothing brutally claptrap about it, you know."
> "But—what does it suggest to you?"
> "Oh, witch-like, mysterious girls or women. Think it over." (Gissing 117)

For the most part leaving its horrors implied, "The Great God Pan" could not sensibly be accused of being "brutally clap-trap." It also had commercial viability, appealing to the "vulgar" as well as the "educated," with its sensational plot hinging on a "witch-like, mysterious" woman presented in intelligent and urbane modern prose.

Machen's career in the first half of the 1890s serves as a microcosm of this overlap between Green's "age of the Story Tellers" and Symons's "Decadent Movement in Literature." The literary tensions of the period are certainly perceptible in the equipoise of Machen's writing and in his refusal to adhere to generic boundaries. It could be argued that this is evidence of a lack of conviction as to which of the prevailing and conflicting streams of literary culture Machen thought he should commit to, as he opted instead to dip his toes tentatively into several to see which was the most comfortable to him. Perhaps a fairer summation, however, is that "The Great God Pan" and to a greater extent *The Three Impostors* are products of the irreconcilable oppositions in the wider literary discourses of literature at the time, and keenly felt commercial demands to be both subversive and popular—a balancing act demanded by circumstances evident across the field of cultural production in the 1890s.

Although there was a new incentive among writers, editors, and publishers to attract readers with risqué work that would never have been countenanced by the morally didactic lending libraries, as Machen would discover first hand, fiction that crossed a line—the exact position of which was still being decided—could find itself attracting opprobrium, outrage, and sometimes even more, rather than increased sales. In May 1889, the seventy-year-old publisher Henry Vizetelly saw his company bankrupted, and he himself received a six-month prison term for publishing unexpurgated translations of Zola (Llewellyn and Heilmann 379).

Despite the very real risks involved in drawing fire from the nation's moral guardians, Machen fought against changes to his text suggested by John Lane with a vigour that reveals no dispassion or timorousness on his part. For example, after a fraught correspondence, Lane eventually backed down on his request that Machen rewrite one specific word in the closing pages of *The Three Impostors*, after Machen presented a robust defence against the suggested edit:

> I have been thinking a good deal over our conversation of a fortnight ago: I mean so far as it has affected my literary reputation, performances etc. The matter is naturally one that interests me strongly, & I have been in some doubt as to the best course to take for the future [. . .] I have made up my mind on the point. I do not propose to alter or soften down *The Three*

Impostors in any way whatsoever. In short I am not going to be "quiltered" in any manner whatsoever. (Brangham 10)[2]

It would be a mistake therefore to conflate acknowledgement of the commercial and practical contingencies of Machen's writing in the first half of the 1890s with an unambiguous privileging of these aspects by Machen himself. Similarly, accommodating some commercial concerns in stylistic choices should not be confused with emotional and intellectual disconnect from one's work. As discussed in further detail below, his financial situation already afforded him some freedom from making these the sole considerations.

When, facilitated by MacLeod, we dispense with the face-value acceptance that Decadent writing operates at a single gear—normally the rarefied meditations of the effete dandy (or its inverse cliché, the penniless bohemian living only for art) shunning the vulgar tastes of the bourgeois—and reintroduce the notion of commerce and market-led artistic decisions, embedded in a literary milieu of writers being excited by the artistic possibilities of "the new style" and publishers being excited about the commercial possibilities of that same style, the motivations behind the balancing act that Machen performs in his two Keynotes volumes becomes clearer. We can perhaps adumbrate an ambitious young writer pitching his work at the market by employing what Lovecraft disparagingly refers to as the "jaunty Stevenson manner" (84), while using the *mise-en-scène* of Decadence to give the work the contemporary *frisson* and relevance that John Lane was looking to exploit commercially. Indeed, it is difficult to imagine a stylistic epithet more incommensurate with Decadence than "jaunty"—an aspect of his writing which particularly problematizes his relationship with the movement. In the same year that John Lane published *The Great God Pan*, Hubert Crackanthorpe wrote a defence of Decadence against the "jaunty courage of ignorance" that emboldened its critics, and contrasted the new mood of the age with the "old jaunty spirit" to which it can "never return" (Crackanthorpe 262, 268).

Far from being dedicated to the avant-garde, Machen's taste in literature was rather conservative. He was an enthusiastic consumer of popular magazines, reminiscing in his memoirs about spending evenings "with a bound volume of *Chambers's Journal, All the Year Round, Cornhill* [where he may well have first encountered Stevenson's short fiction], or *The Welcome Guest*," and describing these magazines as "always a great resource," presumably for his

---

2. "Quiltered" refers to the censorious editor Harry Quilter.

own writing (FOT 35). Not all English writers associated with Decadence, therefore, were "still obviously learning from their French masters" (Thornton 20). Similarly, it is difficult to find any subsequent expression of interest in or affiliation to Decadence from M. P. Shiel, who instead (like Machen) tended to identify publicly with canonical and far less controversial writers of fiction and nonfiction, typically Dickens, Shakespeare, Cervantes, Johnson, and Carlyle—the latter influence particularly evident in his prose style (Shiel 20).

That Machen was ignorant of any explicit agenda by his publisher in presenting the reading public with a construct of British Decadence is evidenced by his suggestion, in a letter to John Lane of November 1895, that he consider M. R. James for a book in the series: "Have you seen 'The Scrap Book of Canon Alberic' in the *National Review* by M. R. James? He should write a 'Keynotes'" (Brangham 14). It is difficult to imagine a figure more challenging to position as a Decadent than the donnish M. R. James. Machen's suggestion in this respect implies that he saw the Keynotes series as a venue for risqué writing of a generally "unhealthy" kind rather than any specific Decadent movement.

Regardless, now as then, an individual author's own views about his or her connection with Decadence were certainly no protection against being accused of nefarious association. Harry Quilter identified Sir Arthur Conan Doyle as a Decadent purely on the basis of his misapprehension that Doyle's novella "The Parasite" had been published in the Keynotes series. Conversely, writers could be considered not clubbable by their peers if they were perceived as not ideologically pure in their dedication to belletrism. Machen was of the opinion that an inopportune expression of admiration for Doyle's new Sherlock Holmes collection at a literary dinner in 1895 had "shocked" Henry Harland, then editor of the *Yellow Book,* to the extent that Machen felt he was "finished" as far as Harland was concerned (and indeed, Machen never was invited to contribute to the exemplarily Decadent journal [Gawsworth 128]). Similarly, M. P. Shiel's biographer, Harold Billings, ascribes Shiel's absence from the pages of the *Yellow Book* to, among other factors, his failure to present himself among John Lane's "young men" as a "dedicated *litterateur*" (138).

I have so far set out the case against either Machen himself or his fiction being Decadent by design or intent up to the publication of *The Three Impostors*. After that novel was completed, however, Machen's creative impulses led him unequivocally towards Decadence, at the time when most of his contemporaries are understood to have been moving anxiously in the concurrent direction.

The Intentional Decadent (or Literary Quixotism)

> In 1895 the literary outlook in England had never been brighter; an engaging and promising novelty full of high vitality pervaded the Press and the publishers' lists, and it was even commencing to invade the stage, when with the arrest of Oscar Wilde the whole renaissance suffered a sudden collapse as if it had been no more than a gaily coloured balloon. (Jackson 53)

It is generally accepted that Wilde's public disgrace and the vituperative repercussions of his downfall led to the Decadent label being "instantly abandoned by those who had briefly adopted it, and ardently denied in retrospect by all those who had never made the mistake of admitting to it" (Stableford 122). Machen, however, fits into neither category; moreover, his output either side of the Wilde trial presents an alternative narrative that cautions against overestimating the extent of the impact of the Wilde trial on literary production beyond Wilde's immediate circle. I have argued above against co-opting Machen as an 1890s Decadent based on his two Keynotes books and his period of comparative success in the first half of that decade when Decadence was in the ascendant. However, his activities in the second half of the decade make it similarly difficult to disentangle him from the claim that Decadence had no bearing on him. Furthermore, and somewhat perversely, Machen's writing became more overtly Decadent at the time it was least critically and commercially strategic to do so.

Machen had already decided upon completion of *The Three Impostors* in early 1894 that he "had squeezed this particular orange to death" (*TNF* 103). When subsequently attempting to fulfil a commission of "a series of horror stories" for a new publication, in tandem with a contribution from H. G. Wells, Machen claims he found himself incapable, despite the prestige and potential revenue of the project: "I remember literally sobbing in a kind of hysteria of despair with my head in my hands; and this shews that there are some men who cannot be helped" (*TNF* 104). He employs "the metaphor of the white road that you see from afar climbing over the hill into unconjectured regions" to account for his inability to write to order:

> For me that is literature; the journey of discovery; the finding of a new world. When once I have toiled painfully up that long road, and have stood on the other side of the dark wood, and have looked upon the land beyond; then all joy, all the delight and thrill and wonder are over for me. Columbus could not discover America twice. (*TNF* 104)

Movingly, it is to this inability to write against his muse and to order that he ascribes his failure to sustain a financially successful career in the long term: "And that is one reason why I beg my bread in my sixtieth year" (*TNF* 105).

It is not, therefore, that Machen had no commercial savvy, or that he wilfully disregarded it as a consideration. Rather, he (so he claims) was simply *incapable* of writing against the grain of his instincts regardless of the potential rewards of doing so. The next project to which his creative animus led him was *The Hill of Dreams*, the "swan song of Decadence" (MacLeod 135). For his source material, instead of looking to Poe and Stevenson, he appropriated his own childhood and early experiences in London. These autobiographical elements in *The Hill of Dreams* have created confusion and obfuscation ever since, with the novel regularly over-imbued with a biographical verisimilitude it does not possess. By 1893, before his successes with John Lane, a string of legacies had given Machen enough financial stability for him and his wife to budget for six years' "comfortable" living in which to develop his literary career (Gawsworth 106). This budget was generous enough to afford the Machens annual holidays in France and the acquisition of an interest in a vineyard in the Touraine (Gawsworth 112). In sharp contrast to Lucian's failure to establish himself as a writer (or even produce a coherent line of fiction), "The Great God Pan" was an unquestionable achievement for "a young man of twenty-eight' (Gawsworth 110): it had received a good deal of press attention, featured in the *Bookman*'s best seller list of March 1895 ("Monthly Report of the Wholesale Book Trade"), and had been complimented by no less a figure than Oscar Wilde as *"un grand succès"* (Gawsworth 128). Machen enjoyed a lifestyle and literary success far removed from that of the penurious Lucian, so sensitively drawn by Machen, a representation which may have reflected the painful memories of his initial—but temporary—period of poverty and travail when he first arrived in London from Wales, but certainly bore little resemblance to Machen's by then settled married life. Wilson typifies the common misreading of *The Hill of Dreams* as autobiographical reportage from the mid-decade, rather than a partial response to financial troubles that had beset him as a younger man in the late 1880s: Machen's life at the time was far from one "limited by the crushing restraints of petty bourgeois semipoverty" (553).

Machen's notebook from the period clearly demonstrates—through his preparatory sketches for ideas that would subsequently develop into *The Hill of Dreams* and *Ornaments in Jade*—that the Wilde trial had no chastening or cautionary effect, or, if it did, not to the point of dissuading him from pursuing the course he had determined upon. His record of his reading in the year 1896 also reminds us that Decadent fiction was still being published, reviewed, and read after the Wilde trial, and evidently fed directly into Machen's own work. It also problematizes the romantic idea that Machen was working in isolation with *The Hill of Dreams*—ploughing a lonely furrow—either thematically or stylistically. Titles recorded by Machen, which are all in some way resonant with the book, include:

- *The Tides Ebb Out to the Night* (1896), "edited" by Hugh Langley, presents itself as the "the journal of a young man, Basil Brooke." The *Athenaeum* disparagingly reviewed it as "a diagnosis of the diseased, self-interested personality of a youth" and "a record of the 'views' and woes of a young Decadent" (Machen, *The Eighteen Nineties Notebook* 98).
- *A Fool and His Heart* (1896), by F. Norreys Connell (pseudonym of the Irish novelist Conal O'Riordan), a semi-autobiographical work that "runs from Dublin to the literary 'Bohemias' of London and the Continent" (Machen, *The Eighteen Nineties Notebook* 80).
- *Aphrodite* (1896) by Pierre Louÿs, the French writer and associate of Wilde (Machen, *The Eighteen Nineties Notebook* 99). The book was described by J. E. Hodder Williams in the pages of the *Speaker* as "probably the most inexcusably revolting piece of fiction published in any country during the last ten years" (110). Williams goes on to lament that the novel "met with enormous success, and the market is now deluged with stories of a similar nature," adding that "there can be no possible excuse for the author who writes, for the publisher who produces, or the bookseller who sells such nauseating pornography." The French edition of *Aphrodite* was the "yellow book" carried by Wilde on the first day of his trial, misreported, occasionally to this day, as a copy of the *Yellow Book* (Lambert and Ratcliffe 80).

I have argued above that Machen did not regard himself as a Decadent writer. It seems somewhat quixotic, then, that far from distancing himself from a movement he did not identify himself with, and moreover, one which was newly toxic as a result of the Wilde trial, Machen seemed now intent on embracing it. Accordingly the protagonist of his new novel, Lucian, recognizes himself to be "'degenerate,' *decadent*" (CF 2.43).

The Wilde trial may have made a dramatic impact on public consciousness, but it seems, in Machen's case at least, to have had little tangible effect on what he chose to write (and, as discussed above, he had determined to change course with his writing at least a year before the trial). It would therefore be misleading to claim that he abandoned Stevensonian horror either due to a new climate of censoriousness or through solidarity with a persecuted artistic minority.

Machen's case is at odds with the interpretation of Decadence as being one of the "last exotic pendants of a hopelessly frumpish Victorianism" (Thornton 7). Despite the "disaster" of the Wilde trial, writers including Machen were still looking forward, pursuing their artistic ambition of not being contained and restrained by moral didacticism and populism; part of an avant-garde continuum rather than a historical anomaly. Machen's place within Decadence is as difficult or easy to determine as the term itself. Machen's position varies depending on how scrupulously we are to define Decadence, or how far we are to attenuate it, on whether it is being employed as a pejorative with implications of callow pretence and preciosity, or rather a positive mark of distinction of those writers of the 1890s committed to progressive forms of fiction in the face of popular indifference, the pioneering harbingers of Modernism. According to his various commentators, Machen has fulfilled all these criteria, but thankfully he is reducible to none of them.

Works Cited

Ashley, Michael. *The Age of the Storytellers: British Popular Fiction Magazines 1880–1950*. London: British Library/Oak Knoll Press, 2006.

Billings, Harold. *M. P. Shiel: A Biography of His Early Years*. Austin, TX: Roger Beacham, 2005.

Brangham, Godfrey. "John Lane and Arthur Machen: A Correspondence." Faunus No. 16 (2007): 3–19.

Canby, Henry Seidel. *The Short Story in English*. New York: Henry Holt, 1909.

Crackanthorpe, Hubert. "Reticence in Literature: Some Roundabout Remarks." *Yellow Book* 2 (1894): 259–69.

Dobson, Roger. "Preface." In *Selected Letters of Arthur Machen*. Ed. Roger Dobson, Godfrey Brangham, and R. A Gilbert. Wellingborough, UK: Aquarian, 1988. 5–8.

"English Literature in 1893." *Athenaeum* No. 3454 (6 January 1894): 17–19.

Fletcher, Ian, and Malcolm Bradbury. "Preface." In *Decadence and the 1890s*, ed. Ian Fletcher. London: Holmes & Meier, 1979. 7–13.

"*The Fool and His Heart.* By F. Norreys Connell." *Athenaeum* No. 3588 (1 August 1896): 156.

Gawsworth, John. *The Life of Arthur Machen.* Leyburn, UK: Tartarus Press, 2013.

Gissing, George. *New Grub Street.* Ed. Stephen Arata. Peterborough, ON: Broadview Press, 2008.

Hughes, William, David Punter, and Andrew Smith. *The Encyclopedia of the Gothic.* New York: John Wiley & Sons, 2015.

Jackson, Holbrook. *The Eighteen Nineties: A Review of Art and Ideas at the Close of the Nineteenth Century.* London: Grant Richards, 1913.

Keating, P. J. *The Haunted Study: A Social History of the English Novel, 1875–1914.* London: Faber & Faber, 2008.

Lambert, J. W., and Michael Ratcliffe. *The Bodley Head, 1887–1987.* London: Bodley Head, 1987.

Llewellyn, Mark, and Ann Heilmann. "George Moore and Literary Censorship: The Textual and Sexual History of 'John Norton' and 'Hugh Monfert.'" *English Literature in Transition, 1880–1920* 50 (2007): 371–92.

Lovecraft, H. P. *The Annotated Supernatural Horror in Literature.* Ed. S. T. Joshi. New York: Hippocampus Press, 2nd ed. 2012.

Machen, Arthur. *Arthur Machen and Montgomery Evans: Letters of a Literary Friendship, 1923–1947.* Kent, OH: Kent State University Press, 1994.

———. *The Eighteen Nineties Notebook.* Leyburn, UK: Friends of Arthur Machen/Tartarus Press, 2016.

———. "Poe the Enchanter." 1910. *Faunus* No. 9 (2002): 55–58.

MacLeod, Kirsten. *Fictions of British Decadence: High Art, Popular Writing and the Fin de Siècle.* New York: Palgrave Macmillan, 2006.

March-Russell, Paul. *The Short Story: An Introduction.* Edinburgh: Edinburgh University Press, 2009.

McDonald, Peter D. *British Literary Culture and Publishing Practice, 1880–1914.* Cambridge: Cambridge University Press, 2002.

"Monthly Report of the Wholesale Book Trade." *Bookman* (London) No. 42 (March 1895): 170.

Quilter, Harry. "The Gospel of Intensity." *Contemporary Review* 67 (June 1895): 761–82.

"Reviews." *Pall Mall Gazette* (1 March 1894): 4.

Shiel, M. P. *Science, Life, and Literature.* Ed. John Gawsworth. London: Williams & Norgate, 1950.

Stableford, Brian M. *Glorious Perversity: The Decline and Fall of Literary Decadence.* San Bernardino, CA: Borgo Press, 1998.

Starrett, Vincent. *Arthur Machen: A Novelist of Ecstasy and Sin.* Chicago: Walter M. Hill, 1918.

Symons, Arthur. "The Decadent Movement in Literature." *Harper's New Monthly Magazine* 87 (November 1893): 858-67.

———. *The Symbolist Movement in Literature.* London: Heinemann, 1899.

Thornton, R. K. R. "'Decadence' in Later Nineteenth-Century England." *Decadence and the 1890s,* ed. Ian Fletcher. New York: Holmes & Meier, 1980. 15-30.

"*The Tides Ebb Out to the Night.* Edited by Hugh Langley." *Athenaeum* No. 3604 (21 November 1896): 713.

Trotter, David. "Introduction." In Machen's *The Three Impostors.* London: Everyman's Library, 1995. xvii-xxxi.

White, Iain. "Introduction." In *The King in the Golden Mask and Other Writings* by Marcel Schwob. Manchester: Carcanet, 1982. 1-13.

Wilde, Oscar. "A 'Jolly' Art Critic." *Pall Mall Gazette* (18 November 1886): 6.

Williams, J. E. Hodder. "New French Fiction." *Speaker* 16 (24 July 1897): 109-10.

Wilson, A. N. *The Victorians.* London: Arrow, 2003.

New Arabian Frights:
Unholy Trinities and the Masks of Helen

Roger Dobson

"Do you think I should waste my time and yours by concocting fictions on a bench in Leicester Square?"—Helen/Miss Lally in *The Three Impostors* (CF 1.400)

"I am not what I seem."—Clara/Teresa in *The Dynamiter* (144)

Every reader of *The Three Impostors* must have pondered on its central conceit: why does Machen fabricate fantastic narratives only to undermine them by revealing they are inventions? The technique was partly to fit his title: the trio of villains not only masquerade as people they are not but provide complex backstories for their characters. Decades before it became fashionable, Machen was playing teasing fictional games with the reader, exploring the art of narrative itself. *The French Lieutenant's Woman* (1969) by John Fowles[1] is the most celebrated example of this genre, boldly admitting it is fiction. In the significantly numbered Chapter 13, Fowles tells his readers everything they have read so far is false and never happened: "This story I am telling is all imagination. These characters I create never existed outside my own mind" (95). Despite this reneging on the tacit contract

---

1. Whether John Fowles ever read Machen is unclear, though *The French Lieutenant's Woman* contains a pun, not necessarily derived from Machen, on Pan—"the great god Man"—in Chapter 5. The first version of *The Magus* (1966) has a passage from A. E. Waite's *Key to the Tarot* (1910) as its epigraph, and Crowley is alluded to. It is interesting to note that both *The French Lieutenant's Woman* and *The Hill of Dreams* contain scenes of auburn-haired Cockney prostitutes beneath a gas-lamp and a naphtha flame. One proves as kind as the other is wicked. Like Machen with his impostors, Fowles experienced the illusion of a character in the flesh. See Eileen Warburton, *John Fowles: A Life in Two Worlds* (New York: Viking, 2004), 269-70. Fowles's fantasy *A Maggot* (1985) is Machenesque in that its mystery remains fiendishly inviolate.

between author and reader we continue, if only to discover what other innovations the author has up his sleeve. His novel famously has two misleading chapters and a dual ending—one happy and one sad—while Fowles himself appears as a minor character.

Our suspension of disbelief is activated every time we pick up a novel. We know Sherlock Holmes, Heathcliff, Mr. Pickwick, Roderick Usher, Catherine Sloper, and Sarah Woodruff never existed, but how often does this occur to us when we are enjoying their exploits? They are so much more engaging than most of the real-life people we know. Machen estimated that Mr. Micawber was born somewhere about 1785, yet how many real people were as alive? The status of fictional characters is hardly ever questioned by us: we simply accept the convention that the world of fiction is worth exploring because we know we shall be entertained, informed, and diverted. On the simplest level, when there is already a good deal in the world to weep about, beings that have never existed have the power to make us cry.

There exist individuals, and we have doubtless all met them, who have no time for fiction. Fiction is all invented and untrue, so why bother? It requires a certain degree of imagination to enter into the spirit of a story. At the other extreme are those strange souls who write to 221B Baker Street in the hope that the great man is still in practice and will be able to aid them in some way. Then there are the folk who live in hope of one day finding the *Necronomicon* on the dusty shelves of a second-hand bookshop. Surely Lovecraft only thought he was writing fantasy: cosmic forces were controlling him and using him as a mouthpiece, though he knew it not. Why, the very name of his grimoire came to him in a dream: surely proof of its existence. Similarly, actors playing nasty pieces of work in television drama can find themselves assaulted by viewers, unwittingly paying tribute to the power of their performances.

It is not clear how much Machen realised he was experimenting with the line dividing fiction from the fiction that overtly declares itself as such. In *The Three Impostors* he is telling lies as all fiction writers, good and bad, do, convincing us that the impossible is true, then dynamiting—a key word in this context—the whole edifice and admitting that the stories are just stories. The process has similarities with that of Ann Radcliffe, whose supernaturalism is ultimately rationalised, much to the annoyance of M. R. James and Lovecraft. As James wrote in "Some Remarks on Ghost Stories," Mrs. Radcliffe explained away her phantoms "with exasperating timidity" (*Haunted Dolls' House* 254). In "Supernatural Horror in Literature" Lovecraft commented that she had "a provoking custom of destroying her own phantoms at the last through laboured mechanical explanations" (36).

Yet how thoroughly Machen destroyed his phantoms, if without mechanical explanations, in the *Impostors!* S. T. Joshi's puzzlement in *The Weird Tale* (1990) is legitimate: why does Machen undermine, and so weaken, his supernatural narratives? Complete consistency is not to be found, or even desired, in Machen. He attacks works with a didactic purpose in his foreword to *The House of Souls* and immediately embarks upon the exceedingly didactic *The Secret Glory*. In *The London Adventure* (1924) he says he cannot read George MacDonald's dream fantasy *Phantastes* (1858) "with any relish, simply because it tells you in the first few sentences that there is not a word of truth it in; that it is an allegory and nothing more" (79). Yet in the *Impostors* the stories are similarly revealed as fantasies. Had he wished, Machen could have made Miss Lally and Miss Leicester recount stories that are not ultimately exposed as fakes. It would surely be enough to suit his title that she and the other impostors had assumed false names. Machen states in the Henry Danielson bibliography that he had the title, from the fanciful *De Tribus Impostoribus*, ready in his notebook from 1885 (26). Interestingly, there seem to be *four* impostors in the book: Joseph Walters refers to "the man calling himself Dr. Lipsius."[2] This suggests that this name is also a pseudonym.

Machen has freely borrowed the manner and the style of Robert Louis Stevenson, from *More New Arabian Nights: The Dynamiter* (1885), but he has also transformed—transmuted perhaps is the more appropriate term—and improved on his model. Stevenson has the greater reputation, but Machen's book is more powerful because he writes not of anarchists but of darker matters. In "Supernatural Horror in Literature" (1927) Lovecraft argued that the work's "merit as a whole is somewhat marred by an imitation of the jaunty Stevenson manner," but the jauntiness is part of the book's charm (92). Who would be without Dyson's slightly pompous observations on life and literature?

The stories in *The Dynamiter* were originally related by Fanny Stevenson in 1883 at La Solitude, a chalet at Hyères, Switzerland, after near-fatal pneumonia and a haemorrhage confined Stevenson to bed. Having caught Egyptian ophthalmia, running wild through the district, he asked Fanny to take a walk each day and recite a tale to him in the evening. Thus Fanny became a real-life Scheherazade. This was the period of Fenian outrages in London, and Fanny invented a series of dynamite tales. Later the stories were written down,

---

2. Similarly, the misguided savant Dr. Black in "The Inmost Light' is pseudonymous, his name created by Dyson.

continued and revised at Skerryvore in Bournemouth, with Stevenson still seated, as he said, on "Charon's pier-head."

Fanny's "Story of the Destroying Angel" is the most effective tale in the book: would that all the stories in *The Dynamiter* measure up to this high standard. It comes as a surprise and a letdown that the story is entirely bogus. According to Roger G. Swearingen's bibliography of Stevenson, Fanny wrote the "Story of the Destroying Angel" and the "Story of the Fair Cuban" and Stevenson "Zero's Tale of the Explosive Bomb." The impetus for the book was the bomb blast in the Victorian railway station cloakroom in 1884. Portmanteaus with dynamite triggered by clockwork mechanism that failed to go off were found the next day at other railway stations. When a bomb detonated in Westminster Hall in the House of Commons early in 1885, Police Constable William Cole and Sergeant Thomas Cox were injured. The two policemen were made the dedicatees of the book.

In *The Dynamiter*, meeting on the northern pavement of Leicester Square after years of separation, Paul Somerset and Edward Challoner adjourn to the Bohemian Cigar Divan in Soho, where they are joined by a third young man about town, Harry Desborough. Prince Florizel of Bohemia, the pre-Ruritanian hero of *New Arabian Nights*, operating under the *nom de plume* of Theophilus Godall, runs the Cigar Divan in Rupert Street. (Rupert Street is a regular Machen locale. He sets scenes in "The Great God Pan" and "The Inmost Light" in the unnamed Florence Restaurant, alluded to in "A Wonderful Woman" and in "The Lost Club" as Azario's. Machen lived in Rupert Street while an actor at the turn of the century.)

In this sequel Prince Florizel is no longer centre stage. At the end of "The Rajah's Diamond" in the *Nights* Stevenson states that through his neglect of his realm a revolution has cost Florizel the throne of Bohemia: "his Highness now keeps a cigar store in Rupert Street, much frequented by other foreign refugees" (206).

Conversing in the Cigar Divan, the three companions Somerset, Challoner, and Desborough are waiting for something to turn up, but all are as "futile as the devil." Challoner plays a fair hand of whist while Somerset, like his creator, has studied as a barrister, though admits he knows little of the law. He resolves that the trio should turn detective—"the only profession for a gentleman," he claims. It could be argued that the vocation of detective is the very last profession a gentleman should pursue; the trio in the book prove laughably incompetent. Somerset's speech on Chance is reflected in Dyson's hymn to fate in the *Impostors*. Somerset says:

Chance, the blind Madonna of the Pagan, rules this terrestrial bustle; and in Chance I place my sole reliance. Chance has brought us three together; when we next separate and go forth our several ways, Chance will continually drag before our eyes a thousand eloquent clues, not to this mystery only [a reward is offered for information about a man in a sealskin coat seen in Green Park–Zero–one of the dynamiters], but to the countless mysteries by which we live surrounded. (Stevenson 7)

After finding the Gold Tiberius, Dyson vows to "go forth like a knight-errant in search of adventure. Not that I shall need to seek; rather adventure will seek me; I shall be like a spider in the midst of his web, responsive to every movement, and ever on the alert" (CF 1.337). These speeches prepare the ground for the coincidences occurring throughout both books. In *The Dynamiter* Stevenson calls London "the city of encounters, the Bagdad of the West" (1). Machen alludes to this in "The Great God Pan," when Villiers, standing outside the Rupert Street restaurant, surveys the passersby with curiosity, thinking, "'London has been called the city of encounters; it is more than that, it is the city of resurrections . . .'" (CF 1.231). One can detect, here and there, subtle touches where Machen pays homage to his predecessors. Significantly, Dyson and Phillipps meet in a tobacconist's shop in Great Queen Street, where Dyson repairs to expound his opinions on literature to anyone willing to lend an ear. Phillipps is presumably the same character—note the unusual spelling of his name—from "The Lost Club," Machen's pastiche of "The Suicide Club," now elevated into an ethnologist and more suited than Dyson to appreciate Miss Lally's scientific discourse on the Black Seal. Machen's unholy trinity, two men and a woman, correspond to the Stevensons' troublemaking trio. Leicester Square, where the heroes of *The Dynamiter* meet, is the scene of Miss Lally's narrative, recounted on a bench, of the Black Seal, and the locus of an abortive bomb attempt by one of the plotters. Clara Luxmore/Asenath Fonblanque spins her web on a Hyde Park bench.

The *Impostors* opens with a woman and two men leaving a house. In the opening "Story of the Destroying Angel," Edward Challoner's adventure begins when he sees an elegantly dressed young woman and two men fleeing from a Chelsea lodging house after an explosion has occurred. The young woman calling herself Asenath Fonblanque spins Challoner the sinister yarn of Mormon avengers; but this is a fantasy to disguise her involvement with Fenian conspirators. The Utah setting of this tale presumably inspired Machen to make the United States the scene of the Richmond/Wilkins narrative, the "Novel of the Dark Valley." Machen's tale has its weaknesses, but how wonderful to think that he wrote what is essentially a Western. Though feeble when compared with Helen's stories of the Black Seal and White Powder, the tale does contain a shocking sadistic scene where half a dozen ruffians, members of Jack Smith's Black Gulf Cañon gang, are stripped naked by a mob of vigilantes and lynched. Wilkins is doused with petroleum—by a woman—and is about to be roasted alive when he is rescued by a sheriff and his posse. Shocking stuff for Victorian readers.

The "Destroying Angel" inspired Conan Doyle to set the second part of his first Sherlock Holmes adventure, *A Study in Scarlet* (1887), a melodrama of persecution, murder, and revenge, among the Mormons of the alkali plain. That great Holmesian Vincent Starrett, in *The Private Life of Sherlock Holmes* (1933), dismisses this subsidiary story as "reminiscent of Bret Harte at his worst," but Holmes is absent from this part of the narrative and perhaps Starrett felt his loss. In view of how the Mormons are portrayed, one wonders how many copies of *The Dynamiter* and *A Study in Scarlet* are to be found in Salt Lake City.

Clara/Asenath and Helen/Miss Lally/Miss Leicester appear as modern-day avatars of Scheherazade, able to weave fabulous fantasies seemingly on the spur of the moment. Miss Fonblanque's name is almost "a fountain of blague": "pretentious but empty talk, nonsense," as the dictionary defines it. Stevenson described the book as an eccentric mixture of blague and seriousness. Black comedy, sinister romance, adventure, mystery, suspense, satire, interpolated stories: the *Arabian Nights* transferred to 1880s London. One can understand why *The Dynamiter* appealed to Machen, but he may have thought he could improve upon the framework.

In the "Destroying Angel" the villain is the elderly Dr. Grierson, who stage-manages Asenath's escape from Utah to London after disposing of her parents in an electric chair he has invented. We can see Professor Moriarty and Dr. Lipsius standing behind Grierson and an earlier villain, the unnamed president of the Suicide Club. Did the chair, years later, influence Nemor's Disintegrator in Doyle's entertaining Professor Challenger yarn "The Disintegration Machine" (1929)? Perhaps, though "the electrocution chair at Sing Sing" is alluded to. Grierson is marked as an unbeliever, even though he assists in the black deeds of the Mormons, disposing of any who rebel against the authority of Brigham Young and the church elders. Asenath tells how she and her parents, dwelling outside the city of Utah, are regarded with suspicion by the elders. Living in fear of their lives, they are "avoided as heretics and half-believers." Brigham Young "that formidable tyrant, was known to look askance upon my father's riches," she explains (Stevenson 22).

Grierson is working on an elixir that will restore his youth, and he proposes to claim Asenath as his bride. Grierson's experiments thus anticipate Dr. Jekyll's researches in *The Strange Case of Dr. Jekyll and Mr Hyde*, which would appear the year after *The Dynamiter*, in 1886. Were it not for Grierson's elixir would we ever have had Jekyll's potion? Drama is intermingled with farce. Grierson's flask explodes, precipitating Asenath's flight from the house in Chelsea, though, as we learn, this is far from being the actual case. Challoner is embarrassed to find himself sceptical of the story, with good reason, and Asenath's response is laughter: Miss Leicester similarly reacts to Dyson's scepticism in the "Novel of the White Powder."

In "Somerset's Adventure: The Superfluous Mansion," Paul Somerset is based, like the young man with the cream tarts in "The Suicide Club," on Stevenson's exuberant cousin, the painter Bob Stevenson. Somerset embarks from the Cigar Divan on the trail of adventure: "In the continual stream of passers-by, on the sealed fronts of houses, on the posters that covered the hoardings, and in every lineament and throb of the great city he saw a mysterious and hopeful hieroglyph" (Stevenson 64). This much anticipates Machen's style. Stevenson calls London "our Babylon": the great metropolis is full of exotic wonders to rival anything in an eastern tale.

Somerset hears the biography of the widow of the Honourable Henry Luxmore, and she turns out to be Clara Luxmore's mother. The old lady has saved Prince Florizel from assassination while he is renting one of her London mansions. Her daughter Clara, we learn, has "Some whim about oppressed nationalities—Ireland, Poland, and the like—[that] has turned her brain" (Stevenson 79). The vagueness of the mother's knowledge about the oppressed minority is part of the joke. The story of Mrs. Luxmore as a young woman, Miss Fanshawe, wandering desolately in London after learning that her family will not support her after she has absconded to the capital, and how she encounters her future husband, surely influenced Machen's similar scene when Miss Lally wanders through London alone and destitute, meeting her saviour in Professor Gregg.

While a tenant of the Superfluous Mansion, Somerset pursues the art of painting, and naturally his room takes on a bohemian character: "The mantelpiece was arrayed with saucepans and empty bottles; on the fire some chops were frying; the floor was littered from end to end with books, clothes, walking-canes, and the materials of the painter's craft" (Stevenson 106). Machen injects a similar vein of humour when Phillipps's primitive Indian knives are dispatched to the dustbin by his landlady.

Minding the mansion, Somerset takes in a mysterious lodger in a sealskin coat—the book's original title was "The Man in the Sealskin Coat"—subsequently revealed as Zero, a Fenian bomber, who turns his room into a terrorist workshop. He relates a blackly comic story, "Zero's Tale of the Explosive Bomb," about his co-conspirator M'Guire, who finds his plan to destroy the statue of Shakespeare in Leicester Square thwarted by police. M'Guire finds himself roaming central London with a Gladstone bag timed to explode. (Stevenson despised Gladstone.) Like the "Destroying Angel," this is one of the more effective episodes in the book, which is as uneven as the thriller it inspired.

M'Guire, desperate to be rid of his deadly burden, encounters a six-year-old girl (which he finds "a God-sent opportunity!"):

"My dear," said he, "would you like a present of a pretty bag?"
The child cried aloud with joy and put out her hands to take it. She had looked first at the bag, like a true child; but most unfortunately, before she had yet received the fatal gift, her eyes fell directly on M'Guire; and no sooner had she seen the poor gentleman's face, than she screamed out and leaped backward, as though she had seen the devil. (Stevenson 123)

In the light of modern terrorist outrages, where children are frequently victims of lunatics with causes, Zero's story is not quite so innocently funny as it once was, but it must be viewed within its period context. What makes Zero's account of the hapless M'Guire amusing is the sympathy he tries to arouse for the bomber: "Put yourself, I beseech you, into the body of that patriot. There he was, friendless and helpless; a man in the very flower of life, for he is not yet forty; with long years of happiness before him; and now condemned, in one moment, to a cruel and revolting death by dynamite!" (122). M'Guire, says Zero, is "the most chivalrous of creatures" (120). Zero sees black as white, and Stevenson does not interpose authorially to show how ridiculous his beliefs are.

M'Guire takes a hansom, planning to leave the bomb inside, to the Embankment, but realises that he has no money for his fare. Mr. Godall, Prince Florizel in disguise, happens to be passing—we accept the coincidence because this is a comedy—and lends M'Guire a sovereign. M'Guire throws his bag into the Thames and falls in after it. He is saved by Godall as the bomb explodes.

In the last interpolated tale, the "Story of the Fair Cuban," the beautiful Teresa Valdevia gives Harry Desborough an account of her adventurous life on an island off the coast of Cuba. "I am not what I seem," says Teresa (Stevenson 144). She is, of course, "the sorceress of Chelsea," Clara Luxmore in another guise: "a mad woman, who jests with the most deadly interests," as M'Guire terms her (Sevenson 201, 57). Her father dies after entering a swamp to bury a cache of jewels; she is persecuted by the high priestess of Hoodoo, Madam Mendizabal, and witnesses a devilish ceremony in the depths of the swamp. After the worshippers are destroyed by a timely tornado, Teresa escapes to the safety of an English yacht owned by the roguish Sir George Greville. It is a rather rambling tale without the power of the "Destroying Angel" but with parallels to *Treasure Island* (which Fanny initially found "tedious") in its exotic setting, the buried jewels, and a heroine replacing Jim Hawkins, with Madam Mendizabal taking Grierson's role in persecuting the heroine. Teresa's face is described as a "piquant triangle, so innocently sly, so saucily attractive" (139). This perhaps influenced Machen in giving Helen her "piquant" face. Clara's code name in a message to M'Guire in Glasgow is "Shining Eye." Machen may have derived Helen's eyes of "shining hazel" from this tiny detail.

In the Hoodoo rite the worshippers call upon the power of evil to smite their enemies. Teresa says: "Death and disease were the favours usually invoked: the death or the disease of enemies or rivals; some calling down these plagues upon the nearest of their own blood, and one [her servant Cora], to whom I swear I had never been less than kind, invoking them upon myself" (165). This episode possibly gave Machen the idea for the ritual in the "Novel of the Dark Valley," where men pay gold to have their enemies murdered by the Black Gulf Cañon gang.

Like the "Destroying Angel," Teresa's tale concerns itself with fear and persecution in an alien, hostile land; a supposedly innocent girl is harassed by evil forces. A double masquerade arises: to get aboard Sir George's yacht Teresa pretends to be Madam Mendizabal, leading the slaves to look upon her with awe.

When Harry seizes a book in Spanish, Teresa is momentarily disconcerted. Alas, she says, thinking rapidly, she has never learned to read. Harry comes across the report of a hurricane in Cuba and convinces himself that this is Teresa's fortuitous tornado. She has Harry accompany a box—muffled ticking comes from within—to a railway station. Realising she is in love with Harry ("I was never nearer Cuba than Penzance" [Stevenson 188]), she has the box returned to her home in Queen Square, Bloomsbury, where it threatens to detonate. The Children's Hospital—the Great Ormond Street Hospital—is next door; but the bomb proves a damp squib, and only dense and choking fumes fill the room. The hospital is saved.

Zero's bomb does explode after he and Paul Somerset leave the Superfluous Mansion, and Zero gloats over the atrocity that will ensure his reputation as a terrorist. Somerset plans to exile him to America, but a brick of dynamite blows Zero up at Euston Station.

At the end of the book all the surviving characters are reunited at the Bohemian Cigar Divan, and M'Guire's death is announced in Stepney. Harry introduces his new wife to Somerset and Challoner; both recognise her, but she pretends never to have met them. "She tells wonderful stories, too; better than a book," Harry informs his friends (201). Godall blackmails Mrs. Luxmore into reconciliation with her daughter, threatening to place Clara behind his counter, "where I doubt not she would prove a great attraction; and your son-in-law shall have a livery and run the errands" (206). All ends happily, as in a theatrical farce. Clara duly repents of her misguided ways: we never hear that she has actually harmed anyone, and so she is permitted a fairy-tale conclusion with her Harry.

As in the *Impostors*, coincidence is stretched beyond breaking point—Machen borrowed Stevenson's vices as well as his virtues—but it is all done with such jollity and verve that the reader scarcely notices. Indeed, the coincidences harm the book less than in Machen's work because it is a comic romp and not to be taken seriously. Only two of the tales in the book are fake, but Machen clearly relished the idea of spinning tales which are ultimately revealed as mere yarns. After all, is not the art of lying the craft of fiction? To get readers to suspend their disbelief and accept the incredible, and then pull the rug out from under them and admit all is invention is a courageous step for a fictioneer.

The flaw in logic shared by both books is why Clara, Helen, and Machen's other impostors should weave such elaborate fictions when all they require is to confuse Stevenson's heroes and discover the bolthole of the young man with spectacles. One wonders whether they accost other strangers across London and pour out further tales. No wonder Grant Richards yearned for a sequel to the *Impostors*. But of course, if they did not weave their tales there would be no books.

"Do you think I should waste my time and yours by concocting fictions on a bench in Leicester Square?" Miss Lally asks Phillipps (CF 1.400). Yet that is precisely what she does. The "Adventure of the Missing Brother" is brief enough to be extemporised, but Helen has surely put much thought into the "Novel of the Black Seal." The tall stranger leading her imaginary (?) brother through Leicester Square can be assumed to be Death. He has a face that seems "devoid of expression or salient feature. It was like a mask" (CF 1.363). Death's mutilated hand seems to relate to the Prologue where Helen has severed part of Walters's hand—a finger perhaps "from the hand that took the Gold Tiberius" (CF 1.330). This is her macabre souvenir for the doctor's museum: an act that is to come. The tall figure and the brother are doubtless figments of Helen's fervid imagination, but it is she who wears a mask.

Like Dyson and Phillipps and her prototype Clara, Helen is not a fully rounded character, but her combination of charm and evil make her the *femme fatale* without equal: a Scheherazade of the sinister. Helen is recognised by Walters as the most deadly of the unholy trinity. Some readers, though not all, may find her as a character more powerful than Dr. Jekyll, for the good doctor needs his potion to locate the evil within himself; Helen holds it within her naturally. Miss Lally and Miss Leicester are what she could be; Helen is what she is. With her blend of bogus kindness and loyalty (she is presumably loyal to her master Lipsius), ruthlessness and sadism, she is the New Woman to end all New Women.

Like Helen, Clara is fanatical in her aims, presenting herself as the innocent victim in her tales. Yet Clara repents of her madness, and all is forgiven at the last. Helen disappears behind the rear of the ruined mansion in the Prologue with her bloodstained parcel and her co-impostors, and, chronologically, that is the last we hear of her. Machen declines to inform us whether Helen takes part in the orgies held in Lipsius's house. Is she the nameless partner who sits by Walters's side? It would be pleasant to think so. Helen certainly responds to the sensual. She saucily offers her hand, "soft and white and warm," for Phillipps to check her pulse on the bench in Leicester Square (CF 1.363): surely one of the most erotic moments in *fin-de-siècle* literature, though the scene must be viewed through Victorian eyes. How much more satisfying than graphic modern descriptions of who put what where.

What, one wonders, did Machen have against the name Helen? We can perhaps see why Helen in "The Great God Pan" is so named—the classical Helen is the daughter of a god; but why did Machen reuse the name in his next book? Does the first syllable of the name suggest the characters' natural habitat? One wonders if any critic would dare advance the proposition that the Helen of "The Great God Pan" and the Helen of the *Impostors* are one and the same; just as, at least unofficially, the Hermit of *Hieroglyphics* and Ambrose of "The White People" may be regarded as the same character. They cannot be the same, of course, if only because of Mrs. Humphry Ward's novel

Robert Elsmere,³ referred to by Dyson in the "Incident of the Private Bar." The book appeared in 1888, the year Helen Vaughan is forced to die by her own hand, and it is clear from Dyson's allusion to the novel, which Machen loathed because he saw it as an attack on Christianity, that it has been available some time. However, if "The Great God Pan" and the *Impostors* are ever adapted for the screen, it would be tempting to make, with the tales chronologically switched, the twin Helens the same character; just as Dyson might replace Villiers or Austin in "The Great God Pan."

One lacuna in the "Novel of the Black Seal" concerns Gregg's two children. Miss Lally reveals nothing about them; their sex, ages, and names remain mysteries. The children are ciphers and rarely mentioned: of course, they may not exist. They are present in the plot only to enable Miss Lally and Gregg to holiday near Caermaen without offending propriety; their ménage might be thought scandalous otherwise. But this contrivance may be a happy accident. Helen's lack of interest in her charges⁴ points to her being devoid of feminine feelings; she is no true woman. She feigns loyalty to Gregg, but beneath her heart is stone.

And what of her pseudonyms? Miss Lally's name presumably stems from "lall" or "lallate," to prattle childishly or babyishly. "Lallation" from the Greek *lalein* (chatter, talk, babble) means to sing lalla or lullaby, as the *Oxford English Dictionary* states. Machen would know Horace's ode to Lalage⁵ ("Chatterbox"),

---

3. On Mrs. Humphry Ward's *Robert Elsmere*, see Machen's letter to Harry Quilter, *Faunus* 6 (Autumn 2000): 40, where he says he would be ashamed to have written that book and Olive Schreiner's *The Story of an African Farm* (1883) "& all such books as deprave and blaspheme the dogmas & morals of the Catholic Church, turning many from the faith." *Robert Elsmere* is not actually an ungodly tract. Mrs. Ward's book, described by her biographer John Sutherland as "probably the best-selling 'quality' novel of the century"—hence Dyson's annoyance—makes the case for non-supernatural Christianity, which Machen would have thought heretical. Elsmere is a young cleric whose faith in miracles and Christ's divinity is eroded by his studies. In *Hieroglyphics* the Hermit warns his "Boswell" (Machen, we infer) to condemn *Robert Elsmere* as inferior literature, but not solely because it contains arguments against the faith.

4. Note the contrast between Miss Lally's attitude and that of the unnamed governess, devoted to Miles and Flora, in *The Turn of the Screw* (1898). Borrowing his mother's Scots idiom, Machen thought the novella "the finest 'ha'nt' in the English language," though he generally regarded James's style as "quite terrible" and the Master's books did not appeal to him.

5. Lalage is the name Sarah Woodruff gives her daughter in *The French Lieutenant's*

a name borrowed by Hardy and Dowson for their poetry. But what of Miss Leicester? The name perhaps commemorates Helen's triumph in Leicester Square. That is, perhaps for some readers, one of the charms of Machen's work: it defies and eludes critical analysis. We are never quite sure that any critical theory is correct. Lipsius warns Walters about scholarly pursuits: "I will know all things; yes, it is a device indeed. But it means this—a life of labour without end, and a desire unsatisfied at last. The scholar has to die, and die saying, 'I know very little!'" (CF 1.446). A fine epitaph for the graves of Machen commentators.

Miss Lally certainly has a sense of humour. She even refers to "our church"—the baggage!—that of All Saints, Kemeys Inferior,[6] high above the Usk. Helen a churchgoer: surely her and Machen's little joke.

One crucial point to consider in the *Impostors* is whether the interpolated stories are entirely fictional. The impostors have documentary evidence to support their tall tales. Wilkins has a newspaper cutting about the Colorado lynchings; Miss Lally explains that she carries Gregg's statement with her always; and Miss Leicester produces Dr. Chambers's conclusions on the astounding properties of the White Powder, which Dyson sees, even if he does not read the report. This evidence lends a pleasing ambiguity to the stories, adding a level of meaning that is absent from *The Dynamiter*. Machen does not press the case for the validity of these documents and rather glosses over their significance. Are we to assume that they have been manufactured by the impostors? If not, their existence hints that some elements of the impostors' tall tales may be authentic. One can posit an alternative version of the book in which the hoaxes contain certain strands of truth. Perhaps Frank Burton thrusts Mathias into the arms of the Iron Maid in order to secure the device for Lipsius's museum. M. R. James stated with regard to the ghostly

---

Woman, who both appears, and signally fails to appear, apart from a phrase, in the novel's dual endings. At one stage in the book an infant begins to lall. The relation to "glossolalia," the gift of tongues, in which Machen took a keen interest, is evident. The American slang terms "lallygag" or "lollygag" (origins unknown), mean fooling around. Miss Lally certainly does that.

6. The church at Kemeys, "grey and severe and quaint, that hovered on the very banks of the river and watched the tides swim and return," as Miss Lally poetically describes it, also features in *Clemendy*'s final story, "The Triumph of Love." Godfrey Brangham went in quest of All Saints some years ago and found only ruins. See Editorial, *Faunus* 10 (Autumn 2003).

tale: "It is not amiss sometimes to leave a loophole for a natural explanation; but, I would say, let the loophole be so narrow as not to be quite practicable" ("Introduction" to *Ghosts and Marvels* [1924]; *Haunted Dolls' House* 248). Machen does the reverse: he makes the loophole the supernatural, rather than the rational. The stories mirror the art of the tale-weaver. Clara and Helen's tales differ from conventional fiction only in the fact that it is admitted that they are inventions.

It would be instructive to know precisely when Machen read *The Dynamiter*: in spring 1885, when it was published, or afterwards? There seems a precedent for the ironic presentation of the impostors' tales in *The Chronicle of Clemendy* (1888). *Clemendy* was a burlesque of the romantic medieval tales Machen loved. The *Impostors* can be seen as a burlesque of the wonder tale. Rabelais mixed humour and satire, giving his name to a type of grotesque bawdiness blended with fantastic romance, and Machen followed suit, eliminating the grossness so as not to offend Victorian sensibilities. *Clemendy*'s naughtiness is so innocuous that certain readers might feel Machen is overly coy.

Several stories in the book are revealed to have protean aspects. After Sir Jenkin Thomas, the mechanical knight who strikes the hours with his axe in the monastic church of Abergavenny, disturbs the monks, lovers, and townsfolk by descending from his tower, the knight is tried for his crimes, one of which is being "in two places at the same time; the which was a pernicious, hurtful and heretical practice, of itself very worthy of the stake"—a clue to what follows (*Chronicle of Clemendy* 78). The knight is consigned to the flames, but the twist is that a company of merry wags has conspired to impersonate Sir Jenkin. Griffith the Delver is amazed by the talk of two monks who, compiling a history, heap up a vast imaginary treasure of gold and jewels in St. Julian's Wood and under the Round Table—the amphitheatre—at Caerleon. Though paradoxically Machen was a champion of tradition, this is his satire on how legend and lies become history. The adventures of Sir Nicholas Kemeys and Sir Dru de Braose are revealed to be pure make-believe: the knights have been revelling, feasting, and making love in Abergavenny when they were supposedly wandering overseas. The story of the miraculous Rose of Cathay, recounted by the mysterious stranger at Penhow Castle, may be intended to be a complete fable, though the matter is left ambiguous. The tale's "hero," Rupert de Launay, uses it to seduce Sir Roger's wife, Eva, and the two elope. The tale-teller is urged to drown the couple when the story is recounted in future to serve a moral warning. He pledges to "make those poor sinners die most miserably and wretchedly; or better still, Eva shall live and turn into a shrew, and so make Rupert's days a burthen unto him" (*Chronicle of Clemendy* 229). Sir Philip Meyrick's battle with the evil magician Maurice Torlesse, who conjures up storms to rage over Gwent, is turned on its head at the end by an alternative version in which Sir Philip, conspiring with Edith Torlesse, murders her father, described as "an honest grave gentleman" (*Chronicle of Clemendy* 301).

Here is Machen manipulating fiction and rewriting tales through his narrators. He subverts romance and demythologises his own mysteries. If the reader does not care for one version of a tale, here is Mr. Machen, that versatile young master of romance, both grave and satirical, to refashion it to your taste. Machen takes the uncharacteristic role of rationalist in providing Jamesian loopholes, which may be viewed as nineteenth-century rationalisations of medieval legends. This adds a further layer to his romantic fables, allowing the reader to decide which interpretation to accept: the now well-established technique of the unreliable narrator, dating back to Poe, taken to ultimate lengths.

Did Machen evolve this technique independently or did *The Dynamiter* provide the impetus? We may never know. And, sadly, we shall never know what Robert Louis Stevenson would have made of *The Three Impostors*. He died in December 1894, the month *The Great God Pan* and *The Inmost Light* was published.

Works Cited

Fowles, John. *The French Lieutenant's Woman*. 1969. London: Vintage, 2010.

James, M. R. *The Haunted Dolls' House and Other Ghost Stories*. Ed. S. T. Joshi. New York: Penguin, 2006.

Lovecraft, H. P. *The Annotated Supernatural Horror in Literature*. Ed. S. T. Joshi. New York: Hippocampus Press, 2nd ed. 2012.

Machen, Arthur. "About My Books." In Henry Danielson. *Arthur Machen: A Bibliography*. London: Henry Danielson, 1923.

———. *The London Adventure; or, The Art of Wanderering*. London: Martin Secker, 1924.

Stevenson, Robert Louis. *New Arabian Nights*. 1882. London: Thomas Nelson & Sons, 1925.

Stevenson, Robert Louis, and Fanny van de Grift Stevenson. *The Dynamiter: More New Arabian Nights*. London: Longmans, Green, 1885.

A Glow in the Sky:
Some Observations on Machen's Style

Jon Preece

In 1970 the theatre director Peter Brook and the poet Ted Hughes were working on a theatrical retelling of the myth of Prometheus. They were wrestling with the problem of language: why languages "lose something of their richness as the years go by," as Brook put it in a BBC Radio Four interview ("Peter Brook, Theatrical Revolutionary", broadcast in May 2015).

They decided they wanted to communicate the play in terms of sound alone. Brook explained: "We went back to the original and found there was more vibration, more tonality, more richness the farther back we went towards the beginning of languages or the very developed ancient languages like ancient Greek."

Brook described how Hughes decided that he would make an "extraordinary attempt" to sit each day in front of a sheet of paper and "just sit and wait and see if by an incredible act of fine awareness he could capture the moment when something was rising up in him to become a word, and before the word took shape the vibration turned into a sound pattern, and before the sound pattern became a recognisable word it was something he could capture with letters; and out of the letters came his name for the language—Orghast."

Brook summed it up: "It was the central sound of what deeply vibrates, like an organ."

Arthur Machen faced the same problem: how to invent "tales . . . to realise my boyish impressions of that wonderful magic Gwent" (*FOT* 19).

"Wonder" and "magic" are what Machen desires to convey—concepts that go back well before language. Furthermore, Machen was also driven to convey something beyond the enchantment: "the vague, indefinable sense of awe and mystery and terror that I had received" (*FOT* 20).

How was Machen to do this? The only tools he had were clodhopping, clumsy words. He would have agreed wholeheartedly with Bernard Malamud, writing of his father's generation, Russian-speaking immigrants in America battling to express themselves in English: "You have some subtle thought and it comes out like a piece of broken bottle" (Davis 49).

Sitting alone in Clarendon Road with his pen above the wastes of empty white paper as he tried to write the great romance, Machen would have had the profoundest sympathy with Ted Hughes waiting for the vibrations of a new language to rise up from within him and huffing and puffing as the syllables plopped out. (*Orghast*, being an experimental and constantly changing work, was never published.)

However, Hughes could draw on the vast experimental examples of the twentieth century—from Gerard Manley Hopkins to James Joyce to Ezra Pound. He also had the anything-goes decade of the 1960s as a further guide. Machen had none of this.

Many writers are first inspired by their contemporaries, or near contemporaries. The twenty-first century looks back to the age of Eliot, Yeats, Pound, and Joyce with awe: there were "Giants in Those Days," as Anthony Burgess entitles the first chapter of his survey *The Novel Now* (1967). Sitting in Clarendon Road, which giants would Machen have admired from his own era? As a novice writer learning his craft, upon whose shoulders might he have wished to stand? Writers who were publishing in the 1880s included Thomas Hardy, George Eliot, Robert Louis Stevenson, and Henry James.

Stevenson did influence Machen. But what if he had chosen Hardy as his model? Hardy was publishing his novels from around 1872 to 1896; and Machen could well have chosen him, as two of Hardy's great themes were the countryside and the clash of ancient and modern. These were two of Machen's great themes, as well, but let's see how Hardy treats them in this passage from *Far from the Madding Crowd* (1874):

> [T]he old barn embodied practices which had suffered no mutilation at the hands of time. Here at least the spirit of the ancient builders was at one with the spirit of the modern beholder. Standing before this abraded pile, the eye regarded its present usage, the mind dwelt upon its past history, with a satisfied sense of functional continuity throughout. (241)

Hardy is describing a building—and no more. The writing is functional only. The verbs are passive; the words are imbued with Victorian pomposity ("abraded" and "beholder"); the phrases avoid the physical act of looking ("the eye regarded"). It is all at a distance. Yet Hardy is dealing with a subject close to Machen's heart: the ancient traditions surviving into the present age. Because Hardy fails to grasp the magic within the core of the scene, he fails to convey it: the old empty barn is just that—empty.

Arthur Machen needs to be set in context—and once we understand where he came from, his achievement becomes all the more astonishing. Machen was born in the middle of the Victorian era—which could have been a disaster for his writing. As G. D. Klingopulos described it: "Nearly all Victorians wrote copiously and had little regard for eighteenth-century ideals of terseness and epigrammatic point" (59).

The fact is that the vast majority of Victorian prose is, to the modern eye, turgid, long-winded, and well-nigh unreadable. Like its décor, common Victorian prose is chock full of the ornate, the stuffed, the gilded, and the pompous. Precious little, comparatively, is read now. When was the last time you read Ruskin? Swinburne? Thomas Carlyle? *Idylls of the King,* anyone? These were the giants of their day, read by millions and praised.

Few novelists escaped this slough. Some writers have lasted, of course, but they had special qualities: Dickens's prose sparks with energy, pungency, and vividness; Emily Brontë's style is blown through with the wind and brutal nature of the moors.

Machen knew their worth, but he also knew how worthless were the vast majority of the hack Victorian novelists churning out their triple-deckers. So for his first great romance Machen turned away from his contemporaries—and into the past. He went even farther back. His first book, *The Chronicle of Clemendy* (1888), begins with an "Epistle Dedicatory": "It were but lost labour on my part (most illustrious) should I presume to give the especial reasons or prerogative instances whereby I am moved to give unto Your Grace these poor gatherings of a scholar's toil" (CF 1.18).

Machen is being deliberately old-fashioned in his style—it is a parody, of course. Many writers find their voice writing in the style of a revered master before daring to create paths of their own. There is a certain charm in the narrative tales that make up *The Chronicle of Clemendy,* but the style itself is self-conscious, slightly awkward, and ever so faintly embarrassed. In his introduction to the 1925 edition Machen is more brutal: the work "drove me on through black fogs of despair and dismal sloughs of hopeless difficulty" (vii). Machen had not found his authorial voice, which is why the writing of *The Chronicle of Clemendy* cost him so much pain.

Part of Machen's problem is that his passion, like his style, is assumed, put on. Dickens's anger at the cruelty of social deprivation was very real, and it powered his voice. In *The Chronicle of Clemendy*, Machen is not driven in such a way, which is why his voice and consequently his style is weak. Like Hardy's description of the old barn, he can admire the wooden structure and wax lyrical—but that is not what he is really after: he is really after the magic, but he cannot grasp it. His eye is superficial; like a Victorian moralist he can see but not touch, and by not touching he cannot convey the feeling of running your finger along the pitted grooves of the ancient timbers.

Machen soon abandoned parody. His early tales then ventured into the contemporary prose of the Victorian era. The style was awkward, to say the least. Take this opening line from the story "A Wonderful Woman" (1890):

> On an isle of refuge, a Patmos mercifully set in the midst of an ever-roaring torrent of hansoms going from the north to the south of London and vice versa, two men, who had not seen each other for many years, met face to face one sultry afternoon in early autumn. They recognised each other simultaneously and shook hands. (CF 1.280)

It does not sound like the Arthur Machen we are used to. So what is going wrong here? For a start, that opening sentence is more than 50 words long. If you tried to speak it aloud you would run out of breath even more quickly than the sentence you are reading has run out of steam. It starts with a five-word sub-clause—which immediately brings the sentence up short, like a rider pulling up a horse. Worse, this five-word hanging clause has nothing to do with the action; it merely tells you the story is taking place on "an isle of refuge." What on earth is that?

The reader is pulled up—and confused. Machen's learning gets the better of him in the next clause: "a Patmos mercifully set in the midst." The reader may think that the printer has mis-typeset "a Patmos," because we now have to go to a dictionary (well, I did, anyway) to find out what "Patmos" means. Immediately following "a Patmos" comes that sniffily declamatory "mercifully set."

"Patmos" turns out to be the Greek island where St. John wrote the Apocalypse. But Machen never explains what exactly is the London "isle of refuge." Is it a traffic island? A pub? A pavement? And if we try to unpack the metaphor, is St. John writing the Apocalypse on it (or possibly "in it," since we do not know what it is)? What has this "refuge" to do with a saint writing a book? The metaphor is, in fact, meaningless.

I concede that I am being too harsh on a rookie writer (which is why I shall leave the dialogue to fend for itself!). But we need to get a sense of this early style of Machen's to appreciate the glory of the later style.

The real reason for this verbosity and why the sentence fails is this: Machen is telling the story from the *outside in*. He is still assuming the mantle of a writer; the prose does not flow from within him to the outside world. One does not get a sense that the writer is in the scene. And if the writer is not in the scene, then neither is the reader.

That 50-word sentence is long-winded and typically Victorian. The Victorians had forgotten the lessons of the breakthrough of the Romantics, whose language was fresh, simple, direct, and full of feeling. More importantly, the Victorians—Bible-worshippers as they were—had forgotten the lessons of that great English writer William Tyndale, whose translation of the Bible in clear, simple prose was so influential that the editors of the Authorised Version followed his style in their edition.

Tyndale declared that his aim was to make the Scripture available to everybody—down to the "boy that driveth the plough" (David Daniell, "Introduction" to *Tyndale's New Testament* viii). Tyndale's directness and immediacy in using English was what made his translation so revolutionary, both linguistically and politically (see Bragg).

Machen's saving grace was that he constantly looked backward—and, luckily for him, it was to the eighteenth century. It is a century he was fond of, and his writings are full of references to it: for example, old houses in forgotten corners of London that have survived from the eighteenth century into the present one (for Machen, that is the unloved nineteenth). It was the age of one of Machen's great heroes, Samuel Johnson (1709-1784), as well as of Edward Gibbon (1737-1794), whose *Decline and Fall of the Roman Empire* was published between 1776 and 1788. You can pick up *Decline and Fall* at any page and find prose that is direct, immediate, and forward moving—such as this example:

> The dangerous secret of the wealth and weakness of the empire had been revealed to the world. New swarms of barbarians, encouraged by the success, and not conceiving themselves bound by the obligation, of their brethren, spread devastation through the Illyrian provinces, and terror as far as the gates of Rome. The defence of the monarchy, which seemed abandoned by the pusillanimous emperor, was assumed by Aemilianus, governor of Pannonia and Maesia; who rallied the scattered forces, and revived the fainting spirit of the troops. The barbarians were unexpectedly attacked, routed, chased and pursued beyond the Danube. (280)

There is a vigour in Gibbon's style that is entirely lacking in most Victorian prose (such as the Hardy passage quoted above). It is clear, informative, direct, and affirmative. There is a sharp dash of humour, too. All these elements are present in Machen's mature prose style. By looking to the past—to the eighteenth century—Machen had inadvertently stumbled upon his way forward as a prose writer.

Machen was fully aware of the problems with Victorian prose. In *Far Off Things* there is a telling passage where Machen recalls a boyhood steeped in reading Victorian magazines, including the *Welcome Guest,* a popular weekly dating from the 1850s. Machen says about the magazine: "I am afraid I should not admire its literature very much, for Sala, the chief contributor, had already acquired those vicious mannerisms which pleased the injudicious. He would speak of Billingsgate as a 'piscatorial bourse', for instance. I am afraid I should find it all terribly old-fashioned" (*FOT* 36).

The irony here is that Machen's contemporaries always thought of Machen as "old-fashioned"—he certainly dressed that way. But underneath the Inverness Cape was a sense that the Victorian style was not for him, and that the "grand manner" of writers such as his beloved De Quincey was one that he could not match. Finally, he did not want to write in a "terribly old-fashioned way."

Let us remind ourselves of Machen's aim: "to realise my boyish impressions" of the "enchanted land" of Gwent (*FOT* 19). Which brings me to another curious fact: that Machen was born *after* Debussy, whose musical "impressionism" is the equivalent of what Machen sought in prose: elusive, yet earthy; delicate, yet precise; simple, yet deep; direct, yet sinuous.

Nevertheless, Debussy still had to write his notes down on a page of manuscript paper just as Machen had to write his words down on paper. However, "impressionism" is easier to assimilate in sound rather than in prose: words do not have the advantage of the sound board of a piano, which echoes and overlays successive chromatic sonorities.

In *Far Off Things* Machen describes the Gwent of his boyhood and youth "as a kind of Fairyland"—but almost at once after saying this, he backtracks: "Fairyland is too precise a word" (*FOT* 21).

Machen had set himself two fundamental problems. First, he had to use words to evoke an impression of fairyland. Words are nothing if not hard sounds, yet they needed to convey an impression of that magic air that flows into the real world when the veil is parted, even for a moment. He had to hint at the mysteries that lie behind the veil of the material world: a Victorian style of thick impasto would obscure what Machen wanted to convey. His style had to be clean and limpid, like glass.

Which brings me to the second problem that Machen set himself: that the kind of story he wanted to tell could not be one of "material incidents": it had to be "suggested to the reader" (*FOT* 20).

Machen shows himself, astonishingly, to be a Modernist. Marcel Proust knew that the traditional story structure was inadequate for what he wanted to convey—the magical impressions of his own boyhood and youth, told in an autobiographical fictional form. However, Proust was decades in the future: Machen was on his own.

It was these boyish impressions about which Machen was passionate, and because he was passionate they fired his vision with the kind of energy Dickens had tapped into. He was no longer assuming the mantle of a writer; he was at last writing from the inside out.

A key text, I think, is "The White People" (1904): specifically the girl's narrative:

> And I came to a hill that I never saw before. I was in a dismal thicket full of black twisted boughs that tore me as I went through them, and I cried out because I was smarting all over, and then I found that I was climbing, and I went up a long way, till at last the thicket stopped and I came out crying just under the top of a big bare place, where there were ugly grey stones lying all about on the grass, and here and there a little twisted, stunted tree came out from under a stone, like a snake. (*CF* 2.195)

The words are short, elemental, and often commonplace—"a long way," for example. The pace is quick, the narrative forward-moving. The clauses flow over the commas—just as the girl stumbles up hill. There are only two sentences in the passage quoted above. The first is short, but it packs a lot in. Most Victorian writers would have used a paragraph or more to convey the sight of this strange landscape. Machen does not wait: as with Gibbon, this scene is swiftly described; and once set down, the action moves on. The reader barely registers the fact that the landscape is unknown—but Machen reveals just how strange it is as the action moves forward.

The second sentence in the passage is longer than the opening sentence of "A Wonderful Woman" quoted earlier; yet it has none of the awkwardness, the pretensions, or the tautology. In "The White People" Machen has the advantage of writing in the voice of a child: the voice is simple, direct, immediate, and engrossing. It draws you in as much as "A Wonderful Woman" makes you keep your distance. It is also spontaneous: the rush of clauses matches the breathlessness of the narrator as she is driven onwards.

The words are simple and elemental: old and ancient. Machen is nearer to Ted Hughes than both would have realised. With this simple, unadorned style Machen is closer to the short, monosyllabic speech of early man—the grunts, the clicks, the yells—and the simple, but chilling, scream. Like Hughes, Machen, too, has travelled back in time.

To the clear prose of Gibbon, Machen added a narrative of strange and odd events to create the unsettling atmosphere it was his desire to convey. If you read that passage again, it is chilling. The protagonist stumbles blindly through a strange landscape where she feels threatened for no apparent reason and is subject to events beyond her control.

It could have come straight out of Kafka: and, indeed, this was the direction that Machen's narrative ambitions had taken him in the late 1890s. He wanted to write a story that would be "a *Robinson Crusoe* of the soul"—the novel that became *The Hill of Dreams*. Without knowing it, Machen was writing about an "existential" hero—or anti-hero—decades before the term "existential" was invented. Aspects of existentialism are found in Dostoevksy and Tolstoy, but it is remarkable how many are found in Machen: a man's alienation from an absurd, cruel, meaningless world; and the burden of "soul-scarring anxieties" that bring with them the "need to distinguish between his authentic and unauthentic self, his obsessive desire to confront his imminent death on one hand and his consuming passion to live on the other" (Karl and Hamalian, "Introduction" 11).

These themes are private, secret, primal, anguished. They are not the themes of imperial Victorian literature; Machen had moved far away from these. It was not until the twentieth century that existentialism and Modernism in literature would resolve themselves into a movement; but in the late 1890s Machen was infusing his stories with existentialist techniques as a by-product of conveying "the vague, indefinable sense of awe and mystery and terror that I had received" (*FOT* 20).

To the clear prose of Gibbon and the terror of "The Great God Pan" and "The White People" Machen has added a lushness of imagery and a sensuality that is new. He then tells the story of a soul adrift alone in a cruel world. This heady mix is the reason that *The Hill of Dreams* is so rich and strange, why it has lasted, and why it has more in common with Kafka and twentieth-century disorders than the nineteenth.

"There was a glow in the sky as if great furnace doors were open": this is the opening sentence of *The Hill of Dreams*. To understand how Machen's prose style works, we can look at this in very close detail.

There was a glow in the sky . . . It is simple and direct. Each word is only one syllable long. The emphasis in the rhythm falls on "glow," "sky," and "great"—words that are long and which require the mouth of the speaker to be open to let the breath out.

There was a glow in the sky as if . . . What happens next? All we have is the "glow." But that word "great" makes the reader anticipate something exciting, or memorable, or impressive. What might we expect? A "blaze"? Or a "sunset," more likely?

That is what the reader thinks *should* come next. But, of course, it does not. The image Machen confronts us with is: *great furnace doors were open.* Are we supposed to be thrilled by this? Or appalled?

. . . *great furnace doors* . . . This image would have meant much more to Machen and his readers than it does to a modern audience. In the Victorian era many industries lived cheek by jowl with the cramped streets of the industrial workers. People knew what furnaces were: fiery, powerful, iron-clad, dangerous. To get some idea of the sulphuric emotion Machen was aiming for, we can look at this famous quotation from Thomas Carlyle, who visited Merthyr in South Wales in 1850. He wrote that the town was filled with such "unguided, hard-worked, fierce, and miserable-looking sons of Adam I never saw before. Ah me! It is like a vision of Hell, and will never leave me, that of these poor creatures broiling, all in sweat and dirt, amid their furnaces, pits, and rolling mills" (Froude 52). We are not looking at a metaphor for the sunset, but at a vision of Hell.

great furnace doors were open . . . The opening sentence is pulled up short and stopped by the adjective "open"—which Machen puts at the end of the phrase. The doors are "open": and if something is open, what do we do? We think "What's inside?"—and we look.

The story is nailed at the start. This is a journey from a "glow" into the hell of a "great furnace." The doors are "open"—and the only way is in. At the beginning of the sentence we may have expected the glory of the sunset; but what we get, in fact, is the hell of fiery destruction.

This is why that opening line is one of the great opening lines of literature. There really are few that can compare with it.

This is not to say that Machen kept up or developed this style. He does lapse into tautology at times, particularly in dialogue. However, Machen worked at this style and eventually it became second nature. I believe that the purest essence of this style is to be found in *Ornaments in Jade* (written in the late 1890s, but published by Alfred A. Knopf in 1924). Consider this passage, from "Midsummer": "He entered the shadow, treading softly, and let the track lead him away from the world. The night became full of whisperings, of dry murmuring noises; it seemed soon as if a stealthy host were beneath the trees, every man tracking another" (CF 2.178).

To me, that passage has the epigrammatic quality of Gibbon: there are no wasted clauses; each clause contains its own self-contained fact that is added to the narrative line—and the line moves on to the next clause and the next fact. The movement of the line is direct. Machen does not give the reader an image and then successive repetitions of the same image with miniscule variations. A man enters a wood; and in the space of several sentences is surrounded by an invisible, phantom host.

One of the most remarkable, hidden aspects of this story is that Machen's prose works wonderfully if you read it out aloud. The words conjure up the magic of the scene Machen desires to convey, and the spoken voice reveals an atmosphere that is very close to the haunted music of Debussy—*Jeux* or some of the *Études,* for example.

Machen gives us glimpses: the flint on the pavement, the face at the window, dry murmurings. These story elements do not need the booming prose of De Quincey (a style Machen loved). They only require the kind of breath that you need to pronounce the French word "tu"; anything more and the delicate candle flame will be extinguished.

Furthermore, Machen is inside the story with you. The prose does not seem as if it is trying; it rarely appears to try at all, unlike that opening passage from "A Wonderful Woman," which tries far too hard to be literature. That Machen finally found a way "to realise my boyish impressions of that wonderful magic Gwent" is the reason his prose has lasted and is enjoyed. He does indeed capture the hidden magic of the ancient hills and woods that, in truth, he never really left and in which his spirit lives still.

Works Cited

Bragg, Melvyn. *The Book of Books*. London: Hodder & Stoughton, 2011.

Burgess, Anthony. *The Novel Now*. London: Faber & Faber, 1967.

Davis, Philip. *Bernard Malamud: A Writer's Life*. Oxford: Oxford University Press, 2007.

Froude, James Anthony. *Thomas Carlyle: A History of His Life in London 1834-1881*. Volume 2. London: Longmans, 1855.

Gibbon, Edward. *The History of the Decline and Fall of the Roman Empire*. 1776-88. London: Everyman's Library, 1993.

Hardy, Thomas. *Far from the Madding Crowd*. London: Smith, Elder & Co., 1874.

Karl, Frederick R., and Leo Hamalian. "Introduction" to *The Existential Imagination*. London: Picador, 1973.

Klingopulos, G. D. *The Pelican Guide to English Literature*. Harmondsworth, UK: Penguin, 1958.

Tyndale, William. *Tyndale's New Testament*. Ed. David Daniell. New Haven: Yale University Press, 1989.

The Secret and the Secrets:
A Look at Machen's *Hieroglyphics*

John Howard

Hieroglyphics (1902) is set in a single room, in a single house, in one of Arthur Machen's favourite North London districts, Barnsbury. Although on the surface a work of nonfiction, *Hieroglyphics*, like much of Machen's genuine fictional output, has a microcosmic setting serving as a counterpoint to thoughts and opinions that can embrace considerably wider settings. From the commonplace and ordinary can come precious gems, and the extraordinary becomes a way of life.

Hieroglyphics is presented as one side of a series of conversations with an unnamed friend, presumably Machen himself. Although a work of nonfictional literary theory, *Hieroglyphics* is thus immediately given a quasi-fictional rationale, and does in fact share many of the characteristics of the author's better-known fiction.

Roger Dobson has pointed out similarities with "The White People." Both works involve reclusive and obscure literary figures who live in old and mouldering houses in North London. Both *Hieroglyphics* and "The White People" are enabled to take place in this setting of apartness and withdrawal from the world, and both are concerned with "ecstasy"—which can be defined as "standing apart."

And into this work of literary theory there also intrudes a hint of the supernatural: "I recall the presence of that hollow, echoing room, the atmosphere with its subtle suggestion of incense sweetening the dank odours of the cellar, and the tone of the voice speaking to me, and I believe that once or twice we both saw visions, and some glimpses at least of certain eternal, ineffable Shapes" (*H* x). Also, in a letter written to the Boswell-like listener by the Hermit, giving him permission to publish the record of their conversations, he says: "Remember: keep the secret, *and the secrets*" (*H* xi).

Machen's other great connected fictional themes, those of "sorcery" and "sanctity," also have their place in *Hieroglyphics*. Each is "an ecstasy, a withdrawal from the common life" (CF 2.185). For Machen this meant true reality. And while his fiction tends to deal with the "sorcerous" side of reality, the dangerous and destructive side, in *Hieroglyphics* he chooses to encounter the "sanctified"—the life-enhancing and constructive—in a theory of literature which uses ecstasy as its starting-point and distinguishing feature.

In my essay "A World of Great Majesty: The Pattern in Arthur Machen's Carpet," I argued that, in his fiction, Machen effectively tried to compensate for what he saw as the weaknesses in contemporary organized religion. So in *Hieroglyphics* he tried to provide a basis for the re-evaluation and enduring worth of true literature and those who write it. In line with the book's title, Machen wished to say that the craft of the writer should be a hierophantic one—as an expounder of sacred mysteries. Authors of true literature are hierophants, and not mere entertainers, and their work is art, and not just entertainment.

While not condemning entertainment and its purveyors (and so consumers), Machen sets out in *Hieroglyphics* to make it clear that true literature, through the hierophantic author, is often, through symbols, seeing and conveying reality as it is. And authors are therefore to be regarded as "priests" of ecstasy: being able, through ecstasy, to produce its feeling in the reader:

> [I]f we, being wondrous, journey through a wonderful world, if all our joys are from above, from the other world where the Shadowy Companion walks, then no mere making of the likeness of the external shape will be our art, no veracious document will be our truth; but to us, initiated, the Symbol will be offered, and we shall take the Sign and adore, beneath the outward and perhaps unlovely accidents, the very Presence and eternal indwelling of God. (H 169-70)

The setting of *Hieroglyphics* in a large and labyrinthine old house is reflected in the structure of the book itself. Machen decides on a theme and asks a question—and then spends the length of a whole book going around in a cyclical argument.

The whole reason for the book is the question, What distinguishes true literature from mere writing, even if interesting writing? The answer, given early on, is ecstasy:

> Yes, for me the answer comes with the one word, Ecstasy. If ecstasy be present, then I say there is fine literature; if it be absent, then, in spite of all the cleverness, all the talents, all the workmanship and observation and

dexterity you may show me, then, I think, we have a product (possibly a very interesting one) which is not fine literature. (*H* 10-11)

And then comes the labyrinthine wandering of Machen's thought and arguments, much livened by the one-sided conversational, if not lecturing, format of the book.

In the scene-setting opening, Machen's Hermit, when he has recovered from the surprise of finding that his talks have been noted down, suggests as a title "Boswell in Barnsbury." Machen's Boswell-like action in recording their conversations, in what he calls the "cyclical mode of discoursing," reinforces the sense of wandering around a large old house, one with many rooms and passages, some neglected, others less so (attributed by Machen to H. N. Coleridge: *H* xii, 5, and 100f.). So Machen hints, in a self-deprecating aside, that the Hermit might be deceived in his search for "real essential knowledge," and the answer to his question (*H* xii).

In *Hieroglyphics*, perhaps the labyrinth—which usually surrounds a centre, a heart, a destination—actually surrounds a void, without allowing it to be fully explored. To Machen, the mystery of literature is only to be approached through cyclical argument or to be found after a journey, a series of discussions (*H* 100). However, in Machen there is also a creative tension and possible contradiction. It can also seem that the experience of the search for the mystery, for ecstasy, is at least as important as—and certainly no less interesting than—the goal itself. The means are as important as the end, and are certainly more obtainable than a fleeting and constantly out-of-reach answer.

Hieroglyphics is as much a book about looking for an answer as it is about providing an unassailable answer in itself. Just as *The London Adventure* is a book about not writing a book called *The London Adventure*, rather than the actual book itself, so *Hieroglyphics* is as much a "hieroglyph" itself, rather than an explanation and revelation (as noted by S. T. Joshi in *The Weird Tale* 35). Machen does get around to answering his question, but not in a way that is satisfactory to all. It is as if Machen said, "I don't really know what ecstasy is, but I recognize it when I see it." His examples are open to question. The process of examining ecstasy, of sifting writing to discover that which is true and fine literature, and that which does not measure up, is not open to question. It just happens.

The labyrinthine setting of *Hieroglyphics*, and the manner in which Machen expounds his theory, have already been noted. It is also worthwhile to note that the literary works that Machen discusses as fine literature—that is, as possessing and giving ecstasy—also seem to be of a wandering, cyclical, if not labyrinthine cast. Machen prefers the expansive in fiction. He lists, in particular, Charles Dickens's *The Pickwick Papers*, Cervantes's *Don Quixote*, and the works of François Rabelais.

These are among his favourite books, mentioned and praised in other connections: Rabelais is drawn on in *The Secret Glory*, Cervantes and Dickens are the subject of the essay "True to Life," reprinted in *The Secret of the Sangraal*. A trawl through the "Periodicals" section of the Goldstone and Sweetser *Bibliography* will reveal many pieces whose titles would seem to refer to these works and authors. They are, doubtless, fine literature by Machen's standards and by his theory of literature. This is perhaps good luck, although of course Machen would also say that this is a coincidence. These books are generally regarded as classics, and the fact that they contain and produce ecstasy in the reader is enough to explain that.

Machen also decides that some other books, which were also highly regarded by many of his contemporaries in the late nineteenth century and have attained classic status now, are not fine literature. Machen insists that they may very well be fine books, but works by such authors as Jane Austen, William Makepeace Thackeray, and George Eliot do not have ecstasy present and are not, therefore, fine literature.

So, for example, Machen's Hermit says:

> I claim, then, that here we have the touchstone which will infallibly separate the higher from the lower in literature, which will range the innumerable multitude of books in two great divisions . . . I will convince you of my belief in my own nostrum by a bold experiment: here is *Pickwick* and here is *Vanity Fair*; the one regarded as a popular "comic" book, the other as a serious masterpiece, showing vast insight into human character; and applying my test, I set Pickwick beside the Odyssey, and *Vanity Fair* on top of the political pamphlet. (H 11)

It may be thought that Machen was being somewhat misogynistic in his choice of literature not to be awarded the prize of being fine literature. After all, he effectively writes off the works of Austen and Eliot. However, I think it is more correct to say that Machen simply did not care for the type of fiction that these authors wrote. Along with Thackeray, Machen discusses the reasons for not allowing their works to be considered fine literature (H 102 *passim*).

But Machen did consider many of the works of one woman, Mary E. Wilkins Freeman, to be fine literature. A New England author little known today except for her ghost stories, for over thirty years from the late 1880s she was a fairly prolific author. Machen in an appendix spends time showing that Wilkins Freeman's work does deserve its place in the canon of fine literature by virtue of its possession of ecstasy:

> So this is my plea for Miss Wilkins. I think that she has indicated this condition of "ecstasies"; she has painted a society, indeed, but a society in which each man stands apart, responsible only for himself and his God. You will note this, if you read her carefully, you will see how this doctrine of awful, individual loneliness prevails so far that it is carried into the necessary and ordinary transactions of social life . . . (H 196)

(Mary Wilkins also published under her married name Mary E. Wilkins Freeman. For further information about her see Solomon's edition of Jewett and Wilkins Freeman and Howard 1999 and 2006.)

In *Hieroglyphics*, Machen realises that, in setting forth his literary theory, he is open to the charge of being subjective. Machen knows the books that he likes and therefore calls them true literature. He then fits them into his literary theory of ecstasy, as they contain that which defines and makes fine literature. This is a circular argument. Therefore, for example, out of two of the greatest writers of the nineteenth century, Charles Dickens and George Eliot, only one of them ever wrote fine literature. And the difference may not have been apparent to most readers!

Machen heads off this accusation by saying that taste is what is subjective, and not art. Thus art is there, and has nothing to do with popularity and enjoyment, "classic" status, and so on. To Machen, how the book is done, and all that follows from that, is not the point:

> You see, I think that the question of liking a book or not liking it has nothing whatever to do with the consideration of fine art. Art is there, if I may say so, just as the Tenth Commandment is there; and if we don't like them, so much the worse for us. . . . But when we leave the utterances of the eternal, universal human ecstasy, which we have agreed to call art, and descend to these lower levels that we are talking of now, it seems to me that the question of liking or not liking counts for a great deal. We must still distinguish . . .
>
> You see how, here again, we come to the generic difference between fine literature and interesting reading-matter. We read the "Odyssey" because we are supernatural, because we hear in it the echoes of the eternal song . . . we read Miss Austen and Thackeray because we like to recognise the faces of our friends aptly reproduced, to see the external face of humanity so deftly mimicked, because we are natural. (H 46, 51)

Thus Machen avoids the charge of subjectivity. It is the art in a piece of writing that determines whether not it should be accepted as fine literature. And art, to Machen, is of the "supernatural"—and speaks to that same quality in humanity. While Machen's staunch adherence to non-Protestant Christianity enables him to claim this high ground of objectivity, it still does require acceptance of, or at least sympathy with, that worldview. As the Hermit says, "you will realise that to make literature it is necessary to be, at all events subconsciously, Catholic" (H 201). This objective base is quite necessary, in that *Hieroglyphics* would otherwise just be an interesting diversion and a labyrinthine shaggy-dog article (which is not, to this reader, intended to be any sort of denigration at all!).

Towards the end of *Hieroglyphics* Machen divides people into two camps: the rationalists and the mystics. He is, of course, on the side of the mystics, and continues to try to prove the objective nature of his literary theory by showing that if rationalism is correct, "then all literature, all that both sides agree in thinking the finest literature, is simple lunacy, and all the world of the arts must go into the region of mania" (H 152).

At the beginning of this section of *Hieroglyphics*, Machen parodies rationalism by giving a series of questions lifted from a rationalist examination paper (H 150-51; see also Joshi 14). And he does precisely that: provides an outrageous and hilarious parody which is great fun to read, but which also necessarily involves the wholesale acceptance of Machen's premises in order to really support and explain his literary theory, and make it credible against all criticism.

Machen describes such a version of rationalism that his views can only be proved to be the correct ones. There must be things that are done and enjoyed without being able to give reasons for doing so, and this does have to be admitted by rationalists (H 153-54).

Machen's literary theory as promulgated in *Hieroglyphics* is effectively only correct if all his premises are accepted. If they are not, then *Hieroglyphics* does become merely very interesting, and is seriously flawed as a work of literary theory in the absolute and dogmatic sense that Machen seems to wish it to be understood and accepted.

As is the case with the acceptance or rejection of a religion or a political stance, it takes more than intellectual argument to convince. Viewpoints accepted on intellectual and logical arguments alone can often he held with a tenacity that is in proportion to the viewpoint's credibility. The heart must be involved, as well as the head.

The two are not in harmony in *Hieroglyphics,* and the Hermit's strong convictions and loquacity are clear symptoms of this (perhaps the "break of some sort" in his early life is relevant! [*H* vi; see also Dobson]). *Hieroglyphics* provides a literary theory, not *the* literary theory, and, as has been seen, too much stands or falls on the necessity of accepting Machen's worldview and understanding of the nature of humanity and its place in a universe created by God.

For all that, *Hieroglyphics* is a fascinating and lively setting-forth of a theory. Machen's view that it is ecstasy that distinguishes fine literature is a viable and defensible one and worth arguing for. (As an aside, it would be interesting to see if the same arguments could be deployed, using twentieth-century literary examples.) But it is Machen's attempts to give his personal views an absolute and universal basis, which by its nature then has to denigrate other views, that causes problems.

In *Hieroglyphics* Machen makes a valuable and timeless definition of fine literature. But it begs the question as to whether such a definition is really needed in the first place, and whether it is worth all the effort that Machen and the "Hermit" put into it.

But perhaps the joke is with Arthur Machen.

The reader is treated to a series of lectures, if not tirades, and may well come to feel that the Hermit is someone whom it would be a good idea not to encounter too often, despite the vehemence and liveliness of his conversation. There is always the nagging possibility that the reader has been taken for a Machenesque ride, and that the Hermit is simply enjoying himself as the long-winded bore at the end of the bar does. (And certainly this reader always emerges from *Hieroglyphics* feeling that he has been the mental equivalent of ten rounds in the ring.)

It is the journey and experience that is the thing, and the labyrinthine quest around the heart of literature is what is eventually left. The reader withdraws from the world in the experience of reading *Hieroglyphics.* The reader thus experiences ecstasy. And whether Machen has proved his point becomes a rather secondary consideration.

Works Cited

Dobson, Roger. "The Hermit and the Mystic: Two Who Are One." In *Machenalia,* ed. R. B. Russell. Lewes, UK: Tartarus Press 1990. 1.5-13.

Goldstone, Adrian, and Wesley D. Sweetser. *A Bibliography of Arthur Machen*. Austin: University of Texas Press, 1965.

Howard, John. "Lavender and Lilac: Ghosts, Visits, and Old Ladies." *Dark Horizons* 38 (Summer 1999): 58–66.

———. "Old England, New England: M. R. James, Mary Wilkins Freeman, and Sarah Orne Jewett." *Wormwood* No. 6 (Spring 2006): 13–23.

———. "A World of Great Majesty." *Avallaunius* No. 17 (Winter 1997): 41–47.

Jewett, Sarah Orne, and Mary E. Wilkins Freeman. *The Short Fiction of Sarah Orne Jewett and Mary Wilkins Freeman*. Ed. Barbara H. Solomon. New York: New American Library, 1979.

Joshi, S. T. "Arthur Machen: The Mystery of the Universe." In *The Weird Tale*. Austin: University of Texas Press, 1990. 12–41.

Machen, Arthur. *Precious Balms*. London: Spurr & Swift, 1924. Contains a selection of contemporary reviews of *Hieroglyphics*.

———. *The Secret of the Sangraal and Other Writings*. Horam, UK: Tartarus Press, 1995.

Sweetser, Wesley D. *Arthur Machen*. New York: Twayne, 1964.

Valentine, Mark *Arthur Machen*. Bridgend, Wales: Seren, 1995.

III. Mysticism, Magic, and Paganism

Arthur Machen's Panic Fears: Western Esotericism and the Irruption of Negative Epistemology

Marco Pasi

Qui perrumpit sepem, illum mordebit serpens.

Introduction: Positive Epistemology

If we were to make a broad generalisation, we could say that Western esotericism is largely based upon a positive epistemology. This has been pointed out by scholars of esotericism such as Andreas Kilcher, who noted that "esotericism is guided by a supreme optimism and universalism concerning knowledge" (143). One common feature of esoteric systems of thought is in fact the idea that, under certain conditions, man is able to have access to aspects of reality that *normally* cannot be the object of perception or experience. These aspects belong to other levels of reality, and esotericism claims to provide access to those levels. This may come, for instance, through intuition, initiation, or revelation.

Instructions as to the way to achieve these deeper, personal experiences of reality may be communicated, often with the claim that their origin is very ancient and that they have been handed down for centuries through an uninterrupted chain of initiates. In the end, the idea is that it is desirable to know these hidden aspects of reality. Perceiving the essence or the inner structure of God, of the universe, of nature, or of history is thought to be one of the supreme goals of human existence. The process of achieving this goal may be dangerous—the amount of esoteric texts devoted to the perils of initiation is vast indeed—but no doubt seems to subsist as to the fact that the goal itself is a positive one, and that no other goal in life may have the same importance.

Two fundamental aspects compose the idea of positive epistemology in esotericism. The first is an obvious confidence in man's epistemological abilities and a belief in the importance of exerting them to the utmost, which in this case largely seems to exceed the limits posed by contemporary mainstream religion or science. The second is the conviction that knowledge, no matter how strongly its "esoteric" varieties, may differ from more common types, is something positive, and that its acquisition brings positive gifts, such as "salvation," "power," "immortality," or "wisdom."

The first aspect, of course, concerns the means of attaining esoteric knowledge; the second one concerns its contents and the value attached to them. Kocku von Stuckrad has focused on the importance of claims to "higher" or "absolute" knowledge in the context of Western esotericism, and has even proposed a new model for its study on the basis of this concept.[1] While it may be somewhat problematic to attach such unique importance to the aspect of knowledge alone, at the expense of other elements which might be equally important, it does seem appropriate to highlight its relevance for the development of esotericism within Western culture.

This relevance adds weight to the point I wish to make here; that is, the fact that esotericism seems to be based on a general paradigm of positive epistemology. In modern esoteric organisations this positive epistemology, as I have defined it, clearly plays an important role. In various brotherhoods, fraternities, and orders, the notion of initiation often lies at the core of their system. Initiation is meant to regenerate the person who experiences it, and to open his consciousness or his perception to a reality that was unattainable for him before. Many different metaphors are used in this context to indicate the process that takes place in the moment of regeneration. One of the most widespread is based on the notion of "light," which is supposed to illuminate the candidate for initiation when the ritual reaches its climax, and to create in him the conditions necessary for the perception of aspects of reality that were supposedly hidden in darkness prior to the initiation. Several authors have observed that the metaphor of light is so powerful in the history of modern Western culture that it has been used in very different, sometimes even contradictory, contexts.[2]

---

1. See von Stuckrad, "Western Esotericism" (esp. 88-92). See also von Stuckrad, *Western Esotericism* 10-11. Von Stuckrad's model relies on the notion of "claims" to absolute knowledge, but also on the "means" to attain it. To this, the idea of certain worldviews specific to esotericism is added.

2. For the uses of the metaphor of light in a religious context, see Kapstein, *The Presence of Light*, a collection of essays that offers a good comparative perspective.

In the second half of the eighteenth century this metaphor was used to describe both the emancipation of humanity from the darkness of ignorance and superstition and the recovery of spiritual truths lost since the fall of Adam. Obviously, the first version alludes to the rationalist project of the Enlightenment, whereas the second one refers to the esoteric endeavours of Illuminism.[3] Some scholars have discussed the complicated, and not always necessarily conflicting, relations between these two different and yet contemporary cultural phenomena. But apart from their many differences, one aspect they certainly shared: this was precisely their being grounded in a positive epistemology, even if the contents of knowledge and the means to obtain it could differ widely in the two movements.

Arthur Machen and the Golden Dawn

The notion of light certainly plays a fundamental role in one of the most famous and influential modern esoteric orders, the Hermetic Order of the Golden Dawn.[4] Candidates who wished to be admitted into the Order were initiated through the ritual of the Neophyte, which therefore gave them their first experience of the esoteric system and served as an introduction to its teachings. The climax of the ritual was achieved when the hoodwink which covered the eyes of the candidate was removed. At this point, one of the officers of the ritual addressed the candidate with these words: "Wanderer in the Wild Darkness, we call thee to the Gentle Light." To this the leading officer of the ritual, the Hierophant, added a dramatic rejoinder, still addressed to the candidate: "Long hast thou dwelt in Darkness—Quit the Night and seek the Day" (Regardie 125-26).

On 21 November 1899, one of the several literary celebrities who would become a member of the Order heard these words for the first time. His name was Arthur Machen, and he chose as his mystical motto "Avallaunius."

---

3. As an introduction on this complicated issue, see Jacques-Chaquin, Bergé, and the bibliographies appended. See also Edelstein; Mannucci, *Gli altri lumi* and *Dai cieli la ragione*; and Ferrone. The literature on this topic is vast, but the classic work exploring the development of Illuminism at the time of the Enlightenment, and their complex relationship, remains Viatte. For some considerations on the ambiguity of the uses of the metaphor of light in this context see, but with caution, Amadou.

4. There is a growing literature on the history, system, and rituals of this important initiatic Order. As an introduction, see Pasi, "Golden Dawn" and Gilbert. The standard history of the Order remains Howe.

The motto was clearly inspired by his love and affection for things Celtic and was a transparent reference to the mythical Avalon.[5] Machen had been convinced to join the Order by his friend Arthur Edward Waite (1857–1942), who was already well known in occult circles for his publications and had been a member of the Golden Dawn for some time (Gilbert 168–73).

Machen at this time was going through a period of depression, as a consequence of the recent loss of his first wife, whom he had loved dearly. Waite thought that joining the Order could offer his friend a cure for, or at least a distraction from, his distress. With hindsight, and quite independently of Machen's personal troubles, we could say that the timing was rather ill chosen. Less than a year after Machen's initiation, a conflict that had been smouldering for some time erupted among the high-ranking members of the Order, eventually leading to schism and even scandal (Howe 203f.).

It is not clear how these events were perceived by members who held a low rank in the hierarchy of the Order, but it seems very likely that the turmoil shattered the mythical aura surrounding its teachings and structure, beginning with the very story of its foundation. Be that as it may, while Machen did succeed in gradually recovering from his personal grief, he never became a particularly dedicated member of the Golden Dawn.[6] He ascended slowly on the initiatic ladder of the Order, and never made it beyond the grade of Practicus (3=8).[7] When Waite, in 1903, created his own Independent and Rectified Rite out of one of the splinter groups resulting from the previous schisms of the Order, Machen decided to follow him for a while; but eventually he ended his membership, though keeping friendly relations with Waite.

In his memories, written some twenty years after the events, Machen observed that the initiation to the Neophyte degree had made a positive impression on him. The "breathless expectation," the sight of the officers of the ritual clad in wondrous clothes, the incense and the dim lights: "all this was strange and admirable indeed" (Gilbert 169). However, the activities and the teachings of the Order, as he came to know them after his first initiation, left him rather cold:

---

5. He had also used the name for the main character of his important novel, *The Hill of Dreams*, which he had written before his initiation in the Golden Dawn but would be published only in 1907.

6, Yet he confessed in one of his later volumes of memories that the membership "did me a great deal of good—for the time" (*TNF* 149).

7. On the initiatic system of the Golden Dawn, see Howe 15–17.

> But as for anything vital in the secret order, for anything that mattered two straws to any reasonable being, there was nothing in it, and less than nothing . . . the society as a society was pure foolishness concerned with impotent and imbecile Abracadabras. It knew nothing whatever about anything and concealed the fact under an impressive ritual and a sonorous phraseology. (*TNF* 151-52)

A harsh judgement indeed for an occultist organisation whose glamour and complexity had fascinated so many sophisticated minds. Machen felt that, despite all its promises of initiatic light, the Order had "shed no ray of any kind on my path" (*TNF* 154). Probably it was not the particular weaknesses of the Golden Dawn as such—for example, the nature of its system or the failure of its members to make it work—that Machen disliked. It seems that he had doubts about the very notion of an initiatic order, and about the knowledge that such an organisation pretended to deliver to its members. If so, his cynical remarks could have been applicable to any other occult organisation as well. In a letter to Waite, dated 24 December 1905—that is to say, in the period when his involvement with the Golden Dawn was coming to an end—he wrote:

> The average secret society presupposes . . . that the initiator is, in a certain sense, superior to the initiated; superior, that is, because he possesses certain information which he imparts to the neophyte; who is, by this process, admitted into a circle of knowledge outside which, (by the hypothesis) he stood, before his initiation. Now, imagine if you will, a society which makes no pretence of knowing anything which the outsider, the neophyte, does not know; which has no temple or circle to which admittance is given; which bids its members look within, & uncover, & remove, & Behold, & Make the Great Interior Entrance—from Within to Within, instead of from Without to Somebody Else's notion of Within. I hasten to say that these are hints & suggestions & not by any means Scientific Information. (*SL* 35)

Is it possible to imagine a secret society that does not impart information previously inaccessible to the new member? Machen seems to be saying that, ideally, the ultimate experience of "Truth," or "Great Interior Entrance," is essentially individualistic and potentially available to everybody. Why then would one need external, hierarchical structures? More conventional occultists might retort that achieving this experience is an art that must be learned: a single seeker without any guide would not even know where to begin or which direction to take, and would easily lose his way. The fact that a "true hermeticist" (Cavaliero 79) like Machen developed a pessimistic, sceptical attitude towards the value of traditional occult organisations, and of the knowledge or the initiatic experience they can offer, introduces us to the central topic of this article, that is to say, the development of a negative epistemology that may be observed in Machen's literary works and that would make its appearance in Western esotericism some years later.

Machen's Great God Pan

In 1894—that is, several years before his initiation into the Golden Dawn—Machen published what some critics have considered one of his best works of fiction: "The Great God Pan." As we will see, in this story the ancient Greek god serves as a symbol for the spiritual reality that lies beyond our senses, to which esotericists and mystics of all times have yearned to gain access. But of course the use of that particular divine entity was not an innocent one; it should be seen in the context of the extraordinary success that the god Pan, after having been mostly neglected by earlier authors in English literature, enjoyed during the nineteenth century, and especially towards the end of it.[8] Ronald Hutton has opportunely shown how the rediscovery of such a "minor" figure of the classical pantheon is also connected to the development of nineteenth-century occultism and to the origins of contemporary neo-paganism (43-51; and, on Machen's use of the image of Pan, 255-56).

Pan was particularly popular among a number of occultists who, like Machen himself, were more or less directly related to the Golden Dawn. Among them one can find Florence Farr, Algernon Blackwood, Aleister Crowley, the latter's disciple and poet Victor Neuburg (who never joined the Golden Dawn but was a member of Crowley's own version of it, the A∴A∴), and Dion For-

---

8. On the use of the image of Pan in English literature, see Merivale. See also the interesting study on literary paganism in late Victorian and Edwardian England by Hallett; the chapter "The Elusiveness of Pan" in Cavaliero (135-41); and, in the context of a discussion of Machen's novel, Valentine 32-33. For a more general survey of the evolution of the image of Pan since antiquity, see Boardman. As is well known, Plutarch, in his *Obsolescence of the Oracles* (*Moralia* 419A-E), reports the strange story that, during the reign of Tiberius, the death of Pan was announced. This story has been interpreted for centuries by Christian apologists as a metaphor for the end of paganism and of its gods, and as an omen for the beginning of a new era, where only one God would rule supreme. It is ironic, and at the same time significant, that when Pan was resuscitated in Western literature and culture, after so many centuries of oblivion, the death of his rival, the Christian god, was announced in turn. Friedrich Nietzsche's famous statement on the death of God was first made only a few years before the publication of Machen's story (in 1882, to be precise; see *The Gay Science*, section 125).

tune.⁹ According to Merivale (220), the glamour of Pan faded after the First World War, but Hutton (50) shows that his literary fortune continued at least until the Second World War. In fact, he had a faithful following in certain esoteric movements even after that period: a significant example is the interest that the Findhorn Community, and in particular its prominent member R. Ogilvie Crombie, paid to the ancient sylvan god (Ogilvie Crombie 82-102).

Now it is important to note that in Machen's story, Pan plays a role that is directly opposed to the one modelled on the perspective of the Romantics and their later occultist emulators, described by Hutton as follows:

> The nineteenth-century English made the god the expression of all the aspects with which the Romantics had invested the natural world: sublime, mysterious and awe-inspiring, benevolent, comforting, and redemptive. He was pitted directly against the perceived ugliness, brutality, and unhealthiness of the new industrial and urban environment and the perceived aridity and philistinism of the new science. He offered both peace and joy, a return—if only for a few hours—to the lost innocence of a sylvan wonderland. (Hutton 44-45)

Machen's biographer and critic, Mark Valentine, expresses a similar opinion and notes that the "the god Pan was to be frequently invoked in the fiction of the Edwardian period and after, usually with a sense of youthful allurement and sometimes a symbol of sexual freedom and license from the stifling moral climate that still clung from the previous century." He adds that Machen's book was "influential in attaching to Pan a new mode": "what had previously been a rustic, rather bucolic image, was now laced with images of illicit sex and cosmopolitan decadence" (32-33).

At the end of this essay I will return to the possible political meaning of the inversion operated by Machen. But let us first take a closer look at Machen's novel. The story begins with a scientific experiment. A scientist, Dr. Raymond, invites a friend of his, Clarke, to witness the final result of many

---

9. All these authors published some literary works in which Pan (or at least a faun-like creature) played a prominent role. I cannot discuss them at length here, but I may at least mention some of them: see Works Cited under Farr; Blackwood; Crowley; Neuburg; Fortune, "A Daughter of Pan" (clearly inspired by Machen's novel) and *The Goat Foot God*. In Dion Fortune's occultist group, the Fraternity of the Inner Light, Pan seems to have played a significant role. Rituals were performed in order to invoke him, and Fortune's collaborator Thomas Penry Evans delivered lectures on topics such as "The Pan Within." See Richardson 109-11 and Hutton 183.

years of research. The experiment is based on the idea that what human beings perceive every day with their senses is but the pale reflection of a deeper reality that cannot be accessed by them under normal conditions. Raymond has developed a theory according to which a surgical operation on the brain would open the "doors of perception" (to borrow William Blake's expression) and unveil this hidden reality. This is how Raymond explains his ideas to Clarke:

> "Look about you, Clarke. You see the mountain, and hill following after hill, as wave on wave, you see the woods and orchards, the fields of ripe corn, and the meadows reaching to the reed-beds by the river. You see me standing here beside you, and hear my voice; but I tell you that all these things . . . are but dreams and shadows: the shadows that hide the real world from our eyes. . . . I do not know whether any human being has ever lifted that veil; but I do know, Clarke, that you and I shall see it lifted this very night from before another's eyes. You may think all this strange nonsense; it may be strange, but it is true, and the ancients knew what lifting the veil means. They called it seeing the god Pan." (CF 1.218)

Pan here seems to be just a metaphor for the spiritual reality that exists beyond our senses; but in fact, as the story unfolds, the reader realises that it is a real, concrete entity as well. The test subject chosen for the experiment is a young girl, Mary, and the operation is indeed performed on her. When she awakens from the anaesthesia, she seems to have lost contact with the material reality around her. Her amazed glance is obviously directed towards unexplored, unknown regions. But suddenly her face shows a fit of "the most awful terror," and she falls "shrieking to the floor." Eventually, Dr. Raymond must realise that she has turned into a "hopeless idiot" (CF 1.223, 224). The vision of Pan has been an experience to strong too bear, and she has irremediably lost her mind.

In the following chapter, these events lie quite some years in the past. Clarke is reading some notes written down during a conversation with a friend, who told him about some strange episodes involving a young girl named Helen Vaughan[10]: a boy has suffered a nervous breakdown, a young

---

10. Initially, she is only mentioned as "Helen V.," but subsequently the reader learns that the V. stands for Vaughan. There is a curious coincidence here with the name of Diana Vaughan, the protagonist of the anti-masonic alleged revelations made in the 1890s by Leo Taxil (pseudonym of Gabriel Jogand-Pagès, 1854-1907) and Dr. Bataille (pseudonym of Charles Hacks [b. 1851]). Diana Vaughan made her first appearance in Dr. Bataille's *Diable au XIXe siècle*, published in instalments between 1892 and 1894. This woman, who appears to be nothing more than a fictional character in

girl has disappeared, and in both cases there seems to be a connection with Helen and with some mysterious entity appearing in the woods. Clarke's reaction to these stories is particularly interesting for us here:

> "My God . . . it is too incredible, too monstrous; such things can never be in this quiet world, where men and women live and die, and struggle, and conquer, or maybe fail, and fall down under sorrow, and grieve and suffer strange fortunes for many a year; but not this . . . , not such things as this. There must be some explanation, some way out of the terror. Why, man, if such a case were possible, our earth would be a nightmare." (CF 1.230)

Clarke is obviously trying to stick to an idealised vision of man's condition on earth. But the reader, who knows better, has already understood that things are not so, and that the "nightmare" threatening "this quiet world" is absolutely real. In the following chapters, we learn more about Helen Vaughan. She is an evil creature, beautiful but dangerous, who ruins the life of all the men who have the misfortune of meeting her. Slowly we begin to understand that there must be some connection between her and the events that have taken place at the beginning of the story. There must be a relationship between her and Mary, but what is it? Helen's victims all end up committing suicide due to some unspeakable horror that seizes them in her presence. An old friend of one of them, named Villiers, follows her traces and is able to discover the part that she plays in the mysterious deaths that occur wherever

---

Bataille's and Taxil's feuilletons, had allegedly been involved in all sorts of diabolic practices with her masonic fellows before converting to Catholicism and denouncing the evil of Freemasonry. See Introvigne 158-226. Interestingly, Machen's friend A. E. Waite took the matter seriously enough to write two books about it, exposing the whole fraud. The first was *Devil-Worship in France*, first published in 1896, and the second, which has remained unpublished until 2003, was *Diana Vaughan and the Question of Modern Palladism*, written the following year (now included in the new edition of Waite, *Devil-Worship in France*). In an essay on Machen, D. Cammarota remarked that in his novel Machen had deliberately taken the name Vaughan from Taxil's books (197). On the basis of the dates of the respective works, this looks possible. This would add an extra layer to the political dimension of Machen's novel, to which I will return at the end of this essay. However this may be, for Machen the name of the character in his story seems also to be linked to Thomas Vaughan, the seventeenth-century Welsh alchemist, whose work Machen had read with interest. But, here again, it is also significant that in Bataille's and Taxil's works a connection was also made between Diana Vaughan and Thomas Vaughan, the former being described as a descendant of the latter. See Introvigne 199.

she goes. He gets in contact with Clarke, who gives him some hints but refuses to unveil all that he knows about the affair. Even without knowing Helen's exact origins, Villiers begins to suspect the truth and explains his conclusions to a friend:

> [I]t is an old story, an old mystery played in our day, and in dim London streets instead of amidst the vineyards and the olive gardens. We know what happened to those who chanced to meet the Great God Pan, and those who are wise know that all symbols are symbols of something, not of nothing. It was, indeed, an exquisite symbol beneath which men long ago veiled their knowledge of the most awful, most secret forces which lie at the heart of all things; forces before which the souls of men must wither and die and blacken, as their bodies blacken under the electric current. Such forces cannot be named, cannot be spoken, cannot be imagined except under a veil and a symbol." (CF 1.260)

The hidden forces of nature referred to by Villiers are clearly akin to the forces of magic, of magnetism, of preterhuman entities one finds abundantly in the esoteric literature. In this literature they may have had negative connotations as well (demons would be an obvious example), but the conviction of the esotericist was that, negative as they might be, he would have (or could potentially acquire) the power to control them. In Machen's story the situation seems to be different. These forces are so uncontrollable, so dangerous, that their use by human beings for practical purposes does not seem to be an option. All one can do is try to keep away from them.

Finally Villiers is able to put an end to Helen's evil doings. He forces her to commit suicide, and thus the order of "this quiet world" is restored. The novel concludes with the text of a letter from Dr. Raymond to Clarke, written after having been informed of Helen's death. He finally reveals that she was actually Mary's daughter, and that her father could not be anyone else than Pan himself, the god summoned at the beginning of the story through the surgical operation upon Mary's brain. Thus it becomes obvious that Mary's vision of Pan after the operation had become so real that it had led to actual sexual intercourse between the two. Helen was therefore only half human.

In his letter Raymond offers his final comments on the tragic events for which he is ultimately responsible:

> I broke open the door of the house of life, without knowing or caring what might pass forth or enter in. . . . What I said Mary would see, she saw, but I forgot that no human eyes could look on such a vision with impunity. And I forgot, as I have just said, that when the house of life is thus thrown open,

there may enter in that for which we have no name, and human flesh may become the veil of a horror one dare not express. I played with energies which I did not understand and you have seen the ending of it. (CF 1.267-68)

Negative Epistemology in Literature and in Esotericism

The basic idea that emerges from Machen's novel is that human beings do not naturally have the capacity of perceiving or interacting with the reality that hides behind the one commonly accessible in everyday life. An access to this reality requires an artificial modification of the brain. But once this modification has taken place, it is discovered that perhaps there was a good reason for the incapacity. The reality that can be accessed after the brain has been modified is far from benevolent; on the contrary, it is a wholly evil reality that produces horror and, ultimately, death and destruction.

The question remains open as to whether the nature of this reality is evil in itself, or only if judged by our standards. Some passages I have quoted may lead one to think that, in the economy of the novel, this deeper reality is composed of extremely powerful forces that become deadly merely because of the sheer amount of energy they possess, which is unbearable for human beings when they come in contact with them. But in other parts of the novel, Machen—paying his tribute to the decadent literary fashion of the day—insists on the moral dimension of this otherworldly agency and on the unspeakable abominations which it produces in our material world.

Whatever may be the case, we are clearly faced here with a model that seems to be the reverse of the positive epistemology referred to at the beginning of this article as predominant in Western esotericism. If in that context we find a positive confidence both in the human capacity of knowing the other reality and in the desirability of such knowledge, here we have neither of the two. Human beings are not able, under normal conditions, to know the other reality; and even if they were, they should better avoid it.

It might seem at first sight that this model of negative epistemology is not necessarily new. For instance, in the fifth century, the Christian philosopher John Cassian could remark that "the air between heaven and earth is so crammed with spirits, never quiet or finding rest, that it is fortunate for men that they are not permitted to see them" (quoted in Hillgarth 58). Here we find both elements I have identified: human beings' incapacity of perceiving phenomena or entities belonging to another level of reality, and the desirability of that situation.

A systematic exploration focusing on the concept of negative epistemology as defined here has, to my knowledge, never been attempted but might produce interesting results and yield many more such examples. But there is an important difference between the religious negative epistemology of Cassian and Machen's literary one. In Machen, the horrific vision of Pan seems to represent the whole of the reality of the other dimension. The presence of a benign God presiding over it, whether knowable or unknowable, does not seem to be included. In the case of a traditional Christian view such as Cassian's, the vision of the "spirits" might be just as horrific, but would nevertheless be potentially and powerfully balanced out by the beatific vision of God. It is the absence of God that makes the pendulum swing towards a fully negative epistemology in Machen's case.

Another interesting example, chronologically and culturally much closer to Machen, is provided by Edward Bulwer-Lytton (1803-1873): Machen himself was one of his admirers (Valentine 31). Bulwer-Lytton exerted an extraordinary influence upon English occultism through his esoteric novels (Pasi, "La Notion" 156-74). *Zanoni*, first published in 1842, was by far his most successful and influential occult novel. It tells a story of love and initiation, and the difficulty for human beings to achieve both at the same time. One of the main characters, Glyndon, is a young man who aspires to initiation into the Rosicrucian mysteries after having met the mysterious Zanoni, an adept belonging to an ancient esoteric fraternity. In the course of the novel Glyndon's attempt at achieving initiation is frustrated by insufficient preparation and determination. During their first encounter, Zanoni, perceiving the young man's curiosity for other dimensions, gives him a warning: "There may be things around us that would be dangerous and hostile to men, if Providence had not placed a wall between them and us, merely by different modifications of matter" (70). It should be noted that, strictly speaking, here it is no longer a mere matter of epistemology, but rather of ontology. The wall that exists between ourselves and the creatures of another reality does not concern only our knowledge of them, but even our concrete interaction. The principle, however, seems to be the same: the fact that humanity does not have access to all reality is not a curse but a gift. A cloud of unknowing protects us from unspecified but very real dangers. Of course Zanoni's warning does not dishearten Glyndon, whose curiosity is aroused even more strongly. He asks Zanoni: "And think you that wall never can be removed? . . . Are the traditions of sorcerer and wizard, universal and immemorial as they are, merely fables?" (70). Zanoni's reply is enigmatic, as befits a mysterious adept: "Perhaps yes,— perhaps no . . . But who, in an age in which the reason has chosen its proper bounds, would be mad enough to break the partition that divides him from the boa and the lion,—to repine at and rebel against the law which confines the shark to the great deep? Enough of these idle speculations" (70).

Well, who would be mad enough? Zanoni is of course talking tongue-in-cheek here, surely with the intention of testing his young interlocutor: a candidate for Rosicrucian initiation not only *would* but *should* be mad enough to "break the partition." And here lies the difference between this model of negative epistemology and Machen's. True, the universe is full of hostile creatures ready to harm poor, ignorant human beings. But while initiation opens the gates to them, it should also teach the way to deal with them safely, even to master them. In the end, Glyndon's initiation fails, and the demons he has not been able to master begin persecuting him; but Zanoni is the obvious counter-example that a successful initiation is possible, and that the other dimensions of reality are hostile only insofar as one does not know how to deal with them. This is precisely what is missing in Machen's story, and in the model of radical negative epistemology introduced by him. There is no successful initiation in "The Great God Pan" to provide a counter-balance against the failure of the experiment at the beginning of the story.

It is only after Machen that we find a similar model of negative epistemology applied to literature again. The most obvious example is H. P. Lovecraft, who, as is well known, was considerably influenced by Machen's work (Joshi 298-300). There is no better specimen of the presence in his writings of negative epistemology than the *incipit* of one of his most famous stories, "The Call of Cthulhu":

> The most merciful thing in the world, I think, is the inability of the human mind to correlate all its contents. We live on a placid island of ignorance in the midst of black seas of infinity, and it was not meant that we should voyage far. The sciences, each straining in its own direction, have hitherto harmed us little; but some day the piecing together of dissociated knowledge will open up such terrifying vistas of reality, and of our frightful position therein, that we shall either go mad from the revelation or flee from the light into the peace and safety of a new dark age. (61)

Here again, the human mind is unable to gain knowledge about important aspects of reality. Science may one day find a way to open our consciousness to them, but this will only lead to "terrifying vistas" and to an awareness of our "frightful position." Obviously, in the economy of Lovecraft's imaginative world, Cthulhu and his fellow monstrous gods incarnate the mysterious forces of the universe that are represented by Pan in Machen's novel. It is also interesting to note that, in the paragraph following the one just quoted, Lovecraft refers explicitly to modern esoteric ideas in connection with this vision of reality:

> Theosophists have guessed at the awesome grandeur of the cosmic cycle wherein our world and human race form transient incidents. They have hinted at strange survivals in terms which would freeze the blood if not masked by a bland optimism. But it is not from them that there came the single glimpse of forbidden eons which chills me when I think of it and maddens me when I dream of it. (61-62)

Lovecraft seems to acknowledge that the theosophical movement created by Madame Blavatsky has been able to approach the awful truth, even if it has not gone very far either.

The negative epistemology we have encountered so far in Machen's and Lovecraft's (and, partially, Bulwer-Lytton's) works could arguably be explained as a logical literary device in the context of horror or supernatural fiction. If the purpose of this literature is to frighten the reader, it should only be normal that its authors avoid optimistic, confident views of other dimensions of reality. This may be true, but even so, we are still dealing with a relatively recent development in the history of this literary genre, for which I cannot find many examples before Machen. On the other hand, it might be interesting to have a look at authors who were presenting themselves not as fiction writers, but as esotericists, in order to see if it is possible to find traces of negative epistemology in them.

The most interesting example I have found in modern esoteric literature is provided by G. I. Gurdjieff (1866?-1949) and his notion of "Kundabuffer."[11] The term was probably coined by Gurdjieff himself, from the words "Kundalini" and "buffer," and refers to an organ that was placed in the human body, at the base of the spine, by a celestial entity when the human race was created. The purpose of this organ was to prevent human beings from knowing their real condition in the economy of the universe.

Gurdjieff believes that the moon is slowly evolving to become a planet in its own right. In order to achieve that goal, she needs an enormous amount of the energy derived from living beings, especially those residing on earth. From the point of view of cosmic evolution, therefore, human beings have no other

---

11. The notion of Kundabuffer has not attracted much attention from scholars working on Gurdjieff, but S. Wellbeloved devotes a short entry to it (113-14).

purpose than that of serving as "food for the moon." All their struggles, all their hopes, all their toils have no real meaning whatsoever, for on a cosmic scale these human beings are to the moon what cattle is for them. This is how Gurdjieff explains the situation:

> The moon is man's big enemy. We serve the moon. Kundabuffer is the moon's representative on earth. We are like the moon's sheep, which it cleans, feeds and shears, and keeps for its own purposes. But when it is hungry it kills a lot of them. All organic life works for the moon. Passive man serves involution; and active man, evolution. (Gurdjieff, *Views from the Real World* 198)

If people were aware of their situation, they would certainly be seized by despair, and probably even commit suicide (Wellbeloved 114). At a certain moment, still in a remote past, the cosmic hierarchy decided to remove the Kundabuffer; but its effects still continue to be felt by human beings, so that they still cannot see clearly what their real situation is and are far from suspecting their role in feeding the moon (Gurdjieff, *Beelzebub* 89-90). Yet their individual awakening from their condition of sleep and ignorance would set them free from their role of moon-food. There is therefore an inner tension between the evolutionary needs of the individual and the evolutionary needs of the universe. However, the two divergent drifts may coexist because it is not expected that the whole of humanity will be able to wake up to reality. Only a minority of strong-willed individuals will achieve that result, while the rest will continue feeding the Moon unwillingly and unconsciously (Ouspensky 93-94).

Here we can see the elements of negative epistemology playing a certain role in Gurdjieff's ideas. Human beings seem to be constitutionally unfit to perceive reality as it really is, and even if this were different, what they would discover would certainly be less than pleasant. Of course this negative epistemology is mitigated by a corresponding positive one, which concerns those individuals who, through Gurdjieff's teachings (the "Work"), are able to overcome the limitations imposed on the rest of mankind, and free themselves from their cosmic predicament.

Concluding Remarks

One could argue that no esoteric doctrine or system of thought could exist on the basis of a negative epistemology alone. Without the *hope* of somehow achieving the goal of spiritual emancipation from a previous condition of inferiority, an esoteric system would hardly be viable. Authors of horror or supernatural stories labour under no such disadvantages, because it is not hope or esoteric teachings that are expected from them, but entertainment. Of course this does not exclude that some of them may also wish to convey esoteric teachings in their writings, or that some of their readers may discover such teachings even when they were not intended. But an absolute negative epistemology, while it can easily stand on its own feet in a horror story, would have difficulties in being convincing within a system of esoteric teachings.

On the other hand, and more importantly, it would be hard to deny that forms of negative epistemology, which to my knowledge are difficult to find in modern Western esotericism before the beginning of the twentieth century, have been integrated into esoteric systems of thought by authors such as Gurdjieff. We could ask ourselves why, and wonder about the possible cultural changes that have prompted such a development. I do not propose to give an answer to these questions here. I would just like to focus again on the appearance of this model in supernatural fiction at the end of the nineteenth century.

The 1890s are considered a special period in the history of England from an artistic and literary point of view (see James Machin in this volume). During the last decade of the Victorian age, the collapse of certainties that had characterised the heyday of scientific naturalism and positivism was acutely felt. It is no coincidence that the artistic and literary fashion of the day took the name of "decadence." More and more people felt that civilisation, or at least Western civilisation, had passed its zenith and was now in decline. One of the most influential books of the decade was Max Nordau's *Degeneration*, which epitomised this feeling. This cultural pessimism was only reinforced by later events such as the First World War. The useless bloodshed and the massacre of millions of human beings, made possible by the latest developments of technology, dealt a heavy blow to the naive faith in science and progress that had been so dominant in the second half of the nineteenth century. The intuitive conviction that Western civilisation represented the best that the history of humanity had produced came to be challenged, along with its colonialist domination of the rest of the world. Between 1918 and 1922 Oswald Spengler published his influential *Decline of the West*, in which he presented Western civilisation as doomed to decline and fall, and his dominant status in the world destined to be taken away from her by some other younger and more ruthless civilisation still in the process of taking shape.

This new cultural climate is important for understanding the birth and the early development of new esoteric currents such as Perennialism (Hanegraaff 1132-35). But it is also important, in my view, for understanding the emergence of forms of negative epistemology among certain esoteric authors and movements. I have tried to show how this attitude made its first appearance in the fiction of Arthur Machen, who was close to esotericism both biographically and by being read widely and with interest by other esoteric authors (for example, Aleister Crowley recommended Machen's books to his students).

As we have seen, this theme later became a conspicuous source of inspiration for another important author of supernatural fiction, H. P. Lovecraft. It has perhaps not been sufficiently emphasised how important it is to have a look at both authors' political attitudes in order to understand the presence of this theme. Both Machen and Lovecraft held strongly conservative ideas (on Machen, see Sweetser 52f.; on Lovecraft, see Joshi 177-79 and passim). They were nostalgic of a mythical, idealised past, in comparison to which their own time represented an obvious involution. Of course, the object of their nostalgia was significantly different: Machen dreamed about the Middle Ages and their unchallenged Catholicism, Lovecraft about the eighteenth century and its Enlightenment. But both believed in the reality of a decline of Western culture. In this respect, it is significant that Machen used Pan to represent the evil of the "other side," because for generations of artists and writers, this god had come to represent wild, unrestrained nature, especially in its sexual aspects: the breaking free of instincts associated with progressive views of social emancipation.

Many years after writing "The Great God Pan," during the Spanish civil war in the 1930s, Machen sided resolutely with the Francoist insurgents, and against the legitimate republican government (Sweetser 53). For him this was an obvious consequence of the defence of traditional religion and values against the attacks of secularism and modernity. The horror that exhales from his stories seems to be a direct effect of the fears that modernity provoked in their author. The monstrous, invisible, all-pervading evil that is constantly threatening the characters in his novels and tales is the same evil that threatens to subvert the traditional values of society and religion. This evil is aptly symbolised by Pan, the god of subversion and one of the ideal ancestors of the Christian arch-enemy. The fear of subversion, of modernity, of change, thus becomes, quite literally, a panic fear. In this sense, the relationship between occultism and modernity is perhaps more complex than has been described by Alex Owen in her important book *The Place of Enchantment*—unless we consider the fear of modernity, and the anti-modern attitudes that may stem from it, as being themselves an essential, albeit paradoxical, phenomenon of modernity. The belief in the decadence of the West, and the consequent distrust in the foundational beliefs of Victorian culture, such as the relentless march of scientific progress, should be seen in connection with the rise of what I have called negative epistemology.

Works Cited

Amadou, Robert. *Illuminisme et contre-illuminisme au XVIIIe siècle.* Paris: Cariscript, 1989.

Bataille, Dr. [pseud.]. *Le Diable au XIXe siècle.* Paris: Delhomme & Briguet, 1892-94. 2 vols.

Bergé, Christine. "Illuminism." In *Dictionary of Gnosis and Western Esotericism*, ed. Wouter J. Hanegraaff et al. Leiden: Brill, 2005. 2.600-606.

Blackwood, Algernon. "The Touch of Pan." 1917. In Blackwood's *Tales of the Uncanny and Supernatural.* London: Spring Books, 1963. 289-310.

Boardman, John. *The Great God Pan: The Survival of an Image.* London: Thames & Hudson, 1998.

Bulwer-Lytton, Edward. *Zanoni.* 1842. Boston: Little, Brown, 1932.

Cammarota, Domenico. "Arthur Machen, Filius Aquarti [sic]." In Machen's *Le creature della terra.* Roma: Fanucci 1987. 189-236.

Cavaliero, Glen. *The Supernatural and English Fiction.* Oxford: Oxford University Press, 1995.

Cevasco, George A., ed. *The 1890s: An Encyclopedia of British Literature, Art, and Culture.* New York: Garland, 1993.

Crowley, Aleister. "Hymn to Pan." 1929-30. In Crowley's *Magick: Liber ABA: Book Four, Parts I-IV.* Boston: Weiser Books, 1997. 121-22.

Edelstein, Dan, ed. *The Super-Enlightenment: Daring to Know Too Much.* Oxford: Voltaire Foundation, 2010.

Farr, Florence. *The Dancing Faun.* London: Elkin Mathews/John Lane, 1894.

Ferrone, Vincenzo. *I profeti dell'Illuminismo: Le metamorfosi della ragione nel tardo settecento italiano.* Rome: Editori Laterza, 1989.

Fortune, Dion. "A Daughter of Pan." 1926. In Fortune's *The Secrets of Doctor Taverner.* Wellingborough, UK: Aquarian Press, 1989. 107-28.

———. *The Goat Foot God.* 1936. Boston: Samuel Weiser, 1994.

Gilbert, Robert A. *The Golden Dawn Scrapbook: The Rise and Fall of a Magical Order*. Boston: Samuel Weiser, 1997.

Gurdjieff, George Ivanovitch. *Beelzebub's Tales to His Grandson: An Objectively Impartial Criticism of the Life of Man*. New York: Penguin Compass, 1999.

———. *Views from the Real World: Early Talks in Moscow, Essentuki, Tiflis, Berlin, London, Paris, New York and Chicago as Recollected by His Pupils*. New York: Penguin Compass, 1984.

Hallett, Jennifer. "Wandering Dreams and Social Marches: Varieties of Paganism in Late Victorian and Edwardian England." *The Pomegranate: The International Journal of Pagan Studies* 8, No. 2 (2006): 161-83.

Hanegraaff, Wouter J. "Tradition." In *Dictionary of Gnosis and Western Esotericism*, ed. W. J. Hanegraaff et al. Leiden: Brill, 2005. 2.1125-35.

Hillgarth, J. N., ed. *Christianity and Paganism, 350-750: The Conversion of Western Europe*. Philadelphia: University of Pennsylvania Press, 1986.

Howe, Ellic. *The Magicians of the Golden Dawn: A Documentary History of a Magical Order 1887-1923*. Wellingborough, UK: Aquarian Press, 1985.

Hutton, Ronald. *The Triumph of the Moon: A History of Modern Pagan Witchcraft*. Oxford: Oxford University Press, 1999.

Introvigne, Massimo. *Satanism: A Social History*. Leiden: Brill, 2016.

Jacques-Chaquin, Nicole. "Illuminisme (Occident Moderne)." In *Dictionnaire critique de l'ésotérisme*, ed. Jean Servier. Paris: Presses Universitaires de France, 1998. 638-40.

Joshi, S. T. *H. P. Lovecraft: A Life*. West Warwick, RI: Necronomicon Press, 1996.

Kapstein, Matthew T., ed. *The Presence of Light: Divine Radiance and Religious Experience*. Chicago: University of Chicago Press, 2004.

Kilcher, Andreas. "Seven Epistemological Theses on Esotericism: Upon the Occasion of the 10th Anniversary of the Amsterdam Chair." In *Hermes in the Academy: Ten Years' Study of Western Esotericism at the University of Amsterdam*, ed. Wouter J. Hanegraaff and Joyce Pijnenburg. Amsterdam: Amsterdam University Press, 2009. 143-48.

Lovecraft, H. P. "The Call of Cthulhu." 1928. In Lovecraft's *The H. P. Lovecraft Omnibus 3: The Haunter of the Dark and Other Tales*. London: HarperCollins, 2000. 61-98.

Mannucci, Erica Joy. *Gli altri lumi: Esoterismo e politica nel Settecento francese*. Palermo: Sellerio Editore, 1988.

———. *Dai cieli la ragione: Gli Illuminati dal Seicento alla Restaurazione*. Rome: L'Officina Tipografica, 1992.

Merivale, Patricia. *Pan the Goat-God: His Myth in Modern Times*. Cambridge, MA: Harvard University Press, 1969.

Neuburg, Victor. *The Triumph of Pan*. London: Equinox, 1910.

Nietzsche, Friedrich. *The Gay Science*. Tr. Walter Kaufmann. New York: Vintage Books, 1974.

Nordau, Max. *Degeneration*. London: Heinemann, 1895.

Ogilvie Crombie, R. "Conversations with Pan." In Alex Walker, *The Kingdom Within: A Guide to the Spiritual Work of the Findhorn Community*. Findhorn, Scotland: Findhorn Press, 1994.

Ouspensky, Piötr Demianovitch. *Fragments d'un enseignement inconnu*. Paris: Stock, 1984.

Owen, Alex. *The Place of Enchantment: British Occultism and the Culture of the Modern*. Chicago: University of Chicago Press, 2004.

Pasi, Marco. "Golden Dawn." In *Dictionnaire critique de l'ésotérisme*, ed. Jean Servier. Paris: Presses Universitaires de France, 1998. 554-56.

———. "La Notion de magie dans le courant occultiste en Angleterre (1875-1947)." Ph.D. diss.: Ecole Pratique des Hautes Etudes (Paris), 2004.

Plutarch. *Moralia*. Tr. Philip H. De Lacy and Benedict Einarson. Volume 7. Cambridge, MA: Harvard University Press (Loeb Classical Library), 1959.

Regardie, Israel, ed. *The Golden Dawn: A Complete Course in Practical Ceremonial Magic*. St. Paul, MN: Llewellyn, 1998.

Richardson, Alan, ed. *Dancers to the Gods: The Magical Records of Charles Seymour and Christine Hartley*. Wellingborough, UK: Aquarian Press, 1985.

Spengler, Oswald. *Der Untergang des Abendlandes: Umrisse einer Morphologie der Weltgeschichte*. Munich: C. H. Beck'sche Verlagsbuchhandlung, 1918-22. 2 vols.

Stuckrad, Kocku von. "Western Esotericism: Towards an Integrative Model of Interpretation." *Religion* 35 (2005): 78-97.

———. *Western Esotericism: A Brief History of Secret Knowledge*. London: Equinox, 2005.

Sweetser, Wesley D. *Arthur Machen*. New York: Twayne, 1964.

Valentine, Mark. *Arthur Machen*. Bridgend, Wales: Seren, 1995.

Viatte, Auguste. *Les Sources occultes du Romantisme: Illuminisme et Théosophie (1770–1820)*. Paris: Librairie Ancienne Honoré Champion, 1928. 2 vols.

Waite, A. E. *Devil-Worship in France; or, The Question of Lucifer*. London: George Redway 1896. Republished, together with a previously unpublished essay, as *Devil-Worship in France with Diana Vaughan and the Question of Modern Palladism*. Boston: Weiser Books, 2003.

Weighell, Ron. "Sorcery and Sanctity: The Spagyric Quest of Arthur Machen." In *Arthur Machen: Artist and Mystic*, ed. Mark Valentine and Roger Dobson. Oxford: Caermaen Books, 1986. 13-17.

Wellbeloved, Sophia. *Gurdjieff: The Key Concepts*. London: Routledge, 2003.

A Fit Symbol for His Meaning: Arthur Machen and the Inexpressible

Karen Joan Kohoutek

[I]t is one thing to dream dreams, and another to interpret them.—Arthur Machen (*FOT* 125-26)

In his work, Arthur Machen was often sensitive to how difficult—perhaps impossible—it can be for artists to truly express what they want to say. This perspective turns up in his commentaries on such diverse writers as Casanova and Dickens, and again when he discusses his own work and career.

Of the failure of words in describing his own life, he says, "I can set down the facts . . . but I am quite conscious that I am not, in the real sense of the word, telling the truth; that is, I am not giving any sense of the very extraordinary atmosphere in which I lived" (*TNF* 150). Instead, he is "doing my best to tell a true tale, and I find that I can make nothing of it."

He made similar comments earlier in the book about Casanova, whose memoirs he translated into English: that Casanova's attempts to speak frankly and truthfully, about love (and, it is implied, sex) in particular, were doomed to failure by his factual approach. Machen says, "The more 'frank,' the more 'outspoken' his page the more the secret escapes from it; the more openly he reveals, the more deeply he conceals the mysteries" (*TNF* 80).

In *Hieroglyphics*, his work of literary philosophy, he wrote: "It is always quite pathetic to me to note how Dickens *felt* the strangeness, the mystery, the haunting that are like a mist about the old Inns of Court, and how utterly unable he was to express his emotions—to find a fit symbol for his meaning" (*H* 57). It is likely that he finds this so poignant because it reflects his sense of his own insufficiency, attempting to express certain things in his art, but being unable to meaningfully communicate them.

Critics often speculate on what compelled an artist to go in a certain direction, to tell a particular story in the way he or she did. In the case of Arthur Machen, he wrote about the inspirations for some of his most famous tales and what spurred him to write at all. As he describes it, his fiction was largely rooted in attempts to convey feelings, rather than ideas, and in particular, a sense of the sublime—although, in using fiction as the vehicle, he found his efforts were insufficient.

While Machen did not use the word "sublime" to describe his artistic philosophy, his stated beliefs clearly align him with thinkers who did, including Immanuel Kant, author of *Critique of Judgment* and other works, and Edmund Burke, whose influential *Philosophical Enquiry into the Origin of Our Ideas of the Sublime and Beautiful* contains many ideas that are similar to Machen's. He would also almost certainly have been sympathetic to Keats's "Negative Capability," the "quality" which most leads to "Achievement," found where one is "capable of being in uncertainties, mysteries, doubts, without any irritable reaching after fact and reason" (261).

Two of Machen's most famous stories, "The Great God Pan" and "The Inmost Light," were published together in 1894, and for each story he later wrote a fairly detailed description of its inspiration. There are similarities in their overall plots, and also their details, attributable to having been written in fairly close temporal proximity to each other. Both even have characters making discoveries while walking down Rupert Street. There are also common themes. In each story, there is a struggle between the scientific imagination and what Machen calls a spiritual point of view, which could easily be seen as a poetic one, concerned with the intangibles of life.

In both "The Great God Pan" and "The Inmost Light," a man, spurred on by a scientific obsession, performs an experiment on a woman. Each of those women is in a relationship of trust with the scientist: in "Pan", she was raised by him since childhood, and she trusts him "entirely" (CF 1.223). In "Light," it is the scientist's wife who undergoes the experiment.

The woman in "Pan," in being able to see some kind of ultimate reality, loses her mind and later gives birth to a daughter who is amoral and apparently soulless. This scientific parthenogenesis can easily be taken as a parody of the Virgin Birth; the victim's name is even Mary. In "The Inmost Light," the object of the experiment is to extract the woman's soul, so her soul is "lost" more directly than in "The Great God Pan."

Not only do the stories share common plot elements, Machen's descriptions of their writing show they are also thematically linked. In his introduction to the 1916 edition of *The Great God Pan*, Machen attributes the story's genesis to the far-off days of his childhood. What he says about symbolism

A Fit Symbol for His Meaning: Arthur Machen and the Inexpressible   163

could work as an elaboration of his comments on Dickens, describing his own position as an artist striving to articulate an emotional response which can, literally, not be put into words.

"It all came from a lonely house standing on the slope of a hill, under a great wood, above a river in the country where I was born" (CF 1.524)–almost a house from a fairy tale. This house, embedded in the natural landscape of his childhood, "became an object of mysterious attraction to me. It became one of the many symbols of the world of wonder that were offered to me, it became . . . a great word in the secret language by which the mysteries were communicated" (CF 1.525). Something which physically exists in the material world, in other words, can operate as a symbol, bearing personal meaning in the same way that a word does within a language. While this is not an uncommon experience, it is not always considered as a factor in artistic production.

Machen elaborates that "the emotions aroused by these external things reverberating in the heart, are indeed the story; or all that signifies in the story. But, our craft being that of letters, we must express what we feel through the medium of words." At that point, once words are being written, "we are forced to devise incidents and circumstances and plots." In so doing, "we translate a hill into a tale, conceive lovers to explain a brook, turn the perfect into the imperfect" (CF 1.525). Unfortunately, despite his efforts, he found "that incident would never convey the meaning intended" (CF 1.528). As a character in the story would put it, "it is hard to be literal" (CF 1.219).

For Machen, this desire to communicate the incommunicable was the essence of literature, and the arts in general. "Artists are rare simply because it is their almost impossible task to translate the emotion of the subconsciousness into the speech of consciousness" (H 96). He commented multiple times on how music, of all the arts, and by virtue of its very abstraction, is truly able to communicate emotional states; for example, "Only by music, if at all, can such things be expressed, since they are ineffable; not to be uttered in any literal or logical speech of men" (FOT 154-55).

The situation, he acknowledged, was different for a writer. As he described it, in an encounter with nature, "this group of pines, this lonely shore . . . has made the soul thrill with an emotion intense but vague in the sense in which music is vague; and the man of letters does his best to realise—rather, perhaps, to actualise—this emotion by inventing a tale about the pines or the sands" (FOT 24).

In the same memoir, he similarly describes an incident that sparked the writing of "The Inmost Light." While walking through a green field, he suddenly came across a row of newly-built suburban homes, "a sudden and violent irruption of red brick" (*FOT* 122). He likens this inspiration directly to the origin of his Pan story, which had been based on a similar experience that "remained in my heart for years." He also adds, almost in passing, that the two stories are companion pieces, the suburban story "originally bound up with" the rural one (*FOT* 123).

In the case of "The Great God Pan," he explains that, after having being "confronted suddenly and for the first time with the awe and solemnity and mystery of the valley of the Usk," and the old house there, he eventually "transliterated it, clumsily enough" into fiction (*FOT* 123). Writing the story, he says, was "an endeavour to pass on the vague, indefinable sense of awe and mystery and terror that I had received," and to "recreate those vague impressions of wonder and awe and mystery that I myself had received from the form and shape of the land of my boyhood and youth" (*FOT* 20).

To Machen, this attempt exposed the "comparative futility [. . .] of the plot, however ingenious, which did not exist to express emotions of one kind or another" (*FOT* 20). In saying that a plot simply "did not exist" that would do what he wanted it to do, he is expanding his personal experience into a belief in the complete insufficiency of words, especially as filtered through narrative, to truly express the very feelings that inspire the use of words and narrative.

In the end, he says of "Pan" that "my real failure" was that "I translated awe, at worst awfulness, into evil" (*FOT* 123). In other words, the narrative he created, with its "incidents and circumstances and plots," could not function as "a fit symbol for his meaning." He followed the same process, "more legitimately" (probably more directly, and consciously) with "the horrid apparition of the crude new houses in the midst of green pastures" (*FOT* 123), which became the cornerstone for "The Inmost Light."

Machen, in a reminiscent mood, may be mythologizing himself to some extent in these memoirs. But there was no real motive for him to lie, as such, about the origins of the tales, and his statements about their compositions are consistent with the general ideas about life and literature found throughout his lifetime of essay-writing.

It is interesting that he connects the two impressions so overtly, considering that the sense of the sublime, in a fairly straightforward sense, is so present in his memory of the valley of Usk, and the suburban homes that "once had frightened me" seem the opposite, representing an intrusion of the ordinary and ugly into a place where he had gone to find the "sweet hillside" and "fair open country" of nature. But the two have a commonality: "the whole matter of imaginative literature depends upon this faculty of seeing the universe, from the aeonian pebble of the wayside to the raw suburban street as something new, unheard of, marvellous, finally, miraculous" (FOT 124).

With "The Great God Pan," the story's origin was in the desire to describe something intangible. In "The Inmost Light," there is an element of dislike—the shock of an aesthetically unpleasing encroachment upon a natural environment. Despite one experience being predominately positive and the other mainly negative, they are in his descriptions more similar than not, each representing to him the presence of mystery underlying everyday life.

In "The Great God Pan," Machen combines his twin obsessions: both the lush beauty of the countryside, associated with the traditional idea of "nature," and the ever-changing mysteries of London, with its landscape shaped by the works of human hands, and affected by human psychology. In his "futile" attempts to wrestle his feelings into words and tales, these are two of the subjects which most inspired those intense emotions, and in "Pan" he adds an element of direct philosophical speculation.

Dr. Raymond, the scientist in "The Great God Pan," quotes Oswald Crollius: "'in every grain of wheat there lies hidden the soul of a star'" (CF 1.220), which echoes a similar aphorism from William Blake's "Auguries of Innocence": "To see a World in a Grain of Sand / And a Heaven in a Wild Flower" (431). To some extent, this saying reflects attitudes that Machen espoused in his real life, but the conclusions he drew were completely different. With Dr. Raymond, he caricatured the kind of scientific temperament that is concerned with lofty abstractions, but is uninterested in the effects of his work on an apparently unimportant individual. This idea is expanded upon in "The Inmost Light," when the scientist purposely removes a human soul, an act that is obviously meant to be seen by the reader as reprehensible, regardless of whether it might have a benefit to science or advancing human knowledge.

The cold unconcern for humanity is made explicit when Raymond admits that he "cared not" about the repercussions of his work, which seems to be at the core of Machen's lifelong critique of scientific curiosity; that is, its tendency to ignore both the bigger picture and the human cost.

The counterpart to Dr. Raymond is a side character, Villiers, who is described as being particularly fond of "useless information" (CF 1.258). At one point in the story he gives an impassioned speech, saying that "all symbols are symbols of something, not of nothing" (CF 1.260). He goes on to say that

"Such forces cannot be named, cannot be spoken, cannot be imagined except under a veil and a symbol, a symbol to the most of us appearing a quaint, poetic fancy, to some a foolish tale" (CF 1.260).

Having Machen's extra-textual statements about the inspiration for this story, his perceived failure to express the sensation he was trying to communicate, and his body of commentary on the difficulty of using language to describe reality (and the individual experience thereof)—it is certainly easy to believe that Villiers is something of a stand-in for Machen at this point. The phrase "foolish tale" even has a meta-textual ring, as if he is explaining what "The Great God Pan" is doing as a story: appearing to be "a quaint, poetic fancy" and "a foolish tale," in the act of attempting to describe the forces that are hidden under a veil. Even his language aligns with some of Machen's more mystical statements about his own life, such as his idea that "everything visible was the veil of an invisible secret" (FOT 24-25).

Dr. Raymond also uses the metaphor of the veil. He believes that all the solid things of the world are "but dreams and shadows: the shadows that hide the real world from our eyes" (CF 1.218), and the true reality he expects to find is "beyond them all as beyond a veil" (CF 1.218). Where he differs from Villiers, and almost certainly from Machen, is in believing that what lies beyond can indeed be named and spoken, and directly experienced, with surgical help.

As in "The Great God Pan," the victim of Dr. Black, the scientist in "The Inmost Light," is a woman who has placed her trust in him. He uses his wife's love for him to manipulate her, along with the generally submissive attitude she has toward him as her husband, which would likely have been socially ingrained. Also similarly to "Pan," he operates on the woman's brain, the symbolic site of the intellect, as opposed to the emotions or the intuition, which are traditionally placed in the heart and the "gut."

In this case, though, the experiment is less abstract than the one in "The Great God Pan," in which the lifting of the veil to expose an ultimate reality was discussed in vaguer terms. Here the object is more concrete, which makes the theme of the work more explicit. Dr. Black discovers the means to remove a human soul, leaving a vacuum eventually filled with an evil that is not clearly defined. It is therefore open to interpretation whether the evil is psychological or metaphysical in nature.

By denying the existence of the soul, as it was traditionally believed in, modern scientific thinking can be seen to have symbolically removed the soul. That concept is made literal here, with the physical extraction of a soul—a metaphorically significant act that is viewed within the story as an abomination.

The soul is seen nakedly, as a beautiful jewel, "a jewel such as Dyson had never dreamed of, and within it shone the blue of far skies, and the green of the sea by the shore, and the red of the ruby, and deep violet rays, and in the middle of all it seemed aflame as if a fountain of fire rose up, and fell, and rose again with sparks like stars for drops" (CF 1.324).

The human soul is depicted here as the ultimate version of the star in a grain of wheat, and a world in a grain of sand. Machen creates a visible symbol of something that is, in reality, completely invisible and intangible, depicting human beings as filled with the titular "inmost light"—that is, generated from within itself, not dependent on the outside reality for its energy. And without the soul, life is seen as merely ugly and sordid.

More than a hundred years after this story's publication, it is still an insult to say that something is "soulless," meaning that it has no life, but is flat and dead, or, in the case of human beings, that they are completely lacking in emotional response or moral compass. It does not seem a coincidence, either, that this symbolic tale plays out in a suburb so new and dull that it is called "a place of no character" (CF 1.304), especially considering Machen's direct comments on the story's origin.

Machen wrote about the composition of some of his other works as well, connecting them to his life experience, with its familiar obsessions. Of *The Three Impostors* he says that he was inspired by his many walks, "those curious researches in the byways of London" (TNF 103). At times, he describes "the City" as a site of the mundane and practical, dedicated to "bread winning", and says of London, "How few there are that can pierce the veils of apparent monotony and meanness!" (CF 1.403). Again, he uses the language of a veil that hides the reality from the casual observer, representing a consistently held belief.

As seen in these examples, his perception of the city was tempered by an awareness of its less sublime qualities. He suffered too much hardship in London to view it with naïve romanticism. Nonetheless, he generally found the experience of London to be sublime in its "infinitude." In the essay "The Joy of London," he wrote: "I do not think there are any more awful concepts presented to the human mind than the eternities and infinitudes of time and space. Not for one moment, it seems to me, can one imagine beginning or end to time, or limit to space; and yet time without beginning or end and space without bounds are conceptions equally intolerable to the soul" (*Secret of the Sangraal* 78).

These comments almost directly echo one of Edmund Burke's major beliefs about that sublime, that "the ideas of eternity, and infinity, are among the most affecting we have, and yet perhaps there is nothing we really understand so little, as of infinity and eternity" (57). Machen brings this rather lofty idea down to earth, continuing, "Here are marked streets and alleys and squares and by-ways, which strike the eye as past numbering. They were all here, in undoubted brick and stone and marble and mortar, and yet one feels that no living man has trodden them all . . . Thus does London make for us a concrete image of the eternal things of space and time and thought" (*Secret of the Sangraal* 78-79). He has taken a way of relating to nature, and the world, which was nurtured in an isolated rural environment, full of natural wonders, where human beings seem small—and translated it onto an immense metropolis, filled with, and shaped by, people, finding the commonality in the two environments, and reminding us that the experience of the sublime can happen in the wild countryside, in the crowded city streets, or in the "raw suburbs."

Perhaps it was impossible to describe these experiences in a way that was perfectly satisfactory to him, and there are likewise readers for whom Machen's translations of emotional response into narrative form is equally lacking. Throughout both his fiction and his memoirs, he links two important metaphysical beliefs: that there is a spiritual reality inside all things (up to and including the human soul inside the human being), and that the impetus of art lies largely in the desire to express an ultimately inexpressible reality:

> If one looks a little more closely into the nature of things it will become pretty plain, I think, that all that really matters and really exists is ineffable; that both the world without us—the tree and the brook and the hill—and the world within us do perpetually and necessarily transcend all our powers of utterance, whether to ourselves or to others. Night and day, sunrise and moonrise, and the noble assemblage of the stars, are continually exhibited to us, and we are forced to confess that not for one moment can we proclaim these appearances adequately. (*FOT* 155)

As such, Machen's work was obviously concerned with the sublime, as described in the works of writers such as Edmund Burke.

In his discussion of the sublime, Burke defined it as that which is "productive of the strongest emotion which the mind is capable of feeling" (36), so that when a person responds to an artistic creation with an experience of awe and intense emotional engagement, rather than with appreciation or a sense of having been entertained, they are in the realm of the sublime. When artists use words as the medium, he says that the difference "between a clear expression, and a strong expression" is that "the former regards the understanding; the latter belongs to the passions. The one describes a thing as it is; the other describes it as it is felt" (159-60). Even though "words undoubtedly have no sort of resemblance to the idea for which they stand" (157), Burke still argued that they could have the emotional effect of the arts, like painting, which are more directly representative, and also nature itself, and even "sometimes a much greater than them" (149).

In fact, as Burke described it, the failure of words in general and literature in particular to express what they exist to express can in fact produce an effect of the sublime on its audience. "Hardly any thing can strike the mind with its greatness, which does not make some sort of approach towards infinity; which nothing can do whilst we are able to perceive its bounds; but to see an object distinctly, and to perceive its bounds, is one and the same thing. A clear idea is therefore another name for a little idea" (38).

The very attempt to understand the inexplicable is a hallmark of the sublime—one of the shortest routes to experiencing it—so the subject matter of these tales seems appropriate to Machen's underlying concerns in telling them. They originated out of his desire to express feelings about particular geographic places, ones which filled him with a sensation of the sublime, as described by Burke and others. To express the inexpressible, he created characters who attempt to understand the inexplicable, within narratives about probing the nature of ultimate reality, and the mysteries of the human soul, with horrific results. In so doing, his approach to the sublime may have served to create the very frisson of the uncanny which, while unsatisfying to his own critical eye, has emotionally engaged readers down to our own time.

Works Cited

Blake, William. *The Complete Writings of William Blake*. Ed. Geoffrey Keynes. London: Nonesuch, 1958.

Burke, Edmund. *A Philosophical Enquiry into the Origin of Our Ideas of the Sublime and Beautiful*. 1757. New York: Oxford University Press, 1998.

Keats, John. *Selected Poems and Letters*. Boston: Houghton Mifflin, 1959.

Machen, Arthur. *The Secret of the Sangraal and Other Writings*. Leyburn, UK: Tartarus Press, 2007.

The Revenge of Vulcan

G. J. Cooling

The Hill of Dreams was considered by Machen to be his masterpiece. This view has been shared by critics and devotees since. The book is partially autobiographical, as there are obvious similarities between the life of Arthur Machen and the "hero" of the book, Lucian Taylor. Indeed, some of the problems that Lucian has in becoming a writer are clearly reflections of Machen's own artistic struggles. However, Lucian ends up being overwhelmed by these difficulties and eventually dies in a doomed attempt to write a masterpiece. Much of the book is taken up with descriptions of Lucian's life in rural Wales, and Machen is bitingly satirical about the parochial nature of that life. This is compared with the scenes of debauchery which Lucian meets on going to London.

Machen was extremely interested in the classical gods (the Victorian era as a whole was more interested in the Greek and Roman gods and mythologies than today's generation). He praised the classical education he received at Hereford Grammar School, where he was top of the class in Classics, and he was often reproached for his fondness for "Latin tags." His first major work—"The Great God Pan"—is about the malign influence of the god Pan upon certain elements in London society. The *femme fatale* figure of Helen Vaughan in "The Great God Pan" was later echoed by several ominously alluring women in *The Hill of Dreams*. The later novel is obviously partly a reverie upon the power of Venus. The country girl (Annie) whom Lucian meets in his hometown is one aspect of Venus, and the prostitute he meets in a London street who suggests a walk is another. We are not told whether the woman in the last scene is the same as the one he meets in a London street, but by her description as half-dressed and having splendid bronze hair, Machen manages to convey the possibility (CF 2.155). More importantly, there is the fact that the whole book is about Lucian's love of an ideal woman, and in this sense that type of ideal woman may be seen as Venus. The title and subject of the book with which Lucian achieves moderate success is *The Amber Statuette*, and this also seems to be a reflection of Venus. Also, the orgies which Lucian saw or imagined in London may be a reflection on this same theme.

In classical mythology, Vulcan—the god of fire—was the husband of Venus, the goddess of love. To give them their Greek names, Hephaestus was married to Aphrodite. Vulcan is supposed to have been extremely jealous of Venus and once caught Venus *in flagrante* with Mars, meshing them with a wire net.

There are many references to flame and fire in *The Hill of Dreams*. The streets of London are described as lit by flames coming from the street lights. The prostitute Lucian meets is described as having flame-coloured hair. In the beginning of the book the Roman fort is described as being invested with fire (CF 2.12). In a rose garden every flower is described as being a flame (CF 2.125). As Lucian learns more and more during his stay in London, Machen writes: "He understood now something of the alchemical symbolism; the crucible and the furnace, the 'Green Dragon', and the 'Son Blessed of the Fire' had, he saw, a peculiar meaning" (CF 2.81). Machen describes one awful scene which glowed into Lucian's memory. The scene is of an orgy and lurid naphtha flames (CF 2.121). One of those who serves the Amber Venus is described as having a fire of bronze hair (CF 2.151).

When we consider that Vulcan was also god of the forge and the furnace, this fire imagery may seem to have a new significance. The first line of the book is "There was a glow in the sky as if great furnace doors were opened" (CF 2.9). Later, as Lucian dreams in bed, "He had seen himself, in a dream, within the Roman fort, working some dark horror, and the furnace doors were opened and a blast of flame from heaven was smitten upon him" (CF 2.12). Even just before Lucian meets Annie on the hill the darkness is described as suddenly glowing because a furnace fire has been lit. The last sentence of the book is "The flaring light shone thorough the dead eyes into the dying brain, and there was a glow within, as if great furnace doors were opened" (CF 2.156).

It may be that Machen intended us to understand the fire in Lucian's brain at the end of the book as a representation of the revenge of the god Vulcan upon the human who dared to love his wife the goddess Venus, and the fires earlier in the book can be seen as warnings from this same god. We can probably also conclude that there is some more esoteric meaning still behind this mythic drama, but this I leave for others to ponder.

Perfume of the Trellised Vine

Ron Weighell

> While yet above the western hills
> The Sun was red, they came to me
> And cried "Your fame the city fills
> For cunning song and minstrelsy,
> And at your peril it were well
> To bring us, ere tomorrow falls,
> A song new fashioned out of hell
> To crown our autumn Bacchanals."
> —Richard Middleton, "Ballad of the Bacchanals,"
> from *Poems and Songs* (34)

In her youth the author, surrealist, and poet Ithell Colquhoun borrowed a copy of Machen's *The House of Souls* but was too disturbed by certain parts of *The Three Impostors* to continue reading. She relates that she found the word Ishakshar so "obsessive" that she had to return the book unfinished.

Later in life, when made of sterner stuff, she overcame her "former squeamishness" and bought a second-hand copy of *The House of Souls*. Only after the purchase did she look in the flyleaf and read the following.

Aleister Crowley.

This book is the property of G. H. Fra Perdurabo
Abbot of Dam-Car.

She had obtained Aleister Crowley's own copy of the book, a stroke of fortune that might well reduce many Machen collectors to quiet tears. It also throws into vivid relief the meteoric rise in bibliophilic status enjoyed by both Crowley and Machen in recent years. Literary fortunes may fluctuate, but it is safe to say that the chance of stumbling upon an extensively inscribed associational copy of either author, lying cheap and unrecognised on the shelves of a London bookshop, have gone forever. And extensively inscribed the volume was, with several passages of "The White People" marked, including the dialogue on the nature of good and evil, and the spells taught by the nurse. On the rear endpaper Crowley had analysed the themes of the story along cabalistic lines.

That Crowley had an interest in Machen's works will not come as a surprise to any Machenite who has seen the Newport Library photocopy of *The House of the Hidden Light*, taken from a rare volume once owned and annotated by Crowley. The full extent of the Beast's familiarity with Machen's works, however, and their influence on some of his most heartfelt writings is not generally known.

It is a unique situation. Crowley himself influenced many writers, providing the basis for a variety of villains in the works of M. R. James, H. R. Wakefield, E. F. Benson, Dion Fortune, Somerset Maugham, Warwick Deeping, and Dennis Wheatley, among others. James Branch Cabell went further. Chapter 22 of his famous *Jurgen*, "As to a veil they broke" (151-58), is based upon Crowley's Gnostic Catholic Mass, with a sly line of humour that revealed a better understanding of the secret nature of the rite than many a serious commentator. Crowley was so delighted that he sent Cabell a copy of *The Book of the Law*.

Most of the stylistic influences acknowledged by Crowley were great poets such as Baudelaire, Byron, and Swinburne. Apart from Sir Richard Burton, who as a traveller, and translator of erotica, was the Beast's hero, he acknowledged few prose teachers. Yet in his writings can be found homages to, or paraphrases of, the works of Machen.

In the punningly titled *Magick in Theory and* [i.e.,Therion] *Practice* (1929), a list of recommended reading for students of his order includes Machen's stories, where they are described as being "of great magical interest" (213). There is evidence that Crowley's interest was not confined to the fiction. He had read and approved of *Hieroglyphics*, for in *Liber Aleph: The Book of Wisdom or Folly*, in which he expresses the heart of his doctrine in the form of one-page chapters, we find that chapter 115, "De Cantu" (on song), contains the words: "Thus, as thy cousin Arthur Machen hath rejoiced to make plain in his book called *Hieroglyphics*, the first Quality of Art is its Ecstasy" (115). It should be pointed out that cousin in the present context means kindred magical spirit!

He was still reading and enjoying Machen towards the end of his life. In a letter to Kenneth Grant dated 16 January 1945, Crowley wrote while in the throes of pleurisy: "*Very* many thanks for Secret Glory; best of his I've read. Criticism when I'm strong enough" (quoted in Grant 14). Crowley's own bitter experiences during school days, and his interest in the Grail legends, would have guaranteed a pungent analysis of the book, but his illness continued, and frustratingly he wrote to Grant on the 21st: "You mustn't tempt me to discuss Secret Glory; too much to say. This pleurisy is a joke, but of the 'Punch' level" (quoted in Grant 15). No record of Crowley's criticism of *The Secret Glory* survives.

I believe Crowley had also steeped himself in *The Hill of Dreams*. The evidence can be found in the most unlikely of places. In 1910 he published the *Bagh-I-Muattar; or, Scented Garden of Abdullah the Satirist of Shiraz*, purporting to be a translation, in the manner of Burton, of Persian erotic (principally homosexual) poetry. It is in fact an accomplished pastiche of Persian verse by Crowley himself, who was proficient in several languages. Aside from a list of demons and their attributes, the main text is exclusively "Persian" in style and subject matter, but a preliminary essay, supposedly by the Reverend P. D. Carey but actually by Crowley himself, begins with a scene glaringly out of keeping with the Victorian Orientalism of the main text.

The scene is a clearing in a wood with sunset blazing red on the horizon. The sun's rays fall on a marble statue of Pan, before which the narrator lies upon the grass, in fevered dreams. Then come hooves treading the turf, and a satyr enters the scene. The narrator is possessed by the god. At this point the description takes on an explicit nature that Machen would certainly not have written, but the red sky, the clearing in the wood, the figure dreaming on the grass in a place which has remnants of Roman occupation, and the manifestation of the Faun conflate two passages of *The Hill of Dreams*: the great opening sentence of the novel, and the episode in the Roman fort. The narrator then reveals that he is not in the clearing, but experiencing a vision from which he awakes to find that he is living in a noisy London square in a world populated by creatures of hell who value only material wealth.

The whole passage reads like Crowley's own, more overtly sexualised gloss on Machen's description of Lucian in London awakening from a dream that he is "within the Roman fort, working some dark horror." An even more intriguing and suggestive echo of Machen occurs in one of Crowley's volumes of mystical poetry, *Liber Liberi vel Lapidis Lazuli*. In section three the reader may be surprised to find:

176   III. MYSTICISM, MAGIC, AND PAGANISM

> There shall be a new flower in the fields, a new vintage in the vineyards.
> The bees shall gather a new honey; the poets shall sing a new song.
> I shall gain The Pain of the Goat for my prize; and the God that sitteth upon the shoulders of Time shall drowse. (*Holy Books* 26)

This will, of course, bring to mind the final page of Machen's "The Red Hand," where Selby shows Dyson and Phillips a magical amulet which he calls The Pain of the Goat. Which reader has not wondered what this shocking object looked like? The answer, I believe, and Crowley's reasons for referring to the object can best be illuminated by a brief diversion into classical history.

In 1752 excavations around Herculaneum revealed the Villa of the Papyri (so named because scrolls of philosophical writings were found there). This magnificent and immense building in its day surpassed any image of luxury and decadence to be found in the Roman chapter of *The Hill of Dreams*. Its garden was surrounded by a 150-metre colonnade decorated with ninety statues of the highest quality and artistic importance. Every one was either an original Greek work in marble or bronze, or the finest possible Roman copy. Many, including the Hermes in Repose, the Drunken Faun, the Sleeping Satyr, and the Wrestlers, have passed into world fame as paradigms of classical artistry. One has become notorious. This was the beautiful marble representation of Pan copulating with a nanny goat. For the sophisticated patricians of Herculaneum this would have been a charmingly amusing piece, the product of some artist's musings on the possible origins of the half-man, half-goat figure of the satyr, such as Norman Douglas recorded in that fascinating grab-bag of myth and folk tales of southern Italy published as *Siren Land* (1911). The more philosophical might also have pondered the implied inversion of the usual method by which gods adopted animal guise to have relations with humans. To the eighteenth-century excavators (their activities hardly deserve the name archaeology) it was an unspeakably shocking object that did not fit into their picture of classical purity. On the orders of the King of Naples it was banished, first into the custody of the sculptor Guiseppe Canart. After Canart's death it was placed in the Gabinetto Segreto of the Portici, now the Museo Archaeologico of Naples.

An exquisite small copy of the Group was executed in terracotta by the neoclassical sculptor and restorer of antiquities Joseph Nollekens. It now resides under lock and key in the British Museum's own "Secret Cabinet" (no doubt to protect our delicate sensibilities). It was undoubtedly this copy, owned by the distinguished collector Charles Townley, from which Sir Richard Payne Knight had a drawing made to be included in a book with a reputation hardly less shadowy and controversial than the Pan Group itself. In 1786 the Society of Dilettantes published, in an edition of eighty copies, "an account of the remains of the worship of Priapus, lately existing at Isernia, in the Kingdom of Naples." The volume also included "A discourse on the worship of Priapus and its connexion with the mystic religion of the ancients." The authors were Richard Payne Knight and William Hamilton. The bulk of the illustrations in the book were of phallic amulets, but the drawing of the Pan Group was featured on page 195. The work was subsequently reissued in revised form, and usually in limited editions.

The subject of the sculpture is often described, euphemistically, as Pan "making love" to a goat, but the Group is clearly an extreme and daring variation on a popular Hellenistic erotic marble symplegmata (groups of two figures entwined together). Often Pan or one of his goatish retinue is depicted struggling to overcome the resistance of a nymph, Bacchante, or even an Hermaphrodite. The present Group should then more rightly be described as representing a rape. Most of the phallic emblems in the Knight-Hamilton book are reductions of large-scale statues in marble or bronze. Variations on the Pan Group exist in small talismanic forms as cameos and intaglios, and were also surely produced as small pendants.

Crowley, who was very rich as a young man and a keen collector of beautiful books, owned a copy of this work and listed it as essential reading in a section of the same list that recommended Machen. In *Golden Twigs* (1988), a fine collection of short stories based on themes from *The Golden Bough* (1890), he describes a room full of statues, including the Pan Group, which he describes as the work of an "Unknown Master of Herculaneum." This is I think a conclusion as to the work's quality that Crowley would not have arrived at by looking at the book illustration alone. I think he had gained access to the Gabinetto Segretto and seen the sculpture for himself.

It is very likely that Machen handled at least one copy of the book during his time working for Redway. Given the dealer's interest in books on magical and erotic themes, editions of a work combining both would have passed through the shop regularly. He also credits Payne Knight with the idea behind his "Novel of the White Powder" (in his notes to the Danielson bibliography) (27). In any case, I think it likely that the Pan Group was the inspiration for the Pain of the Goat, that "revolting obscenity" held in the keeping of those who were "little higher than the beasts," and which so shocked the sensibilities of those three gentlemen. That Crowley identified the Pain of the Goat in just this way is shown by the use of the phrase in a poem whose prologue takes the form of a sensuous adoration of the God Pan, and by a later passage which is clearly inspired in part by the ancient writings gathered as *The Priapeia*, which were devoted to the subject of Priapus. An edition was published in 1890, edited by L. C. Smithers and Sir Richard Burton. A section concerning bestiality actually refers to "antique monuments" representing the subject depicted in the Pan group.

Perhaps the most elaborate and extensive tribute to Machen in Crowley's work occurs in *Konx Om Pax*, published in 1907. The section entitled "The Wake World" is an account of a journey through a strange magical world couched in the naive chatter of a young girl who does not understand the real nature of the initiations she undergoes. She meets a "fairy prince" who gives her an amethyst ring and tells her, "Whenever you want me, look into the ring and call me ever so softly by name, and kiss the ring and worship it, and then look ever so deep down into it, and I will come to you" (4). He leads her to a green place where a snake lays biting its own tail. They travel to an emerald palace, where she sees a black stone pillar that casts a fountain of pearls. Later they cross a bleak heath where a slab of grey granite lies in the form of an animal. The girl recounts that "we did all the most beautiful wicked things you can imagine, yet all the time we knew they were good and right" (11).

Although the symbolism of the fairy world explored by the young girl is that of the Golden Dawn magical society and the Tarot, the tone of the girl's narrative and the reference to the subversion of traditional forms of good and evil seem to me deeply influenced by "The White People." Why was Crowley so taken with Machen's work? Of course Crowley was a good enough writer himself to recognise a master when he saw one, but he also considered "cousin" Machen—the early Machen of *The Hill of Dreams*, *The Three Impostors*, and "The White People"—as a kindred spirit in the evocation of magical paganism. They both belonged to an artistic brotherhood that could be traced back to the Arcadian vistas of Annibale Carracci and the bronzes of Andrea Briosco, the patinated surfaces of whose little satyrs and satyresses seemed to reflect the warmer sunlight of a lost classical world.

Another of their kin was Austin Osman Spare. Like Machen, Spare tasted brief success in his youth but fell into relative neglect and poverty through the inability to compromise his principles. Both were mystics who, like Blake, experienced strange visions in the byways of London. Both joined magical societies (for Spare it was Crowley's Silver Star) but eventually left to find their own ways through—or towards?—the Great Mystery. Spare elected for sorcery, conjuring out of the subconscious onto canvas and paper forms satyric and menacing. Indeed, with their melting masses of distorted limbs and malevolent faces, seductive naiads and images of Pan, Spare's drawings are still the definitive illustrations of the early Machen's literary world, for both men created, from an essentially dark palette, strange beauty.

The young Machen, Crowley and Spare all drew inspiration from a classical tradition, the fabulously rich literary and visual vocabulary of Greece and Rome. Pan and the Bacchic Mysteries, in particular, furnished them with unforgettable images of ecstasy, desire, and terror. The goat-foot god and his retinue stalk and prance through the works of all three masters, the inspiration for some of their finest works. Crowley's "Hymn to Pan," Spare's depictions of "Satyrs Gathering," and Machen's "Great God Pan" are high-water marks of pagan-inspired art.

Crowley and Spare stayed true to the ancient path they had chosen. For a while, at least, Machen was of their number, but in the end he chose another path. Nevertheless, the divergence has been exaggerated. Spare's art can be frightening, but the man himself was a sociable animal lover who enjoyed his pint in the pub. Crowley's title of Wickedest Man in the World was coined before that World contained Belsen, Bosnia, and Rwanda, and was the opinion of *John Bull*, the populist rag that demonstrated its nose for truth by swallowing the Angel of Mons story whole. In its original form, or in its modern manifestation as the *Sun* newspaper, any enemy of John Bull is a friend of mine. Machen on the other hand has been, somewhat simplistically, claimed for orthodox Christianity, but his own definition of his faith would have left any clergyman, Anglican or otherwise, frothing at the mouth.

He had some harsh words to say of occultism, but where his prejudices got the better of him he could be an unreliable and untrustworthy source. His inability, for instance, to see worth in any mystical tradition but the Christian prevented him from gaining valuable insight into his own visionary experiences. His contempt for the Theosophical Society made him condemn G. R. S. Mead out of hand—"I don't think he was a solid man"—when in fact Mead's works on Gnostic and Hermetic texts are still included in scholarly bibliographies and even referred to with respect, a remarkable feat for a man working before the discovery and translation of the Nag Hammadi texts. Being a member of the Theosophical Society did not prevent Mead from being a greater scholar than Machen, but he had sinned against Machen's religious prejudices and was damned for it.

In fact, for all his attacks on "balderdash," Machen remained wonderfully non-rational himself, taking a lively and informed interest in such "Fortean" subjects as ghosts, poltergeists, and weird coincidences. All religions, mystical and magical practices alike, answer a need in the human heart with which common sense or logic have precisely nothing to do. Machen may have forgotten that at times when railing against the beliefs of others, but to his eternal credit he never ceased to embody it when discussing his own.

Machen always had a slightly ambiguous attitude to ancient magic, but it could be said that this was good for his fiction. As in the case of M. R. James, that mixture of attraction to and fear of his subject matter produced a genuine sense of awe and terror that is sometimes lacking in the exposition of the initiated devotee. Crowley's essay in *Konx Om Pax* may use the linguistic style of "The White People," but never for a second does it capture the haunting, creepy atmosphere of the original. It may also be true that Machen's later work deserves more praise than it has received, suffering as it does by comparison with the sheer quality of the early stories, but in a sense this merely underlines what many of us already know: that however fine and admirable the later work is, his greatest achievements came when he conjured the old gods and hymned matters pagan. Some may believe that his life traced a path out of darkness into light, but for those of us who, like Swinburne, follow where "the hoofed heel of a satyr crushes the chestnut husk at the chestnut's root," he cast aside his deepest inspiration, and was never quite as great again.

For who would not, like some ancient Adorer of Dionysus, gladly swap all the frankincense and myrrh in the world to enter once more the Garden of Avallaunius, and breath again the "perfume of the trellised vine."

Works Cited

Branch Cabell, James. *Jurgen*. New York: Robert M. McBride & Co., 1919.
Middleton, Richard. *Poems and Songs*. London: T. Fisher Unwin. 1912.
Crowley, Aleister. *The Holy Books*. Dallas: Sangreal Foundation, 1972.
———. *Konx Om Pax*. New York: Walter Scott Publishing Co., 1907.
———. *Liber Aleph: The Book of Wisdom or Folly*. West Point, CA: Thelema Publishing Co., 1962.
———. *Magick in Theory and Practice*. New York: Dover Publications, 1976.
Grant, Kenneth. *Remembering Aleister Crowley*. London: Skoob, 1991.
Machen, Arthur. "About My Books." In Henry Danielson. *Arthur Machen: A Bibliography*. London: Henry Danielson, 1923.

Of Sacred Groves and Ancient Mysteries: Parallel Themes in the Writings of Arthur Machen and John Buchan

Peter Bell

> Language should give its aid, expressing by the very cadence and rhythm that which cannot be told in explicit words, but which is so momentous for the truth.—John Buchan, "Nature and the Art of Words" (133)

John Buchan and Arthur Machen, superficially, offer great contrast: Buchan, bestselling novelist, university graduate, successful man-of-the-world, doyen of the Imperial establishment and Governor-General of Canada; Machen, struggling bohemian writer, frequently impecunious, stranger to ambition, living much of his life in London. They were contemporaries—Machen 1863-1947, Buchan 1875-1940—writing at a cultural watershed, when the religiously defined certainties of the nineteenth century were under challenge from modernity. The new frontiers of scientific rationalism assailed not only religion but also the quasi-mystical faith of romanticism, threatening what many artists revered as the spirituality of existence, especially man's kinship with Nature. It is not surprising that, alongside "realism," the era spawned a literary genre broadly definable as "supernatural" but equally marked by mystical and occult themes, exemplified by writers as diverse as Sheridan Le Fanu, Robert Louis Stevenson, Vernon Lee, Algernon Blackwood, Walter de la Mare, H. P. Lovecraft, and John Cowper Powys. Preeminent amongst these visionaries is, of course, Arthur Machen. Perhaps less well-recognised in the field, if only due to his primary association with adventure fiction, is John Buchan. Yet Buchan's supernatural tales, mostly set within a numinous Scottish landscape of dark, forbidding moors, are as evocative as Machen's macabre tales, located in the equally eerie hills of Wales, and address comparable themes.

Buchan's stories appeared in four, by no means mainly supernatural, collections: *Grey Weather: Moorland Tales of My Own People* (1899); *The Watcher by the Threshold and Other Tales* (1902); *The Moon Endureth: Tales and Fancies* (1912); and *The Runagates Club* (1928). The Reverend James C. G. Greig, of the John Buchan Society, in his erudite introduction to Buchan's *Supernatural Tales* (1997), notes that, whilst at Oxford in the 1890s, Buchan reviewed books for John Lane, at the Bodley Head publishing house, suggesting intriguingly that in the climate of the day he "acquired an acquaintance with writing such as that of the occultist Arthur Machen" (ix). The aim of this article is to explore the presence within Buchan's stories of ideas that resonate with Machen's early writing, and which may even show direct influence.

Buchan's connection with Lane is also noted by Andrew Lownie in his biography, *John Buchan: The Presbyterian Cavalier* (1995). Shortly after Buchan entered Oxford in 1895, Lane approached him to succeed Richard Le Galliene as literary adviser, "a job which largely involved reading and commenting on scripts submitted to the firm" (Lownie 41). Lane also agreed to publish Buchan's own work. These were notable accolades for a twenty-year-old aspiring writer; unsurprisingly, Buchan seized the advisor's role with alacrity, "relishing the contact the job would bring with some of the leading writers of the day" (Lownie 44). It further introduced him to new authors patronised by Lane, who in 1894 had published *The Great God Pan and The Inmost Light*; and, a year later, *The Three Impostors*, including within its narrative two of Machen's finest weird tales, "Novel of the White Powder" and "Novel of the Black Seal." Indeed, *The Great God Pan* was debated by Brasenose College's Crocodiles Club, a literary discussion society of which Buchan became president in 1896; another being *Island Night's Entertainments* by Robert Louis Stevenson. It is tempting to speculate that the inclusion of Machen's volume reflected the new president's professional interest in Lane's dark protégé, though the furore over the controversial publication is in itself probably enough to explain its inclusion on the Club's agenda.

Machen's influence, according to Lownie, is evident in Buchan's early publications, especially the essay collection *Scholar-Gipsies* (1896), an eclectic mix, "the baggage of a vagrant in letters and life" (vii) in Buchan's words. Six had previously appeared, since 1893, in *Macmillan's Magazine*. The collection includes cameos of local characters, scenes of rural life, and vivid evocations of the landscape of the Scotish Borders, as well as speculations on the art of pastoral writing, the writer's relationship with nature, and modernity's challenge to the rural idyll; several being quasi-fictional. It captures the spirit of the Upper Tweed Valley, with which Buchan kept throughout his life an emotional and literary relationship comparable to Machen's nostalgia for Gwent. Since 1889 Machen had been publishing in magazines like *St. James's Gazette*, atmospheric pieces such as "Rus in Urbe," composed as an "exile from his native land" (50). Amongst Buchan's pieces bearing comparison with Machen is the title story, identifying the spiritual vision shared by writer and country rambler; "Urban Greenery," which sketches the borderland between town and country; and "An Afternoon," in which by an ancient fort in a wooded fastness a boy encounters a strange lady who bewails the effect of urban barbarism upon rural innocence, and beholds an apocalyptic sunset: "The crimson heart of evening was glowing like a furnace." Despite obvious parallels with Machen, however, these pieces were already in gestation before Buchan knew Machen's work, and point rather to a common sensibility than direct influence. The likening of the setting sun to a furnace calls to mind Machen's recurrent use of this image, but it is a metaphor a sensitive observer might naturally apply to such fiery magnificence.

The title piece, "Scholar-Gipsies," Lownie suggests, shows Buchan's empathy with those torn "between urban and rural life, between the world of scholarship and success and the meditative opportunities of nature" (44). Buchan would develop the Machen-like theme of conflict between mystic and worldly callings in later works, including his melancholy novel *Sick Heart River* (1941), dictated on his deathbed. Another example is the short story "Fountainblue" (*The Watcher by the Threshold*), about a successful man-of-the-world visiting his boyhood paradise on the western coast of Scotland, caught between the surface glitter of life and more primeval longings found in the wilds. There is a superficial similarity to Machen, but Buchan treats the conflict with significantly different emphasis. If Machen tended to opt for primeval sensitivity and eschewed ambition, Buchan could not escape his Presbyterian conscience and the Protestant work ethic. It should be further noted that, at this stage, Machen had yet to publish the works that most significantly engage with such ideas. "A Fragment of Life" did not appear until 1904, and *The Hill of Dreams* until 1907.

Buchan's next book for Lane, *Grey Weather* (1899), collected together fiction which, as with the essays, he had already largely written. They were likewise inspired by the Borders and based partly on local yarns. It is an evocative rendering of the wilds, infused with mystical and supernatural lore, lent authenticity by frequent use of local dialect. Its mood is similar to that of *Scholar-Gipsies*, representing the young Buchan's tribute to his own roots and the tremendous spiritual impact of the Scottish landscape. Its dedication, to his sister, states: "In Memory of Old Moorland Days." They are tales which, in all likelihood, stood as they had been written and were certainly conceived before Machen's forays into the pastoral. Lane was keen to discuss an already existent body of largely unpublished work, doubtless because it suited the theme of the Arcady Library. Buchan, in the essay "Men of the Uplands," had even likened the community of the Tweed Valley to Arcady.

There is certainly nothing in *Scholar-Gipsies* or *Grey Weather* to suggest derivation from the grim horror of "The Great God Pan." Mark Valentine has argued that Machen's novel fuses the sinister with the "pastoral poems-in-prose," summoning "a mystery which arises from the remote fastness of mystic Gwent, a mystery that was to make Machen's name and identify him ever after as a master of the macabre" (24). *Grey Weather* reveals that Buchan was already a master of the sinister-pastoral, though the mood, if akin to anyone, recalls Sir Walter Scott and displays an independent authorial voice. There is, however, a shared perception, deriving from each writer's rapport with the numinous and ominous, apprehended in the landscape around them; and also a common talent for projecting that vision through a poetic, darkly romantic sensibility, and a talent for evocative prose.

"The Herd of Standlan" recounts a herdsman's rescue of a man fallen to disaster in an ill-reputed pool in a ravine in the hills: the Black Linn, an "Inferno on the brink of Paradise"; a place "always black with damp and shadow," where "the hoot of owls and the croak of hooded crows is seldom absent," where "in winter sheep stray and are never more heard of, and where more than once an unwary shepherd has gone to his account" (*Supernatural Tales* 287).[1] The shepherd, on a night "misty and nae mune visible," witnesses eldritch visions: "Witches and bogles and brownies and things oot o' the Bible, and leviathans and brazen bulls—a' cam fleerin' and flauntin' on the tap o' the water straucht afore me," then "an auld wife wi' a mutch and a hale procession o' auld wives" (*ST* 292). The tale is notable for the way Buchan conjures from the forbidding landscape a credible supernatural vision, rooted in authentic folklore, and conveys an air of brooding menace.

Buchan's talent for imbuing events with menacing portent is exemplified in "Summer Weather." During an intolerable heat wave a man is viciously attacked, alone on the moors, by his loyal collie, suddenly crazy in the hot weather. The dog attacks repeatedly, despite relentless battering by his master, the terror described in fearful, compelling language. It flees to a village, and

---

1. Hereafter abbreviated in the text as *ST*.

the master, fearing for the safety of others, follows and confronts it again, shooting it dead. Buchan's depiction of these simple events excels itself in the way the final struggle and the killing assume quasi-supernatural imagery, the dog, with "two glaring eyes," like a demon from hell: it "loomed up before him in proportions almost gigantic; it seemed to leap to and fro, and blot out the summer heavens" (*Grey Weather* 171-72). The dreadful heat in which he has to exert all his energy is likewise hellishly described. The story conveys a powerful sense of the sinister, unpredictable face of Nature.

Buchan and Machen, through their heritage, shared three cultural influences: Celtic, classical, and Christian.

Buchan, a Scot, and Machen, Welsh with Scottish on his mother's side, carried within their soul the ancestral memory of the Celts—that pre-modern sensitivity imbuing the world with a spirituality atrophied within civilisation. Both writers inhabited an emotional plane in which phantoms, fairies, demons, lost races, ancient rites, portents, sacraments, and mystic epiphanies lay beneath the surface, awaiting only a bard's skill to give them form. The communion between landscape and transcendence is crucial to this heritage. Both writers possessed the rare talent for rendering through the alchemy of words a sense of unutterable, revealed truth present in Nature. Buchan has been praised for the influence of landscape on the rhythms of his sentences, lending his writing extraordinary force. Indeed, *Scholar-Gipsies* includes an essay addressing this very concept, "Nature and the Art of Words." Machen, recounting his "indescribable emotion" before an autumn landscape, once defined literature as "the art of describing the indescribable; the art of exhibiting symbols which may hint at the ineffable mysteries behind them; the art of the veil which reveals what it conceals" ("Beneath the Barley" 370).

Both writers early acquired a fascinated knowledge of classical culture. Machen grew up in a region steeped in Roman survival. John Gawsworth records in his biography that Machen's grandfather entertained "an archaeologist and antiquarian who burrowed and delved in his papers pertaining to the Roman occupation, writing his *Isca Silurum*, at the Priory" (2). Whilst at Hereford Cathedral School, Machen excelled in Classics and Divinity. Enthusiasm for the classics led to a juvenile poem *Eleusinia*, inspired by a his father's copy of *Smith's Classical Dictionary*. Buchan was a young admirer of Walter Pater's *Plato and Platonism*, fulfilling his passion for the classics at the universities of Glasgow and Oxford. Buchan's sense of classical doom is well defined by Greig: "That sensitivity to the incalculable, sometimes uncanny *deus absconditus*, the God—to the ancient Greeks the gods—behind Nature in all her moods—*Benigna* and *Maligna*—pervades the short stories" (viii).

Both were clergymen's sons: Buchan's father a minister of the Free Church of Scotland, Machen's father, and grandfather, Anglicans. Christianity exerted a powerful force on the young writers, sitting perhaps uneasily with Celtic and classical paganism; yet this very tension weaving rich strands in the tapestry of their visions. Each writer's response, however, was distinctive: all his life, Buchan felt a conflict between his mystical, pagan empathies and his Calvinist conscience; whilst Machen, enamoured of the mystic glory of ritual, reinforced his faith, gravitating towards High Church. While Buchan was unable to renounce his dour Presbyterian heritage, Machen's religion became part of a broader mystical vision, in which he saw the whole universe as "a tremendous sacrament; a mystic, ineffable force" (Valentine 43).

To these formative influences must be added the zeitgeist of *fin-de-siècle* England, a cauldron of seething, innovative ideas, linked by a rejection of convention and fascination with the *Unheimlich*. This was the era of Symbolism and Decadence, of Oscar Wilde and *The Picture of Dorian Gray*, of Celtic revivalism, of W. B. Yeats and William Sharp, whose Celtic fantasies began appearing in 1895 under the pseudonym Fiona Macleod. Lane, through 1894-97, was publishing Aubrey Beardsley's and Henry Harland's *Yellow Book*, an eclectic mix of the decadent, fantastic, and aesthetic; whilst in the Keynotes series he was introducing controversial, esoteric works, the fifth being "The Great God Pan." Central to the scene was aesthete Richard Le Gallienne, whom Buchan, as noted, succeeded as Lane's reader—an exalted affirmation, surely, of the talented young writer's empathy with the era and the literary ambience which Lane was pioneering.

Machen was an admirer of Wilde's strange imagination, even meeting him; while both wrote tales of comparable mood to *The Picture of Dorian Gray*. Buchan was an early contributor to the *Yellow Book* with, in 1896, "A Journey of Little Profit." Reprinted in *Grey Weather*, this is a quasi-supernatural tale about a drunken herdsman's temptation by the Devil in an ancient, desolate, crumbling house. Whilst quintessentially Buchan, his atmospheric description of the setting is on the same wavelength as Machen's eerie evocations of Bertholly House in "The Great God Pan." Buchan and his sister, Anna, were fascinated by the *Yellow Book*, such that Anna would sit in a darkened room burning incense, much to the chagrin of their father, the Reverend John Buchan. Buchan contributed two further pieces, "At the Article of Death" (reprinted in *Grey Weather*) and "A Captain of Salvation." Machen later distanced himself from the era, seeking more the mystical than the weird and decadent, dismissing the days when "Yellow Bookery was at its yellowest," suggesting, rather disingenuously, that 'The Great God Pan' merely "profited by the noise" (Valentine 29-30). Though not himself a contributor to the journal, he cannot so easily be detached from the context in which it flourished.

Finally, overarching the literary scene was Robert Louis Stevenson, whose innovative style, arcane narratives, and outré themes set the tone for a new generation of writers interested in the weird and fantastic. Stevenson's paramount influence upon the two can be seen in the structure and style of Machen's *The Three Impostors* and Buchan's *The Runagates Club,* and is evident in the weird content of various tales, with madness and mysterious drugs prominent in the trend of *Dr. Jekyll and Mr. Hyde*. Machen's "Novel of the White Powder" and Buchan's "A Lucid Interval" deal with personality-changing drugs; while split personality underlies Buchan's most well-known supernatural tales, "The Watcher by the Threshold" and "Tendebant Manus," the latter of which concerns a man's self-identification with a brother killed—like Buchan's younger brother—in the Great War.

The image of Pan or Faun in the works of Machen and Buchan merits some discussion. As Mark Valentine has argued, the image is central to the era's ambience, with writers as diverse as Saki, Blackwood, Forster, Dunsany, Huxley, Lawrence, and Benson playing on the theme. Lane published in the 1890s Kenneth Grahame's *Pagan Papers* and the Keynotes title *The Dancing Faun* by Florence Farr. The enigmatic god, in varied manifestations, is present in classical and Celtic culture, a capricious, awe-inspiring nature spirit. (Interestingly, in *Scholar-Gipsies* Buchan records a local belief attributing evil to "what sentimentalists name the Woodland Pan, what plain people call the Old Adam, or plainer still, the Devil." [68]) Yet by the turn of the century, Pan had become a specific symbol of sexual licentiousness. Machen and his grim novel may be unwittingly responsible, Valentine argues, for transforming "a rustic, rather bucolic image" into an image of "illicit sex and cosmopolitan decadence" (32-33).

The imagery of Faun appears in two of Buchan's stories: "The Green Glen" (*The Moon Endureth*) and "The Wind in the Portico" (*The Runagates Club*). "The Green Glen" begins with the narrator's boyhood memory of a mysterious hidden valley of "indescribable greenness," its "still slopes and folds" seeming to "stretch to eternity" (ST 261); flowing through it is the significantly named Fawn. Discovering "a rude mound, embanked like some Roman fort," panic overwhelms him: "The green hills shut me in, and the awe of them brooded over me. I was mortally afraid, and not ashamed of my fear. I could not give a name to it, but something uncanny was in the air: not terrible exactly, or threatening, but inhumanly strange" (ST 261). Returning as a man, drawn by the "delicious desolation," he reads in a volume of local history a baleful rhyme: *"Ubi Faunus fluit, Spes mortalis ruit"* (Where Fawn flows, Man's hope goes) (ST 263). Buchan conjures a seductive, yet sinister, pastoral scene, infused with Roman survival and the mystery of Faun. There are echoes of Machen in its evocation of Roman heritage and a mystic landscape. It recalls the description in *The Hill of Dreams*, published five years previously, of the Roman fort where Lucian awakes from his dream—"the gleaming bodily vision of a strayed faun"—and flees in awestricken panic (CF 2.19).

Buchan works hard to build an antiquarian context: the Glen is perhaps the lost *Fauni Castellum*, a station on the Roman road; a broken satyr's head is found in an unidentified local earthwork, perhaps originating from the site; iniquity surrounds clerics—rather obviously named John of Fawn and Andrew de Faun—who, in the past, usurped the ancient shrine, *diabolos convocandi*. A head "pronounced by the most experienced archaeologists of the district to be that of a faun or satyr" is also featured in "The Great God Pan" (CF 1.228). Buchan's denouement, however, is flat: two lovers re-enact, unwittingly, an ancient tragedy; at a tryst in the Glen the woman utters the same words spoken by an ancestor in similar circumstances, dying in her suitor's arms. The story leaves an impression of awkward contrivance, as if Buchan were merely using the strange setting and associations with the deity to tell a different tale, a dynastic romance, reminiscent of Scott rather than Machen. The mystical aura is dissipated; and for all its effort to establish the profane, the story lacks the understated demonic menace of "The Great God Pan." It is a very different tale—though probably influenced by Machen's novel—but more a part of the wider context of literary paganism, revealing as much affinity with Kenneth Grahame, whom Buchan greatly admired, as with Machen.

"The Wind in the Portico" is one of Buchan's most Machen-like stories. It is the only supernatural tale he wrote set in the Welsh borders, in Shropshire; lying, as the narrator states, "between Ludlow and the hills, in a shallow valley full of woods" (ST 196). The large house, in which the strange events occur, lies in a park through which flows the River Vaun, hence its name, Vauncastle. The mysterious inhabitant, Dubellay, a loner obsessed by Roman antiquity, is a character not unlike Dr. Raymond in "The Great God Pan" or Professor Gregg in "Novel of the Black Seal." An antiquarian, visiting Vauncastle to consult a rare, variant edition of Theocritus, becomes fascinated by his host's oddity and by the discovery that the house is faced on one side by a Roman portico, where a warm wind always seems to blow. It is, in fact, a sacrificial shrine to the Pan-deity, Vaunus, once locally worshipped; and the heat, it transpires, is not some form of hypocaust, as he imagines, but a consuming fire that destroys Dubellay. He finds "a naked body, already charred and black," beside a hideous image of the deity, "the ultimate horror of fear, the last dementia of cruelty made manifest in stone," glowing "like a sun in hell" (ST 213, 216). Again, the satyr's head in "The Great God Pan" springs to mind: "a stone head of grotesque appearance," built into the wall above a door; never had Dr. Phillips "received such a vivid presentment of intense evil" (CF 1.228). Affinity with Machen's macabre vision is reinforced by Buchan's dourly sketched setting: Vauncastle stands amidst bleak hills and unfriendly woods, "dark and cloudy, as if they were hiding secrets," a landscape "not only sad, but ominous" (ST 198). This story did not appear until 1928, three decades after Machen's grim masterpieces, perhaps indicative of a lasting legacy within Buchan's literary consciousness.

Interestingly, the cover of *Grey Weather*, published in Lane's Arcady Library, bore an image of a goat-footed Pan. There is, however, no reason to think this expressed a tribute by Buchan to Machen's tale. It represented a fashionable icon, put there by the publisher perhaps for commercial reasons, or simply because it was consistent with the bucolic concept of Arcady rather than the decadence. As Lownie argues, Buchan's book was "rather more rooted in the pastoral than the other writers who used Pan as a symbol of revolt against convention and urban life" (59).

Greig offers shrewd insights into the critical significance within Buchan's tales of the sacred grove, or *temenos*, stemming from his interest in the classics. Sir James George Frazer's *The Golden Bough*, published in 1890–1915, with its themes of ritual and sacrifice, is also crucial; and at Oxford Buchan studied pre-Christian cults. Although parallels with Machen exist and motifs are repeated, especially that of ancient mysteries impinging on the present, most reflect his own perspective. *Golden Bough* lore, for example, underpins the human sacrificial ritual practised by the fearsome tribe in "No Man's Land" (*The Watcher by the Threshold*), a story which, in other respects, as argued below, certainly resonates with Machen. A similar ritual appears in Buchan's novel *The Dancing Floor* (1926). In "The Grove of Ashtaroth" (*The Moon Endureth*), we see how pagan themes similar to those fascinating Machen affected Buchan differently, exercising the Scot's Presbyterian conscience. Set in South Africa—realised as potently as his portrayal of Scotland—it tells of the building of a house in an exquisite grove that turns out to have been a former shrine to the goddess Ashtaroth, indicated by a strange obelisk. Its spell obsessively fascinates the owner, of Judaeo-Christian background, but dismays the narrator, who instigates the razing of the unholy site, only to realise that this Christian duty has violated something more profound, that he has "driven something lovely and adorable from its last refuge on earth." The story ending, perhaps, in its meditation on barbarism, resonates with Machen-like sensibility, but it is quintessentially Buchan.

Machen is perhaps most noted for his demonic representation of the "Little People" or "Fairy Folk," a crucial part of Welsh, Scotish, and Irish folklore—possibly ancestral memory of hostile races exiled into remote regions of the hills. Machen was here engaging with another aspect of the era, inherent in Celtic culture, then undergoing a revival. Richard Doyle's 1870 publication *In Fairyland*, with its violent, gruesome images of capricious fairies, accompanied by William Allingham's chilling verse—"Up the airy mountain, / Down the rushy glen, / We dare not a-hunting, / For fear of little men"—exercised a lasting impact; the same year J. Sheridan Le Fanu's alarming tale "The Child That Went with the Fairies" appeared, anonymously, in *All the Year Round*. H. G. Wells built on such images in *The Time Machine* (1895) with his sinister troglodyte race, the Morlocks. Buchan's forays into this territory—as with Pan—fitted into the wider perspective, and the topic was endemic in Celtic-Scottish legend. Fiona Macleod's Celtic fantasies, then popular, are replete with such lore. Buchan's early writings are infused with references to similar myths.

In "The Moor Song"(*Grey Weather*; reprinted in *The Moon Endureth* as "The Rime of True Thomas"), a shepherd is lectured by a whaup (curlew) on man's ignorance of Nature's mysteries:

> "But the blue hawk that lives in the corrie o' the Dreichil can speak o' kelpies and the dwarfs that bide in the hill. The heron, the lang solemn fellow, kens o' the greenwood fairies and the wood elfins, and the wild geese that squatter on the tap o' the Muneraw will croak to ye of the merrymaidens and the girls o' the pool." (*Grey Weather* 255)

Buchan is here articulating local folklore, in a meditative piece about the folly of ambition and spiritual awakening, which may resonate with Machen but is not directly influenced. Another story, "No Man's Land" (*The Watcher by the Threshold*), however, shows a distinct similarity to Machen's sinister portrayal of the fairy folk in "The Novel of the Black Seal" and "The Shining Pyramid," published in 1895 in the magazine *Unknown World*, edited by occult scholar A. E. Waite.

Buchan's menacing tale is of an Oxford don, Mr. Graves, schooled in Celtic and Nordic folklore. He visits a remote Scottish fastness of moor and mountain, following hints from a pupil, a dropout, "dreeing his weird in the Backwoods," obsessed with dark legend (ST 80). The youth impresses upon him that the Celtic legend of the Brownie has authentic credentials: this "little swart man of uncommon strength and cleverness, who does good and ill indiscriminately, and then disappears" is a degenerate descendant of the ancient inhabitants, the Picts (ST 80-81). He introduces him to an old book:

> The early part consisted of folk-tales and folk-sayings, some of them wholly obscure, some of them with a glint of meaning, but all of them with some hint of a mystery in the hills. I heard the Brownie story in countless versions. Now the thing was a friendly little man, who wore grey breeches, and lived on brose; now he was a twisted being, the sight of which made the ewes miscarry in the lambing time. But the second part was the stranger, for it was made up of actual tales, most of them with date and place appended. It was a most Bedlamite catalogue of horrors, which, if true, made the wholesome moors a place instinct with tragedy. Some told of children carried away from villages, even from towns, on the verge of the uplands. In almost every case they were girls, and the strange fact was their utter disappearance. Two little girls would be coming home from school, would be seen last by a neighbour just where the road crossed a patch of heath or entered a wood and then—no human eye ever saw them again. Children's cries had startled outlying shepherds in the night, and when they had rushed to the door they could hear nothing but the night wind. (ST 81)

The parallels with "Novel of the Black Seal" are striking. In Machen's tale the ethnologist, Professor Gregg—not unlike the name Gray—opines that much folklore is "but an exaggerated account of events that really happened" (CF 1.391), that stories of disappearances, changelings, and demons might originate from memories of a race which had "fallen out of the grand march of evolution" (CF 1.392), degenerate and strangely powerful: "What if the obscure and horrible race of the hills survived, still remained haunting wild places and barren hills, and now and then repeating the evil of Gothic legend" (CF 1.393). Gregg cites reports of local people who had "vanished strangely from the earth":

> They would be seen by a peasant in the fields walking towards some green and rounded hillock, and seen no more on earth; and there are stories of mothers who have left a child quietly sleeping, with the cottage door rudely barred with a piece of wood, and have returned, not to find the plump and

rosy little Saxon, but a thin and wizened creature, with sallow skin and black, piercing eyes, the child of another race. (CF 1.391)

A mysterious disappearance is likewise featured in "The Great God Pan," where a woman "vanished in broad sunlight"; "they saw her walking in a meadow, and a few moments later, she was not there" (CF 1.230).

Both stories refer to books of strange lore that contain more truth than man realises. Gray encounters "a large leather-bound book" lettered in "rococo style," *Glimpses of the Unknown*; readings from the grim volume were "not pleasant"; indeed, rarely had the scholar "heard anything so well fitted to shatter sensitive nerves" (ST 81). Professor Gregg's assistant, Miss Lally, finds "an old quarto, printed by the Stephani, containing the three books of Pomponius Mela," an "odd mixture of fact and fantasy" (CF 1.376). In a chapter on Solinus she reads of a folk, dwelling "in remote and secret places," celebrating "foul mysteries on savage hills," who "hiss rather than speak," shun sunlight and have nought in common with humankind "save the face" (CF 1.376). Buchan's account of the ancient Picts is very close:

> Then suddenly in the hollow trough of mist before me, where things could still be half discerned, there appeared a figure. It was little and squat and dark; naked, apparently, but so rough with hair that it wore the appearance of a skin-covered being. It crossed my line of vision, not staying for a moment, but in its face and eyes there seemed to lurk an elder world of mystery and barbarism, a troll-like life which was too horrible for words. (ST 95)

Similar imagery occurs in "The Shining Pyramid," which Buchan would doubtless also have read. In a hollow in the hills, beholding the fairy folk, the onlookers see that "there were things like faces and human limbs," yet "no fellow soul or human thing stirred in all that tossing and hissing host" (CF 1.505).

Similarity is evident, moreover, in reports of the speech of the alien folk. Gray hears, "as through acres of mist," a sound of speech, vaguely human, yet a "mere craziness—the cry of a weasel or a hill-bird distorted by my ears," making "the nerves tense and the heart timorous," the "strangest jumble of vowels and consonants"; perhaps "some maniac talking Jabberwock to himself," a belated traveller "whose wits had given out in fear," or a shepherd "whiling the way with nonsense" (ST 94). Interestingly, both cite an identical phrase of Homer's: "articulate-speaking men" (CF 1.392/ST 94). Gray recognises that, though degenerate, this is just about what he is hearing, and later converses with them, but only by using a lost Celtic dialect. Gregg wonders whether Homer "knew or had heard of men whose speech was so rude that it could hardly be termed articulate; and on my hypothesis of a race who had lagged far behind the rest, I could easily conceive that such a folk would speak a jargon but little removed from the inarticulate noises of brute beasts" (CF 1.393). He describes it elsewhere, concerning the idiot boy Cradock, born of miscegenation between the fairy folk and his mother, as "the very speech of Hell" (CF 1.381).

Gregg's research, like Gray's, postulates real ancient origins for the legend of the little people, deriving from degenerate races, and refers to the ancient Turanians. This is expressed even more explicitly in "The Shining Pyramid": "the very probable belief that they represent a tradition of the prehistoric Turanian inhabitants of the country, who were cave dwellers" (CF 1.510). The narrator realises he is searching for "a being under four feet in height, accustomed to live in darkness, possessing stone instruments, and familiar with the Mongolian cast of features" (CF 1.510). This dovetails with Buchan's squat Picts, who inhabit caves in the hillside, as does the evidence of stone implements, which is featured as evidence in both tales. In "No Man's Land" a shepherd reveals a flint-head arrow, which Gray finds the more remarkable in that he estimates its age as of recent date. A stone axe is presented as similar evidence in "Novel of the Black Seal," while in "The Shining Pyramid" the strange folk employ arrowheads as a form of semaphore. The troglodyte communities in both tales suggest a kinship with Wells' Morlocks.

Buchan's story is set in a fictional Allermuir, based on the ancient Pictish Manaan, which roughly corresponds to the Borders, Dumfries and Galloway; possibly the story he was reputedly working on during a walking tour of the Galloway hills in 1897. He brings to the tale all his talent for evoking through powerful prose an impression of a forbidding landscape, in which all manner of terror might emerge. The mountain fastness Gray seeks is the ominous-sounding Scarts O' the Muneraw, a shunned region, equivalent to Machen's dread Grey Hills in "Novel of the Black Seal," a barren, savage territory "all strange and unvisited, and more unknown to Englishmen than the very heart of Africa" (CF 1.375). Buchan skilfully uses the raw cadences of Gaelic dialect, spoken by a fearful shepherd, to express the dark ambience of this fell domain:

> D'ye see yon corrie at the east that runs straucht up the side? It looks a bit scart, but it's sae deep that it's aye derk at the bottom o't. Weel, at the tap o' the rig it meets anither corrie that runs doun the ither side, and that one they ca' the Scarts. There is a sort o' burn in it that flows intil the Dule and sae intil the Aller, and, indeed, if ye were gaun there it would be from Aller Glen that your best road wad lie. But it's an ill bit, and ye'll be sair guidit if ye try't. (ST 91-92)

Like Machen, Buchan approaches landscape with a mixture of reverence for its magnificence and awe at its secret terrors. Gray begins his venture to the hills seduced by the beauty of nature:

> The morning was breaking over the bleak hills. Little clouds drifted athwart the corries, and wisps of haze fluttered from the peaks. A great rosy flush lay over one side of the glen, which caught the edge of the sluggish bog-pools and turned them to fire. Never had I seen the mountain-land so clear, for far back into the east and west I saw mountain-tops set as close as flowers in a border, black crags seamed with silver lines which I knew for mighty waterfalls, and below at my feet the lower slopes fresh with the dewy green of spring. (ST 91)

Forestalled by a sudden change to dreich weather, on his "long and toilsome retreat" (ST 92), the mood changes dramatically; panic before a hostile wilderness is perfectly realised in Buchan's prose:

> Now, in the thick weather I had crossed the glen much lower down than in the morning, and the result was that the hill on which I stood was one of the giants which, with the Muneraw for centre, guard the watershed. Had I taken the proper way, the Nick o' the Threshes would have lead me to the Caulds, and then once over the bog a little ridge was all that stood before me and the glen of Farawa. But instead I had come a wild cross-country road, and was now, though I did not know it, nearly as far from my destination as at the start . . . I took what seemed to me the way I had come, and began to descend steeply. Then something made me halt, and the next instant I was lying on my face trying painfully to retrace my steps. For I had found myself slipping, and before I could stop, my feet were dangling over a precipice with Heaven alone knows how many yards of sheer mist between me and the bottom. Then I tried keeping the ridge, and took that to the right, which I thought would bring me nearer home. It was no good trying to think out a direction, for in the fog my brain was running round, and I seemed to stand on a pin-point of space where the laws of the compass had ceased to hold. (ST 93-94)

Despite the similarities of plot and mood, however, Buchan develops his story differently from Machen, and is ultimately less effective. The power of Machen's horror lies in his restriction of information, allowing the reader's imagination full rein. The peril of the little folk is the greater for being indirect, understated, conveyed by subtle glimpses, creating "an aura of menace and hideousness about them, in a masterpiece of macabre allusiveness" (Valentine 41). Buchan builds up his terror subtly at first, recounting the ramblings of a shepherd, torn between religious mania and alcohol as a salve against the powers of darkness, obsessed with the struggle between God and the Devil. He seeks to deter Gray from the area, indicating a hill with a Gaelic name meaning the "Place of the Little Men": "I saw something in the first year o' my herding here which put the terror o' God on me, and makes me a fearfu' man to this day" (ST 90). He tells of sheep ravaged in ways no poacher would use; and "stories o' faces seen in the mist, and queer things that have knocked against me in the snaw, wad ye believe me?" (ST 88). When these accounts are dismissed as old wives' tales by the scholar, the shepherd reminds him "ye're no in the toun just now, but in the thick of the wild hills" (ST 88). The mystery is dissipated, however, by the long, graphic account of Gray's experience at the hands of the Picts, who capture him and try to suborn him into perpetrating a sacrificial killing of a woman; here Buchan moves into adventure story mode. Gray, having escaped Houdini-like from bonds, returns in a spirit of scientific zeal, leaving an unfinished journal, rather in the manner of Gregg, setting out upon his "final trial and encounter" (CF 1.399) with the "Little People."

The other four tales in *The Watcher by the Threshold* exhibit, to lesser degree, Machen-like themes, especially the title story. Set also in the ancient realm of Manaan, "old, sorrowful and uncanny," framed in "dank mysterious woods," a "sullen relic of a lost barbarism" (ST 2, 4), the strange tale gains much from its morbid location. Ladlaw, like Dubellay, is an obsessed Romanist, gripped by the occult version of the Emperor Justinian's life, as told by Procopius in his *Secret History*. It is a tale of dual personality, caused perhaps by insanity, or maybe possession. Ladlaw suffers from an affliction of the left—sinister—side, which cannot be explained medically. His friend's plight causes the narrator to recall tales from his Calvinist upbringing in a renewed light, having come to believe that "Science had docketed and analysed and explained the Devil out of the world" (ST 16). To the local minister, the once respected Ladlaw "now appeared a horrible kind of genius, a brilliant and malignant satyr" (ST 28). The story becomes essentially a battle between the Christian and the pagan, typifying Buchan's engagement with his own Presbyterian background.

Calvinistic resonance is apparent in another story in the collection, "The Outgoing of the Tide," concerning witchcraft, an idea developed further in the novel *Witch Wood* (1927), not a theme that attracted Machen, though Professor Gregg widens his account of the fairy legend to include "myths darker still; the dread of witch and wizard, the lurid evil of the Sabbath, and the hint of demons who lingered with the daughters of men" (CF 1.391). "Fountainblue," already mentioned, deals with ambition versus innocence. "The Far Islands," also set in Western Scotland, in which the narrator experiences a recurrent hallucination of distant isles—essentially Tir na Nog—only reached as he dies in battle, contains Machen-like overtones, with its elegiac melancholy and its mysticism, but it is essentially, like "Fountainblue," inspired by Buchan's own Scottish-Celtic soul.

To conclude, a comparison of Machen and Buchan reveals certain common themes, ideas, and motifs: madness and split personality; books of occult lore; sacred groves and ritual; Roman survival; the spirit of Pan; lost races and fairy folk; numinous landscape; and mystical experience. Much stemmed from similar immersion in Celtic, classical, and Christian lore, and from the two writers' intimate, nostalgic relationship with their rural roots, in an era of threatening modernity. They cannot, however, be divorced from the zeitgeist; similar concepts can be found in many late Victorian and Edwardian authors, some of whom had signal influence upon the aspiring young writers. Care must be taken not to attribute ideas within Buchan's writing solely or mainly to Machen. Machen's influence, though, is prominent in at least two stories, "No Man's Land" and "The Wind in the Portico," and in varying degrees in several other tales. This does not mean Buchan was not his own master, for he develops his plots differently, consistent with his unique personal experience, especially the culture of Calvinist Scotland. Ultimately, Machen and Buchan shared a common sensibility, a perception of existence as communion with the ineffable. And both were gifted with the rare ability to imbue their prose with the tones appropriate to that vision. Both, indeed, stood "amidst sacraments and mysteries full of awe" (CF 1.369).

Works Cited

Buchan, John. *Grey Weather*. London: John Lane/The Bodley Head, 1899.

———. *Scholar-Gipsies*. London: John Lane/The Bodley Head, 3rd ed. 1927.

———. *Supernatural Tales*. Ed. James C. G. Greig. Edinburgh: B & W Publishing, 1997.

Doyle, Richard. *In Fairyland: A Series of Pictures from the Elf-World*. Exeter: Webb & Bower, 1979.

Gawsworth, John. *The Life of Arthur Machen*. Ed. Roger Dobson. Leyburn, UK: Tartarus Press, 1995.

Lownie, Andrew. *John Buchan: The Presbyterian Cavalier*. Edinburgh: Canongate Classics, 1995.

Machen, Arthur. "Beneath the Barley: A Note on the Origins of *Eleusinia*." 1931. In John Gawsworth. *The Life of Arthur Machen*. Ed. Roger Dobson. Leyburn, UK: Tartarus Press, 2005. 369–70.

———. "Rus in Urbe." 1890. In *Rus in Urbe and Other Stories*. Lewes, UK: Tartarus Press, 1992.

Valentine, Mark. *Arthur Machen*. Bridgend, Wales: Seren, 1995.

Beyond the Veil of Reality: Mysticism in Arthur Machen's "The White People"

Emily Foster

Introduction

Arthur Machen, a student of occult medievalism, Celtic folklore, and pagan legends, created fiction that synthesised the magical, mystical, and mythological. An air of mystery and strangeness, which stems from Machen's underlying religious and spiritual principles, pervades each of his stories. His fantastical fiction centers on a mythology involving hidden subterranean races that subsist in dark, supernatural worlds. We are faced with "mystical figures of awe and woe" (Scarborough 248), which take the form of dark, primitive beings that live beyond the realms of human existence; fairies and demons hold a sinister disposition. Rather than deal with quaint, wholesome folklore, Machen concentrated on the sinister aspects of ancient myths. He was thus concerned with the sense of awe and terror that derive from tales associated with the supernatural.

Machen, however, also held pantheistic beliefs, in which he saw every spring, every cloud, and every hilltop as some unearthly divinity of being (Scarborough 228). He was prepared to reconcile pantheistic spirituality with other forms of spirituality, so as to explore the mysteries that lie beyond the depths of our existence. As a child, growing up in the alluring landscape of Caerleon-on-Usk, he was fascinated by the discoveries in the region of strange pagan sculptures and inscribed stones dating back to the Roman occupation. His lifelong curiosity in the ancient world infused his writing with a belief that there is supernatural significance in the trees, stones, hills, and streams that form our natural world. For Machen, as he describes in the first volume of his autobiography *Far Off Things* (1922), the Welsh landscape became a spiritual realm of mystery and beauty; a place where he could "fall into a reverie or meditation, as if it had been a fragment of paradise or fairyland" (*FOT* 25). Yet the landscape in his fiction also takes on a more unsettling persona, as nature becomes host to malevolent spirits. The countryside that surrounds Machen's characters is deceptive, as beyond its outward appearance is another land in which pagan rituals and ceremonies predominate. The nymphs, fairies, and ethereal beings that inhabit this other world possess dark, supernatural powers that can affect not only people's minds, but also their unsuspecting souls.

Machen's stories thus espouse a belief that beyond the monotony of our everyday life is a land far stranger and mysterious. Devoted to both Anglo-Catholic beliefs and the powers of mysticism, he sought "to restore the sense of wonder and mystery into our perception of the world" (Joshi 13). He was intent in ensuring that his religious dogma would not give way to the dominant materialism of the age. By suffusing his writing with mystical and spiritual values and drawing on elements of Catholicism and the ancient Celtic Church, Machen was able to pursue his own spiritual quest.

Ecstasy and Sin: A Mystical Vision

One of Machen's stories that draws heavily on these pantheistic ideas and mystical experiences is arguably his most successful tale of terror, "The White People" (1904). Written in 1899 but not published until 1904, this story focuses on the diary of an adolescent girl, in which she recounts her "most secret secrets" (CF 2.193). Brought up by a nurse who participates in supernatural rituals, the girl from a young age witnesses the wonderful white people that live within the depths of the wood: "They were a kind of creamy white like the old ivory figure in the drawing-room; one was a beautiful lady with kind dark eyes, and a grave face, and long black hair, and she smiled such a strange sad smile at the other, who laughed and came to her" (CF 2.194).

Machen's description of ivory-white figures that dance and sing around the "pool" alludes, as S. T. Joshi argues, to a possible witch cult, which indoctrinates people into their supernatural orgies (22). These occultist worshippers within this hidden land captivate and hypnotise those who enter their realm. The people who are drawn into this world of magic and mysticism fall into a trance-like state. Although the nurse tries to persuade the girl that she had been dreaming, the girl knows that she has not and she is made "not to say a word about it to anybody" (CF 2.194), otherwise she will be thrown into the black pit. It is evident that what the girl has seen is beyond the veil of reality and holds possibilities for the kind of evil that protagonists Ambrose and Cotgrave discuss in the prologue of the story.

In the very first line of the narrative, Ambrose sets out what he considers to be the only two states of reality in life: "'Sorcery and sanctity,' said Ambrose, 'these are the only realities. Each is an ecstasy, a withdrawal from the common life'" (CF 2.185). It is only through reaching a state of ecstasy that we can remove ourselves from the false world in which we live. Machen therefore presents us with the idea that the material life we lead is not a true existence, but rather a veil that stops us from being able to reach our true state of being. We should seek to lift the veil and go beyond our everyday life in order to reach, as Vincent Starrett argues, a strange, mystical borderland, "somewhere between Dreams and Death, peopled with shades, beings, spirits, ghosts, men, women, souls" (18). Machen uses Ambrose to voice his own spiritual views and to claim that through ecstasy, we are able to move our body, mind, and soul towards a higher, mystical existence.

Evelyn Underhill writes of the significance of ecstasy in relation to mysticism. She contends that "Mystics of all ages have agreed in regarding such ecstasy as an exceptionally favourable state," a state in which "man's spirit catches up to its immediate vision of the divine" (428). Thus, through ecstasy, man is entranced and becomes "wholly unconscious of the external world" (427), therefore withdrawing from the normalities of everyday life. Machen had established a friendship with Underhill through their membership of the Hermetic Order of the Golden Dawn, and had assisted her with her key work, *Mysticism* (1911), which she dedicated to him and his wife Purefoy. For Machen, the ecstasy to which he introduces us through Ambrose is a transcendental state in which humanity must enter a spiritual realm to awaken and reach its divine self. Although Machen still strongly held the belief that Christianity had the ability to transport mankind to a sublime condition and the possibility of oneness with God, as Nicholas Freeman argues, he did not feel that the Church of England could provide access to it (244). We might see Machen's concept as the Gnostic transcendence of the demiurge. However, there is little evidence in "The White People" to suggest he had the Gnostic lexicon in mind.

This spiritual world, which can only be reached through ecstasy, is, as Ambrose continues to explain, not just confined to the supremely good. The "supremely wicked, necessarily, have their portion in it" (CF 2.185). Under Ambrose's logic, a man may be infinitely wicked without realising it, as the form of wickedness that he is asserting exists, is always unconscious. In this sense, the ordinary man can never understand the real nature of evil or the true meaning of sin, as these religious notions subsist beyond the mundanity of our empirical realm. The average murderer or the everyday person who steals a loaf of bread does not commit true sin. Rather, sin is conceivable when your cat or dog begins to talk to you, or when the flowers in your garden begin to sing to you. As Ambrose explains to Cotgrave, sin transcends our natural human existence and cannot be understood in relation to the social laws of our society:

> "Certainly; because the true evil has nothing to do with social life or social laws, or if it has, only incidentally and accidentally. It is a lonely passion of the soul—or a passion of the lonely soul—whichever you like. If, by chance, we understand it, and grasp its full significance, then, indeed, it will fill us with horror and with awe. . . ." (CF 2.190)

To be able to grasp sin in its full significance, Ambrose is stating that we must rid ourselves of all the elements we consider to pervade the normal existence of our life. However, our higher senses have been blinded by our material life, so we would be unable to recognise sin or real evil even if we encountered it. To wholly appreciate Ambrose's view that the true essence of sin can only be reached through a mystical journey by the individual, we can reflect on Underhill's conception of "the purification of the self." Underhill explains that "the normal self as it exists in the normal world—the 'old Adam' of St. Paul—is wholly incapable of supersensual adventure" (240). This is due to the fact that "we do not know ourselves; hence do not know the true character of our senses; hence attribute wrong values to their suggestions and declarations concerning our relation to the external world" (240). We are unable to awaken our senses to the ineffable beauty and mystery of the world without detaching ourselves from the sham material lives that we lead. In light of Underhill's claims that "man has built a false universe," and that our inner self "craves for harmony with the Absolute Truth" (240), we can perceive that Machen, through Ambrose, is stating that a belief in mysticism is the only way we can find, for ourselves, the true Order of Reality. This view is particularly clear in part of his autobiography *Far Off Things*: "Man . . . is by his nature designed to look upward, to gaze into the heavens that are all about him, to discern the eternal in things temporal . . . We receive, each one of us, the magic bean, and if we will plant it it will undoubtedly grow and become our ladder to the stars and the cloud castles" (FOT 125).

Machen is highlighting humanity's natural instinct to want to pursue a mystic union with God. We all have the ability within us to achieve spiritual Enlightenment. However, in "The White People" Machen emphasises the dangers of pursuing Enlightenment through nature; or, at least, of following the wrong path within nature. He mixes pantheistic beliefs with ideas of mysticism to explore how the magic of a transcendental landscape can quickly lead man onto a path of moral corruption. In "'the taking of heaven by storm'" (CF 2.188), Ambrose proclaims that a human being, in "'an effort to gain the ecstasy and the knowledge that pertain alone to angels'" (CF 2.188), will, through his effort become a demon. Thus, the power of nature enables humans to transcend into a supernatural realm, but in gaining entry into a "'higher sphere in a forbidden manner'" (CF 2.188), they risk sacrificing their souls.

Into a Distant, Unknown Land

Machen states that in his boyhood and youth, he viewed the countryside around him "as a kind of fairyland" (FOT 21). It was a place in which he came near to the spirit of St. Thomas Aquinas: *Adoro te devote, latens Deitas*. From his childhood, Machen believed he saw "that of God" in the historic landscape of Gwent. He was fascinated by the magical power of the hills, the maze of unknown brooks and the long stretches of wild land. Thus, from very early in his life, the hidden realms of nature enchanted him:

> But, looking back, I believe that, as a child, I realised something of the spirit of the mystic injunction. Everywhere, through the darkness and the mists of childish understanding, and yet by the light of the child's illumination, I saw *latens dietas*; the whole earth, down to the very pebbles, was but the veil of a quickening and adorable mystery. (FOT 26)

Therefore the countryside where he spent hours exploring and getting lost as a child stimulated and nurtured his belief in mysticism. He believed that the landscape was alive with hidden secrets and mysteries. "The White People" closely draws on the idea that the landscape around us can act as a portal into another mystical realm. In the girl's narrative, we are informed that at the age of nearly fourteen, she decided to go on a very "singular adventure, so strange that the day on which it happened is always called the White Day" (CF 2.195). Her adventure leads her into what she terms as a "new country," where she must battle her way through "thorny thickets on the hills" and "dark woods full of creeping thorns" (CF 2.195). As she goes through that dark place, that appears to be a never-ending journey into the unknown, she comes to a part of the landscape that is strange and unfamiliar. The girl likens the place to the "wicked voorish dome in Deep Dendo" (CP 2.195), which is a reference to the Desolation of Voor in Thule. The term "ultima Thule" denotes a place located beyond the "borders of the known world," and thus the "wicked voorish dome" lies in a cavern, under the desolation. Machen, in this part of the narrative, is alluding to the fact that the girl, having journeyed far into the depths of the earth, has entered a distant, unknown land. However, the features of this landscape are sinister, where the rocks and stones can come alive and entrance the girl into a state of dizziness and confusion:

> I got quite dizzy and queer in the head, and everything began to be hazy and not clear, and I saw little sparks of blue light, and the stones looked as if they were springing and dancing and twisting as they went round and round and round . . . and I danced and danced along, and sang extraordinary songs that came into my head. (CF 2.197)

It is implied that the girl, by surpassing the ordinary bounds of our existence and by singing wicked songs and performing wicked dances, transcends into a state of ecstasy where her condemned soul is associated with the kind of evil and wickedness that Ambrose has already described. Although this ecstatic episode is imbued in pagan colour, as the girl fully connects with the natural world around her we are also reminded that this journey has led the girl into the hands of evil: "I was afraid something had happened to me, and I remembered nurse's tale of the poor girl who went into the hollow pit, and was carried away at last by the black man. I knew I had gone into a hollow pit too, and perhaps it was the same, and I had done something dreadful" (CF 2.203).

Although we are informed that the girl is aware she has entered a realm that will ultimately lead to her religious downfall, Machen leaves it ambiguous as to whether the girl has followed that path of her own free will. We only know that from a young age she was able to speak strange mythological languages and could see white faces that looked at her when she was lying in her cradle. The nurse, conscious of the girl's ability to see and connect with the spiritual world, decides to take her to a place beyond the wood where the girl can watch and be part of the rituals and ceremonies. Furthermore, when the girl is eight, the nurse shows her how to make a little man out of clay, which is able to invoke the spirits so as to bring change to the person who has created it: "And she said that if one loved very much, the clay man was very good, and if one did certain things with it, and if one hated it very much, it was just as good" (CF 2.208). However, the girl is not old enough to understand the true nature of what her nurse is showing or teaching her. She believes it is all a game where they can pretend all sorts of things without doing any sort of harm. We are therefore left in doubt as to whether it was her upbringing or, more importantly, the nurse's influence which has led the girl to follow a path of sinful ecstasy within the mystical landscape, rather than a conscious choice.

It is interesting to speculate that one reason for this ambiguity surrounding the girl's journey into wickedness and evil may be related to Max Nordau's influential treatise *Degeneration*. Originally published in German in 1892 as *Entartung* and translated into English in 1895, Nordau's book was an attack against decadent and degenerate artists. Central to his argument was the idea that the first sign of degeneracy is "moral insanity" (Eckersley 279-80), and he relates this degenerate state to what he perceives to be mysticism. In attempting to understand the psychology of mysticism, he provides a comprehensive definition of what he sees the religious belief to encompass:

> Now, this state of mind, in which a man is straining to see, thinks he sees, but does not see—in which a man is forced to construct thoughts out of presentations which befool and mock consciousness like will-o'-the wisps or marsh vapours—in which a man fancies that he perceives inexplicable relations between distinct phenomena and ambiguous formless shadows—this is the condition of mind that is called Mysticism. (Nordau 57)

For Nordau, mysticism is a principal characteristic of degeneration. The mystic suffers from a weakness of the mind, in which he produces "false judgements respecting the objective universe, respecting the qualities of things and their relations to each other" (56). Nordau argues that it is easy to distinguish between the healthy man and a man who is suffering from a mystic state. The healthy man is able to "obtain sharply defined presentations from his own immediate perceptions, and to comprehend their real connection," whilst "the mystic, on the contrary, mixes his cloudy half-formed liminal representations with his immediate perceptions, which are thereby disturbed and obscured" (69). Thus, Nordau's idea of mysticism is rooted in biology and science rather than in spirituality. His beliefs highlight a significant shift in the climate of spiritual beliefs during the 1890s, whereby, as Adrian Eckersley states, "the function of the priest as society's moral guardian was steadily and imperceptibly being taking over by the medical man" (277). If we apply Nordau's theory of degeneration and mysticism to "The White People," the girl would be seen as suffering from a weakness of the mind, in which she enters an eccentric state, where her view of the external world is distorted and blurred. From a "Nordauian" perspective, the girl in Machen's story would be classed as suffering from hysterical fits, as she "gives way to all kinds of dream-fancies" (Nordau 59). Her mystical adventure into the realm of sin and evil would merely be perceived as her inability to comprehend the difference between the landscape she was exploring and the unstable presentations of her mind. Thus, the mist that surrounds our understanding of whether the girl has entered the supernatural realm of her free will might relate to the shift in attitudes and sensibilities of the time. Machen may be certain of his ground but content with an ambivalent narrative, leaving the reader to follow his own convictions.

On the other hand, Machen fought passionately against notions of scientific materialism and was determined to champion in his writing what he considered to be the true form of mysticism. Although he leaves us with a number of questions, including what choices—subject to her free will—would have enabled the girl to obtain salvation in this transcendental universe, "The White People" is a powerful story that displays his conviction in the efficacy of a mystically, spiritual existence. Although the girl, in time, "poisoned" herself through her connection with the divine, mystical realm that she had discovered, Ambrose stresses the importance of the fact that she had "something more than imagination" (CF 2.220). She was not just a girl suffering from an over-emotional state of mind; she was a girl who could escape into the wonders and horrors of the ineffable mysteries that lie beyond the landscape.

Conclusion

Machen, in exploring the complexity of numerous religious concepts in "The White People," toys with the idea that original sin is not a purely metaphysical construct. He imbues his narrative with an artistic, ethereal gossamer of magical and mystical beings that not merely arise from the earth, but are the essence of the earth. Machen's spiritual world, in this sense, is effectively aestheticised, as within the mystical beauty of the landscape we are able to discover both spiritual holiness and wickedness. The mounds and the hollows and the valleys in "The White People" are not just geographical features of the countryside; they are mysterious places that hold wonderful secrets and have the means of inducing, in the person who enters them, a state of ecstasy. This ecstasy, through the mysticism of nature, allows the characters in his fiction to transcend our material world. Therefore Machen, as Mark Valentine maintains, was wholly concerned with "the intermingling of this world and another of far vaster significance" (126). He manages to merge pantheistic ideas and pagan themes with a wholesome belief in mysticism, so as to create a gateway within the landscape that permits us to transcend into a higher, spiritual realm. His writing emphasises the fact that science and materialism only deal with the surface of things. For Machen, our true purpose is to recognise that there are unfathomable mysteries in our world, which, if we discover them, can be both wondrous and terrifying.

Works Cited

Eckersley, Adrian. "A Theme in the Early Work of Arthur Machen: 'Degeneration.'" *English Literature in Translation* 35 (1992): 277-87.

Freeman, Nicholas. "Arthur Machen: Ecstasy and Epiphany." *Literature and Theology* 24 (2010): 242-55.

Joshi, S. T. "Arthur Machen: The Mystery of the Universe." In *The Weird Tale*. Austin: University of Texas Press, 1990.

Machen, Arthur. "The White People." In *The White People and Other Weird Stories*. Ed. S. T. Joshi. New York: Penguin, 2011.

Nordau, Max. *Degeneration*. 1895. Mansfield Centre, UK: Martino Publishing, 2014.

Scarborough, Dorothy. *The Supernatural in Modern English Fiction*. 1917. n.p.: Forgotten Books, 2012.

Starrett, Vincent. *Arthur Machen: A Novelist of Ecstasy and Sin*. 1918.

Underhill, Evelyn. *Mysticism, A Study in the Nature and Development of Man's Spiritual Consciousness*. 1911. n.p.: Forgotten Books, 2012.

Valentine, Mark. *Arthur Machen*. Bridgend, Wales: Seren, 1995.

Sanctity Plus Sorcery:
The Curious Christianity of Arthur Machen

Iain Smith

For many readers, Arthur Machen is a fantasy writer synonymous with paganism, earth mysteries, and the Great God Pan; however, dig a little deeper beyond the usual anthology stories and you will soon unveil one of the most Christian writers of his era. Just as J. R. R. Tolkien's Middle Earth is full of Christian symbolism in an ostensibly pagan setting, so Machen's curious tales of transcendence and ecstasy are suffused with the Christian mysticism of his core beliefs. In fact, it is fair to say that much of the power of Machen's stories is directly due to his almost mediaeval Christian mindset; i.e., he genuinely believes in—and fears—the powers of evil. Of the major writers of his era, only C. S. Lewis and G. K. Chesterton rival him for their commitment to the faith; but, unlike them, Machen had an unusually strong interest in paganism, from the classical-era mystery cults to the more exotic secret magical orders of his day. In his stories, both were often viewed through the perspective of the other; his paganism was seen through a critical Christian lens, whereas his Christianity was usually referenced through ritual, mysticism, and quasi-pagan imagery such as the Holy Grail. Although he was a self-professed Christian for most of, if not all, his life, it would seem that he also had a very healthy respect for the paganism of antiquity, in both the positive and negative senses of the word.

Perhaps one reason this spiritual dialectic is so rarely acknowledged is that, to appreciate it fully, one must be familiar with the substantial legacy of a six-decade writing career (roughly 1881-1943) over a wide range of fiction and nonfiction genres. Most of his well-known horror/fantasy stories date from the 1890s, and there is little nonfiction surviving from that period to give a balancing picture of his Christian beliefs; in contrast, the bulk of his later work consists of essays, journalism, memoirs, and book introductions in which his religious ideas are often explored in repetitive detail. As his later stories often contain a pronounced spiritual dimension too, it is reasonable to conclude that he became more strongly Christian in his worldview later in life, whereas as a younger man there seemed to be considerable conflict between the religion he was brought up with and his fascination with alternative pagan and occult traditions. Within this general (and not uncommon) pattern, we can detect much subtle variation—enough to provide us with a sketch of his spiritual journey, with the proviso, of course, that this is based only upon the written evidence he chose to publish. The deeper mysteries of his spirituality have, alas, died with him.

It is easy to see whence Arthur Machen's Christianity originally came: his father was a vicar in the minor rural parish of Llanddewi Fach on the Welsh Borders. But can we also detect a source there for his equally vibrant pagan themes? Although Machen's early life was something of a rural idyll (he often declared that an early inspiration was the natural beauty of his homeland), his teenage years were blighted by poverty, as his father's living was low even compared to the typical income for a late nineteenth-century rural clergyman. At first he enjoyed the privilege of a place in the well-respected Hereford Cathedral School, but his hopes of a university education were dashed because his father could not afford the fees. So instead, Machen followed the typical path of the literary autodidact and educated himself through extensive reading. It is easy to see how his fertile, creative mind and a taste for the wilder fantasies of De Quincey, Poe, and Robert Louis Stevenson could lead him to a tendency for the exotic. Factor in the frustrations at his situation in life and the usual adolescent dilemmas, and his fascination for the occult looks increasingly like the growing pains of a sensitive literary spirit. It is perhaps significant that his first (self-)published work was *Eleusinia*, a poem about the pagan Greek mysteries.

By 1884, Machen had left Llanddewi and was living in London with the intention of fulfilling his dream of becoming a writer. As well as trying his hand at teaching and translation work, he catalogued rare occult works for the publisher George Redway, coming across many an obscure text to fire his imagination. As a result, his first major works, "The Great God Pan," "The Inmost Light," and *The Three Impostors*, were packed full of weird occult imagery and about as Decadent as they come. They certainly represent the high-water mark of his desire to shock as a horror writer in the heady world of 1890s London. In these works, the powers of darkness seem to be everywhere and even to have the upper hand. As Machen was later to comment: "Here [. . .] was my real failure; I translated awe, at worst awfulness, into evil; again, I say, one dreams in fire and works in clay" (*FOT* 123).

We do not know whether Machen was a serious, practising Christian during this period, but the strong sense of fascination/repulsion with sex, paganism, and the forbidden in "The Great God Pan" tells its own story. Is Machen subconsciously writing himself a warning here about the dangers of meddling with unknown powers? He certainly seems to revel in the transgression as a mere voyeur. Tellingly, there seems to be an obscure religious reference in the text, hidden among the classical allusions (Nelson). In Chapter 1, the character Clarke has a dream in which he receives a premonition about the results of Dr. Raymond's doomed experiment: "And in that moment, the sacrament of body and soul was dissolved, and a voice seemed to cry 'Let us go hence'" (CF 1.222). This vision can be interpreted as a reference to the story of the destruction of the Second Temple in Jerusalem as recorded by the Romano-Jewish historian Josephus. Writing circa 90 CE, he describes the Divine Presence leaving the building before the legionaries arrived with the words "We are departing hence." As Machen seems to be suggesting that Mary will literally lose her soul when the experiment is complete, he appears to be viewing the story through a Judaeo-Christian filter and intimating that the whole exercise is doomed from the start.

In the same chapter, Machen introduces one of his central lifelong themes: that everyday reality consists of "dreams and shadows that hide the real world from our eyes." It is the attempt to lift the veil and to see things as they really are that causes the dreadful consequences in the story. This may sound like some mysterious hidden knowledge, but in fact the idea comes from the very cornerstone of Western civilization: Plato, the hugely influential Athenian philosopher who spoke of a realm of ideal forms beyond space and time. He proposed that only the idea (the ideal form) was real and that the particular is only apparent. In his famous allegory of the cave (from the *Republic*, Book 7), he described mankind as being like a population of prisoners chained in a cave, seeing only shadows and thinking them to be reality; one man breaks free, leaves the cave, and sees the real world as it is, but upon his return he is rejected by the others. He has been dazzled by the light, appears to have gone mad, and is unable to convince them of what he has seen. Reading his many reformulations of Plato's idealism, I cannot help feeling that Machen, in his wilder fantasies, may well have seen himself as that strange madman trying to show the truth to his readers.

Although Machen was clearly fascinated by this ideal realm, he also believed that somehow it would be sinful for mortal man to try to lift the veil that hides it—an idea he developed most famously in the preamble to "The

White People," where he writes of "sanctity" and "sorcery" as being two opposing ideals. By sorcery, he means the use of magical or other means to penetrate the veil and to access or exploit forbidden knowledge. This idea is, of course, the main theme in "The Great God Pan" and underlies its companion story "The Inmost Light," where an unfortunate woman's soul is imprisoned in a gemstone. It is also in *The Three Impostors*: Professor Gregg should never have tried to track down the little people, and the white powder should have been left well alone.

This is clearly an obsessive theme for Machen that may well suggest his internal between the desire for "forbidden" spiritual knowledge and the morality of his religion. With his strong Christian background, Machen would surely have felt that this kind of sorcery was essentially wrong. The Bible condemns it, although many of the activities of the great prophets and holy men of Jewish tradition do appear to be like magic to modern eyes, but as they are said to be done through the power of God and his agents, they are considered lawful. Perhaps the most famous Bible story on the subject is in 1 Samuel, where the great King Saul hires the Witch of Endor to raise the spirit of the dead prophet Samuel. He wants advice on a critical battle with the Philistines, but almost predictably his transgression ends in tears. Although the Bible took a dim view of sorcery, it should be noted that the early Church did not have any such problem with Plato. As it spread the gospel from its Jewish homeland through the gentile Roman Empire, it engaged directly with classical philosophy and, far from condemning Plato, Socrates, Aristotle, and others, it acknowledged many of their insights and incorporated much of their thinking into its developing theology and ethics/morality from St. Paul onwards (Hill).

Despite the warnings in Machen's stories though, this period was also the high point of his interest in the occult, and he was sufficiently fascinated with this supposedly forbidden knowledge to become, for some time, a member of the legendary Hermetic Order of the Golden Dawn. Ever keen to mix his sanctity with a touch of sorcery, he was initiated as Frater Avallaunius in 1899, but how seriously he took these magical practices remains unclear. Like many a Freemason, he may just have been in it for the social side and professional contacts. After all, where else could a fantasy/horror writer explore the occult on equal terms with the likes of W. B. Yeats, Algernon Blackwood, and Aleister Crowley? In addition, it may have been something of a welcome distraction from the pains of nursing his first wife through her final illness. In *Things Near and Far*, he mentions that he indulged in certain magical practices after her death, of which he subsequently felt ashamed. The details are not mentioned, but he soon found the easy camaraderie of his side-career as a travelling actor with the Benson Company to be a more satisfying balm, and we can detect a move away from sorcery and back towards sanctity as the new century rolled on.

The other lifelong theme of Machen's work from the 1890s onwards was the desire to achieve a state of ecstasy in literature. Like the notion of the ideal form, it is another classical affectation (probably acquired during his private school education at Hereford) and in ancient Greek times was originally referred to as *ekstasis*: the idea of stepping outside of oneself. It originally referred to ritual activity in which, under the influence of music, drugs, and alcohol, the participants would move beyond their normal consciousness and attain a godlike state of transcendence.

As with Plato's ideal world (co-opted into Christian ideas of God's eternal word via the Jewish philosopher Philo of Alexandria), the idea of spiritual ecstasy became a central idea of Christian mysticism, associated with St. Teresa of Ávila and St. Francis of Assisi. Machen is unique in extending this idea into a metaphor for defining great literature. Whilst it is obvious that the act of reading always involves some kind of entry into another person's consciousness, most people do not feel such a complete loss of self-identity with even the most gripping page-turner: you may feel transported in some way, but that is hardly comparable to the ecstasies of St. Teresa. Still, Machen develops the idea at some length in *Hieroglyphics*, an intriguing work of literary criticism incorporating some fictional elements. His idea of ecstasy is a much more general feeling of "awe, mystery, sense of the unknown" that goes well beyond the self-transcendence of both pagan and Christian ideas of the term (H 11); however, it clearly inspired many of his greatest works of the 1890s, from the exquisite "A Fragment of Life" to his masterpiece *The Hill of Dreams*. In these stories, the direct horror element of the earlier books becomes increasingly toned down and a more mysterious note of the sublime enters the writing, which could be more conveniently described as Symbolist rather than Decadent.

A particularly interesting group of short stories from this period were later collected in *Ornaments in Jade* (1924). They betray the wide range of Machen's religious influences, from the out-and-out paganism of "Midsummer" to the Christian imagery of "The Holy Things." What is perhaps even more surprising to find is the Islamic flavour in the "The Rose Garden," a story that clearly betrays the influence of Sufism (the mystical expression of Islam) in its central metaphor and also in its invocation of the far-off domes of

"Ispahan" (CF 2.158). He seemed to return to Sufism again in "The Moth and the Flame," a later article for the *Observer* (reprinted in Wagstaffe), in which he speculates on why moths are attracted to destroy themselves in candle flames. Clearly no entomologist, he speculates from a theological point of view that the moths are drawn to annihilate themselves in God. This is not a Christian metaphor, but it is a common one in Sufism, perhaps best known in "The Moth and the Flame," a story by the Persian poet Fariduddin Attar (most easily found in Fadiman and Frager's *Essential Sufism*). I'm sure that it would not spoil the poetry of all this to point out that the primitive optics of a moth's eyes are confused by the extreme contrast between the flame and the surrounding darkness—they probably think that they are flying into a deeper darkness (perhaps the real mystery here is why natural selection has not yet weeded this out).

The medieval Jewish mysticism of the Kabbalah is another theme, often mentioned in Machen's correspondence with fellow seeker A. E. Waite and used as a central metaphor in his late stories "The Tree of Life" and "Out of the Picture" from *The Children of the Pool* (1936). He also discussed the Kabbalah approvingly in a 1929 *Bookman* review of Waite's exhaustive book on the subject, where he notes its parallels with some aspects of Christianity. It is therefore clear that Machen's religious interests were pretty broad-ranging and that despite the often dogmatic tone of many of his theological pronouncements, he clearly had at least an academic interest in the other Abrahamic religions, as well as the Christian/pagan dialectic that fuelled his art.

The first decade of the twentieth century saw Machen rebuilding his life in the wake of his first wife's death and experiencing a passionate revival of interest in his Christian faith. This is reflected in many of his essays from this period, including a whole series of religious articles for the *Academy* in 1907-08. "Ecclesia Anglicana I & II" are particularly interesting, as they reveal the intensity of his personal brand of sacramental, hierarchical, and ritualistic belief. Machen also expressed many strongly anti-Protestant views in his writings, and in a letter to his spiritual confidant A. E. Waite (from around October 1902) he actually revealed an intention to go to over to Rome (*Selected Letters* 32), although in the end he decided to remain a member of the Church of England, i.e., a Protestant (though still a "Catholic" as distinct from a "Roman Catholic").

It was also in this period that Machen wrote his first explicitly Christian fictional work, *The Secret Glory* (not published as a complete book until 1922). As a weird blend of the boarding school novel and the journey of mystical spiritual awakening, it predates J. K. Rowling's Harry Potter novels by over ninety years; but rather than coming from a long line of magicians, the protagonist turns out to be descended from a long line of guardians of the Holy Grail. Machen himself was fascinated with the Grail image, which is one of the most complex and multifaceted symbols in mediaeval literature. Although it appears to be an essentially Christian concept (dateable only to the twelfth century and usually associated with the supposed chalice of the Last Supper), it also has strong roots in pagan myth; indeed, many scholars have directly associated it with the "magic cauldron" archetype of Celtic myth (as, for example, in the "Branwen Daughter of Llyr" story from the *Mabinogion*).

Machen and A. E. Waite spent considerable time researching this topic, and in his "Secret of the Sangraal" essays Machen proposed an interesting theory that the Grail myths represent a survival in some way of the liturgy of the early Celtic Church (i.e., the original Romano-British version of Christianity that survived the pagan Anglo-Saxon invasions of the post-Roman period in Wales and Ireland and was supposedly "replaced" by Roman Catholicism after the Synod of Whitby in 664 CE). Although Machen is right to stress the essentially Christian nature of the Grail, there is little evidence to support the idea of a Dark Ages "Celtic" church being substantially different to the Roman Catholic version; indeed, it has been suggested in a thought-provoking essay by "Ignatius" (2015) that the roots of this idea actually lie in Protestant anti-Rome propaganda from the Elizabethan era.

Perhaps Machen's most intensely Christian phase was during the First World War, when his religious fervour was combined with a heartfelt patriotism. At the start of the conflict in 1914, he was making ends meet by working as a journalist at the London *Evening News*. Like many, he was caught up in the jingoistic fever and, rather than seeing it as a clash of imperial powers, he began to see it as a crusade against "German frightfulness." After news started coming through of German atrocities in Belgium, he began writing a series of short patriotic stories for the paper. One of these propaganda tales, "The Bowmen," was to become his most famous piece of fiction, helping to create the myth of the "Angels of Mons." In the face of its notoriety in portraying the ghostly bowmen of Agincourt, many overlook the fact that, with its invocation of St. George to help the English cause, it is an excellent example of Machen's religiosity in print.

As well as these patriotic potboilers, Machen also produced one of his most exquisite works in "The Great Return," published in 1915. In the story, he revisits his Holy Grail obsessions and imagines its return to spread hope and religious revival in a deadly time of war. It is a quite remarkable piece with a vivid and inspiring sense of religious transcendence. Here is the sense of ecstasy in literature he often spoke of, but in a blatantly Christian setting rather than the pagan themes of his 1890s classics. Look a bit closer, however, and the exotic ritual activity described in it is rather suggestive of the sort of thing you might encounter in a secret magical order. It certainly feels more Golden Dawn than Church of England.

Machen also produced a small book based upon a series of his *Evening News* articles called *War and the Christian Faith* (1918), which, to judge from the title (chosen by the publisher), should have been one of his most explicitly Christian works. However, instead of justifying the conflict in terms of religious doctrine, ethics, or morality as you might expect, he develops a rather rambling polemic that the brutality and horror of the war are not actually a valid argument for atheism. The original articles were probably intended to address a popular feeling along the lines of "How could a loving God allow this sort of thing?" (revived, of course, in World War II after the liberation of the Nazi concentration camps) rather than offering any specific moral or ethical justification for an English Christian to kill a German Christian over a political dispute. With that reservation, it is actually quite revealing of Machen's religious ideas and, unusually for him, it does actually mention Jesus briefly—and rather curiously—under the title "The Grand Master" rather than the more usual "Lord." This is the language of Freemasonry, or even the Golden Dawn, rather than Anglicanism, and is possibly some kind of coded reference. As with "The Great Return," Machen may well have been sending a message to the cognoscenti.

It is interesting that a reticence to discuss directly the person of Jesus Christ (usually considered an important feature of Christianity!) is absolutely typical of Machen's writing on the subject, which usually revolves around symbols and metaphors such as the Holy Grail and very rarely anything Christological. Indeed, references to core Christian beliefs such as the Nicene Creed and the doctrine of atonement are conspicuous by their rarity. It seems clear that, judging from his writings upon religion, he has very little interest in the subject of Jesus at all, but is more focused upon the idea of an infinite and transcendent God, ecstasy, and religious idealism. It would seem that his Christianity is very much of an abstracted mystical kind, but whether he is a mystical Christian or a Christian mystic is a moot point.

Whatever the details of his faith at this time, Machen found his patriotic fervour sorely tested by the horrific casualty lists of the Battle of the Somme in 1916; and by the time of *The Terror* (1917), in which the beasts of heaven and earth turn against mankind for its transgressions, there is a real sense of despair in his writing. Although an obscure story, even by Machen's standards, it anticipates Alfred Hitchcock's film *The Birds* and indeed the whole popular horror subgenre of Mother Nature turning on us.

As the war drew to a close and the 'Twenties entered a new phase of optimism, Machen's star seemed to be rising, with considerable interest in his work in America; but sadly, his new-found popularity was not matched by a new burst of creativity. Instead, he focused on nonfiction work and journalism, in much of which he continued to discuss his religious ideas in some detail. However, there was one last flowering of Machen's storytelling with his long-neglected, late tales in the collection *The Children of the Pool*, his novel *The Green Round*, and most important of all, "N," his cryptically titled late masterpiece, written as the only new story in the 1936 collection *The Cosy Room*.

For many Machen enthusiasts, "N" is one of his finest works, dealing explicitly with his favourite theme of lifting the veil to a world beyond. The story has been much admired and discussed elsewhere (for example, Howard and, in this volume, Miller), but for the purposes of this piece I would like to focus on the rich collection of unusual religious themes that stud the text. I'm sure that, like most readers of "N," I had not come across the word "perichoresis" before reading this story. It is the term used in the Eastern Greek Orthodox Church for the interpenetration and coexistence of the three hypostases of the Holy Trinity (i.e., Father, Son, and Holy Ghost). In the Western Roman Catholic tradition it is known as "circumincession" and is often visualised in the stained glass of Gothic cathedrals with a special type of rondel called a triskele.

This might seem like a pretty outré idea for a monotheistic faith, but it is central to the Nicene Creed of 325 CE, the core doctrine in all mainstream varieties of Christianity. Miller has suggested that the term also has specific occult meanings, but it seems fairly clear that Machen is using it as a Christian metaphor for the interpenetration of some kind of ecstatic realm (as represented by the story's fantastic garden of unearthly beauty) into our everyday reality. The final part of the story is actually rather chilling, in which the protagonists speculate upon whom they are sharing their reality with—a theme also explored independently by H. P. Lovecraft in his marvellous story "From Beyond" (1920).

It is also worth noting that Machen uses the Eastern rather than the Western Church term here. Benham has previously suggested that Machen "might have found a more suitable home within the jurisdiction of the Eastern Churches" (1), and he quotes Machen's reference to the iconostasis in "The Charm of Old Churches." It is interesting that in *War and the Christian Faith* Machen also quotes "the creed of St. Athanasius" (a key figure in Eastern theology and the Alexandrian defender of the Nicean Creed, but not its originator) rather than referring directly to this central tenet of Christianity itself (22). This is a nice distinction, but it seems to me that Machen is actually more inclined towards Christian mysticism (which was always more deeply embedded in the Eastern Church) than any particular attraction to its doctrines.

As an aside, in the English mystical movement of the High Middle Ages one of the key figures was Richard Rolle of Hampole. Is it a coincidence that in "N" the author of the fictional *A London Walk: Meditations in the Streets of the Metropolis* is the Revd. Thomas Hampole? Christopher Palmer remarked upon this connection in his introduction to the Duckworth *Collected Machen*; and as "Hampole" is such a rare and unusual name (it refers to the name of the obscure nunnery outside of Doncaster where Rolle was laid to rest), I am inclined to agree with him and see it as another of Machen's coded messages to fellow travellers.

It may also be significant that Machen's parallel world in "N" is far from some kind of paradise. As attractive as it may seem, it is clearly not a spiritually desirable place to be and, in the story, the Revd. Hampole is so shocked by its manifestation into his life that he experiences "a revulsion of terror." Here we are back to the idea of "sorcery and sanctity" and Machen's fascination/repulsion with the ecstatic opposition to his favoured Christianity. Although he carried on writing to his death, this tale is by far the most intense late expression of his credo.

Arthur Machen endured the Second World War stoically in the comparative safety of Amersham and died on the 15th of December 1947. Despite his great age of eighty-four, he remained fascinated with his religious quest to the end. According to Reynolds and Charlton, he still found a moment to question the origins of St. Wandragesilaus (the patron saint of Bixley in Norfolk) on his deathbed (188). The story that he converted to Roman Catholicism *in extremis* is, however, untrue: Arthur Machen remained an Anglican communicant until the very end.

So, after reviewing the evidence in Machen's writing, we are left with a picture of a man with a complex and, on the surface at least, somewhat contradictory spirituality. Although he often presented the image of being nothing more than a typical High Church Anglican and, certainly in his later years, was a regular and enthusiastic churchgoer, he was also clearly fascinated by the world of classical paganism and indeed many other areas of spirituality which would, at first glance, seem to be in conflict with his professed faith.

It should be remembered, however, that although Christianity is a monotheistic religion, it is far from the monolithic creed that some of its more zealous proponents would like us to believe. In its early development, up to the Council of Nicea in 325, it evolved from being the Jewish sect of Jesus of Nazareth's original followers to the official state religion of the Roman Empire—a process which entailed the absorption of many pagan Greek and Roman ideas from the philosophy and religious thought of late antiquity (see Wilson). The second-century Catechetical School of Alexandria, headed by the great Christian philosophers Clement and Origen, was a major catalyst in this process, and later the same city was also home to St. Athanasius, who, as already noted, was a key figure in the establishment of Trinitarian Doctrine in Nicene Christianity (Vermes). In subsequent centuries, it developed even farther from its origins in Judaism, with many competing orthodoxies and mystical traditions of its own. Viewed from this perspective, Machen's idea of Christianity as a secure framework for his extended spiritual explorations looks much more like an informed and sincere response to the complexities and contradictions of the faith of his father. As is only appropriate, let us leave the last word on this spiritual journey to Machen himself, by quoting from his conclusion to *War and the Christian Faith*:

> But as it is certain that those who make the adventure of beauty are not deluded, so it is certain that those who make the greater adventure of God are not deluded. And it is probable that this would be much clearer to many if the Faith were presented, not as a system of morals with certain supernatural sanctions, but as the supreme end of life, the key to all mysteries, the fulfilment of all desires, the quest of all quests. (61-62)

Works Cited

Benham, Patrick. "Editorial." *Avallaunius* No. 17 (1997): 1-2.

Fadiman, James, and Robert Frager. *Essential Sufism*. San Francisco: HarperSanFrancisco, 2000.

Goldstone, Adrian, and Wesley Sweetser. *A Bibliography of Arthur Machen*. Austin: University of Texas Press, 1965.

Hill, Jonathan. *The Crucible of Christianity: The Forging of a World Faith*. Oxford: Lion, 2010.

Howard, John. "Interpenetrations: Ecstasy and Boundaries in the Works of Arthur Machen." *Faunus* No. 26 (Autumn 2012): 39-48.

"Ignatius." "Arthur Machen, Anglicanism, and the Legend of the 'Celtic' Church." *Faunus* No. 31 (Spring 2015): 3-19.

The Mabinogion. Tr. Jeffrey Gantz. London: Penguin, 1976.

Machen, Arthur. "The Charm of Old Churches." *Faunus* No. 27 (Spring 2013): 3-11.

———. "Ecclesia Anglicana." 1907. *Faunus* No. 29 (Spring 2014): 50-57; No. 30 (Autumn 2014): 49-56.

———. "*The Holy Kabalah* by A. E. Waite." 1929. *Faunus* No. 31 (Spring 2015): 29-31.

———. "The Secret of the Sangraal." 1025. In *The Secret of the Sangraal.* Horam: Tartarus Press, 1995. 1-34.

———. *War and the Christian Faith.* 1918. *Avallaunius* No. 17 (1997): 20-40.

Nelson, Dale J. "Clarke's Dream in 'The Great God Pan'—Two Classical Allusions." *Avallaunius* No. 7 (1991): 19-24.

Palmer, Christopher. "Introduction" to *The Collected Machen.* London: Duckworth, 1988.

Plato. *The Republic.* Tr. H. D. P. Lee and Desmond Lee. London: Penguin, 2007.

Reynolds, Aidan, and William Charlton. *Arthur Machen: A Short Account of His Life and Work.* 1963. Oxford: Caermaen, 1988.

Vermes, Geza. *Christian Beginnings:" From Nazareth to Nicea, AD 30-325.* London: Penguin, 2012.

Wagstaffe, Nick. "The Moth and the Flame: A Discussion Provoked by Arthur Machen's Writings in the 'Observer' 1926." *Faunus* No. 29 (Spring 2014): 38-45.

Wilson, Ian. *Jesus: The Evidence.* London: Pan, 1984.

"The Abyss of All Being": "The Great God Pan" and the Death of Metaphysics

Geoffrey Reiter

At no point in his writing career did Arthur Machen ever lose his interest in exploring the distinctions between the material world and the spiritual world. This theme is the glue that binds together his work at all phases of his life. Whether concealed within the ancient misty groves of southern Wales or crouching around the corner of a dingy London alley, the supernatural world in Machen's fiction is always hidden just out of sight, waiting for a fleeting moment in which to reveal itself. "His purpose," observes Wesley Sweetser, "both as an artist and as a humanist was to discover, behind the ordinary, the extraordinary and transcendental meaning" (132). Yet these incursions of the supernatural, of "the extraordinary and transcendental," do not necessarily perform the same functions in all his stories. While no one doubts the ecstatic mysticism of his twentieth-century work, Machen biographers, critics, and scholars are less in accord about his earlier work, particularly the horror fiction of the early 1890s. And in no case is the subject less settled than in the question of how to understand the tale that is arguably Machen's most famous, his novella "The Great God Pan."

Interpretations of "The Great God Pan" are probably as numerous as its interpreters, but roughly speaking, two major camps emerge. Some believe that the book is at its heart a meditation born out of late Victorian anxieties about atheistic materialism and its implications for the human soul (or lack thereof). Others maintain that "The Great God Pan" affirms the existence of a supernatural world beyond the veil of our ordinary sensory experience, much as his later writings do, even if the emphasis here is on numinous terror rather than transcendent ecstasy.

Advocates of this latter position often invoke *Hieroglyphics*, Machen's manifesto on literature, which he wrote in 1899 and saw published in 1902.

In an oft-quoted passage, Machen asserts that the defining characteristic of literature is its ability to provoke a sense of ecstasy:

> If ecstasy be present, then I say there is fine literature, if it be absent, then, in spite of all the cleverness, all the talents, all the workmanship and observation and dexterity you may show me, then, I think, we have a product (possibly a very interesting one), which is not fine literature.
>   . . . I have chosen this word as the representative of many. Substitute, if you like, rapture, beauty, adoration, wonder, awe, mystery, sense of the unknown, desire for the unknown. All and each will convey what I mean; for some particular case one term may be more appropriate than another, but in every case there will be that withdrawal from the common life and the common consciousness which justifies my choice of "ecstasy" as the best symbol of my meaning. (H 11)

S. T. Joshi calls this work "a transparent elucidation of his own literary goals" (13). Sweetser believes that "the standards of *Hieroglyphics* represent, to a great extent, simply a rationalization of what Machen had been trying to accomplish in the field of art" (99). Glen Cavaliero too finds ecstasy to be "a tenet that underlies all Machen's more thoughtful writing in the supernaturalist vein" (76).

In these readings, "The Great God Pan" represents the dark face of a two-sided coin, while Machen's later work more or less flips it. The supernatural trappings of Machen's oeuvre from the 1890s could be just as ecstatic as his later Grail fiction, but it is an ecstasy of fear they elicit. Many critics thus posit a transcendent evil as concomitant to the supernal good manifest in the twentieth-century writings. Machen's own commentary on the text might be seen to support this understanding. In *Far Off Things* he would claim that, while exploring his native Welsh countryside in his youth, "I saw the lonely house between the dark forest and the silver river, and years after I wrote 'The Great God Pan,' an endeavor to pass on the vague, indefinable sense of awe and mystery and terror that I had received" (*FOT* 19–20). In the same text, with the customarily self-effacing tone he often adopts when analyzing his own work, he identifies "The Great God Pan" as an unsuccessful experiment. Rather than effectively capturing "the awe and solemnity and mystery of the valley of Usk, and of the house called Bartholly hanging solitary between the deep forest and the winding esses of the river," he "transliterated it, clumsily enough, in the story of 'The Great God Pan,' which as a friendly critic once said, 'does at least make one believe in the devil, if it does nothing else.' Here, of course, was my real failure; I translated awe, at worst awfulness, into evil" (*FOT* 123).

Following his lead, many Machen critics and aficionados identify "The Great God Pan" as a fine exposition of evil. For Jill Tedford Owens, "Machen resurrected Pan to embody ... evil" (120), an evil that "is terrible ... a primordial, transcendental evil which lurks beneath the exterior of material reality" (119-20). In his preface to the Penguin Classics edition of Machen's works, filmmaker Guillermo del Toro follows a similar track, asserting that "In 'The Great God Pan' ... [e]vil is never dormant—it gestates.... And no matter how wicked or perverse we can be, somewhere in a long forgotten realm a mad God awaits, leering—and ready to embrace us all" (ix). Interpreters in this vein appear to be suggesting that the supernatural elements in Machen's work from the early 1890s exist not only as a plot device in a quasi-Gothic work of fiction but as an outworking of the same belief in the transcendent that so readily characterizes his later work (fictional or otherwise). As the Ambrose Meyrick of Machen's "The White People" will later explain, the world has room for both "[s]orcery and sanctity," true evil and true good, and "[e]ach is an ecstasy" (CF 2.185).

Yet ultimately, as some other critics have recognized, the portrayal of Machen as a mystic who opposes science and materialism at all costs fits quite poorly with many of his best-known works. In "The Great God Pan" and other works from the first phase of Machen's mature writing, the early 1890s, hidden realms and spiritual worlds are sites of abject terror. This terror might be labelled "ecstasy" for convenience's sake (though Machen never uses the term in "The Great God Pan"), but it is hardly indicative of any philosophical mysticism. Indeed, it would appear to spring from a rejection (perhaps reluctant?) of the supernatural, which may be why many later devotees of weird fiction would love his early horrors so much—they are not the work of a Christian author with a belief system buttressed by an eschatological hope, but rather of a skeptic who views the unknown with horror instead of wonder. This denial of a mystic and meaningful cosmos can be seen in many aspects of the work, most creatively in Machen's repeated allusion to the seventeenth-century writers known as the Metaphysical poets.

In a letter written on October 1, 1899, to the French writer Paul-Jean Toulet, who translated "The Great God Pan" into French, Machen explained:

> Je ne sais vous si êtes mystique. J'ai toujours été catholique (anglican, pas romain), et un catholique est naturellement attaché au mysticisme et tant que système. Mais j'avoue que je n'avais que des préoccupations artistiques quand j'écrivis Pan et la *Poudre Blanche* (dans les *Trois Imposteurs*). Alors je n'aurais pu croire un instant que d'aussi étranges événements fussent jamais arrivés dans

la vie réelle ou meme aient jamais été susceptibles de s'y produire. Mais depuis, et tous récemment, il s'est produit dans ma propre existence des *expériences* qui ont tout à fait changé mon point de vue à ce sujet. Je ne dis pas évidemment que toutes les circonstances de la *Poudre Blanche* se soient produites en réalité comme je les ai racontées, mais je les crois désormais très possible. Je suis tout à fait convaincu même qu'il n'y a rien d'impossible sur terre. J'ai à peine besoin d'ajouter, je suppose, qu'aucune des *expériences* que j'ai faites n'a de rapports avec de telles impostures que le Spiritualisme et la Théosophie. Mais je crois que nous vivons dans un monde de grands mystères, de choses insoupçonnées et tout à fait stupéfiantes. (Martineau 53-54; emphasis in original)

This letter reveals several important points about the development of Machen's thought. First, it shows that at the time he wrote "The Great God Pan" and *The Three Impostors* he was a skeptic. While Machen admits his lifelong Anglicanism ("J'ai toujours été catholique"), this comes across as a peripheral matter at best, an inheritance from his father rather than an active system of belief. He was mystic only insofar as any High Churchman would be mystic, and he apparently rejected the supernatural: "Alors je n'aurais pu croire un instant que d'aussi étranges événements fussent jamais arrivés dans la vie réelle ou meme aient jamais été susceptibles de s'y produire." Here Machen appears to be talking about the supernatural in general, and not the kind of horrific events of his earlier novels.[1] In other words, Machen is writing this letter from a time of belief (late 1899) reflecting on a time of unbelief (1890-95).

---

1. Reynolds and Charlton point out that Machen would later encounter people resembling the more fanciful characters of *The Three Impostors* (72), members of the Order of the Golden Dawn. Machen discusses these events in *Things Near and Far*, and the letter might have those encounters partly in mind, but he is also clearly making a more substantial claim. Indeed, Machen's account in *Things Near and Far* suggests that his dealings with the Order were an effect, rather than a cause, of these "strange events": "I must say that I did not seek the Order merely in quest of odd entertainment. As I have stated in the chapter before this, I had experienced strange things—they still appear to me strange—of body, mind and spirit, and I supposed that the Order, dimly heard of, might give me some light and guidance and leading on these matters. But, as I have noted, I was mistaken" (*TNF* 152-53). Machen discusses the "strange things" in the ninth chapter of *Things Near and Far*, which is where he describes the mysterious process he used to alleviate the pain of his wife Amy's death, "a more raging pain than that of any toothache" (132). Even then, however, this mystical process appears to be but one of many ways in which he found "the world . . . presented to me at a new angle" (*TNF* 122).

This is a highly significant fact that few scholars have sufficiently recognized: despite his interest in occult subjects and his religious upbringing, at the beginning of the *fin de siècle* Machen was, for all intents and purposes, an agnostic, at least in regard to mysticism and the supernatural. He did not believe encroachments from other worlds into our own were possible, if any such other worlds even existed. Such a revelation leads to another question: if indeed Machen did not believe in the supernatural, why did he write about it so much? What does it represent in his earliest works of weird fiction? The answer to these questions lies in a close reading of the way in which the supernatural functions in Machen's earliest horrors such as "The Great God Pan"—as a symbolic representation of the psychic consequences that the doubts of materialist skepticism can have on the human person.

The crux of the tale, so shocking to late Victorian audiences, lies in what to make of its eponymous symbol, the god Pan. To Raymond, at least initially, Pan clearly represents some form of sublime reception of a trans-materialistic world. It is a form of alchemical scientific Platonism in which the substances of this world

> are but dreams and shadows: the shadows that hide the real world from our eyes. There *is* a real world, but it is beyond this glamour and this vision, beyond these "chases in Arras, dreams in a career," beyond them all as beyond a veil. I do not know whether any human being has ever lifted that veil; but I do know, Clarke, that you and I shall see it lifted this very night from before another's eyes. You may think this all strange nonsense; it may be strange, but it is true, and the ancients knew what lifting the veil means. They called it seeing the god Pan. (CF 1.218)

Raymond, though a scientist, speaks in purely metaphysical terms here. His comparison of the material world to shadows corresponds to Plato's allegory of the cave. His quotation derives from "Dotage," by the Metaphysical poet George Herbert, for whom this life is filled with transient pleasures only:

> False-glozing pleasures, casks of happiness,
> Foolish night-fires, women's and children's wishes,
> Chases in arras, gilded emptiness,
> Shadows well mounted, dreams in a career,
> Embroidered lies, nothing between two dishes;
> These are the pleasures here. (Martz 151)

Herbert laments that most people are "brute beasts" (152) who choose such pleasures of

> a loathsome den
> Before a Court, ev'n that above so clear,
> Where are no sorrows, but delights more true
> Than miseries are here! (152)

Raymond, like George Herbert, is looking for a world which makes the mundane material world pale in comparison. For Herbert, of course, the Platonistic yearning is fused to the Christian conception of heaven. Raymond, adopting the Greek symbol of Pan and referring to his temple acolytes, keeps the imagery purely pagan. Both writers, however, envision a realm exponentially grander than the physical realm, and both long to experience it.

Yet even from the start, there are clearly problems with Raymond's pursuit of his ideal spiritual world. His utilitarian treatment of Mary, for instance, reveals that his interests are by no means purely altruistic. And even in his own superlative claims, his project begins to appear rather suspect. The final result of Raymond's experience is not transcendent glory but abject horror, and Mary's reaction represents a consummate weird fiction moment:

> Suddenly, as they watched, they heard a long-drawn sigh, and suddenly did the colour that had vanished return to the girl's cheeks, and suddenly her eyes opened. Clarke quailed before them. They shone with an awful light, looking far away, and a great wonder fell upon her face, and her hands stretched out as if to touch what was invisible; but in an instant the wonder faded, and gave place to the most awful terror. The muscles of her face were hideously convulsed, she shook from head to foot; the soul seemed struggling and shuddering within the house of flesh. It was a horrible sight, and Clarke rushed forward, as she fell shrieking to the floor. (CF 1.223-24)

Even after this horrific occurrence, Raymond cannot accept failure: "'Yes,' said the doctor [to Clarke], still quite cool, 'it is a great pity; she is a hopeless idiot. However, it could not be helped; and, after all, she has seen the Great God Pan'" (CF 1.224).

The results of the experiment, and Dr. Raymond's initial reaction to those results, suggest a profound angst in the face of late Victorian science. As a scientist, Raymond appears oblivious to the metaphysical consequences of his experiments. Not only does he refuse to believe that his experiment could undermine a stable conception of the spiritual world, he actually believes his work will *unite* the physical world and the spiritual world. The initial ambiguity of his project allows him to interpret the results favorably—Mary has indeed "seen the Great God Pan." Yet he is only able to draw this conclusion by ignoring the actual evidence, the convulsions and cries and "awful terror." Mary cannot tell him what she has experienced, so he assumes that he has succeeded in bridging the gulf between the realm of matter and the realm of spirit. Even if he has succeeded, however, the spiritual realm to which he has connected is not the glorious world he might have been expecting.

A close examination of "The Great God Pan" reveals that the Pan symbol may reflect something that was even more disturbing to the *fin-de-siècle* mind than transcendent evil—namely, nothing. Specifically, the book's imagery represents the ways in which materialist science has stripped away the spiritual world entirely, leaving only the material world and, beyond that, the entire annihilation of consciousness and existence. It is this fear that animates "The Great God Pan" and drives its terror. Men like Raymond may have hoped that science could shed new light on spiritual dimensions, but instead their work results only in a frightening betrayal, the revelation that there are no such dimensions. As Sage Leslie-McCarthy points out, "Raymond's assumption that understanding the other world could be a matter of simple surgery demonstrates a materialistic worldview that denies the essence of the very spiritual world he is attempting to connect with" (39).

Fears about the ramifications of such a materialistic cosmos found their apex (or perhaps their nadir) in the late Victorian obsession with degeneration, the dread that the evolutionary process might turn "backward" and result in a devolution. Many critics have observed that "The Great God Pan," as well as several other works in Machen's oeuvre of the 1890s, broaches the theme of degeneration—though not all interpreters agree on this point. The key lies in how readers understand Helen Vaughan's "suicide." Is it a hyperbolized depiction of degeneration as Victorians understood the notion, or is her dissolution drawn instead from earlier sources? Charlton and Reynolds long ago noted that Machen is likely appropriating the language of the seventeenth-century alchemist Thomas Vaughan in his descriptions (46). Jake Poller further contends that this scene derives perhaps exclusively from Vaughan and alchemical speculation; he castigates critics like Adrian Eckersley and Susan J. Navarette for "committing an error that infuriated Machen, namely rationalizing the supernatural and explaining it in terms of pseudo-science" ("Theme" 26).

Yet surely this is a false dichotomy. No one at this point can doubt that Machen's depiction was heavily influenced by Thomas Vaughan, a fellow Welshman whose works he had read. Helen's name derives (in part) from this connection, and in her death she does travel backward along the chain of being toward the "Horrible Inexpressible *Darknesse*" that Vaughan describes in his work *Lumen de Lumine* (328). But even if Poller is correct in asserting that Machen was little aware of writers cited by Eckersley and Navarette, fears of degeneration were so pervasive by the time Machen moved to London that he could scarcely have avoided knowledge of them and the implications of materialist evolutionary biology on the understanding of human development. In her book *The Gothic Body*, Kelly Hurley observes just how much *fin-de-siècle* writers in the Gothic mode wedded their preternatural horrors to the scientific currents (and anxieties) of the age. The resulting emphasis on the "abhuman" (a term Hurley derives from weird fiction writer William Hope Hodgson) can be seen in the renaissance of Gothicism in the 1880s and '90s.

Whatever occultic influences Machen may have derived from Thomas Vaughan, it seems unlikely to be a coincidence that "The Great God Pan" appeared in the same time as other works so horrifically drawing out the unsettling scientific implications of the human subject's biological instability. Machen need not have read theoreticians like Morel, Lombroso, or Nordau to have known about degeneration; he could easily enough have derived it second-hand from fellow horror practitioners such as Robert Louis Stevenson (whom no one discounts as one of Machen's influences). In her book, Hurley examines Helen Vaughan's dissolution in the light of T. H. Huxley's 1868 essay "On the Physical Basis of Life." "To be a Thing," she observes, "is to inhabit a body having no recognizable or definite form, but it is unmistakably to inhabit a *material* body. . . . Within a materialist reality, there are nothing but Things: matter subjected, provisionally, to the contingency of forms" (31). Poller too acknowledges Huxley's work, maintaining that Helen's transformation into protoplasm is an attack on "the scientising of the supernatural" (27). But this need be no contradiction to degeneration readings. Vaughan's "First Matter," his "Horrible Inexpressible *Darknesse*," his "*Tenebræ Activæ*" can, by his own admission, also be identified as "*Nihil* or *Nothing*" (328-29). As C. S. Lewis pointed out some time ago, there was little distinction to be made in the Renaissance between alchemists (like Vaughan) and scientists (75-79). So Machen's account of Helen's death can be seen to invoke both seventeenth-century alchemy and nineteenth-century science. And while Vaughan's understanding differs in key ways from *fin-de-siècle* materialist degeneration beliefs, in some sense anyway they both end in *nothing*.

In distinguishing between these two approaches, a critical question emerges: does Machen truly *believe* in Vaughan's first matter, or indeed in malevolent supernatural intrusion at all? We may not know for certain, but his statements to Toulet suggest otherwise, as does the strong tendency of his

1890s horrors to reduce the apparent spiritual component of humans into raw material forms. This tendency finds its apex in the companion piece to "The Great God Pan," "The Inmost Light," in which Agnes Black's soul *literally* becomes matter, "a cinder, black and crumbling to the touch" (CF 1.327). In "The Great God Pan," then, as Hurley observes, what makes Helen so terrifying is not only that she—a seemingly human woman—is in actuality a Thing, but that she is so little different from anyone else. All humans, materialistically speaking, are Things in the same way she is, and the path she travels backward is the one that we have traveled forward.

Read this way, Machen is thus portraying a world in which science has destroyed the soul, physics has devoured metaphysics. One of the primary ways Machen dramatizes this conflict is in his characters' names. The seemingly generic name Helen Vaughan is in fact one of Machen's most brilliant creations. As Adrian Eckserley notes, she is given "a good pagan name" to contrast the "good Christian name" of her mother Mary ("Panic" 70). From the start, then, Machen is already implying a degeneration from the high-minded spiritual world of Christianity to pagan Greece, not the philosophical paganism of Plato or Aristotle but the bacchic polytheism of Pan-worship, beneath which lies raw nature stripped of any religious sensibility. One might also see the abysmal traces of "hell" in her name—"hell in Vaughan." Her surname, of course, derives in part from Thomas Vaughan. Yet it is also the surname of Thomas Vaughan's brother, Henry the Silurist, who would write so memorably in "The World," "I saw Eternity the other night / Like a great *Ring* of pure and endless light" (Martz 324). Like his spiritual and literary model George Herbert, Henry Vaughan sought out a Christian Platonic heaven. Herbert's unsaved men in "Dotage" are "brute beasts" who chase "Shadows well mounted," and Vaughan shares with Herbert a frustration for such people:

> O fools (said I) thus to prefer dark night
>   Before true light!
> To live in grots and caves, and hate the day
>   Because it shows the way,
> The way, which from this dead and dark abode
>   Leads up to God . . . (325)

Such high-minded aspirations have no fulfillment in "The Great God Pan." Thomas Vaughan's own researches into dark "First Matter" were, to his mind, part of a grander plan to understand the subtle forces of the world as God had created them and then to manipulate those forces toward a Neoplatonic ascent to greater perfection. His brother Henry expresses such desires imagistically in Metaphysical poems like "The World," "The Retreat," "Resurrection and Immortality," or countless others. But such transcendence is nowhere to be found in the dark, fragmented climax of Machen's work; instead, the reader (like Dr. Matheson, who narrates Helen's death) is left only with darkness, with abyss . . . with *nothing*.

Machen's penchant for naming characters in "The Great God Pan" after Metaphysical poets may seem singularly out of place, yet it is an important aspect of the novella. The term "Metaphysical poets" is retroactively applied to a group of English poets writing from the late Elizabethan period through the Restoration, among the most famous being John Donne, George Herbert, and Andrew Marvell. The term was first used by Samuel Johnson[2] in the first volume of his *Lives of the English Poets* (1779-81) during his discussion of Abraham Cowley, in which Johnson asserts, "The metaphysical poets were men of learning, and to show their learning was their whole endeavour" (200). Johnson criticizes the Metaphysicals because, in their effort to show off their wit, their poetry and ideals become inventive rather than imitative. T. S. Eliot would later help resuscitate their reputation for those very reasons. As Metaphysical poets, they sought not only to display their learning and ingenuity, but also to explore the tensions of human existence and the nature of the world—the intellectual domain of metaphysics, the philosophical examination of reality.

While Machen wrote "The Great God Pan" several decades prior to the revival of interest in Metaphysical poetry, he was certainly familiar with their work and likely knew of the term. He frequently quoted Samuel Johnson and even portrayed him as an actor. And the term, though infrequent, was in use at the *fin de siècle*: the 1890 edition of *Encyclopaedia Britannica* specifically applies it to Henry Vaughan, listing him in the company of the other two Metaphysicals to whom Machen alludes, Richard Crashaw and George Herbert (115-16). Yet the Metaphysicals fare poorly in Machen's little book. Machen quotes George Herbert's "Dotage" early on, but it is from the mouth of the deluded Dr. Raymond. Later, a character named Herbert marries Helen, only to find his life brought to utter ruin. He finally dies, and his "life was all a tragedy, and a tragedy of a stranger sort than they put on the boards" (CF 1.240). Another individual who meets a similar fate is named Crashaw. This

---

2. Johnson here is likely alluding to an earlier comment by John Dryden (Gardner 15).

name no doubt refers to the Roman Catholic Metaphysical poet Richard Crashaw. Like George Herbert and Henry Vaughan (and unlike some other Metaphysicals), Crashaw was devoutly religious. Like Vaughan, he was heavily influenced by Herbert, and the title and content of his poetry collection *Steps to the Temple* is a direct reference to Herbert's own posthumous volume *The Temple*. His work often alludes to Christian mystics, as in his depiction of Teresa of Ávila in "The Flaming Heart," and according to one recent critic, "His poetry amounts to the most sustained endeavor among English poets to render—and by rendering stimulate—ecstasy" (Rambuss xxii). In Machen's tale, Crashaw commits suicide after visiting Helen, his face "an infernal medley of passions" and "a devil's face" (CF 1.255). And then, of course, there are the references to Vaughan—Thomas, certainly, but also doubtless Henry, who hailed from the same Welsh region as Machen himself and who furnishes the degenerate Helen with her surname. By the book's end, a character named for *one* Metaphysical poet has lured two others into annihilation before joining them herself. All told, "The Great God Pan" racks up some substantial Metaphysical carnage in its few pages.

The motivation behind Machen's naming is appallingly simple: "The Great God Pan" is narrating the death of metaphysics. Of course, a materialistic worldview is not intrinsically opposed to the field of metaphysics; on the contrary, many atheist philosophers (in the nineteenth century and afterwards) develop quite intricate metaphysical systems. But at the heart of metaphysics lies a search for unity, for a coherent, organized understanding of reality. Writing at about the time "The Great God Pan" was published, the British idealist philosopher F. H. Bradley defined metaphysics as "an attempt to know reality as against mere appearance, or the study of first principles or ultimate truths, or again the effort to comprehend the universe, not simply piecemeal or by fragments, but somehow as a whole" (1). The world of "The Great God Pan" is inimical to such a definition of metaphysics. It is a piecemeal book from varied perspectives whose last chapter is aptly titled "The Fragments." There is no fundamental reality beneath Helen's transformations, only dissolution and darkness. Christine Ferguson has observed that many Victorians opposed the scientific positivism of their day for fear "that antimetaphysical zeal might eliminate morality and produce social disintegration.... A science absolved of its obligation to metaphysics must become dehumanized, for the idea of the person ... as a vessel for a soul is profoundly metaphysical" (468-69). In Ferguson's reading, Helen Vaughan becomes the decadent embodiment of scientific positivism taken to its farthest measure, and her "metamorphic flight from a stable order of meaning represents the ultimate fulfillment of decadent experimentalism" (476). In other words, *fin-de-siècle* science culminates in a collapse of metaphysics, "a stable order of meaning."

The character of Villiers problematizes this reading somewhat in his discussion of the Pan symbol. He tells his friend Austin,

> We know what happened to those who chanced to meet the Great God Pan, and those who are wise know that all symbols are symbols of something, not of nothing. It was, indeed, an exquisite symbol beneath which men long ago veiled their knowledge of the most awful, most secret forces which lie at the heart of all things; forces before which the souls of men must wither and die and blacken, as their bodies blacken under the electric current. Such forces cannot be named, cannot be spoken, cannot be imagined except under a veil and a symbol, a symbol to the most of us appearing a quaint, poetic fancy, to some a foolish tale. But you and I, at all events, have known something of the terror that may dwell in the secret place of life, manifested under human flesh; that which is without form taking to itself a form. (CF 1.260)

If indeed, as Villiers says, "all symbols are symbols of something, not nothing," how can Pan represent the nothingness of a materialistic worldview in the text? It is first worth noting a possible irony that might subvert this assertion from the start. For while there was no *Metaphysical* poet named Villiers, there *was* a seventeenth-century poet by that name: George Villiers, Second Duke of Buckingham. This Villiers was more of a satirist and playwright, but among his more comic performances is a brief work entitled "Upon Nothing." His end is ultimately to ridicule such "nothings" as "French truth" and "Kings promises" and "whores vows" (149). But he begins by describing his subject matter in this way:

> Nothing, thou elder-brother, even to shade,
> Who hadst a being ere the world was made,
> And well fixt alone, of ending not Afraid.
>
> Ere time and place were, time and place were not,
> When primitive nothing something straight begat;
> Then all proceeded from the great united what! (147)

While Machen was unquestionably familiar with Herbert, Crashaw, and Henry Vaughan, his knowledge of the more obscure Duke of Buckingham is less certain. Moreover, recent scholars maintain that this particular poem was actually the sole product of John Wilmot, Earl of Rochester (Hume and Love

329). But the attribution of this work to Buckingham was commonplace in Machen's day: Katherine Thomson and John Cockburn Thomson, in their well-regarded book *The Wits and Beaux of Society*—published in 1860 but readily in print in the 1890s—levied the "atheistic" poem as evidence of Buckingham's religious "inconsistency" (Wharton 32).[3] So it is intriguing that he would choose to provide a name for the *de facto* protagonist and spokesperson in his tale, an evident *flâneur*,[4] that matched a decidedly non-Metaphysical and aloof poet, a poet who actually wrote an ode (however satirical) to Nothing![5]

The *textual* answer to Villiers's assertion about the nature of symbols, however, lies in following Machen's Chinese box usage of symbolism.[6] In his book, characters often attempt to articulate what exactly Pan signifies, but they are never able to do so with any clarity. Raymond initially believes the experience will be a positive, transcendent one for Mary, proclaiming that he "will level utterly the solid wall of sense, and probably, for the first time since man was made, a spirit will gaze on a spirit-world" (CF 1.220). What this means, however, he cannot tell: "I can complete the communication between this world of sense and—we shall be able to finish the sentence later on" (CF 1.220). By the end of the book, Raymond regrets his actions but believes he has succeeded, writing to Clarke,

> What I said Mary would see, she saw, but I forgot that no human eyes could look on such a vision with impunity. And I forgot, as I have just said, that when the house of life is thus thrown open, there may enter in that for which we have no name, and human flesh may become the veil of a horror one dare not express. I played with energies which I did not understand, and you have seen the ending of it. (CF 1.268)

Raymond's claim to have "forgotten" such terrors is weak, especially given his own admission that he was "playing with energies which [he] did not

---

3. Katherine Thomson and her son John Cockburn Thomson wrote the book under the pseudonyms Grace and Philip Wharton.

4. For more discussion on the Villiers character as *flâneur*, see Leslie-McCarthy.

5. The first word in his play *The Restoration*, and also the first word in the second volume of his 1775 *Works* (the volume in which "Upon Nothing" appears) is, in fact, also "NOTHING" (3).

6. Machen himself uses the metaphor of Chinese boxes in "The Great God Pan" when Villiers ruminates, "A case like this is like a nest of Chinese boxes; you open one after another and find a quainter workmanship in every box" (CF 1.234).

understand." His assertion that Mary saw what he said she would can only be accurate if he is using the same symbol—Pan—to represent two different things: a positive life energy principle (his first definition) and a negative energy principle (his second definition).

The second interpretation of the Pan symbol quickly becomes the dominant one in the story. It is Villiers's interpretation—"the terror that may dwell in the secret place of life"—and Raymond's later interpretation—"a horror one dare not express." It is also Clarke's interpretation. Notwithstanding his "Memoirs to Prove the Existence of the Devil," Clarke grows increasingly terrified as the events of the story unfold. At the end, he writes to Raymond about walking by Helen's old house in a small Welsh town: "I looked over the meadow where once had stood the older temple of the 'God of the Deeps,' and saw a house gleaming in the sunlight. It was the house where Helen had lived" (CF 1.265). Clarke sees elsewhere in the town a pillar whose Latin inscription may be translated, "To the great god Nodens (the god of the Great Deep or Abyss), Flavius Senilis has erected this pillar on account of the marriage which he saw beneath the shade" (CF 1.267). Nodens, an obscure British god, is here implicitly associated with Pan.[7] The "marriage . . . beneath the shade" hints at an encounter with "Pan," much like Mary's. And the language of the passage mirrors the language Machen uses in the first chapter, when Clarke witnesses the experiment. In the midst of Raymond's bizarre fusion of Victorian science and ancient paganism, the smells in the air put Clarke into a trance-like state, where he recalls a walk he took many years prior. At first he encounters only the beauties of nature, but then,

> Clarke, in the deep folds of dream, was conscious that the path from his father's house had led him into an undiscovered country, and he was wondering at the strangeness of it all, when suddenly, in place of the hum and murmur of the summer, an infinite silence seemed to fall on all things, and the wood was hushed, and for a moment in time he stood face to face there with a presence, that was neither man nor beast, neither the living nor the dead, but all things mingled, the form of all things but devoid of all form. And in that moment, the sacrament of body and soul was dissolved, and a

---

7. The actual nature of the god Nodens remains confusing. He has been identified as a variant of other Celtic gods or heroes and has been linked to Roman gods such as Mars or Neptune. As Valerie J. Hutchinson has noted, however, symbological connections do exist between Nodens and Bacchus (15, 431), and thus Machen's implicit identification of Nodens and Pan is not wholly imaginative.

voice seemed to cry "Let us go hence," and then the darkness of darkness beyond the stars, the darkness of everlasting. (CF 1.222)

In this early vision, the being "neither man nor beast" who is "the form of *all things* but devoid of all form" is clearly Pan, who is depicted as a cross between human and animal and whose name, literally, means "all things." In his vision, Clarke is in "cool shaded places, deep in the green depths" (CF 1.222), a description which is echoed by the pillar inscription to "the god of the Great Deep . . . on account of the marriage . . . beneath the shade" (CF 1.267).

Yet once again, in Clarke's dream, we can see the progressive stripping away of symbols and meanings and metaphysics, until at last nothing at all remains. The path Clarke follows begins in "his father's house" (CF 1.222), which at least connotes safety and civilization, and may more specifically indicate church or the traditional Christian faith. But the path leads "to an undiscovered country" (CF 1.222), an allusion to Hamlet's famous "To be or not to be" monologue.[8] In Shakespeare,

> that dread of something after death,
> The undiscovered country, from whose bourn
> No traveller returns, puzzles the will,
> And makes us rather bear those ills we have
> Than fly to others that we know not of . . . (3.1.79-83)

As Hamlet fears what might lie beyond death, "the undiscovered country," so in "The Great God Pan" Clarke's path leads him from the safe confines of his ancestral faith into a world of deeper and darker knowledge. Beneath civilized Christianity, he first finds nature, beautiful and enchanting. But farther in, that nature grows darker, until he is in the silent realm of the Pan-symbol. And Pan's voice beckons him to follow to the ultimate depths, "the darkness of darkness beyond the stars, the darkness of everlasting."

This darkness is deeper than any hell or any mystery religion. This is the darkness of a cosmos without metaphysics. Villiers is both right and wrong when he asserts that "all symbols are symbols of something, not of nothing." The Great God Pan is used by its characters to represent something unspeakable and transcendent. Initially, in Raymond's mind, this transcendence is a positive spiritual force, but it is ultimately revealed to be transcendent evil.

---

8. Shakespeare is not traditionally reckoned as a Metaphysical poet. However, he lived around the same time as the earliest such poets, and certainly Hamlet's musings here touch on questions of metaphysics.

And yet, what exactly is meant by this transcendent evil force? Is Machen really positing a sort of maltheism or dark Satanism, in which spiritual evil exists without a countervailing spiritual good? Jill Tedford Owens seems to think so, asserting that "Machen resurrected Pan to embody ... evil" (120). In making her case, Owens cites Patricia Merivale's sweeping examination of Pan literature in which Merivale condemns Machen for playing fast and loose with the symbol: while appreciating the innovation of a horrific Pan figure, she, unlike Owens, believes that "Machen did not make the best of the material" (166) by "leaving out the hoofs and the murky odour" (167). Owens believes that despite "vagueness in his description of Pan," Machen's use of the symbol is ultimately "concrete" (120), while Merivale wants the malevolent god to have a more active incarnation. Either way, *too* complete an incarnation would be inappropriate for Machen's purposes, as his own comments, and the story itself, indicate. "Evil" in the world of "The Great God Pan" is not any religious formulation of devil, god, or devil-god, but rather an encounter with something more horrifying than the devil himself—a world without the devil, without God, without anything beneath the tapestry of nature.

This is the pure cosmic horror that lies at the core of so many of the best weird tales. Machen would eventually claim a mystical version of the Christian religion and assert that literature at its purest represented a quest to effect ecstasy. The germs of those inclinations are doubtless present even in works like "The Great God Pan." But the underlying dread of Helen Vaughan's universe lies not in the disclosure that she is *evil*, for a sublime evil could suggest the existence of a concomitant supernal good. Machen may not have been *happy* about skepticism or scientific materialism, but he seems in the early 1890s to have been caught up in the midst of it and, in his fiction, teased out its implications vividly. The reason H. P. Lovecraft would be so enamored of Arthur Machen's "The Great God Pan," why he would praise its "cumulative suspense and ultimate horror" (63) and later draw so heavily upon it in works like "The Dunwich Horror," is that its terrors arise from a similar source as his own. It is the fear of an empty cosmos indifferent to human existence. The Machen who wrote this tale knew well the horror of an anti-metaphysical reality; he had the soul of a mystic but the mind of an atheist, one who could not bear the possibility that there might be nothing beyond "the abyss of all being."

Works Cited

Bradley, F. H. *Appearance and Reality: A Metaphysical Essay.* London: Sonnenschein, 1893.

Buckingham, George Villiers, Duke of. *Plays, Poems, and Miscellaneous Writings Associated with George Villiers, Second Duke of Buckingham.* Ed. Robert D. Hume and Harold Love. Vol. 2. Oxford: Oxford University Press, 2007.

Cavaliero, Glen. *The Supernatural and English Fiction.* Oxford: Oxford University Press, 1995.

del Toro, Guillermo. "Foreword: The Ecstasy of St. Arthur." In Machen's *The White People and Other Weird Stories.* New York: Penguin, 2011. vii-ix.

Eckersley, Adrian. "The Panic God." *Wormwood* No. 3 (Autumn 2004): 63-75.

———. "A Theme in the Early Work of Arthur Machen: 'Degeneration.'" *English Literature in Transition* 35 (1992): 277-87.

Encyclopaedia Britannica. Vol. 24. New York: Henry G. Allen, 1890.

Ferguson, Christine. "Decadence as Scientific Fulfillment." *PMLA* 117 (2002): 465-78.

Gardner, Helen. "Introduction" to *The Metaphysical Poets.* 1957. 2nd rev. ed. Harmondsworth, UK: Penguin, 1972. 15-29.

Hurley, Kelly. *The Gothic Body: Sexuality, Materialism, and Degeneration at the Fin de Siècle.* Cambridge: Cambridge University Press, 1996.

Hutchinson, Valerie J. *Bacchus in Roman Britain: The Evidence for His Cult.* B.A.R. British Series 151. Oxford: B.A.R., 1986. 2 vols.

Johnson, Samuel. *The Lives of the Most Eminent English Poets; with Critical Observations on Their Works.* Vol. 1. Ed. Roger Lonsdale. Oxford: Clarendon Press, 2006.

Joshi, S. T. *The Weird Tale.* Austin: University of Texas Press, 1990.

Leslie-McCarthy, Sage. "Chance Encounters: The Detective as 'Expert' in Arthur Machen's 'The Great God Pan'." *Australasian Victorian Studies Journal* 13, No. 1 (2008): 35-45.

Lewis, C. S. *The Abolition of Man.* 1944. New York: Harper, 2015.

Lovecraft, H. P. *The Annotated Supernatural Horror in Literature.* Ed. S. T. Joshi. New York: Hippocampus, 2000.

Martineau, Henri. "Arthur Machen et P. J. Toulet: Une Correspondence Inédite." *Mercure de France* 281 (1 January 1938): 47-61.

Martz, Louis, ed. *George Herbert and Henry Vaughan*. Oxford: Oxford University Press, 1986.

Merivale, Patricia. *Pan the Goat-God: His Myth in Modern Times*. Cambridge, MA: Harvard University Press, 1969.

Navarette, Susan J. *The Shape of Fear: Horror and the Fin de Siècle Culture of Decadence*. Lexington: University Press of Kentucky, 1998.

Owens, Jill Tedford. "Arthur Machen's Supernaturalism: The Decadent Variety." *University of Mississippi Studies in English* 8 (1990): 117-26.

Poller, Jake. "The Transmutations of Arthur Machen: Alchemy in 'The Great God Pan' and *The Three Impostors*." *Literature and Theology* 29, No. 1 (March 2015): 18-32.

Rambuss, Richard, ed. *The English Poems of Richard Crashaw*. Minneapolis: University of Minnesota Press, 2013.

Reynolds, Aidan, and William Charlton. *Arthur Machen: A Short Account of His Life and Work*. London: John Baker, 1963.

Shakespeare, William. *Hamlet*. Ed. G. R. Hibbard. Oxford: Oxford University Press, 1994.

Sweetser, Wesley D. *Arthur Machen*. New York: Twayne, 1964.

Vaughan, Thomas. *The Works of Thomas Vaughan*. Ed. Alan Rudrum with Jennifer Drake-Brockman. Oxford: Clarendon Press, 1984.

Wharton, Grace and Philip. *The Wits and Beaux of Society*. Vol. 1. London: James Hogg, 1860.

Arthur Machen and King Arthur, Sovereigns of Dream: A Personal Interpretation

Donald Sidney-Fryer

Dedicated,
with love and gratitude,
To Fritz and Jonquil Leiber,
who first showed D. S. F.
the full splendor of Arthur Machen
by letting him read their copy
of *The Hill of Dreams*

Preface

The specifically *modern* weird story, properly speaking (whether concerned with supernatural horror or not), grew out of the romance/fantasy tradition. In both the greater and the lesser aspects of this tradition, Arthur Machen (1863-1947) occupies an unique and monumental position not only by virtue of his literary works but by virtue of the aesthetic pattern and significance of his life itself.

In the following pages we attempt to define something of Machen's achievement (both as a person and as an artist) in connection with the local traditions of King Arthur in the West Country of Britain, as well as with the historical evidence (recent and mostly archaeological) supporting the reality of an actual Arthur or "Artorius" who may have lived in the late 400s A.D. to the mid-500s.

King Arthur undoubtedly ruled far longer and more magnificently during the Middle Ages than he ever did in his own historical period. His tremen-

---

Donald Sidney-Fryer's celebration of Arthur Machen and the Arthurian Mythos was published in 1976 and reflects contemporary appreciation of the subject. Views on some aspects of the history and literature have developed since that time, but we have kept the work unchanged as a poetic reflection of a particular moment.—ED.

dous figure dominates the metrical romances (he is always there at least in the background) that flourished in the High Middle Ages; and thus his contribution (as an utmost symbol of romance) to the romance culture of the High Middle Ages must not be underestimated.

The specifically Romantic period or movement has ordinarily been conceived as embracing (more or less) the last decade of the 1700s (signalized by the French Revolution), the entirety of the 1800s, and the first 25 or 30 years of the 1900s (ending, possibly, with the Great Depression of 1929 or, at its latest, with World War II).

The last flowering of Late Romanticism (in terms of a sizable group) occurred primarily in California and included (among others) that small company of dedicated romanticists (or "Romantists," according to the usage of that magisterial romancer F. Marion Crawford) now known as the West Coast Romantics (principally Ambrose Bierce, George Sterling, Nora May French, and Clark Ashton Smith); and this last flowering more or less embraced the four decades from 1890 until 1930.

The specifically romance/Romance tradition that we propose here would cover not only the usual connotation of this Romantic period or movement but would also include the Renaissance of the 1400s and 1500s, in addition to the romance culture of the 1100s and 1200s, the beginning of romance and romanticism in our modern sense.

But in a larger and historically more inclusive sense, the romance tradition began of course with the Fall of Rome (whether 410, 455, 476, or 546/547) and the onset of the Dark Ages, and above all with the immediate sense of understandable nostalgia for the ancient Imperium Romanum on the part of the former Roman population still inhabiting the now fallen Western Roman Empire. One of the principal ingredients or "constants" of romanticism has always been the vague and ill-defined "emotion" of nostalgia, an unquenchable hankering after past magnificence, vanished beauty, and lost splendor. Thus, once the political sovereignty of Rome had become a thing of the past, we have the conditions for the first Romanticism (with emphasis on the "Roman"). Further, while we may recognize the beginning of romance and romanticism (in our modern sense) in the romance culture (and most pivotally in the medieval metrical romances) of the 1100s and 1200s (the true flowering of the Middle Ages), we should also recognize the Dark Ages as a period of "proto-romance" and as a time when the foundations of medieval romanticism were established.

Nowadays it is quite well-known that in the development of the metrical romances (as well as of the later romances in prose) of the Middle Ages, the semi-fabulous world of King Arthur, his court, and his Keltic dominions exercised the single most important influence, thanks to the *Historia Regum Britanniae* (c. 1135) by Geoffrey of Monmouth, and thanks as well to *Li Romanz de Brut* (1155), Wace's translations into the standard European languages of that time. These translations opened up for the medieval writers of romance a whole new world for their imaginative development. Among other results (and again thanks primarily to Geoffrey of Monmouth), the historical Arthur became transformed into another Charlemagne with a "glamorous" imperial court and a vast imperial domain.

The last flowering of Late Romanticism that occurred in the case of the life and the works of Arthur Machen was radically generic and reached back for its roots into the Late Roman period of Latinized Britain. Indeed, the older classicistic romanticism (common to Machen's time and of which his work is a modern extension) had just about run its course apart from some last-minute developments of great and unique artistic significance. Certainly Machen's work represents one of the finest as well as one of the most individual of these last-minute developments of classicistic romanticism.

This ROMANticism that is peculiar to Machen was able to emerge only because of the very fortunate juxtaposition of Machen and Caerleon-on-Usk ... old Caerleon, which had once been the "Castra Legionis" or "City of the Legions" and later one of the imperial camelots or capitals of King Arthur ... that same Artorius whose towering figure illumines the early Dark Ages, that very same period of "proto-romance" when Rome fell and the Western Roman Empire collapsed (into the shards and fragments of innumerable independent successor states), and when the selfsame foundations of medieval romanticism were established.

Arthur Machen—the high priest of Late Romantic prose fiction (or at least sharing that honor with Joseph Conrad)—stands virtually by himself in his profound symbolic and psychological understanding of the moral and ethical responsibilities that had become inherent in modern romance; and this latter development is actually very much in the tradition of Edmund Spenser and his great epic-romance-allegory *The Faerie Queene*.

Considerably before Hermann Hesse and the post-World War II vogue for the German poet's work, Machen had pioneered the romance of alienation, especially as crystallized by his magisterial novel *The Hill of Dreams*. He had pioneered in his own life (that is, during his early London period) by fulfilling the role of an archetypal Steppenwolf long before Hesse conceptualized the basic character pattern in *Steppenwolf* and other novels. What was to save Machen (as it was not to save later the French Existentialists), in the face of terrible circumstances and vicissitudes, was his quiet and abiding sense of self-humor. This inherent sense of self-humor was one of the few but singularly important "graces" permitted to Machen in his pilgrimage through life; and in this he was fortunate: he did not die as does Lucian Taylor (Machen's fictional alter ego) from an accidental overdose of laudanum in the final pages of *The Hill of Dreams*.

Incidentally, Machen certainly takes his own place among the great Romantic and Victorian masters of prose (and such writers would include at least Thomas Carlyle, John Ruskin, Matthew Arnold, Walter Pater, Robert Louis Stevenson, Rudyard Kipling, and Joseph Conrad). In some respects—for example, simply as a fictioneer—Machen's only serious runner-up would be Conrad, who is quite a different writer from Machen.

The present monograph seeks to honor the romance and fantasy tradition of the Western world by demonstrating just how Arthur Machen (both directly and indirectly) drew upon the particularly Late Roman and Arthurian traditions of his native Caerleon in order to define a significant and ultimate stage in the Late Romanticism developing during the late 1800s and early 1900s.

The achievement of Arthur Machen in life and letters has been notoriously difficult to define because (among others) of its Catholic quality of "ineffability" (a word and concept only recently having become acceptable again to many intellectuals). But we firmly believe that it is only in connection with the Arthurian tradition that it is possible to grasp something of the full meaning behind Machen's tremendous achievement as a "myth-maker" or *fantaisiste*. We do not mean by this a literal one-to-one parallelism between the Arthurian cycles of legendry on the one hand and Machen's fiction on the other; nor do we mean a literal usage of familiar characters and stage props directly lifted from Victorian or (for that matter) medieval fictional formulations of the Arthurian Mythos. But what we do intend here is a matter more elusive and subtle, that of an actual transference by Machen of something of the spirit of Arthurian splendor still lingering in Caerleon-on-Usk. By its very nature, such a piece of magic or artistry cannot be argued conclusively, cannot be presented in terms of incontrovertible proofs, because proofs of such a nature do not exist, and further, because the evidence for the most part does in no way warrant such a presentation.

What we proffer here then is frankly an aesthetic speculation, a construct of suggestive probability, an obvious "gallimaufry" of some historical fact, some selective aspects of fiction (or myth), and some plain and simple guesswork of the most elementary type.

In putting together the present monograph, we have drawn not only from the books mentioned in the text (and the standard encyclopedias and other reference works) but just as much upon the various Arthurian articles in that unique and invaluable compendium *Man, Myth and Magic* (subtitled the "Illustrated Encyclopaedia of the Supernatural") and of but recent publication. However, the divers conclusions and premises in regard to the Arthurian materials are for the most part strictly those of the present writer. We have also drawn upon (and here more immediately) an actual visit to the West Country of Britain during the first week of April 1972, with two English friends, Jack and Audrey Hesketh; to both of these friends we are singularly indebted for making that experience possible.

The real Arthur may or may not have been a sovereign. He does appear to have acted as *imperator atque dux bellorum* for the remnant of the Romanized Britons, and he does appear to have won a period of peace or semi-peace—the not inconsiderable respite of what seemed in retrospect a "golden age"—during the often desperate British defense against the Saxons and other Germanic invaders of what we today call England. He certainly was a paramount and paragon "sovereign of dreams" during the High Middle Ages.

Arthur Machen may have been forced by circumstances to assume the role of literary Jack-of-all-trades; but his fortitude and his quiet good humor in the face of tragedy or adversity made him his own aristocrat, his own best person, his own outstanding alchemical experiment. Despite his own creative agony, despite both popular and critical neglect and what seemed to Machen at the time as artistic failure, his fortitude and perseverance as a writer mark him out as a true Prince of Letters. In spite of the contemporary presence of such other excellent fantasy writers as C. S. Lewis, J. R. R. Tolkien, and Charles Williams in English alone, Machen's preeminence as a myth-maker (particularly in the difficult genre of self-myth as exemplified in the form of an autobiographical fiction) crowns him as a veritable "sovereign of dreams" in the opinion of many connoisseurs and, in the opinion of the present writer, no less a "sovereign of dreams" than King Arthur himself.

—Donald Sidney-Fryer.

Sacramento, California, Thursday,
14 August 1975, the 14th anniversary of the death of Clark Ashton Smith.

I. Arthur Machen, Geoffrey of Monmouth, and Caerleon

It is altogether fitting that we embark our Late Romantic personalities-on-parade first with Arthur Llewelyn Jones-Machen, alias Arthur Machen, truly "The Last of the Arthurians." As much as any who have managed to outlast the age in which they were born—instinctively feeling as outsiders therefrom—and who have suffered singular bitterness and (on occasion) breadless days on behalf of their chosen art, Arthur Machen surely deserves our special respect and honor for being the truly classic Odd Man Out, raised to the nth degree. This kind and courageous man, retaining as much good cheer and quiet self-humor as possible, found and developed the strength of heart and mind and character to transcend both personal tragedy and artistic failure, as well as both popular and critical neglect, in a truly remarkable way. Although he killed himself (so to speak) as a practising writer before this final phase, he ended his life as the archetypal Great Old Man of Letters, often visited by sympathetic admirers who sometimes came from afar and who appreciated Machen's genius as unique to their times. He was, incidentally, a wonderful host and raconteur. If nothing else, Machen had developed into a great human being; moreover, one who had rendered the humanities an awesome service by preserving, in a singularly pure and intrinsic way, something of the ancient British-Keltic spirit into an alien age (the twentieth century). In his own peculiar and proper way he had lived much of his best creative life as an artist-martyr or as a hermetic alchemist of letters, becoming his own best book (or work of art) himself in the end. A wondrous transformation, indeed!

In addition, he had achieved through his fiction, at the only truly popular moment of his entire writing career, what only another and earlier Welshman had been able to accomplish. (We must emphasize here that a true Welsh person is descended from the really British or British-Keltic race existing in England, as well as in the Scottish Lowlands, before the Saxons and other ancestors of the present-day English had invaded the island.) This other and earlier Welshman had been the bishop Geoffrey of Monmouth, and thus of Machen's own homeland of Gwent. Geoffrey (at least to himself) certainly was no conscious forger, but he had his *Historia Regum Britanniæ* (or *History of the Kings of Britain*, written originally in Latin prose about 1135) a deliberately mythopoetico-historical account (a personal poetic myth, if you will) "published" and accepted immediately among a majority of his contemporaries as actual history. His fantastic history begins with the well-chosen fiction that Britain was first settled by Brutus, the great-grandson of the Trojan hero Aeneas, and then finishes with an astonishing account of King Arthur, whom Geoffrey portrays as the conqueror of Pict, Scot, Saxon, and Roman. The book proved a brilliant success for that time.

Geoffrey's magnificent main chronicle of an imperial King Arthur conferred (or so it seemed to his contemporaries) an authentic historical dignity on the Arthurian myths and legends. Although he does not go so far as to state the analogy in such obvious terms, he implies that Arthur (as an archimperial figure and as a military leader fighting for decades against savage invading outlanders) was indeed comparable to Charlemagne, High King of the Germans and the Franks, Restorer of the Roman Empire of the West, and (hence) Holy Roman Emperor (as crowned at the hand—and therefore certainly with the pronounced official approval—of Pope Leo III on Christmas Day, 800 A.D., in Rome).

In some strange and subtle way the distinct feeling haunts Geoffrey's pages (although he is nowhere so bold as to state this explicitly) that Arthur had in a sense functioned, at least symbolically, as the Last of the Roman Emperors of the West. The chronicle depicts Arthur as head of a brilliant, imperial, cosmopolitan court centered in ancient Caerleon-on-Usk (Arthur's coronation capital) and as master of Western Europe including certain portions of the Scandinavian world (e.g., Denmark and Norway) in addition to large islands in the West (e.g., Ireland and Iceland).

Up to a certain point Geoffrey seems plausible enough (apart, of course, from the obvious accounts of hypernatural marvels). Recent "Arthurian" archaeology and recent reconsideration of the Arthurian Mythos would seem to bear out, at least in broad terms, some of Geoffrey's allegations. But he loses credibility with the modern reader when he depicts Arthur as master of a vast empire stretching from Iceland to Norway (in the north) and from Ireland to Britain and Gaul (lying further south). What might actually lie behind such a grandiose allegation? Arthur evidently reunited the Britons everywhere (whether in Britain or in Brittany across the Channel) under a strong central government centered in Western Britain. He had restored in effect the former province of Britannia. Considering the time in which he lived and the peculiar difficulties under which he had to operate, that was a tremendous thing to do! By reuniting the Britons everywhere and then acting as their suzerain, Arthur would have ruled over a fair piece of turf, at least the areas Cambria (what we today call Wales), Cornwall, Devon, Somerset, Dorset, Cumberland, Westmoreland, Lancashire, Cheshire, the Scottish Lowlands, the two isles of Mona in the Irish Sea (today called Man and Anglesey), Brittany, Armorica (later called Normandy), the Channel Islands, as well as those fragments presumably left over from the lost land of Lyonnesse, the Cassiterides of Roman times, the 500 islands and islets of the Scilly archipelago lying immediately due west or southwest of Land's-End at the tip of Cornwall.

Now all this would have constituted an "empire" of some kind. Arthur may also have fostered strong ties, both political and cultural, with the Irish or Goidelic Kelts (the Gaels), to whom he and his fellow Britons were related as "cousin" Kelts. Geoffrey may have worked from written or oral traditions that, taking all these "facts" and factors into account, could not have avoided construing Arthur in other than "imperial" terms. Geoffrey would then have been merely continuing and developing further this "imperial" tradition in a perfectly logical way. Granting the basic premise of Arthur's Brythonic empire, what would have struck the imagination of someone like Geoffrey, living as he did so much closer to Arthur's time than ourselves? Arthur had in effect restored more than the former province of Britannia: he had thus restored a substantial and strategic fragment—to wit, the actual northwestern corner—of the former Roman Empire of the West. Again, that was a tremendous thing to do! Given these premises, it is easy to see how Geoffrey and his contemporaries, whether they were actually conscious of the process or not, would have instinctively conceived of Arthur in terms of the departed splendor and pomp of the imperial Caesars. Given these terms, we cannot only generously pardon, but we can actually applaud Geoffrey for extrapolating Arthur's "real" empire into a vast North Atlantic and Western European domain.

This then was the deliberately mythopoetic "fact" that Geoffrey perpetrated, an imperial myth still potent in the reigns of the Welsh-descended Tudors (particularly Henry VII, Henry VIII, and Elizabeth I). This last period significantly marks the span of the English Renaissance: from 1485, when Henry VII took power, to 1603, when Elizabeth I died (although some scholars extend the span to 1625, thus including the reign of James I, the first of the Stuart kings). Geoffrey's account formed the inner core (the so-called Matter of Britain) around which so much myth and legend had already cycled and from which the romancers of the High Middle Ages were to borrow many hints. His "history" was accepted, quoted, and followed by most later historians; and credibility in it was maintained into the Late Middle Ages and the early Continental Renaissance. This imperial myth had proven equally potent in the reigns of the earlier Anglo-Norman kings beginning with William the Conqueror, and it is obvious that Geoffrey formulated the myth the way he did purposefully for his fellow "Britons" (*exoterically* for the inhabitants of

England living in his own time, but *esoterically* for his *true* fellow Britons: the Welsh, the Cornish, and the Bretons).

Now Machen during World War I had written and published one short fantasy—a poetic parable more mystic than patriotic in any narrowly chauvinistic or jingoistic sense—which his English contemporaries had immediately picked up as a historical report of an actual miracle; to wit, "The Bowmen." This was in 1914. In this brief and, in its way, brilliant story, he hymns some ghostly bowmen from Crécy and Agincourt necromantically evoked out of England's earlier days but now fighting in the British ranks during the retreat from Mons in France in 1914. His imaginary tale was accepted as factual by much of the British public; and when garnished with sword-brandishing saviors on horseback, this became the celebrated legend of those "Angels of Mons" fighting on the British side. So, in effect, Machen too had created, willy-nilly, a myth for his fellow Britons. Next to Geoffrey of Monmouth's *History*, and possibly on an equal footing with it in this regard, Machen's tale can be described as one of the most successful works of fiction ever composed.

However, Machen never received just recognition for this exploit. It did not really help his writing career, which would be over and done with by the later 1920s, when he achieved a considerable vogue in the U.S., thanks to such discriminating American enthusiasts as Vincent Starrett and Carl Van Vechten. To the end of his life he would be described as the man who claimed to have invented the tale of the Angels of Mons!

Machen had been born on March 3rd, 1863, in Caerleon-on-Usk, in southeastern Wales, not far from the "Severn Sea" to the south or southeast (the inner estuary of the Severn River), and the very heartland of ancient Britain. Machen, the inheritor of a vast and immemorially old spiritual legacy from the Welsh, the true Britons, described his birthplace in various novels and stories, but possibly he has done so the most compactly in the "Novel of the Black Seal," one of the major narrative units in the picaresque "gallimaufry" *The Three Impostors* (1895). Here he shadows his own Caerleon under the name of "Caermaen"—and here are the relevant passages, in some of his at once most simple and most lyrical prose:

> It was one evening after dinner that the word came.
> "I hope you can make your preparations without much trouble," he said suddenly to me. "We shall be leaving here in a week's time."
> "Really!" I said in astonishment. "Where are we going?"
> "I have taken a country house in the west of England, not far from Caermaen, a quiet little town, once a city, and the headquarters of a Roman legion.

It is very dull there, but the country is pretty, and the air is wholesome."

I detected a glint in his eyes, and guessed that this sudden move had some relation to our conversation of a few days before.

*****

The days passed quickly; I could see that the professor was all quivering with suppressed excitement, and I could scarce credit the eager appetence of his glance as we left the old manorhouse behind us and began our journey. We set out at midday, and it was in the dusk of the evening that we arrived at a little county station. I was tired and excited, and the drive through the lanes seems all a dream. First the deserted streets of a forgotten village, while I heard Professor Gregg's voice talking of the Augustan Legion and the clash of arms, and all the tremendous pomp that followed the eagles; then the broad river swimming to full tide with the last afterglow glimmering dustily in the yellow water, the wide meadow, the cornfields whitening, and the deep lane winding on the slope between the hills and the water. At last we began to ascend, and the air grew rarer. I looked down and saw the pure white mist tracking the outline of the river like a shroud, and a vague and shadowy country; imaginations and fantasy of swelling hills and hanging woods, and half-shaped outlines of hills beyond, and in the distance the glare of the furnace fire [of the setting sun] on the mountain, growing by turns a pillar of shining flame and fading to a dull point of red. We were slowly mounting a carriage drive, and then there came to me the cool breath and the secret of the great wood that was above us; I seemed to wander in its deepest depths, and there was the sound of trickling water, the scent of the green leaves, and the breath of the summer night. The carriage stopped at last, and I could scarcely distinguish the form of the house as I waited a moment at the pillared porch. The rest of the evening seemed a dream of strange things bounded by the great silence of the wood and the valley and the river.

The next morning, when I awoke and looked out of the bow window of the big, old-fashioned bedroom, I saw under a grey sky a country that was still all mystery. The long, lovely valley, with the river winding in and out below, crossed in mid-vision by a mediaeval bridge of vaulted and buttressed stone, the clear presence of the rising ground beyond, and the woods that I had only seen in shadow the night before, seemed tinged with enchantment, and the soft breath of air that sighed in at the opened pane was like no other wind. I looked across the valley, and beyond, hill followed upon hill as wave on wave, and here a faint blue pillar of smoke rose still in the morning air from the chimney of an ancient grey farmhouse, there was a rugged height crowned with dark firs, and in the distance I saw the white streak of a road that climbed and vanished into some unimagined country. But the boundary of all was a great wall of mountain, vast in the west, and ending like a fortress with a steep ascent and a domed tumulus clear against the sky. (CF 1.372-73)

This then was the country of Gwent, or Monmouthshire, the ancient Siluria. This then was the town of Caerleon, the "Castra Legionis" or fabled "City of the Legions" where Machen was born; and according to Geoffrey of Monmouth, one of the imperial camelots or capitals of Arthur, King of the Britons.

II. In the Forest of Nodens

Siluria, or southeastern Cambria, was thus the country of the Silurians, the ancient British-Keltic folk of the woods and forests. Most of the Brythonic Kelts lived originally as forest folk, and many of the Silurians still dwelt in the forests and mountains of southeastern Cambria all through the Roman occupation. The Silurians were hunters, fishermen, and skilled iron-miners, and they hunted, among other prey, both the red deer and the wild boar. Their skill as hunting men made them dangerous and unpredictable foes. Yet the Silurians were also skilled fishermen and were definitely at home in the water, paddling about in their peculiar braided and caulked coracles. To this day one of the greatest forests in this region that have survived is the old Forest of Dean, formerly the Forest of Nodens (the hunter-god Nuada of the Silver Hand) whose shadowy depths preserved his chosen people, the Silurians, from the worst effects of the successive invasions of Britain by outlanders, beginning with the Romans.

The Forest thus protected them from complete colonization and pacification by the Romans, such as obtained over most of lowland Britain. Make no mistake about it: the Romans did materially change the face of the British land with the network they founded and developed of cities, towns, and forts all the way to the Antonine's Wall lying north of Hadrian's by a good piece of ground. Antonine's Wall stretched from the Firth of Clyde on the west to the Firth of Forth on the east. The Forest of Nodens similarly protected the Silurians from the worst immediate effects of the continuing invasions by the Saxons. These Germanic barbarians were primarily cattle-herding people and country-dwellers who preferred the open grasslands to the Roman towns and villas, and who also preferred to live in their own tribal communities in the lowlands beside the rivers with their heavy but fertile soils favored for Saxon agriculture. For these basic reasons they settled early in the extensive open country of Kent south of London, or in the central-to-southeastern stretch of Britain's southern coast (the "Saxon Shore" separated from the continent of Europe by the "Narrow Seas").

In 1018 Canute, the Danish king of England, granted the Forest a royal charter, upholding the ancient Verderer's Court which persists to this day. The Forest of Nodens again preserved this ancient Cambrian people from the worst conditions resulting from the Norman Conquest of England under William the Conqueror in 1066. The now Forest of Dean became one of William's favorite hunting grounds. Since it was a royal forest, the inhabitants of Dean were spared much of the degradation of petty feudalism.

The Silurians then witnessed a long succession of English kings in their more pleasant moods. Now there ensued the pageantry of the royal hunt as the king would pursue the red deer and other wild creatures of the woods. Eventually the Silurians witnessed a Welsh-descended prince, one of their own ancient British-Keltic race, ascend to the throne of Britain (in fulfillment of an elder prophecy) and found an imperial dynasty, the House of Tudor. The last Tudor monarch in direct line of descent ruled as Elizabeth I, one of England's finest sovereigns, and the mystical Astraea returned to turn "dull time" for a substantial respite into a golden and goddess-inspired age.

"Happy the eye / 'Twixt the Severn and Wye." The bare outline of the Forest of Dean's history is endorsed in this old rime, reminding us of how the old woods have indeed palpably preserved and protected the Silurians from the worst effects of Time's changes. In the ancient forest depths, in the shadow of the olden oaks and beeches, something of the original British-Keltic spirit still remained as if by some predestined magic, and passed uniquely to Arthur Machen, born in Caerleon-on-Usk, and one of antique Wales' most illustrious offspring.

This Caerleon, the little town in which Machen was born, had once stood in Roman times as Isca Silurum, or "Isca of the Silurians," and as possibly the single most distinguished city in southern Wales. Although Caerwent, or Venta Silurum (8 to 10 miles to the east, just inland along the northern shore of "Severn Sea")—the "Market of the Silurians"—was the "cantonal" or local administrative capital for southern Cambria; Caerleon was one of the three legionary fortresses for the whole of Britannia: the other two were located at Eburacum, or York, in the Midlands, and at Chester, or Caerleon-upon-Dee, called Ceva by the Romans, and located in northeastern Cambria. Isca was, moreover, a cosmopolitan community thanks to the presence of the Imperial Augustan Legion, or "Legio II Augusta," a cosmopolitan gathering of professional soldiers who had brought with them their altars and cults of such gods and goddesses as Mithras, Isis, Horus, Osiris, Diana (the Artemis of the Ephesians on the west coast of Asia Minor), and Jupiter Dolichenus, a Syrian divinity.

Although the Romans had been in the country in one way or another since

55 B.C., it was not until about a hundred years or so afterwards that they began to settle and civilize Britain in earnest. The central Roman government maintained some official representation or control in this province until about 410 A.D. Britannia protected the northwestern sector of the Imperium Romanum.

III. "Caer Nodentis"

North and east of Isca Silurum there stretched the mysterious Forest of Nodens. East of Venta Silurum, further up the Severn, again along the river's northern shore, and just within the southeastern corner of the Forest (which virtually came to the water's edge), there stood the imposing Temple of Nodens upon its own hill.[1] This was an elaborate and quite sizable temple compound comprising various buildings and set within an older, pre-Roman, Iron-Age fortress, a spot sacred to Nodens from time immemorial.

South of the temple compound, across the Severn, all along her eastern and then southeastern shore (stretching from Glevum or Gloucester on the north to the great southeastern "bend" in the Severn Estuary, more or less marked by the mouth of the River Brue or Uxella), there lay the great estates of the landed Britanno-Roman gentry (actually large farms) with their elegant and stately villas, which were also well-heated, well-watered, well-ventilated, and quite livable, comfortable, and eminently "modern." The Britanno-Romans had carefully modeled their country houses upon the Roman villa, which they skillfully modified to suit the new non-Mediterranean surroundings. The placement of "Caer Nodentis" (as we shall call it after the Welsh fashion) virtually on the river facilitated all approaches by water. The temple served as a focus for the immediate countryside on both banks of the river, and it was common for people to ferry back and forth.

Caer Nodentis was the greatest of all Romano-British temples, a center of healing and pilgrimage, with an elaborately appointed hostelry, or "villa," with baths, healing cubicles, priests' quarters, and so forth—and all built in the fourth century A.D. within the prehistoric earthwork fortress and above the remains of an early Roman iron mine.

---

1. The main axis of the Hill of Nodens is more northeast and southwest than north and south. However, we have presented the discussion of the Hill and Temple (area) of Nodens in simple terms of north and south for ease of presentation as well as for ease of understanding. The ground-plan accompanying this monograph (for which sketch we are indebted to Jack Hesketh of New Ash Green, near Dartford, Kent, England) indicates the specifically correct compass directions.

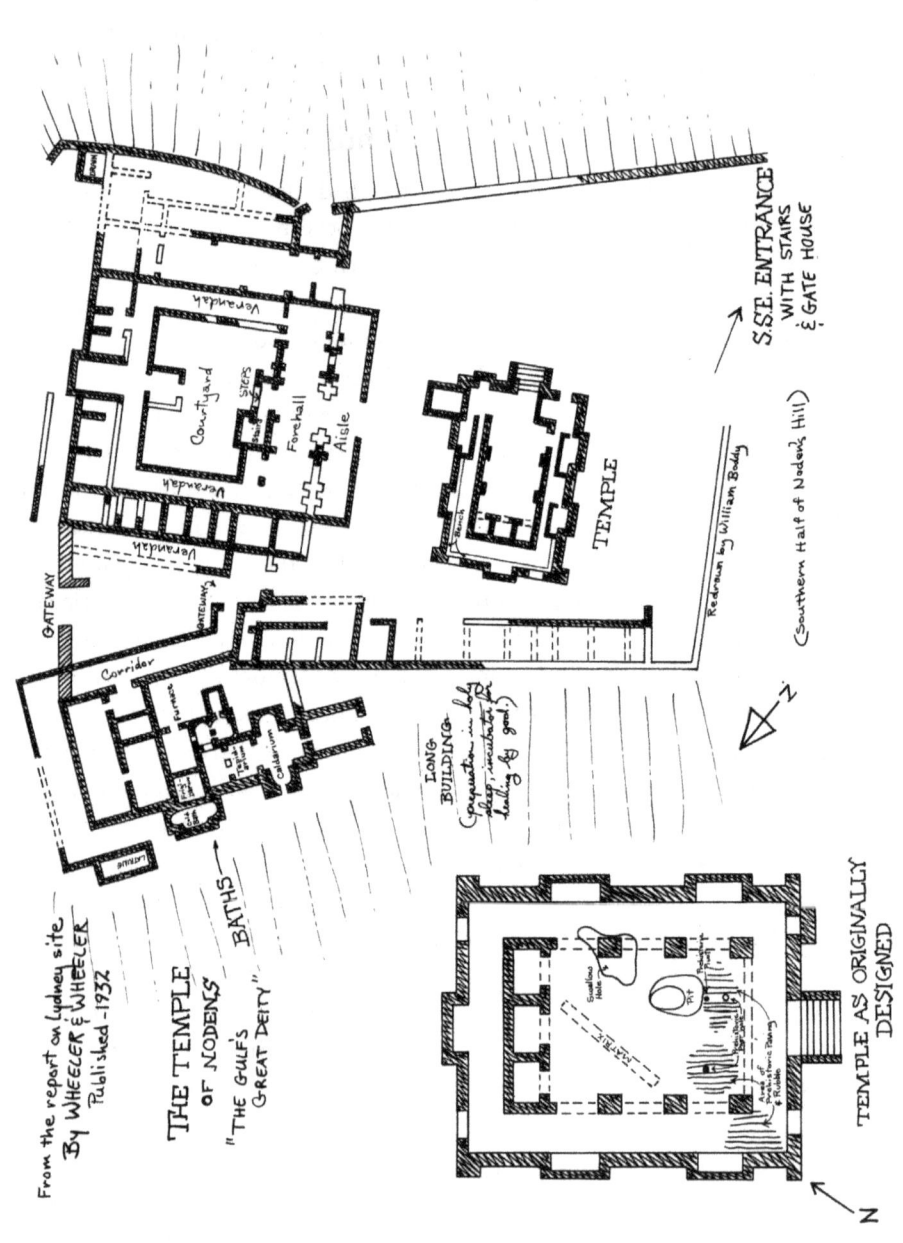

To the ruins of this temple located on its own hill within Lydney Park, the present writer (then in Britain during a long sojourn of half pleasure and half business) came early in the first week of April 1972, together with two English friends Jack and Audrey Hesketh, during our pilgrimage to the Arthur Machen country and to the West Country at large. First on our itinerary was the Temple of Nodens, not far from the new Severn Bridge that goes over the river just west of Bristol, one of the largest modem cities in the West Country. We had first been apprised of this Britanno-Roman relic through its mention by Machen in a number of his tales as well as in various autobiographical materials. But we were eager to see the temple not only because of this association with and mention by Machen but just as much for its own intrinsic and unique historico-cultural interest.

Here was centered the cult of the Severn river god Nodens, "Lord of the Abyss" and "the gulf's great deity" and also (in another of this divinity's attributes) Nuada of the Silver Hand, god of the forest and the forest-depths. The Severn is presumably named after Sabrina, the daughter of Locrine, who, when pursued by her angered stepmother Gwendolen, drowned herself in the river to which she bequeathed her name. Nodens was the greatest god of the Silures, or Silurians. But Nodens was also a marine divinity and the particular genius loci of the Bristol Channel, or Gulf of Nodens, with the inner gulf, or Severn Sea, extending west about as far as Cardiff, and with the outer gulf extending as far west as St. George's Channel on the north and the Atlantic Ocean on the south.

In addition to the Hill of Nodens (and now Camp Hill), there stands another smaller hill, once crowned by a Roman watchtower and separated from Camp Hill by a ravine some 28 yards in width. Although the location functioned primarily as a shrine, the civil authorities in Caerwent, or Venta Silurum, maintained a military station here, as well as in the watch-tower on the smaller adjacent hill (for the practical, everyday purpose of protecting the shrine from any immediate man-made perils and alarms), through most of the Roman occupation of Britain. The ravine forks below the temple park. Since the river once came to the foot of Nodens Hill, the tide would have gushed into the creek that flows down from the hills farther to the north. Today, between the base of the main hill and the edge of the Severn River (lying thus on the southeast), there lies an alluvial plain given over to farming. Among the present native trees marking the temple site are some huge, well-matured oaks and beeches, 300 or 400 years old, and well garlanded with mistletoe, that mystic plant cherished by the ancient Gallic and British Druids. The only alien among the native trees here is the Spanish chestnut brought over by the

Romans from the Continent, along with the "fallow deer."

As noted, Nodens had at least three main but related attributes: he was a sea god, a river god, and a forest god, and was thus three times a god of the abyss or of the depths. But in one further significant and quite literal aspect he functioned as lord of the void, or voids. Most gods have their benign and overt attributes, their outer selves, imaged as divine men or women or both; this represents their exoteric side. However, they also have their unknown and mysterious attributes, and sometimes possibly malign; this represents their esoteric side. The former administers to the worshippers and is often and usually the object of popular cults. The latter administers as it were to the secret and unknown concerns of the initiates, priests, and mysteriarchs. This esoteric aspect is your true "unknown and unknowable god," and Nodens too had his hidden and unknown self who presided over and within the manifold caves and caverns that abound in the hills and mountains of Wales (including those of southern Cambria), either opening to the outer air or located in hidden places far underground. Over these upper caverns and these subterranean places, Nodens presided as the unseen, unheard, and unknown deity, truly the Lord of the Abyss (a divinity whose presence is *known of* and *felt* but who yet remains *unknown*). Appropriately enough, there is at least one (and partially man-made) hollow space beneath the Temple of Nodens, to wit, an early Roman iron mine, abandoned during the later Latin occupation and presently walled off with cement.

The Severn River's tidal bore presented a palpable manifestation of the god's divinity. His priests, once they learned how to foretell the arrival of the mystic wave peculiarly associated with Nodens, gained the confidence of simple men, and thus the cult grew. The Temple of Nodens was at once the largest and yet most intimate relic of its type in the whole of Roman Britain, and his shrine is more than an ordinary ruin. Barring its firing by the Saxons (an event that may or may not have happened), the buildings would have continued in use in some way throughout the Middle Ages and into the Renaissance, like a great deal of Roman architecture both in Britain and in Europe. Already commanding a large popular cult during the earlier Roman times in Britain, the Lord Nodens became even more popular (especially as a healer) during the "Keltic Revival" of the latter 300s and early 400s.

This revival came about as a direct result of the first major Saxon and related Germanic attacks on Britain's eastern and southeastern shores during the years 367, 368, and 369. These attacks (which the Britanno-Romans vigorously repulsed, and which had no real effect on the continuing prosperity of the province) also had another and singularly practical result: the Britanno-Romans now proceeded to erect walls around most of their cities, towns, and villas. Walls already existed around the great legionary fortresses and the smaller camps that were situated all over Roman Britain, as well as around those towns located near such dangerous milieux as Hadrian's Wall or the mountains in the west or northwest where the Roman influence had at best proven superficial. But most of the towns and cities were not protected by walls because hitherto they had proven unnecessary: the civil communities had had the security afforded by the highly mobile presence of the three great legions stationed in the island. One by one, the legions were to be called away for duty on the Continent, where the Western Roman Empire was crumbling beneath the attacks of barbarian invaders. But now the Britanno-Romans with commendable and sensible dispatch erected walls and bastions around most of their settlements. A major series of maritime defenses and forts—established earlier in the 300s against Saxon pirates—continued in use along Britain's eastern and southeastern shores, all the way from the Wash (about 100 miles almost directly north of London) to the Thames, and then from the Thames to the white cliffs of Dover, and then finally from Dover to Portsmouth and the Isle of Wight; to the same earlier period there also belonged a new fort at Cardiff southwest of Caerleon and a fleet station at Holyhead on the Isle of Anglesey just off the northwestern coast of Wales. Thus, with good reason, the Hill of Nodens and the adjacent hill with watch-tower possessed their own garrisons and substantial fortifications.

It must be remembered that, although the upper classes in Britain had become largely Christian (at least superficially), following the imperial example of Constantine the Great (sole emperor 323–337), himself proclaimed emperor in Britain, yet the British cult of the young Nazarene carpenter-god Jesus Christ was at best only minimal at that time, and only one of many religions. The Christian cult was, in addition, only the latest in a long series of "exotic" religions imported from the Orient and including the cults of Isis, Horus, Osiris, Mithras, the Asiatic Diana, and Jupiter Dolichenus. It should not surprise the reader therefore that in times of such genuine peril, whenas not only a people's way of life was threatened but also its very life stood in danger of annihilation, the people should have turned to their own native divinities with renewed trust and inspiration. The religious life of the province was especially rich and variegated, and formed three main groups of cults: the official or imperial cults (these involved at least the dead emperors deified while alive, the living emperor or emperors, and the imperial household); the imported cults (these involved at least the main divinities from the Oriental, Greek, and Roman pantheons); and the native cults (these involved all the local British deities throughout the island, an amazing and typically Keltic multiplicity of gods and goddesses). These various kinds of religious life survived all over the country up to the latest period of Roman Britain, especially in the southwest.

Although the cult of Nodens became even more elaborate during Late Roman times, here was the site of an oracle and a shrine long before the arrival of the Romans. But it was particularly during the Keltic Revival of the later 300s and early 400s that Caer Nodentis received its greatest following and appanage. Replacing the much older Keltic shrine but still honoring the same god or principle, the Romano-Britons now constructed in 384 A.D. a splendid congeries of buildings in Roman style primarily on the southern half of the hill. The entire hill itself was protected on the north (where it joins a wooded plateau) by a double fortification, each with its own outer fosse. The outer wall was pre-Roman and built of earth, the inner wall was Roman and built at least partially of stone. Heavy gates led through both walls.

The northern half (for the most part unexcavated) of the hilltop was evidently used as a courtyard but possessed few structures and was probably naturally landscaped. The southern half of the hill was dominated by the temple building itself and by the large-scale two-story luxurious hotel-villa where both ordinary pilgrims and important dignitaries could find lodging. The temple itself, built to be used in winter, was originally enclosed and was not of the colonnaded Mediterranean type. It measured 93 feet in length and 76 feet in width, and was unique for the period in having six side chapels.

Nodens was depicted in typical Roman mosaic design on the floor of his temple, surrounded by salmon and sea serpents (or conger eels, much esteemed as a comestible by the Romans). He was portrayed as coronetted and rising up from his own river, standing in his chariot drawn by four horses and accompanied by Tritons bearing coracle paddles. In appearance Nodens resembled the Roman god of the sea, Neptunus, but without the beard. As a marine god, he held or inspired the gift of prophecy, and as such he was definitely a power or divinity to be propitiated.

Popularly Nodens was a god of health and healing in the manner of the Greek deity Aesculapius. Like Mercury, he was also a god of good luck. According to the *interpretatio romana*, the Romans likened him, in his "sylvan" aspect, to Sylvanus, one of the Latin divinities of the woods. Originally in the temple floor there was located the so-called Oracle of Nodens, a circular opening 9 inches across and environed by a broad red band in turn enclosed by two other bands of blue. The coins recovered from within the temple floor (and close to this oracular orifice) range from the reign of Augustus to that of Arcadius (about 377-408), the Roman Emperor of the East, from 383 into 408 A.D.

In addition to the gates opening onto the forest at the north, there was also an entrance to the hill-top located with stairs and gate-house at the southeast (for the devotees coming by river). Here, after climbing the stairs, one would find himself in an open area bounded on the west by the temple. The main entrance into the temple building (which runs more or less on an east-west axis) is on the east. There was also an open area to the north of the temple, and between the temple and the hotel-villa. West of the temple there lay a long low building, the healing house or *abaton*, with individual rooms or cubicles where the devotees of Lord Nodens (many of them cripples and other kinds of invalids) would await the healing presence of the god. Indeed, the evidence suggests that Caer Nodentis was a kind of British-Keltic Lourdes, and many miraculous cures resulted there over time. North of the *abaton* and west of the hotel-villa there arose the obligatory bath building which, like the *abaton*, overlooked the ravine (separating the Hill of Nodens from the watchtower hill) and which included the caldarium, tepidarium, and frigidarium. The pilgrims who came to Caer Nodentis would first negotiate with the resident priesthood, would probably find lodging for the night if they had come for "the cure," and before retiring to their individual chambers in the *abaton* to await the god, would go through a complete cleansing ritual in the baths.

There were also other and smaller edifices, such as the quarters where the priests and acolytes lived, studied, and maintained their own private cults and mysteries. The buildings were roofed with heavy, Mediterranean-type red tile, bits of which one can still easily see scattered here and there on the southern half of the hill-top. Altogether, the Shrine of Nodens presented an imposing and rather mysterious appearance, half hidden by the primordial Forest of Nodens, which stretched away from the temple to the north and west. Wales, like most of Britain at that time, was heavily covered with all manner of huge, beautiful, and olden trees, most of them deciduous: the spring and autumn glory of leaves much have been breathtaking. Not even the truly splendiferous temple and great baths dedicated to Lady Sulis, sovereign queen above all waters, and the presiding divinity of Aquae Sulis (or Bath), formed a more magnificent architectural entourage than "Caer Nodentis." The Romans likened this goddess of the hot springs and medicinal waters to Minerva, or Pallas Athena. It is indeed an odd coincidence that in Roman Britain—as in the

Britain of later times—the great metropolis was London, and the fashionable spa in the West Country was Bath (or Aquae Sulis), which stood south-southeast of Caer Nodentis and the northwestern bank of the Severn.

Long after the last official Roman legion had departed from Britain and the Latin speech itself had become a dead language, the name of Nodens was remembered, until his own river gradually wandered away from the shrine now left standing alone amid the low forested hills that marked the southeastern corner of the Forest of Nodens.

The Forest, once a vasty and primordial woods, became in time only a fragment of its former self, but it had more than served its purpose by preserving Nodens' chosen people into an age completely different from that which had known his charismatic worship. The unknown and potentially malign aspect of the god would not have been directed against his own people, the Silurians and other forest folk, but (on behalf of their preservation) against the successive tides of outland invaders.

There is the possibility that the Saxons fired the temple compound in their final push westward and after the golden age of peace and order brought about by King Arthur's victories. But there is no conclusive evidence for such a burning, and in all likelihood the buildings would have continued in use into the Renaissance. We think the Saxons would have respected Caer Nodentis (as they did the shrine at Glastonbury or Avalon) and would have allowed it to function in its own immediate locality as previously. However, the fact remains that both Caer Nodentis and Caerleon continued under the direct political control of the Welsh until the Norman Conquest, that is, for half a millennium.

Both Cambria, or Wales, and Cornwall maintained a quasi-independent status for centuries before their eventual absorption into what was to become the mainstream of English culture and life. Both the Welsh and the Cornish managed to maintain much of their own peculiar way of life into modern times: their language, their customs, their arts, their poetry, and their music.

In 1670, the Hill of Nodens, now Camp Hill, was enclosed in Lydney Park, just south of the little town of Sydney. As recently as the eighteenth century, many of the walls in the old temple compound were still at least 8 feet high. Today they are only about 3 feet high, but still demonstrate the solid building skill of the Britanno-Romans. One can still clearly see how they constructed the walls with forest stone well cemented together. Today Caer Nodentis is still part of Lydney Park, Lydney, Gloucestershire, on private property owned presently by Lord and Lady Bledisloe, who live in the (comparatively) modern manor house on the hill just to the east of the old Hill of Nodens.

Before we proceed on our pilgrimage from the Temple of Nodens on into ancient Caerleon-on-Usk, we mention in passing—for the benefit of interested readers—two basic books to apprehend properly the archaeological site and its cultural significance. First, the *Report on the Excavation of the Prehistoric, Roman, and Post-Roman Site in Lydney Park, Gloucestershire*, by Messieurs Wheeler and Wheeler, and published by Oxford University Press, 1932. Second, the *Roman Antiquities at Lydney Park, Gloucestershire*, by Reverend William Hiley Bathurst, and published by Longmans, Green & Co., London, 1879. The former is an excellent report on the exemplary excavations conducted by Sir Mortimer Wheeler in modern times. Unfortunately it completely or virtually ignores the considerable folklore relative to Nodens in the immediate neighborhood of Camp Hill and handed down orally from generation to generation. The latter title makes up for the cultural/anthropological omissions of the modern report and forms a fascinating compendium of the vicinage's oral traditions as extant in Bathurst's lifetime. This is a book that would have been known to the young Arthur Machen, since his references to Nodens in both his fiction and his autobiographical materials draw upon virtually the same folklore.

IV. Caerleon-on-Usk

And now at last we come to "Caer Leon" or "Castra Legionis" on the river Usk, whereby there hangs full many a tale; indeed the full ROMANtic heritage of which, like wings summoned out of time, descended upon the exquisite sense, sensibility, and sensitivity of Arthur Machen.[2]

---

2. As in the case of the Hill and Temple (area) of Nodens, the main axis of the Roman fortress as well as the city of Isca Silurum (that is, the two thus lying side by side) is really northeast and southwest and not north and south. We present the discussion of Britanno-Roman Caerleon in simple terms of north and south for ease of presentation and of understanding. The illustration accompanying this monograph and showing "Early Isca Silurum" clearly demonstrates the half-circle of the river Usk sweeping on the south around the city.

It has only been since after World War II and after Machen's death that modern archaeologists have known for a certainty (thanks to recent discoveries) that the city (as distinct from the fortress) did exist, and did indeed constitute a fair-sized community. However, when Machen grew up in Caerleon and then later when he wrote *The Hill of Dreams*, he had to work from local traditions about the Roman antiquities and from his own artistic intuition. It is clear from his descriptions of Isca Silurum that he knew perfectly well that the town itself existed in the form that modern archaeolo-

Although Julius Caesar came into Britain in 55 B.C., the Romans did not begin their conquest in earnest until sometime just a little less than one hundred years later under the emperor Claudius in 43 A.D. In a scant thirty years the Romans succeeded in superimposing their civilization over most of what is now England. The reduction of Cymru, or Cambria, the western mountain heartland of ancient Britain, remained until the last. Then in 75 A.D. the commander Julius Frontinus began the conquest of the Silurians. About the same year the Romans built the foundation of the fortress at Isca Silurum, the Isca or Usk of the Silurians, taking the name thus from the river.

The Silurians had already marked the general position of the fortress as one of strategic value by the presence of the 17-acre prehistoric Iron-Age earthwork fort (today called Lodge Camp or Belinstock) on the hill just to the northwest (and possibly the original for Machen's "hill of dreams"). The Romans moreover chose the site for its approachability by river and for its command over the coastal area as well as of the routes into the hinterland, that is, the wilder and more remote mountainous areas of northern and central Wales. A network of smaller (auxiliary) forts in southern and central Wales depended upon the fortress at Caerleon.

A large rectangle with rounded corners, the fortress measured 1630 feet (running east and west) and 1375 feet (running north and south), and covered about 50 acres. It occupied a terrace in a broad bend of the Usk, and together with various other stone buildings, it accommodated some 6,000 men in 64 substantial barrack blocks.

The wall or walls (mainly a rampart of clay with thick stone facing and superstructure) environing the fortress rose about 20 feet to a crenellated parapet, with a ditch moat 30 feet wide and 8 feet deep in turn surrounding them, providing thus for both defense and the removal of effluents. Attached interval and corner turrets rose every 150 feet. A gateway stood symmetrically situated in each side of the rectangle, and each gate had twin arched portals between towers.

In addition to the 64 barracks the fortress possessed numerous administrative offices, stores, and other buildings. The subsidiary streets had side drains and the major streets had deep central sewers. Seven-inch lead pipes provided the running water. All the buildings (including the towers and turrets) possessed heavy, Mediterranean-type tile roofs, and were grouped in three main sections or divisions.

---

gy has discovered and confirmed. This last revelation represents one of the great archaeological finds of the twentieth century.

The headquarters or *principia* lay in the middle of the central section. It had a chapel of the standards or *aedes,* and its great basilica measured 210 feet by 90 feet. Its great courtyard lies principally beneath the parish church and churchyard of St. Cadoc's, which in turn lies virtually at the heart of modern Caerleon.

To the rear of the headquarters (that is, toward the west) there stood the residence of the commander, or *legatus.* The real King Arthur would certainly have inhabited this building among other imposing residences within the overall area of camp and city combined. In the central section the workshops or *fabrica* lay to one side of the commander's residence, and a drill hall (flanked by "magazines") lay on the other.

Twenty-four barracks lay in the western section and a like number lay in the eastern one. Each barracks block typically measured 250 feet long, with one third of its area appropriated for the centurion; the remaining area provided for the men's quarters, with a veranda in front.

The front or eastern section included a large hospital of typical legionary pattern measuring about 230 feet square, together with a commodious bathhouse (containing a long exercise hall, lavish cold-water and hot-water baths, and a *palaestra* with a sizable swimming pool 135 feet long, 19 feet wide, and 4 feet deep).

Both south and north of the headquarters there lay a group of eight barracks each, the southern group lying just adjacent to the principia, and the northern group lying adjacent to the fortress's northern gate. Between the northern group and the principia there lay the stabling for the 120 mounted scouts who made up the full legionary complement. This would later have provided the stables for at least some of Arthur's "knights" or *equites cataphractarii.*

We have described the fortress in some detail since this part of Caerleon would have played an especially important role in the life of Arthurian Britain.

South of the fortress (between it and the river now flowing west), the Romans began building the town of Isca about 100 A.D. The settlement covered more than 100 acres and accommodated some 12,000 people. It soon possessed a wide range of impressive buildings.

The town, incidentally, did not develop (like so many communities of the Western American frontier) willy-nilly as a random agglomeration of buildings but as a planned settlement. It boasted handsome temples to Diana, Mithras, Jupiter Dolichenus, and other divinities both native and imported, an indication of its cosmopolitan character.

Southwest of the fortress there lay a walled parade ground 700 by 500 feet for the use of the resident legion, and one of the few areas within the city proper which would have been available for new construction during the regimes of Aurelius Ambrosius and Rex Artorius.

Across from the parade ground, and southeast of the fortress, there stood Isca's military amphitheatre used for both military and civic events. It measured 222 feet long 192 feet wide, and some 30 feet high, thus overtopping the fortress walls. Immediately southwest of the amphitheatre there lay a large public bath-house. South of the walled parade ground and the city's forum there lay the principal area of the civilian settlement. East and south of the city, along the banks of the Usk, there lay the military and civilian warehouses with their wharves.

Unlike Venta Silurum, the cantonal capital to the east or northeast by some 8 miles, Isca Silurum flourished as something more than a marketplace or administrative center. Its preeminence and entire characteristic development was due completely to the fact of its being one of the three permanent legionary bases and specifically the home of the Second Augustan Legion. Curiously, the official emblem of the Second Legion duplicates one of the standard symbols of modern astrology: the Capricorn, that elegantly mythical creature compounded of half-goat above and half-fish below.

Isca Silurum, almost from the very beginning of the Roman occupation of Britain, was thus an important and strategic provincial city of the Roman frontier. But, as noted, it also very much possessed a charisma and mystique all its own. However similar it may have appeared in a general way to other Roman cities, it retained (according to a variety of reports then and later) a character very much its own, and that curious atmosphere of "otherwhere" typical of the West Country.

The civilian settlement at Isca, like that of so many classical Roman cities, had two main streets (one running east and west, the other north and south) that bisected each other at right angles. This bisection resulted in four uneven quarters. The great walled parade ground dominated the quarter on the northwest, and in the northeastern quarter, near the fortress's southern gate, the legionary amphitheatre (flanked just south or southwest by the good-sized public baths) stood at the entrance to Isca's forum, which lay beyond surrounded with basilicas, theatres, temples, and other civic buildings. Most of the civilian population lived in the two larger quarters on the south: east of the southeastern quarter as well as south of this same quarter, and then of the quarter on the southwest, Isca's considerable waterfront area with wharves and warehouses (mixed in with civilian residences and probably military stations, particularly at the water's edge) lay generously displayed.

After or around the time of the first severe barbarian assaults of 367–69 A.D., the Britons living in Caerleon refurbished the substantial walls (with attached interval and corner turrets placed probably every 150 feet) around the city proper similar to the defenses enclosing the fortress lying just to the north. The waterfront areas too would have received some kind of fortification system consisting of divers bits of walls and towers and turrets alternating with portcullis-type gates and smaller pastern-type doors. The Britanno-Romans, we can be confident, made sure of Isca's defenses.

When Caesar Honorius (then in Ravenna north of Rome) declared Britain a free province in 410—when much of the former Western Empire had already collapsed—Isca Silurum as a Roman city was thus more than three centuries old.

The Welsh derived the very name of the town in later times from "Castra Legionis" (the Camp or Camps of the Legion): Caerleon, or "Caer Leon" (the Castle or Fort of the Legion). Hence, by Late Roman and certainly by Arthurian times, the civilian and military communities had fused together to be transformed into that golden and glittering "capital" deep in the west of Britain, the legendary "City of the Legions" where something of the ancient imperial splendor still abode.

Mention has already been made of Caerleon's military amphitheatre, whose arena measured 184 feet by 137. It could accommodate around 6,000 persons, or an entire legion (for the purposes of military education). And legend has associated it with King Arthur's Round Table (whatever may have lain originally behind *that*). Certainly, had there been a real "emperor and leader in battles" named Artorius, and had he made Caerleon one of his camelots or capitals, this ancient monument (today maintained for the public by the Department of the Environment) would have played its part in large public gathering during the time of Arthur's Britain.

The later Welsh historian Geoffrey of Monmouth, writing in his *History of the Kings of Britain* in the twelfth century, depicts Caerleon as the setting for King Arthur's imperial coronation. Although some scholars and critics have considered Geoffrey "a reckless forger" and his magnum opus a fable pretending to be history, recent research suggests that, allowing for some pardonable *cultural* or patriotic exaggeration on the good bishop's part, he may very well have worked from some genuine historical sources no longer extant (and not only just that certain ancient book in British that he cites, which could have really existed, when all is said and done).

Now, when Geoffrey knew Caerleon the city would still have had a fair show of ancient architecture. Even the less imaginative Gerald of Barry (who saw Caerleon in 1188) writes of temples and theatres, immense palaces, remarkable hot baths, and other buildings, all enclosed in fine walls; in short, a town of prodigious size and substantial architecture that would have impressed a sensitive and knowledgeable person of that time as a considerable "relic" left over from the former Roman Empire.

It is worth noting some peculiar coincidences here. Geoffrey of Monmouth's father had Arthur for his name. His son derived his greatest fame in writing about *King* Arthur. According to Geoffrey as well as various local traditions, Caerleon was one of the British warchief's headquarters. And *Arthur* Machen, who was to extend and extrapolate certain elements and aspects of the Arthurian Mythos in his poetic fantasies (possibly most notably in "The Great Return"), was born in Caerleon and, it will be noted, largely from ancient British-Keltic stock.

V. Roman Britain and the Western Roman Empire

But now Caerleon must be seen against the larger background of Roman Britain and the Western Roman Empire. By 410 A.D., when much of the Western Roman Empire had already collapsed, and when Caesar Honorius (the puppet emperor of the Romanized barbarian general Stilicho until the latter's death in 408) declared to the Britons that the defense of their province now depended upon their own initiative (and that in effect Britannia was now a free realm), the impossible happened.

The general Alaric with a large barbarian host entered and sacked the great imperial city of Rome, an event that, while perhaps unavoidable, caused a profound shock throughout the Roman and Romanized populations in what was left of the Western Empire. The emperor Honorius and his court had taken refuge in Ravenna in the north of Italy, and it was plain that if Mother Rome could herself no longer look to her own defenses, then the Romans themselves could have no thought for the safety or protection of Rome's far-away northwestern frontier.

Ironically enough, the latest surviving Roman coin found in Caerleon does not honor Caesar Honorius but dates to the reign of Arcadius (but before 395). During the time of the first major sacking of Rome, whilst Honorius had removed to Ravenna, Arcadius was ruling from Constantinople, the ancient Byzantium, as the Eastern Emperor. Two further major sackings of

Rome were to occur in the mid-400s and mid-500s. In 476 the barbarian Odoacer deposed the last official Western Roman Emperor, Romulus Augustulus. By 547 it is written that for a while the city of Rome remained actually deserted!

Meanwhile the Romano-Britons were having their own problems. Britain, or Britannia, during the fourth century A.D. had remained a wealthy and integral part of the Roman Empire. Left to its own devices in 410, the government of Roman Britain during the 420s evidently enlisted Saxon warriors from Germany to strengthen the British defenses.

But sometime during the 420s to 440s the Saxon and other Germanic barbarians rebelled—that is, *mutinied*—against the nominal Britanno-Roman dominion. A contemporary Gallic chronicle could even say that in 441-42 Britain (actually East Britain) had been reduced to the dominion of the Saxons. This report would have of course been greatly exaggerated, but it undoubtedly captures something of the dread felt by British refugees making the report. The Romano-Britons (from Eastern Britain) fled into Western Britain and into Armorica, the ancient double peninsula of Brittany and Normandy, on the northwest of Gaul.

The Britons then made the signal mistake of hiring further Saxons to fight and contain the rebelling Saxons already in Britain. These mercenaries in their turn rebelled or mutinied, and in collaboration with further Germanic barbarians took the occasion evidently to mount a full-scale invasion and settlement of at least Eastern Britain.

Three main routes of penetration by the Anglo-Saxons (along estuaries and other waterways) are prominent: along the Thames, the Wash, and the Humber. The invasion up the Thames in particularly linked with the Jutish heroes Hengest and Horsa, and with their dealings with the chief British ruler Vortigern in the mid-fifth century. The later English scholar Bede places the time of Hengest and Horsa's invasion somewhere between 450 and 455. Hengest and his son (or grandson) Aesc established the Jutish kingdom of Kent, or Cantwara, a name borrowed from the British tribe of the Cantii. The wars of Hengest and Aesc seem principally to concern their conquest and settlement of Kent.

From the writings of the sixth-century monk Gildas (associated with the early Christian monastery at Glastonbury), as well as from other contemporary or near-contemporary accounts, we may vaguely perceive a great federated attack by the Saxons and other Germanic tribes (and not just into Eastern Britain) in the later fifth century. This attack ruined what remained of the

Roman towns at least in much of Eastern Britain and spread devastation over vast stretches of the country. The Britons now drew back into their mountain strongholds in the west, the southwest, the northwest, and the north of Britain, while probably still holding both York and London. Between them and the Saxons in the east, a desolate no-man's-land ran down the middle of the country.

The fifty or sixty years between the mid-fifth to the early sixth century, many of them grim for the Britons, were years of intermittent warfare that destroyed much of the Roman economy and technology. Whilst something of Roman civilization still survived in the west, most of Eastern Britain now lay beyond the effective recovery and repair of the Britanno-Romans. The net result of the ravages (beyond the destruction of Eastern Britain and the settlement of Brittany by the Britons or Bretons) was to thin out virtually to extinction the educated Romanized classes: their last efforts, decisive and considerable, produced the careers of Ambrosius Aurelianus and Arthur, the fabled "King of the Britons." The post-Arthurian Welsh kings and tribes surviving in the west were Britons with but an inconsiderable trace of Roman civilization or language. The ravages that occurred circa 450-500/510 had one further important result. Because of the devastation spread over large areas of the country, there was now plenty of room for the settlement of the Saxons and other invaders.

In that long struggle with the barbarians the Britons found two outstanding and ingenious leaders from the Romanized remnant. Of Ambrosius Aurelianus it may be said he made a successful resistance; and on the foundation of this defense the Britons chose Arthur again and again to lead them against the invaders. This series of twelve great battles culminated in a signal victory at Mons Badonicus around 500 or 510, and won for the Western Britons some thirty or forty years of peace or semi-peace.

Thus the British won the war under Arthur's leadership, and Arthur restored the forms of Roman imperial government. They contained the Saxons within substantial and clearly defined reservations. Arthur's "empire" of united Brythons on both sides of the "Narrow Seas" lasted some thirty to fifty years (estimates vary). At his death his realm fragmented into a large number of small independent successor states.

Also, sometime following his death, starting in 547 and gaining new impetus in 552, the Anglo-Saxons continued the expansion of their territory westward, and always at the expense of the Brythons. The Saxon and other Germanic federates rebelled once again (say, from the mid-fifth century on into the early seventh). In one generation they subdued most of the former province of Britannia and began its transformation into England. (Some authorities give the approximate dates 552-615 for this further period of conquest by the Saxons.)

From that time onward, the independent native British were confined to the west (mainly Cambria and Dumnonia or Cornwall, Devon, and Somerset) and to the north (areas such as the Scottish Lowlands and the Lake District).

According to a recent monograph devoted to the subject, *The Age of Arthur* (1973), John Morris sums up the achievement of the real historical Arthur or Artorius in the following words:

> His triumph was the last victory of western Rome; his short-lived empire created the future nations of the English and the Welsh; and it was during his reign and under his authority that the Scots first came to Scotland [from northern Erin or Ireland]. His victory and his defeat turned Roman Britain into Great Britain. (xiii)

What then were the basic British holdings during the regimes of Aurelianus and Artorius?

There were some five or more principal Welsh "kingdoms" or geographical areas that spread from southwestern Britain all the way up through the Scottish Lowlands to the Grampian Mountains north of Antonine's Wall (this latter is in the same latitude as Edinburgh).

There was Cambria or Wales with three main kingdoms: Gwynedd or Venedotia in the north, Dyfed in the south, and between them (lying more in the east of central Wales) Powys. There was also the area in southeastern Cambria, Siluria or Gwent, which included Caerleon and Caerwent and the Forest of Dean. To the east and north of Gwent, there lay the great protected inner valley of the Severn (mainly north of Glevum or Gloucester).

The Britons held Cheshire and Lancashire and then further north Cumberland and Westmoreland. These last two areas southwest of Hadrian's Wall comprised the kingdom of Rheged.

North of the Wall (that is, in the eastern Scottish Lowlands) there was the large kingdom of Gododin (also called Manau Guotodin) or Lothian; in the western Scottish Lowlands there were other smaller kingdoms. Drawing a line from the Tyne or the Tees to Silchester (west of London)—virtually down the middle of Britain—we may regard everything east as belonging to the Anglo-Saxons and other invaders.

The Britons would probably still have held the land just around Eburacum or York, say, somewhere between the Humber River on the south and the Tees River on the north.

They would still have held Winchester, Vindocladia, the Isle of Wight, Calleva or Silchester, London, and the naval control of the Thames to Vagniacae and Rutupiae and in the series of Roman forts built along the lower Thames out to the "German Sea" (lying on the east or northeast of Britain).

They would still have held the heavily forested Chiltern Hills, which lay north and northwest of London, and which served as a natural defense against the settlements of the Northern Angles in the land just north of the Wash as well as those of the East Angles and the East Saxons inhabiting the lands northeast of London, that is, lying between the Wash and the general London area.

The heavily fortified Britanno-Roman city of Londinium served of course as its own defense against the South Saxon settlements in southeastern Britain, particularly the chieftain Aelle's own isolated but populous kingdom in Sussex between the "Narrow Seas" and the uninhabited forest of Anderida, or the Weald. Aelle founded his own kingdom sometime between 477 and 491, when he stormed and sacked the fortified town of Anderida or Pevensey.

VI. Arthurian Britain

It has only been recently that more and more scholars have come to realize that a real historical figure does indeed stand behind the King Arthur of myth and legend, and that for excellent reasons he should be legended. In restoring for the nonce a substantial portion of the Western Roman Empire, Arthur as a Britanno-Roman hero deserved—indeed could not have avoided—the mythicizing that for centuries and centuries kept his name and something of his real ancient renown alive in people's imaginations in lieu of any actual historical evidence available to the modern world until recently. A pretty piece of magic for someone who has been described as "a semi-barbaric chief"!

The following collation of dates and events in regard to Arthurian Britain is the present writer's own personal interpretation, and represents a conflation of varying sources (history, legend, archaeology, traditions, folklore, and summaries of divers schools of thought). While many of the dates are frankly tentative, we have tried nonetheless to create some kind of consistency between the historical Artorius and the legendary "King Arthur" by aligning them with certain main outlines and facts of that almost obliterated and certainly chaotic period of history.

According to Geoffrey of Monmouth, Arthur was born in 505 and died in 542. However, the consensus of modern scholarship suggests around 470 for Arthur's birth. This date would allow a more extended period of time than 505, in order to accommodate the press of events in Arthur's lifetime, but we shall use this latter date elsewhere. Arthur was crowned king in Silchester (the Calleva of Roman times) at age fifteen. This would give us 485 or around 485, a year in which we may also posit the death of Arthur's father Uther Pendragon (if there is indeed any historical reality to such a kingly father-figure for Arthur's own immediate progeniture), as well as the first of Arthur's "twelve great battles" against the Saxons. These last three events might all be connected.

At least one modern novelist, Mary Stewart in her best-selling novel *The Hollow Hills* (1973), has adroitly and astutely connected them. In her telling Uther Pendragon, virtually on his deathbed, commands the British forces against the Saxons in a great battle near Hadrian's Wall at Caer Luguvallium. Arthur literally saves the day for his own British by the heroism and fiery enthusiasm of his fighting. Uther dies during the subsequent victory feast within the old Roman fort. Arthur is recognized as king by virtue of a magic sword in a mysterious forest chapel. All these events transpire during the same day and night. The year is around 485.

The neighborhood of Caerleon-on-Usk witnessed Arthur's ninth great battle against the Saxons: we shall posit 505 for this event. If the myths and legends relative to this battle at Isca Silurum reflect any truth, the defense of this proud and ancient city (the one-time military capital) would have called forth an especially valiant display of desperate and heroical fighting on the part of Arthur and the Britons.

The prolonged and intermittent fighting betwixt Saxons and Britons lasted from 450 into 500 or 510, and culminated at last at Mount Badonicus where the British won overwhelmingly against the Saxons, returned them to their clearly defined reservations, and presently enjoyed a long period of peace or semi-peace before the inevitable reduction of most of Britain to the dominion of the Saxons.

Various dates have been suggested for the battle at Mount Badonicus (also called Mount Badon, Mons Badonicus, and Badon Hill): 490, 500, 510, 512, 514, 516. We have chosen the year 510, as this would allow more than thirty years for the "imperial reign" of Arthur, a respite of peace that, in retrospect, would appear a magical and "golden" age. The precise location of Mount Badonicus is not known, but it may have been at Bath, or possibly somewhere southeast of Bath, or possibly it might have been Salsbury Hill at Batheaston.

Twenty-five years of Arthur fighting victoriously against the Saxons (circa 485 to 510) does not seem a necessarily unrealistic length of time for what must have proven a bitterly desperate struggle for the beleaguered British. Charlemagne spent thirty years in subduing the Saxons in the later 700s on the basis of intermittent warfare.

We would posit 510 or 512 as the year in which Arthur would have been crowned as Caesar Augustus Artorius—the Roman Emperor of the West—at "Caer Leon" on Usk. As a proper military, administrative, commercial, and courtly ambiance it would naturally have suggested itself to the British of that time. It was a former military capital, a wealthy community with a long-established cosmopolitan character, a well-protected municipality (that is, a Roman town still extant and intact as compared to many Roman towns in Eastern Britain that lay desolate and ruinous), and a seat of the ancient Brythonic stock situated in the still unconquered West Country of Britannia (and moreover in the very mountain heartland of Cymru or Cambria). Arthur came along just in time to take advantage of all the previous Britanno-Roman efforts against the Anglo-Saxons, and his twenty-five years of vigilance against the barbarian invaders represents approximately the latter half of the fifty or sixty years between 450 and 510.

At the time of his imperial coronation Arthur would have numbered among his contemporaries the following key historical figures: Symmachus, the Pope at the Lateran Palace in Rome; Theodoric, King of the Ostrogoths, and the Byzantine Emperor's Viceroy in Italy; Anastasius I, Emperor of the East, ruling from Constantinopolis and surrounded by imperial splendor; and Kavadh I, the Shah of Iran and the Sasanian Empire, ruling from the double city of Ctesiphon (on both sides of the lower Tigris River) in ancient Mesopotamia (20 miles southeast of the later Bagdad) and surrounded by no less imperial magnificence.

Whether or not any of these would have recognized (or even been aware of) the Welsh *ameráudur* or emperor is today a moot question, since early in the fifth century the Teutonic conquest of Gaul had virtually cut Britain off from Rome and the Mediterranean.

There in the "sunset realms" of Britain the Britanno-Romans would have been conscious of preserving a cultural continuity directly from Late Roman times. By the time of Arthur's Britain they were already far enough away from those irremeable days that they would certainly have perceived with acute nostalgia the vanished peace and order of the Imperium Romanum and the whole way of life that had gone with it.

Whilst Arthur's reign (imperial or merely royal) would have marked a revival of Keltic art and architecture, and the earliest transformation of Late Roman society into "proto-medieval," the Romano-Britons would especially have reverenced the forms of Roman imperial ritual as a charismatic survival from the Western Roman Empire. This would have represented in effect some of the earliest ROMANticism—properly speaking—even though most modern phases of Romanticism stem from the High Middle Ages and the whole way of life symbolized through the metrical romances of the trouvères, and the songs of the troubadours and minnesingers.

As one of the three former legionary bases in Britain, Caerleon would have retained a strong civic pride as a custodian and protector of the Late Roman culture as well as of the revised Kelticism symbolized by such a *native* ruler as Arthur, a revised Kelticism also seen in the contemporary hero-cult in verse concerning Arthur fostered and maintained by the native Welsh bards according to immemorial custom.

The mixed Roman and (revived) Keltic style that would have prevailed in the Romano-British world in the age of Arthur might be symbolized best for us by the following simple and purely verbal examples. Segontium became Caer Segontium, then later Caer Seint, then still later Caernarvon (after the Welsh "Caernarfon," i.e., Caer yn Arton, the fort in the land over against the island of Mona or Angelesy). Venta Silurum became Caer Venta or Caerwent. Isca Silurum, Caer Legionis or "Caer Leon." Maridunum, Caer Maridunum, then Caer Myrrdyn, then finally Carmarthen (this area is strongly associated with the poet-prince-magician "Myrrdyn" or Merlin, the name so closely linked with Arthur's in later legend).

This curious mingling of the classical (Roman) with the native (Keltic) continued on in various forms during most of the Middle Ages. Geoffrey of Monmouth brought a strong "classicizing" influence upon the Arthurian lore bequeathed to the Britons of his time, and from this peculiar mixture the later Arthurian Mythos derives much of its characteristic aesthetic (together with a considerable admixture from the Age of Chivalry, it must be emphasized).

In the saga of the historical Artorius there remains now to record only the final Battle of Camlann, or Camlaun (identified by some scholars as "Camogdelanna")—"in which Arthur and Medraut fell"—dated by some to 537, and by others (including Geoffrey of Monmouth) to 542. Compare this with the Arthur of legend, reported as "sore wounded" whilst fighting against

Medraut (or Mordred) in a last battle on the River Camel in Cornwall. And this is the last we hear of the Welsh *ameráudur*—in any kind of historical way—until the High Middle Ages and Geoffrey of Monmouth.

At the time of Arthur's death Justinian the Great was reigning from Byzantium as Emperor of the East (he had succeeded Justin I, who in turn had succeeded Anastasius I), and Chosroes or Khosrau I (at least as great a ruler as Justinian) had succeeded his father Kavadh I as the Shah of Iran and the Sasanian Empire. Then sometime between 547 (signalized by the death of King Maelgwyn of Gwynedd) or 552 and 615, the Saxons conquered further but always (it should be stressed) against the fierce opposition of the British, or as the newcomers called them, the Welsh who lived in the west and the north. By 570 the Welsh still held a little less than half of Britain, although they evidently had lost London by this time.

VII. The Arthurian Country at Large

We have now pursued the career of certain elements and locales in the work and life of Arthur Machen as related to Caerleon and what we may call the specifically *local* Arthur Machen country. Next we shall continue to follow some of these (mainly certain aspects of the Arthurian Mythos) into what we might call the Arthur Machen (and surely the "Arthurian") country *at large*. To wit, the world (cultural and geographical, and surviving through radically diverse political systems over a period of millennia) of the Brythonic or British-Keltic empire, and then, beyond that, the Keltic world of Gael and Brython combined, including most particularly ancient Erin, or Ireland, the Hibernia or Ivernia of Roman usage.

First, we open an atlas to the British Isles and quickly focus in on the country around the Bristol Estuary and the western end of the English Channel. Glance at Scotland, Ireland, and the Isle of Man (called Mona in Roman times) in the upper Irish Sea; here have lived from ancient times the Goidelic or Gaelic Kelts, cousins to the Brythonic Kelts. Now look over Wales (including also the Isle of Anglesey, just northwest of Wales, and also called Mona in Roman times) bounded by the Dee and the Severn (and at one time by Offa's Dyke, the Anglo-Saxon wall connecting the two rivers, and keeping the Welsh within the traditional boundaries of their native mountain heartland), Monmouth or Monmouthshire, Gloucester, Somerset, Devon, Cornwall, and the Scilly Isles. And then glance over to Brittany and Normandy (the ancient Armorica), and just west of Armorica, the Channel Islands. These are some of the ancient lands where the Brythons have dwelt since both before and after the decline of Roman Britain; and according to myth and legend, these lands form but a fragment of Arthur's Empire, which in its own turn had been but a fragment of the Western Roman Empire, which in yet its own turn had only been the other half of the Imperium Romanum, stretching from the British Isles on the far west to venerable Mesopotamia on the far east. Both the Gaels and the Britons had myths and legends that told of their Avalons and Avilions, remarkably Hesperides-like or Atlantis-like islands arising from those depths of the North Atlantic Ocean that lay to the west or southwest of Britain and Gaul.

(Between 500 and 550, the Brythonic Kelts primarily inhabited the western peninsulas and highlands from Cornwall and Wales on through the scenically spectacular Lake District (an old Keltic mountain heartland from which the much later English Romantic poets were to derive both inspiration and a name) and then on through the Scottish Lowlands about as far north as Antonine's Wall and "Caer Eidyn," or Edinburgh.)

Secondly, we draw a line from Caer Nodentis in Lydney Park, Gloucestershire (this would be a point roughly midway betwixt the Wye and the city of Gloucester on the Severn) south-southeast to the city of Bath (the Aquae Sulis of Roman times); then, another line from Aquae Sulis but going southwest to Glastonbury (the ancient island-valley of Avalon); and then, another line from Avalon (or "Glastonia"—one of its names in medieval Latin) but going northeast or north-northeast back to "Caer Nodentis." Thus you will have a triangle that lies at the very heart of the cultural Brythonic empire, and which keynotes an immediate area where extraordinary spiritual and mystical activity has taken place from pre-Roman to post-Christian times and into the twentith century. This area is moreover intensely connected with certain main aspects and elements in the Arthurian Mythos. Keep this triangle in mind, since it will serve as the geographical touchstone or triangular homebase (as it were) from which we shall now explore some of those same principal aspects, elements, and locales important in Arthurian Britain.

By an odd coincidence, the distance between the Wye and the city of Gloucester on the Severn—upon a line running from southwest to northeast—measures roughly the same as the distance between Caer Nodentis and Aquae Sulis, and then between Aquae Sulis and Glastonbury; that is, the original distance is approximately the same in length as the "eastern" or "southern" sides of our triangular homebase.

VIII. Cadbury Castle

Straight in a line as the bird flies, about 12 miles southeast of Glastonbury, we come into the neighborhood of the River Cam and the village of Queen's Camel (formerly known as just Camel) and thus to Cadbury Castle. This earthwork fort (pre-Roman Iron-Age, like that to the northwest of Caerleon, or like that at Caer Nodentis) stands on a solitary hill some 500 feet high and overlooks the Vale of Avalon with Glastonbury Tor in the distance to the northwest. During the reign of Henry VIII, the antiquarian John Leland recorded the fact that the local people referred to Cadbury Castle as "Camalat" and as once the home of King Arthur. Out of all the sites that might have been the original for the legendary Camelot, this particular place has one of the best claims to a real enduring tradition.[3]

The question of Camelot seems to be curiously intertwined (linguistically at least) with that of Camlann or Camlaun, as well as with other places and place-names where *cam* or *camel* occur. If *cam* or *camel* has any meaning in Welsh or Cornish beyond "twisted" or "crooked," it may have been a generic word for stream or river in that the course of most rivers is twisted, or twisting, or making loops or "esses." Curiously enough, in many poems and stories that depict or mention Camelot, there is usually a river that goes near or fairly near its walls, and that features rather prominently in the given narrative.

According to legend, Camelot was the capital where King Arthur ruled over the Britons, during the time of the terrible Saxon invasions but before the overall Saxon conquest of England. The oldest existing records or stories of Arthur do not mention Camelot. He is first mentioned as ruling there in *Lancelot*, the metrical romance by Chrétien de Troyes, written sometime between 1160 and 1180, and hence after the first appearance in Latin prose (c. 1135) of Geoffrey's *History of the Kings of Britain*. "Camelot" happens to make a good rime with "Lancelot" in Norman French (where the final "t" is not pronounced) as well as in modern English. Chrétien de Troyes may simply have picked up the name of Camel, or Camlann/Camlaun (or as Camalann/Camalaun), and Frenchified it easily enough into "Camelot."

In *Le Morte d'Arthur* (published in 1485), his classic redaction of the Arthurian Mythos in English prose, Sir Thomas Malory depicts Camelot as the chief metropolis of the realm (rather like London), sometimes equated with

---

3. The principal source for this chapter is the article "Camelot and Arthurian Britain" by Geoffrey Ashe in *Man, Myth and Magic*.

Winchester but in one context located north of Carlisle (Caer Luguvallium). Some scholars have proposed the modern city of Colchester as the site of Camelot; in Roman times it bore the name of Camulodunum; but since that area of East Anglia was occupied by the barbarian invaders almost from the start of the Germanic invasions, the Britons would have needed to spend a great deal of energy to make Camulodumun an important capital for Arthur so far from the West Country still occupied and controlled by the Kelts. Thus, beyond the purely linguistic coincidence of the name, Camulodunum has little to recommend it as Camelot.

Just north of Antonine's Wall and then due west of the inner Firth of Forth (not far from Caer Eidyn; i.e., Edinburgh) there once rose a Roman fortress called Camelon or, in the Keltic style, "Caer Camelon." This general area saw some considerable Arthurian activity; immediately outside Caer Eidyn is the mountain called Arthur's Seat (from whose summit he is supposed to have surveyed the surrounding countryside) not far from which Arthur and his Britons fought one of his "twelve great battles" against the Saxons. The name of Camelon is (coincidentally) close to that of Cam(a)laun, and whilst this Roman frontier fortress was probably no more Camelot than Colchester, it seems safe to assume that the Arthurian Britons may have used it to defend their own realm's northern frontier inherited from the Romans. It may even have figured in some signal way in Arthur's own saga.

Yet another theory places Camelot near Tintagel where in a pre-Norman castle Arthur is supposed to have been born. Again, without placing absolute credence in the legend of his birth, or in the theory that here in this particular spot there once a rose the legendary Camelot, so much tradition has associated Tintagel with Arthur that it does seem safe to assume it did possess some real and important connection with him.

If Camelot does have any meaning beyond a generic usage as capital or headquarters (and any particular town and/or fortress under Arthur's rule could have functioned in that capacity even if only temporarily), then the two best geographical candidates must share the specific honor between them, as they often do in some of the legends. We stress the double honor, since the overall concept of Camelot has at least two main aspects as Arthur's capital.

In some accounts Camelot is primarily a great castellated palace with a village or town attached in order to serve the needs of Arthur's court. In other accounts Camelot is a genuine and heavily fortified city similar to London (although nowhere near as large) with Arthur's "gorgeous palace" featured as one of the main architectural attractions. The best candidate for Camelot as a genuine city is probably Arthur Machen's own birthplace Caerleon-on-Usk. The city is located on, and derives its Roman name from, the Usk; and while no site as yet discovered at Caerleon has preserved any vestiges of Arthur's royal palace, we cannot presently rule out the possibility that such may not have existed there.

The best candidate for Camelot as a "great castellated palace" is undoubtedly Cadbury Castle. The River Cam and the village of Queen's Camel lie close enough to the Castle so that they figure geographically in the traditional local references to, and accounts of, King Arthur. Thus it remains Cadbury Castle "in the neighborhood of" or "not far from" the River Cam and the village of Camel or Queen's Camel.

The Castle's ramparts enclose an area of 18 acres atop the 500-foot-high hill, and the summit plateau (which local folklore of vast antiquity calls King Arthur's Palace) did actually support at least one elaborate timber structure once upon a time. During the first quarter of the sixth century (a part of Arthur's presumed period) a wealthy and powerful British lord or leader did use the hilltop as a stronghold, and erected at least one substantial timber building on the summit plateau. This edifice (as visualized in basic restoration on paper) has an immediate affinity with the great hall of later medieval usage. Recent archaeology has revealed a large rectangular ground-plan (wider east and west than north and south) and with about the eastern third of its area originally walled off by some kind of screen. (This last feature also has its mediaeval affinity.)

Moreover, the same British ruler and/or war-chief secured his woodland fortress with strong fortifications indeed. He completely refurbished the original, pre-Roman, Iron Age defenses of earthwork by superimposing an enormous "drystone" type of rampart (featuring a type of tower both similar to and yet different from that of the Roman fortress-camps) and all done in a peculiarly Keltic style of architecture. These walls remain without "known contemporary parallels anywhere else in Britain" (Cavendish 331). The warchief lived quite securely and comfortably within what must have been (from the available evidence) an elaborate series of hills upon the summit plateau, enclosed as they were inside the far-reaching round of outer battlements. It is known that either the lord or his household acting for him imported luxuries from the eastern Mediterranean and also probably from the Middle East.

This "Camalat" was then easily the largest, strongest, and most elaborate of all the known British fortresses in Arthurian times (apart, of course, from the walled cities and forts in the West Country left over from Late Roman days). The remaining usable acreage on top of the hill could easily have accommodated (within tents and pavilions) a large entourage, military and otherwise, whenas circumstances relative to the omnipresent Anglo-Saxon threat served to gather them there (this last must have been fairly often). Details of the specific buildings and fortifications still possess distinct analogies with Britanno-Roman architecture (but not the placement of the entrance to the great hall at the southwest and northeast). But the overall conception of the stronghold would have definitely appeared to us as non-Roman, however obvious its ultimate immediate evolution from Roman models in certain selected aspects. The typically native Brythonic, purely timber architecture of the main group of buildings, as well as the general plan of the fortress (a kind of donjon or inner castle surrounded by a series of vast outer courtyards, in turn environed by "many-towered" ramparts of mixed stone and timber construction), rather curiously foreshadows the typical castle of the later Middle Ages.

It is not hard to imagine the Welsh *ameráudur* living in this typically British woodland fortress of the early Dark Ages—this Brythonic Versailles, as it were—attended by an entourage of British warriors and knights, bard and minstrels, astrologers and priests (whether Christian or Druid, or both).

Recent archaeology suggests a genuine historic link between this Brythonic stronghold and Glastonbury Tor some 12 miles to the northwest. Significantly, both places lie within sight of each other. In the graveyard of early Glastonbury Abbey—according to an ancient local tradition—his followers buried "Rex Arthurius" after his famous last Battle of Camlaun in 542 A.D. Although it may seem at first as though we are straying far afield from Arthur Machen and from matters strictly Machenesque, we must spend some little time and space next at Glastonbury.

In its own right it is a mystical milieu of supreme importance—it has been termed quite properly a prime spiritual "acupuncture point" on the planet Earth—and during the High Middle Ages, Glastonbury's greatest period, it contributed tremendously both to the local renown and the international cult centered around King Arthur.

IX. Glastonbury and Avalon

The Tor, or Avalon Tor, rises high above the small town of Glastonbury in Somerset, internationally famous for its ruined Abbey, one of the greatest Christian foundations in all Western Europe.[4] The town lies upon (or

---

4. This chapter is heavily indebted to the article "Glastonbury" by Geoffrey Ashe in *Man, Myth and Magic*.

actually just off) the River Brue. Like "Camelot" or Cadbury Castle some 12 miles to the southeast, this hill attains a height of some 500 feet above sea level and looks out over a broad stretch of low-lying country on all sides, the ancient island-vale of Avalon. Built more specifically on the site of the island proper of Avalon, Glastonbury Abbey is allegedly the first Christian foundation in Britain and the last resting place of King Arthur. In addition, the Abbey is the focus of a large tapestry of myth and legend, and in some special sense a repository of pre-Christian mysteries.

The main legend relative to the Abbey tells how in the first century A.D. Joseph of Arimathea (the rich man who buried Christ) transports the Holy Grail (used at the Last Supper of Christ and his apostles) to the Island of Avalon. In obedience to a vision Joseph and his companions build a wattle chapel, the so-called Old Church dedicated to the Virgin Mary, and still standing in the High Middle Ages as an object of the profoundest veneration. How did this Arimathean story come about? Was it a symbolic literary fiction, a deliberate monastic fraud, or a genuine rediscovery of an elder tradition?

The main legend relative to the Tor is that of the ancient Isle of Avalon. The original "island" of Avalon and its immediate neighborhood have served as a holy place, a burial ground, and a residence. To the original Brythons it was a place of the greatest religious awe, the literally *enchanted* Isle of Avalon, consecrated to the shades of the dead: the "ynys apfalon" or "ynysapfalon annwn." The Abbey site itself is rich in both Christian and pre-Christian burials; this evidently was the original burial site for which Avalon was first used and from which there evolved much of the "otherworldly" character of the Avalon legends. The earthwork of Ponter's Ball (to the east) may be a vestige of the Keltic sanctuary's boundary that defined the original limits of the island.

As for "Avalon," this is usually interpreted as the "place of apples" like the Garden of the Hesperides in classical mythology; the Irish Kelts (the Gaels) also told of an Avalon as Isle of the Blest, and a "place of apples" likewise, lying somewhere in the Atlantic Ocean west or southwest of the British Isles. A later name was no longer "ynys apfalon" but "ynys vitrin" or the Isle of Glass ("Glastonbury" is an Anglo-Saxon version of this): that is, an "Isle" reflected in the "Glass" or mirror of the surrounding waters.

Geology would seem to indicate quite definitely that before drainage, and especially during Late Roman times and the subsequent Dark Ages, the Tor with its environing lesser hills must often have been virtually isolated. Indeed, most of this region used to be subject to flooding, with permanent lagoons, marshes, and forested islets. Thus at the beginning of the Christian era Glastonbury was almost a true island, surrounded as it was by lagoons and rivers: with its original flora and fauna the area must have presented an appearance of wild "primordial" beauty.

The island of Avalon, the otherworldly apple orchard, was thus a pre-Christian religious center and for the Brythons an "Isle of the Dead" and a Gate into Annwn, the realm of shades and faery folk. In some of the Brythonic folklore Avalon is indeed equated with Annwn, and to distinguish it from other Avalonian concepts the real Avalon should therefore be more properly termed Avalon Annwn. Apple trees have grown on the Tor at various times, and in the pre-Christian era wild apple orchards may have originally flourished here. Any apples from such sacred trees would have possessed a mystical significance for the Kelts. At least one surviving legend (relative to the Welsh saint Collen) preserves presently undatable folklore about the Tor as an entrance to Annwn the Underworld, and as a home for Gwyn-ap-Nudd, lord of the faery folk, leader of the Wild Hunt, and sometimes the "son" of Nodens (hence, a later aspect or incarnation of the same principle or divinity).

Gwyn-ap-Nudd and his "home" on Avalon may preserve a memory of a shrine to Nodens or some closely related god here in Roman times. There may have been tales or legends of the Tor as a hollow hill. Hence, Nodens or Nudd, Lord of the Abyss or of the "void" (the "hollow place" lying below the earth's surface), provides an easy and logical transition to—and transformation into—Annwn the Underworld (and part of the Keltic concept of the Otherworld). We can safely postulate therefore a pre-Christian shrine on the Tor. Significantly, the Christian monks during the later Middle Ages built a chapel with a tower on top of the Tor and dedicated it to St. Michael, vanquisher of the "evil powers." Only the tower still stands.

Traces of inhabitants on the Abbey site in Roman times have been recently found but no indication of their religion. This might have been some kind of simple residence for pre-Christian holy men, say, a hermitage or abbey of Druids. Recent excavations on the Tor have revealed human settlement there also, notably around 500 A.D., part of the Arthurian period. Indeed, in the time of Arthur a typical timber-built citadel stood atop the Tor. We shall call this stronghold "Caer Avalon Annwn" after the Welsh fashion. Such a citadel would have safeguarded this holy spot from overt physical damage during the early Dark Ages, above all a period of turmoil, danger, and chaos. Since Christianity was still only one religion among many and had not as yet become paramount in the Western world, we could have seen (during the age of Arthur) both on the Tor or close to it—that is, existing at one and the same time—the Keltic pre-Christian shrine, the Brythonic citadel, and the early Christian monastery with the Old Church.

A Keltic pre-Christian monastery would have more than likely stood on the future site of Glastonbury Abbey (just as the well-organized colleges of Druids among the Irish Kelts were easily converted to Christian monasteries). By the sixth century Christian hermits were living on the spot and worshipping in the Old Church. The simultaneous presence of a Christian Keltic monastery near the Tor, and of a timbered Brythonic citadel atop the Tor, is closely paralleled by that of the Christian Keltic monastery on Tintagel Headland, as well as of the presumed Brythonic citadel upon whose site the later Norman castle was built.

As for Glastonbury Abbey it was certainly founded by British Christians on the present site before the Saxon conquest. Archaeologically a date early in the sixth century appears likely. Although St. Patrick reorganized the little community and gave it a monastic rule, no saint of the Dark Ages is credited with Glastonbury's foundation. The monastery is simply there in some form, its origins unexplained and further back still. Hence it is arguable that the Old Church and a small group of hermits may have been there *before* the 500s. Or it is equally arguable that the Church and Abbey were founded within a pre-existing Druid abbey; or, if the latter had been destroyed, then upon the site of the same pre-Christian hermitage.

The West Saxons conquered central Somerset in 658. Their Christian king Cenwalh maintained Glastonbury without a break. It thus became the first major institution in which Teuton and Kelt co-existed and cooperated. It is the one place in Britain with Christian continuity stretching back without a break to King Arthur, to the Romans, and to the apostolic age itself. It is a kind of national shrine, with a spiritual character uniquely its own. The British monks were unable to tell the Saxons any clear story of the Abbey's foundation; this had already been lost in antiquity.

Whenever its foundation, and whatever the site's pre-Christian antecedents, one fact from the Abbey's earlier history seems to remain a fact. According to a very old local tradition, King Arthur was buried in the Abbey's graveyard after his famous last battle, wherever that took place. His alleged exhumation in 1190 served to affix the name of Avalon on the map after it had evidently been lost to the general recognizance.

In 1184 most of the then Abbey (including the Old Church) burnt down, and in the course of the rebuilding the monks who were digging at the site discovered a coffin together with a stone slab and a lead cross, inscribed HIC IACET SEPULTUS INCLITUS REX ARTURIUS IN INSULA AVALONIA: "Here lies ensepulchred the famous King Arthur in the Island of Avalon." The coffin, made from a hollowed-out oak log, contained the bones of a large man with a damaged skull, as well as some smaller bones (and some tresses of blond hair) understood to be those of Queen Guinivere, Arthur's second wife. Perhaps the most valuable contemporary account of this exhumation is that of Geraldus Cambrensis; he was a skeptic about King Arthur at a time whenas most people were indiscriminately credulous.

The monks appropriately enshrined the relics in a casket that Edward I re-interred before the new high altar. However, the contents of the casket were tragically dispersed and lost at the Abbey's dissolution in 1539 during the reign of Henry VIII. The Abbey's dissolution in itself constitutes a tragic loss of the first magnitude: the main church alone, whether as an ecclesiastical locus or simply as a piece of superb Gothic architecture, was in every way at least as great as the cathedral of Westminster Abbey.

In 1962 and 1963, C. A. Ralegh Radford re-excavated the area of the original disinterment, and among other evidence he discovered "the stone lining of an important grave at a great depth." Ralegh Radford was thus able to prove (though not conclusively—which, given the particular evidence, should not be surprising) that this may very well indeed have been the original grave of the real Arthur.

If it is indeed true that Cadbury Castle near Queen's Camel forms the original locus for the legendary Camelot, its closeness to Glastonbury may be more than a mere coincidence.

Before we leave Glastonbury, we must note certain aspects of the Arthurian Avalon legends inspired ultimately by the pre-Christian Isle of Avalon. There are two main concepts of Avalon: there is the island-vale of Avalon Annwn where the real King Arthur was buried, and there is the Avalon depicted by Geoffrey of Monmouth as an Island of the Blest in the Atlantic Ocean rather like a Garden of the Hesperides. This last idealized Avalon is very similar to—if not the same as—the Avalon legended by the Irish Kelts to lie in the western ocean (i.e., somewhere in the Atlantic). Just as the historical Arthur was taken to the real geographical Avalon, Geoffrey's idealized Avalon in the Atlantic is again Arthur's last earthly destination, where he is taken for his wounds to be healed. This occurs in a later work of Geoffrey's, his *Vita Merlini*. Geoffrey possessed (it should be emphasized) an especially poetic quality of imagination, and in its pronounced *poeticalness*, distinctly Welsh or Keltic.

In some versions the idealized (ocean-situated) Avalon is ruled over by Morganne Le Fay. Could she be a memory of a "lady of Avalon" who once lived in Caer Avalon Annwn, or a goddess peculiar to Avalon? Here we see a fictional/mythical extrapolation in the classic "scientifictional" manner. The real island of Avalon is removed to an unspecified location in the Atlantic, and the Brythonic goddess (possibly Morrigu) is extrapolated into a medieval enchantress. Whatever else the real Avalon may have been, it remained for the Keltic imaginative tradition a place of great magic-making, as well as a perfectly logical "smithy" for the production of Caliburn or Excalibur, Arthur's magic sword.

As a traditional burial ground sacred to the British Kelts (not even Christianity could prevent that particular pre-Christian cultural continuity) it was close enough to Arthur's last great battle (whether near "Camelot" at Cadbury Castle, or near "Camelot" at Caerleon-on-Usk in Gwent, or near Tintagel and Camelford in Cornwall) to be the officially logical choice for the inhumation of Caesar Augustus Artorius with due mystical and imperial splendors. The traditional barge in most of the legends, which bears the dead or dying Arthur to Avalon, is very likely the reminiscence of a real vessel that did bear Arthur to Avalon for burial there.

Looking back through the mists of time, can we not somehow see that military flotilla with Arthur's funeral barge in its midst proceeding just off the northern coast of Devon and then into the mouth of the River Brue that flows by Glastonbury? This was the gloriously sad and ultimate public moment in Arthur's career: the little navy paddling up the river into the haunted island-vale of Avalon Annwn, past the forested islets and the brooding marshes, over the great misty lagoons, directly to the Isle of the Dead, and the Gate into Annwn the Underworld or *Other*world.

X. Cornwall and Tintagel

Now going due southwest, we leave Glastonbury, pass through Devon, and come into the ancient land of Cornwall (or "Cornua"), proceeding immediately to Tintagel Headland, a place of unique and spectacular senic beauty high above the western sea.[5] In the later 400s A.D., and before the

---

[5]. Sometime after the presumed Brythonic hill-top stronghold but before the later Norman castle, another castle was built (this is archaeologically attested), thus indicating a virtually continuous residence by politically eminent persons upon Tintagel Headland.

final ascendancy of the Brythonic Kelts under the aegis of King Arthur, great numbers of the Romano-Britons had fled before the invading Saxons from eastern and southeastern Britain into the West Country and beyond, settling in Wales, Cornwall, Devon, Westmoreland, Cumberland, lower Scotland, and Brittany. Indeed, Cornwall together with Wales and Brittany remained a sanctuary for the Britons long after most of England had yielded to the dominance (political and cultural) of the Anglo-Saxons. The Cornish preserved their own language virtually into modern times, and even much of their culture into the twentieth century.

If Arthur were indeed born at Tintagel, as many traditions and legends aver, then the area would naturally have loomed large during his early manhood and later maturity, especially during his career as *imperator atque dux bellorum*. The strategic position of Tintagel far in the west of England (the Brythonic territories par excellence) alone would have assured its importance during the Arthurian period. Although no trace has yet emerged of the pre-Norman "castle" where Arthur was reputedly born, it has now become a fact (thanks to recent archaeology) that the Headland certainly did have inhabitants at this period. A community of British monks (Christians, not Druids) lived here then, and the imported pottery used by their monastery has provided paramount clues to the dating and interpretation of other places, including Arthur's "Camelot" at Cadbury Castle.

The later medieval castle at Tintagel stands close by the remains of the Keltic monastery, and it may very well have been constructed upon the remains of a typical Brythonic hill-top citadel dating from Arthur's time or somewhat before. This Headland is in many respects a very special area, and while it may not have been a place of sacred awe to the Brythons in the manner of Avalon Annwn to the northeast, it does possess its own unique aura. The spot is a natural one for habitation of some kind, and especially desirable as a location for some Arthurian chieftain's hill-fort. Such a fortress (and let us call it "Caer Tintagel" after the Welsh fashion), like Caer Avalon Annwn, would have afforded protection not only to the monastery also on the Headland but to the overall area as well. The simultaneous presence of Christian monastery and Brythonic citadel in the same immediate area is closely paralleled (as we have noted earlier) by that of the monastery and stronghold on the ancient Isle of Avalon.

At a further hill-top dwelling in Cornwall—to wit, Castle Dore—recent archaeology indicates that a Brythonic stronghold (similar to, but not as large as, Cadbury Castle) stood there during the sixth century, i.e., during Arthur's period. Some West Country chieftain built a timber hall within a preexisting Iron Age earthenwork hill-fort, like that at "Caer Nodentis," or like the 17-acre hill northwest of Caerleon's Roman fortress, or like the 18-acre hill of Cadbury Castle. Some scholars have suggested that this chieftain may have furnished the original (historical) model for the King Mark figuring in the romance of Tristram and Yseult. Further hill-top dwellings and strongholds of Arthur's period are known to have existed in both Cornwall and Wales.

Tintagel Headland lies only some 5 miles northwest of the small town of Camelford and the River Camel area. This overall neighborhood is literally permeated with the atmosphere of the sea lying immediately to the west. Again, like Caer Nodentis and the island-vale of Avalon Annwn, this vicinage possesses its own haunted and haunting aura. According to various legends as well as local traditions, the River Camel region is the general area where Arthur fought his famous and fatal "last battle." Certainly, like most of Cornwall, it would have provided a striking background for such an event. The bards at least were following a sound story-telling instinct when they located the last battle here.

The rugged and rocky Cornish coast, the farms on upland plains and in river valleys, the desolate marshes and moors near the sea, the brooding moors lying inland, the outbreaks of stone on old hills and mountains, the variegated clumps of wood, thickets, and other shrubbery—the "poetic" coloring with gemlike hues of blue and/or green pervading the sea, the sky, and the land on a clear day—all possess a wonderfully picturesque quality well suited to the "spirit" of the legend, even if not necessarily to the "letter" of any available historical evidence.

Apart from his final voyage to Avalon, this is the last we see of the real historical Arthur (by now in his later sixties or early seventies) while he is yet alive: the great Welsh *ameráudur* riding forth from Caer Tintagel to the "Last Great Battle of the West"—an event that will loom in later legend like a Brythonic Ragnarok, poignantly symbolizing the final moments of the British-Keltic revival as well as its twilight, which transpired at one and the same time during the period circa 500–550 A.D.

XI. Lyonnesse and Brittany

Now we leave the land of that final fatal encounter of Brython against Brython, and heading again due southwest we pass the towns of Camborne ("Cam-Bourne"), St. Ives, and Penzance, and then come directly to the southwestern extremity of Britain, that curious rocky promontory sculptured by wind and wave into fantastical shapes, to wit, Land's End, with the western sea immediately beyond.

Just some 25 miles due west southwest of Land's End (at the westernmost tip of Cornwall) there lies the small archipelago called the Isles of Scilly; and according to ancient Cornish tradition, they represent the fragments of a larger land called Lyonnesse long lost beneath the waves, but which once stretched from Land's End up to the Scillies, and which also included St. Michael's Mount not far from Penzance.

These islands possess at times a semi-tropical climate, and to the ancient mainland Brythons they must have seemed a veritable paradise. They once contained valuable deposits of tin which both the Phoenicians and the Romans mined; and from this fact there came their Latin name of the Cassiterides, or Isles of Tin. There inheres something peculiarly "Atlantean" in the name of Lyonnesse (as in that of Yss, the island-city that appears and submerges in Breton legendry), vaguely suggesting a survival of some kind from the far-off Empire of Atlantis (such as Plato hath devised), as though Lyonnesse or the Isles of Scilly were somehow the actual remnants of a former Atlantean colony. Lyonnesse (easily semi-independent by virtue of her environing waters and treacherous reefs and rocks) would nonetheless have borne fealty to Arthur, since the inhabitants of the Scilly Isles were at least kindred to the mainland Brythons.

Now we depart from Lyonnesse and head southeast, crossing over the western reaches of the English Channel (or the "Narrow Seas" as they were known in Roman and post-Roman times), and then coming to the peninsulas of Brittany and Normandy, the Armorica of Roman times. An earlier (pre-Keltic) race had lived in Brittany and had built such curious and mysterious megalithic monuments as menhirs, dolmens, and cromlechs; these are most numerous at Carnac and Morbihan. Thus, even before the arrival of the Britons, the peninsula already possessed its own unique aura of otherworldly myth and magic.

The ancient Keltic people in the region of Brittany came under Roman control in 51 B.C. Brittany, or Little Britain, received its name from the Britanno-Roman tribes who settled in Armorica during the second half of the 400s, fleeing before the Anglo-Saxon invaders of eastern and southeastern Britain. By Armorica (from *ar-mor* or *on sea*) we mean Brittany and Western Normandy. It was the lower peninsula that became known as Brittany, with an Upper Brittany and a Lower Brittany, and the home of the "Bretons" (i.e., Britons), or Armorican Brythons. According to various traditions and legends, these definitely counted as among the lands over which King Arthur ruled as Brythonic suzerain. The Channel Islands, just west of Normandy or Upper Armorica, also purportedly formed part of Arthur's Empire.

Before, during, and after Arthur's time, Western Britain and Brittany carried on considerable cultural exchange. Ireland, Britain, and Gaul all possessed varying types of Druids and Druidry, as they later did of Christians and Christianity. On the southern coast of Cornwall and not far from that country's western tip at Land's End, there stands St. Michael's Mount just offshore from the little town of Marazion. (Again, according to ancient Cornish tradition, this Mount represents a remnant of the lost land of Lyonnesse.) The Gulf of St. Malo lies between Brittany and Normandy, and in its (inner) southeastern corner there stands the majestic mass of Mont-Saint-Michel, again just offshore. During the High Middle Ages, these two Benedictine abbeys were closely connected: in name, religion, and general monastic culture.

Rennes, the immemorial capital of Brittany, was named after the Gallic tribe of the Redones or Redonians once resident there. In Roman times the city was known as Condate, or Condate Redonum (the "Condate of the Redonians"). The Forest of Paimpont lies southwest of Rennes; this is the modern remnant of the ancient Forest of Brocéliande, so closely associated in the Arthurian Mythos with Merlin and Arthur (as is much of Brittany). According to one legend the Lady Vivienne ensnared none other than Prince Merlin (the "uncle" and advisor of King Arthur) and imprisoned him in one of the hoary oaks of Brocéliande.

It was here in Brittany (as well as in Western Normandy) that the earliest cycles of poetic narratives about "li re Artus" (first in Breton and then in Norman French) developed subsequently to Arthurian Britain. Thus, "The Bretons have a strong Druidic and Arthurian tradition from classical and mediaeval times . . ." In addition to the enchantments of the Forest of Brocéliande, they had their famous prophecying "Druidesses" on the Ile de Seine.

> It was only at the beginning of the present century, however, that Druidry became an organized force in Brittany. For several years now the annual August Eisteddfod [that peculiarly Keltic gathering of bards, musicians, and entertainers] has been held beside the beautiful lake at Paimpont, in the midst of the old forest area of Brocéliande. (Cavendish 6.723)

The Breton mythology in general has characteristics uniquely its own, just as modern Breton literature written in French is unique in modern French literature for its keenly mystical and cosmic feeling and quality. Thus, Brittany can justly and proudly claim the distinction of acting as the first medium for the transmission of the Arthurian Mythos into the culture of the High Middle Ages, and for thus influencing (in a signal manner) the subsequent development of romance in general throughout Europe. Moreover, the Bretons' bardic and musical culture has remained alive and vigorous into the twentieth century, and has produced outstanding and highly original harpist-singer-poets, some of them popular at least throughout Europe.

XII. Bards, Druids, and Arthur's Later Fame

This then was the Arthurian country at large: the world (cultural and geographical, and surviving through radically diverse political systems over a period of millennia) of the Brythonic (or British-Keltic) empire, and then, beyond that, the Keltic world of Gael and Brython combined, including Ivernia or Ireland.[6]

This cultural Brythonic empire, stretching from the Grampian Mountains in Scotland on the north all the way to Brittany across the "Narrow Seas" on the south, may then actually reflect a Britanno-Roman dominion once ruled by a Rex Imperator Artorius. Even if not politically, at least *culturally* he would have claimed kinship with all these Brythonic lands and peoples to whom he certainly would have been known contemporaneously. The real King Arthur, however great he may actually have been during his life, became infinitely greater after his death, thanks to the peculiar cycles of myth and legend that the various Brythonic peoples wove around his name and exploits.

However, this particularly Keltic tradition would have commenced in Arthur's case whilst he was very much alive, and in fact early in his public or military career. Arthur's court would naturally have attracted the greatest bards, musicians, and sages of his time. Hence the Arthurian Mythos would have begun in the age of Arthur itself.

Throughout the post-Roman Keltic world of Western Europe (whether Gaelic or Brythonic) the bards and seers, unlike the more famous but also more mysterious Druids, continued in positions of power and authority. Certainly in Arthurian society, with its curious and unique mixture of transformed Romanism and revived Kelticism, the bards occupied a singularly

---

6. This chapter is heavily indebted to the two articles (under the uniform heading) "Druids," the first by Stuart Piggott and the second by Ross Nichols, respectively, in *Man, Myth and Magic*.

important place. The traditions relating to the Druids are curiously intertwined with those relating to the bards. Even though the Druids are supposed to have been abolished or driven underground (that is, either exterminated or banished to divers hinterlands devoid of political or economic importance to the Romans), various of their traditions continued on in specific ways: thus, for example, the bards evidently captured something of the particularly "Druidic magic" in their poetry.

Geoffrey Ashe has well summarized the importance of the bards in Arthurian times:

> A great chieftain's title depended partly on the appropriate bard's knowledge of his ancestry. The loyalty of his vassals depended on the bard's success in keeping them convinced of his prowess, wisdom, and generosity. Poet-sages of legend like Merlin and Taliesin have real if shadowy originals. It is because of these highly respected figures . . . that the tradition of Arthur himself, and of a British heroic age associated with him, was handed down to supply the material of mediaeval romance. (Cavendish 1.393)

The condition of the Druids during this post-Roman period of revived Kelticism is (due to lack of direct evidence) more problematical, since they are frequently confused with the bards and seers. The Druids often incorporated within themselves the functions of bards and poets, and like the bards they spent anywhere from twelve to twenty years in the oral tradition of memorizing verses (as recorded by Julius Caesar in *De Bello Gallico*).

The Druids—the priestly caste in Gaul, Britain, and Ireland—were originally (before the arrival of the Romans) the authoritative class in Keltic society, and in Ireland at least they took precedence over king and warriors.

The Keltic or Druidic beliefs in regard to the immortality of the soul evidently seemed rather outré to the classical world (and pointedly unfamiliar): an otherworld that was a magic recreation of life just as on Earth but in another place. Hence an Avalon "here" has as its counterpart an Avalon "there" or "otherwhere." To accommodate this concept within classical thought, the Graeco-Roman philosophers used the Pythagorean doctrine of the transmigration of souls, although Druidic belief nowhere implies this.

Druidry has consistently claimed a considerable antiquity, going back at least to the New Stone Age. In Stonehenge, Avebury, and other stone circles throughout the West Country, modern Druids recognize the elder temples in which their forebears regarded the sun, moon, and stars with wonder and awe. Specific connections with India's early Aryan culture seem clear: reverence for the sun, moon, and other heavenly bodies; circle dancing in a clockwise direction; the existence of a sacred caste composed of sages; the burning of the dead; wisdom-teaching and the imparting of sacred lore through the medium of long memorized poems; and the cult revolving around certain animals.

According to Julius Caesar, "The young are taught to repeat a great number of verses by heart and often spend twenty years upon this institution. . . . The Druids teach likewise many things related to the stars and their motions, the magnitude of the world [that is, the cosmos] and of our Earth, the nature of things, and the power and prerogatives of the immortal Gods" (*De Bello Gallico* 6.15). Both Britain and Ireland rather than Gaul, evidently, were the traditional training places of this caste who knew, and presided over, the contemporary arts and sciences and imparted them, who acted as political advisers to rulers, who were exempt from war and who often acted as heralds of peace, as well as being priests of a religion.

The term *druid* or *dru-wid* presupposes a Gallic *druvis* (from *druvids*) and probably relates to the Greek *drus*—an oak tree—with the ending the same as the Inda-European root *wid* or "to know" (and surviving in modern English in such a phrase as "to wit"). In his depiction of the Druidic mistletoe ceremony, Pliny makes an immediate link between oak trees and the Druids; in this ritual the Druid would cut mistletoe from an oak tree with a knife or sickle of gold upon the sixth day of the new moon. The oak tree in some mystic way evidently symbolized (for the Druids) wisdom or at least knowledge. Hence, *dru-wid* can mean either deep knowledge or knowledge of the oak *or* both. Of course, *deep* knowledge can be the same as, or can lead to, true wisdom.

Woodland sanctuaries are characteristically Keltic, such as those at Caer Nodentis and Avalon Annwn. According to Julius Caesar, there was an Archdruid for the whole of Gaul who convened annual meetings in a sacred woodland sanctuary within the territory of the Carnutes tribe. Archaeology does indeed bear witness to such sites, generally just simple cleared areas in the forest (identified in Gaul by such names as nemeton), sometimes enclosed with a palisade and/or bank and ditch. A reasonable possibility exists that there was an Archdruid for the entirety of Britain as well as a similar ecclesiastic for Ireland, both of these probably elected by constituent groups of sages and elders.

The noble classes largely supplied the personnel for the Druid caste. Their instruction in the oral tradition of memorizing verses could last anywhere from twelve to twenty years. Such traditional instruction for bards and poets was archetypally Keltic. It continued in Ireland up to the late 1600s and in Scotland up to the 1700s.

The Druids thus functioned as the acknowledged repositories of traditional lore and wisdom, particularly of customary law. They also incorporated within themselves something of the prophetic powers of the seers due to their practical knowledge of the calendar. They were directly responsible for animal and human sacrifice when they required that for their magic-making. To judge from the surviving fragments of a monumental calendar-inscription from Coligny in Gaul and other evidence, the Druids possessed considerable calendrical expertise, and they had long recognized the practical problems of reconciling the solar and lunar cycles. Like most shamans, they also possessed considerable knowledge of herbs and their medicinal properties.

Modern archaeology would seem to vindicate the traditional Druidic beliefs at Stonehenge and other stone circles; and we can add the obvious deductions from their structure: circular dancing, fivefold teachings, processions, and a death-and-rebirth cult of the sun, together with male and female emblems. These phenomena would seem to indicate a cult remarkably like that of traditional Druidic ideas.

The Druids urged their peoples to fight the Romans when Julius Caesar invaded Gaul and Britain. In Gaul the Druids rapidly lost influence as the Roman military advanced. The Latins either exterminated them or forced them to flee, knowing them immediately for a dangerous and seditious influence. It was their seditious influence, just as much as their practice of human sacrifice (and sometimes on a large scale, it might be added), which caused the Romans to proscribe their religion, and to banish and/or exterminate them with no mercy shown.

However, numerous Gallo-Roman altars and shrines, together with various inscriptions, demonstrate that cult functionaries of lesser standing (who could also be considered Druids) continued to preside at the various native temples and holy spots throughout the non-Christian period of the Roman Empire. In Britain the Roman general Julius Agricola destroyed the Brythonic Druids in 78 A.D., but the Gaelic Druids continued in Ireland until their conversion to Christianity during the 400s.

Again, in Britain as in Gaul, lesser cult functionaries (again, virtually the same as Druids but posing no threat to the civil authorities of the Roman administration) continued at native shrines (such as at "Caer Nodentis," Aquae Sulis, or the island-vale of Avalon Annwn) before as well as during the first and largely superficial Christianization of the Britons (the Late Roman and Arthurian periods).

It is fascinating and important to note that there were great Druidesses as well as great Druids. In Gaul and in Ireland at least they often enjoyed considerable prestige and power, sometimes comparable to what the male Druids enjoyed. The essential function of the ancient Druids then was clearly to sustain—by magical or "shamanistic" means—the prosperity of tribe and land. As the tribal repositories of traditional Keltic learning and sentiment, the Druids embodied the specific "barbarian" element that classical civilization could not assimilate and naturalize.

How far was Druidry driven out by the Romans? It survived in the remote parts of Wales, in Scotland beyond the Lowlands, and in Ireland. It developed the deeply poetic traditions of the fifth, sixth, and subsequent centuries, the same poetic traditions that later were to nurture the Arthurian legendry.

Later references depict the remnants of the original Druids as no more than magicians and medicine-men on the fringes of Roman-Keltic culture, and even Druidesses appear as no more than common fortune-tellers. The original Druidry may also have survived by simply going underground: that is, in the Romanized areas much of the former priesthood may simply have continued on under the guise of being lesser cult functionaries at the native shrines, or they may have transformed themselves into bards, seers, and so forth.

And now we come to the question of the Druids vis-à-vis the Christian monks during Late Roman, Arthurian, and post-Arthurian times. Apart from the one great difference in their respective central conceptualization of deity—the one Christian god versus the Keltic multiplicity of gods and goddesses—there are a number of reasonably close parallels between them. For example, the Holy Trinity of Christian doctrine versus the curious use of, and emphasis upon, the "triad" within the Welsh storytelling tradition of Arthur's time and after (possibly stemming originally from Druidic poetic practice). For a more strategic example, the Christian concept of an immortal soul and an afterlife is not that dissimilar (in broad outline) from the Druidic beliefs of an immortal soul and a Keltic otherworld. Many articles of faith among the Kelts before the advent of Christianity seem to have prepared the way for the later Jesus cult. There is the distinct implication of some kind of cooperative coexistence then between the native Druidry and the early Keltic Church of the British Isles.

The Keltic Church in Britain and Ireland (almost out of touch with the Church in Europe) developed along its own lines and possessed its own (and rather different) character. Monasteries rather than dioceses provided its foundation; abbots rather than bishops furnished the main authority; the monks rather than the secular clergy set the tone. The three chief Christian centers of Arthurian Britain were evidently Llantwit Major (in southern Wales), Amesbury, and Glastonbury; these were all monasteries, and no bishop claimed any of them as his seat.

The Keltic monks of the British Isles had far greater freedom than their Continental brethren. More democratic in outlook, they wandered widely, and because their importance made the Keltic nuns important as well, Keltic society held women in greater esteem than among European Christians. In scholarship and literature the Keltic monks of Britain and Ireland excelled and produced outstanding manuscripts.

In Ireland as well as in the less Romanized western parts of Britain, the Church did not need to contend—as formerly on the Continent—with a powerful and firmly established non-Christian priesthood. The Keltic monks did not view their old religion as "Satanic," and preserved much mythology and speculation of a type that passed into virtually permanent eclipse elsewhere.

The greater freedom, greater individuality, and more democratic outlook of the Keltic Church in the British Isles than of Christianity in Europe—as well as the superior esteem accorded women and women ecclesiastics—probably reflect a natural evolution from the times and conditions of the Druids and of Druidry.

In early Irish literature (surviving through Christian sources) the Druids or "Magi" who are depicted as malignant magicians bitterly opposed to the introduction of the new faith probably represent the die-hard remnant of those Druids not easily converted or convertible to the new cult. The *filid* or "seers"—who also practiced divination and are often confused with the true Druids in the early Irish hero-sagas—assumed an honored place in early Irish Christian society as literary men and historians. Significantly many contests between Druids and Christians take place over the possession of land. This (besides its literal meaning) could easily signify the struggle between the two creeds for the domination over the territory of souls.

Just as the well-organized colleges of Druids among the Irish Kelts were easily converted into Christian monasteries, Druidic abbeys may more than likely have stood on the future sites of Glastonbury Abbey and the monastery inhabited by British monks on Tintagel Headland. It is also a distinct and logical possibility that Druidic abbeys may have preceded the Christian monasteries (at least) at St. Michael's Mount near Marazion in Cornwall, at Mont-Saint-Michel just northeast of Brittany, at Iona Island just west of Scotland, and so forth.

In the event that he does not symbolize a real historical personage, what then precisely would the poet-sage and poet-magician Merlin have represented at Arthur's court *if not the Druidic element itself par excellence?* Significantly, Merlin is never shown in the later legendry as in conflict with Christianity. The strongest and most fascinating *magical* elements in the Arthurian Mythos are but rarely Christian; they are primarily *non*-Christian.

It could only have been with the full cooperation of all classes indigenous to the Brythonic society of his time that the historical Arthur would have been enabled to achieve what he did. Needless to say, he would most particularly have needed the active support of the Druids, bards, and seers, in addition to the support and approbation of the wealthy and noble classes on the one hand and of the Keltic Church on the other. In both Britain and Brittany (or Little Britain) it was the bards who kept Arthur's immediate *later fame* alive.

The Eisteddfod—the Welsh musical convention and contest—goes back to an unknown date, at least before the reign of King Hoel the Good (circa 950 A.D.), whose Pencerrd or Chief Poet already had a special chair in the court. Some kind of Eisteddfod, patronized by Lord Rhys, took place at Cardigan Castle in 1176, but nothing is later recorded until 1450 at Carmarthen (indubitably under the excorporate aegis of Prince Merlinus, whose presence at least consistently in legend has always been closely linked with Caer Maridunum). The next recorded meeting took place at Caerwys in the north in 1523, and then another in 1568 when a committee (appointed by Queen Elizabeth) examined bards and granted licenses to wander and earn money by performances. Assuredly is it significant that this happened in the reign of Elizabeth I; the Tudors, it will be remembered, claimed Welsh nobility among their immediate ancestry. Thus, apart from these few recorded Eisteddfods, the earlier tradition against written records has prevented our knowing much more until the eighteenth-century almanacs begin to advertise meetings.

Organized with the assistance of Wales, the modern Bards of Cornwall form a considerable group that revives the extinct Cornish language (among other activities). The Bards are of two classes, language and non-language members. Uniquely bardic, their impressive robes are of deep blue. They implement some of their usual ceremonies at the stone circles of Cornwall or in the great halls of Arthur built at Tintagel in the twentieth century for the Arthurian Order.

In view of the Keltic imaginative concept (quintessentially Druidic) of the immortality of the soul that will continue living in an otherworld, it is easy to understand how an Avalon "here" or in Britain can also be an Avalon "there" or somewhere indefinite west of Britain in the North Atlantic (the Avalon in

Geoffrey of Monmouth's *Vita Merlini* as well as that island sacred to the mystical consciousness of the Irish Kelts). But . . . this Avalon located in the western ocean as conceived by Gaelic or Brythonic Kelts . . . could this not be some kind of racial memory of an Atlantis long since submerged beneath the ocean's waves?

XIII. A King Arthur Summary

Conjectures about Arthur's mail-clad cavalry are based on the facts of fifth-century warfare and revolve around the conception of Arthur as the creator of a band of knights. Now "knight" is a word that for us in the twentieth century, as in the nineteenth (the Romantic period par excellence), has a preeminently medieval coloring. However, the knight of the Middle Ages was in fact only a survival or revival of the Late Roman *eques cataphractarius*, clad in a shirt of mail, with arm-pieces and leg-pieces attached. This armor (embryonically "medieval," it will be noted) made the Roman horseman "invulnerable" (according to the Roman historians Ammianus and Vegetius).

Thus, one of the best popular theories explains the knights of the Round Table by contending that the historical Arthur turned the tide against the Germanic invaders with an innovative cavalry force, a personal corps of armored riders. It is a fact that the Romans developed heavy mailed cavalry during the last period of the Western Roman Empire. It is also a fact that the Anglo-Saxons were not horsemen (at least at first), and thus a highly trained group of armored British horsemen, possessing therefore a militarily technological advantage, could well have put them to flight.

From clues in early Welsh poetry, and from the results of recent excavation, an explicit picture is formed of Arthur's knights. They went into combat wearing coats of mail over thick leather tunics with thick leather breeches attached. They carried lances, long-bladed swords, and circular shields. They rode horses that were sometimes also armored. The actual style of armor would have developed from the Late Roman mode of heavy mail, to which would have been added typically Keltic and therefore largely abstract patterns of decoration. Many of the knights would have been Christian (at least nominally). These would have attended Christian service before battle. Their nonmilitary clothing would have consisted of breeches, tunics, and robes of simple but colorful design. They wore golden ornaments and jewelry.

While the civil authorities would probably still have tolerated and even protected the native cults and cult sites, the new Christian faith would have provided a unifying and inspirational impetus of which the older native beliefs were incapable. The Grail stories, while superficially Christian, actually reflect the Druidic preoccupation with the inherent Keltic sense of otherwhere. Thus, while Christianity was probably already well on its way to becoming the principal religion of the land, the older and increasingly dispossessed native religion began to show up as an unmistakable element in the continuing Brythonic mythology of Arthur's period. Some of this early Christian activity was unusual enough to harmonize with the strange "otherworldly" atmosphere of the later Grail romances, if not with their imagery in detail.

The upper Britanno-Roman classes, for the most part Christian somewhat before the end of Roman rule, produced such outstanding figures as St. Patrick. The containment of the Anglo-Saxons during Arthur's reign permitted a much wider flowering of Christianity and Christian culture both in Britain and in Ireland than what would otherwise have obtained. Ireland above all became the most cultured and most thoroughly Christianized country of Western Europe during the Dark Ages and owed much to the British-Keltic saints.

In his monograph *King Arthur's Avalon*, Geoffrey Ashe has adroitly summarized the case for a "great" historical Arthur with unusual clarity and insight, and he deserves to be quoted in full:

> The salient point about the mass of Arthurian oddments is the grandiose geography. Nobody else except the Devil is renowned through so much of Britain. From Land's End [in Cornwall] to the Grampian foothills [in Scotland], Arthur's name "cleaves to cairn and cromlech." We hear of the Cornish fortress at Kelliwic; of a Cornish hill called Bann Arthur and a stream called the River of Arthur's Kitchen; of Cadbury and its noble shades; of the lake Llyn Bertog in Merioneth, where Arthur slew a monster, and his horse left a hoof-print on the rock; of a cave by Marchlyn Mawr in Carnarvon, where his treasure lies hidden (woe to any intruder who touches it); of a cave at Caerleon, and another near [Mount] Snowdon, where his warriors lie asleep till he need them; of still another cave in the Eildon hills, close to Melrose Abbey, where some say he is sleeping himself; of the mount outside Edinburgh called Arthur's Seat; of Arthur's Stone, and Arthur's Fold, as far north as Perth; and many more such places. Arthur seems to be everywhere.
>
> The first natural deduction is that Arthur really was everywhere: that he flashed from end to end of his crumbling country on that terrible armoured charger, rallying the faint hearts, reconciling the factions [no mean task, *that!*], and pouncing on the bewildered heathen; with Kay and Bedivere riding beside him. And the second deduction . . . is that the man who bequeathed such a towering legend was no ordinary human being. Even if most

of the Arthur stories were borrowed or fabricated, it is still necessary to explain why they should ever have been attached to Arthur. Even if the bards vested him with the attributes of a god, the question still remains: Why him in particular? To which there is no adequate answer but the readiest one—because he deserved it. (91)

Thus, it can be readily seen how Arthur's historical period and court could easily have prompted at least something of the immediate imagery and narrative "staples" (to say nothing of the "strange" atmosphere which is peculiarly Keltic) featured in the later medieval romances. Also, it can be readily seen how in a genuinely historical way the British culture or manner of living in Arthur's period fore-shadows the later Middle Ages and contains in a fashion more than embryonic much that will become common in medieval times. Nor can there be much doubt that the peculiar coloring of the Arthurian Mythos, especially in its grand and Ragnarok-like finale, reflects something of the real poignancy and nostalgia that would gather—retrospectively in myth and legend—to the period of British history circa 500-550, a period which was after all, in a strict historical sense, the Keltic Twilight.

Nor is it at all bizarre that Geoffrey of Monmouth should have stressed the "imperial" characteristics of King Arthur and his dominions. While this "imperialism" may reflect something of a historical reality peculiar to Arthur and his times, it surely reflects the real British-Roman imperial tradition before Arthur, and which he would have inherited as a natural consequence of historical evolution: beginning at least with Constantine the Great (proclaimed Caesar Augustus at Eburacum or York) and continuing later through Magnus Maximus (Spanish-born but an "adopted" Briton) and then later through Aurelius Ambrosius (or as the later myths fashion his name, Ambrosius Aurelianius), one of Arthur's immediate Britanno-Romanized predecessors.

Arthur's career may be divided into three main parts; and again we must emphasize that these dates are purely provisional. From 470 into 485 he would have been prince; from 485 into 510/512, king, from 510/512 into 537/542, emperor. In many tales about Arthur (including various modern novels), the first fifteen or sixteen years of his life are deliberately "mysterious." To avoid being murdered or harmed in any way, and so that he can have a "normal" childhood and adolescence, he is taken out of Britain and raised by foster parents, with his identity remaining a secret. Later still, he returns (still young) and spends time away from the political centers and factionalism of the Britons. Then he appears miraculously and as a great fighter at around the age of fifteen or sixteen. This could be fiction, but it could also reflect some folklore or genuine historical tradition known to earlier periods but lost before our modern era.

Spenser in his great epic-romance-allegory *The Faerie Queene* (published 1590-1609) presents, among other main narrative threads, a myth of "Arthure, before he was king" and as "the image of a brave knight." He therefore depicts *Prince* Arthur during his lengthy sojourn in "Faerie lond." Now it is a fact that in the characterization of *his* fictional Faeryland Spenser would have portrayed not only something of his native Britain but also, and particularly, something of his "adopted" country of Ireland, or Ivernia (which he personifies in Book V as "Irena"), where he lived for long periods of his adult life (approximately 1580-89, 1591-95, and 1597-98), if not the majority of his adult life. Thus, in ways both subtle and overt, Spenser's Faeryland is an uniquely Irish one; and it must be admitted that the Irish countryside to this day can be "heartbreakingly" beautiful. Now, depicting Prince Arthur as adventuring in Faeryland, which is Ireland in particular, may have been based by Spenser on some Arthurian tradition current in his contemporary Britain (the Age of Elizabeth I) but lost since that time. Not that the tradition would have necessarily emphasized Ireland to the neglect of other Keltic lands. The tradition may have preserved a memory of Arthur passing most of his first fifteen or sixteen years in the various Brythonic or Gaelic realms: Cornwall, Brittany, the Channel Islands, Lyonnesse, modern England's northwest (i.e., Westmoreland and Cumberland), the Scottish Lowlands, the Isles of Man and Anglesey, the Hebrides, the Orkneys, and of course Ireland.

There are still some remaining aspects relative to the Arthurian Mythos that we need to discuss before we return to Caerleon-on-Usk and Arthur Machen.

As a concept of the creative collective imagination of Western man, the Arthurian Mythos has passed through two principal stages. The early Welsh tradition celebrated an idealized Britain or Britannia where Arthur and his knights had flourished. England was then "Logria," and the Cymry or Welsh had the dominion over it. Then the Cymry lost Logria, and the West Country (notably Wales and Cornwall) almost alone preserved the lingering vestiges of Arthurian splendor. Some day, however—or so it was prophesied—Arthur would come back as a Keltic Messiah and would then subdue the English or Anglo-Saxons. This then was the tradition promulgated by Geoffrey of Monmouth when, in the 1130s, he indited and published his *History of the Kings of Britain*; this compilation did everything to implant an exaggerated and highly glamorized Arthurian realm in the minds of readers outside Wales.

The second principal stage began with the popularization of the Mythos by non-Keltic romancers. However, with this popularization Arthur became something far more than a purely regional hero. The Plantagenet kings of England claimed to possess his birthplace, his chief cities, and his grave, and they posed as his legitimate successors in their dominion of the whole of Britain. Edward I displayed Arthur's alleged remains at Glastonbury to demonstrate once and for all that he would never come back as the Keltic or Welsh Messiah. Significantly, no Welshman ever disputed Glastonbury's claim to possessing Arthur's grave.

Geoffrey Ashe has again well summarized the final purely political formulation of the Mythos as follows:

> Both aspects of Arthur were adroitly united by Henry Tudor. He stressed his own Welsh ancestry, and marched to overthrow Richard III under the standard of the Red Dragon. When he became king as Henry VII, he allowed his propagandists to construe the event as fulfilling the prophecy of Arthur's return—meaning, now, not that the Welsh had conquered the English, but that a true "British" prince had saved the whole land from civil war and restored its ancient Arthurian glory. (Cavendish 1.396)

The great poetic exponent of this Tudor myth is Edmund Spenser who, in *The Faerie Queene*, portrays the England of Elizabeth I as the magnificent kingdom of the Britons restored.

Spenser would have of course been familiar with the classic redaction of the Arthurian Mythos in English prose *Le Morte d'Arthur* by Sir Thomas Malory, published more than a century before in 1485 in London. William Caxton, the first English printer, had printed and published that particular masterpiece, the first great surviving piece of English literary prose. Malory had evidently written *Le Morte d'Arthur* during the last twenty years of his life, which he spent in prison. From Book XXI we quote Chapter VII in full:

OF THE OPINION OF SOME MEN
OF THE DEATH OF KING ARTHUR

Yet some men say in many parts of England that King Arthur is not dead, but had by the will of our Lord Jesu into another place; and men say that he shall come again, and he shall win the holy cross. I will not say it shall be so, but rather I will say: here in this world he changed his life. But many men say that there is written upon his tomb this verse:

Hic jacet Arthurus, Rex quondam, Rexque futurus.
[Here lies Arthur, the once and future King.]

The original inscription on the lead cross found during the exhumation of King Arthur in 1190 at Glastonbury Abbey had read: *Hic iacet sepultus incli-*

tus rex Arturius in insula Avalonia. It is fascinating to see how Malory has refashioned the original inscription to read: *Hic iacet Arthurus, rex quondam, rexque futurus.* (The Welsh and English forms of Arthur's name have changed the original Latin form of Artorius or Arturius into Arthurus.) Thus, his regal title contains the ancient Welsh prophecy within a singularly compact form: "King formerly, and King to be."

In fact—and in a sense not quite foreseen by Geoffrey of Monmouth and his contemporaries of the twelfth century—the later generations of the Middle Ages vindicated the ancient Brythonic prophecy. King Arthur had indeed returned and was to enjoy a greater and longer reign than any he had enjoyed in his own proper and historical period—in the minds and imaginations of not only his fellow later "British" peoples but also, and more extensively, in minds and imaginations throughout Western Europe.

From the twelfth to the fifteenth centuries, the "magick" of Arthur and his Britain grew greater with every retelling in verse and prose from generation to generation—no matter the transformation in externals—and in a truly marvelous fashion not even those early Welsh prophets, bards, and seers could have conceived.

Thus, when people began to doubt his historical reality in modern times (say, from the first Elizabethan age to the first half of the twentieth century, and then on into the Second Elizabethan Age)—at least on the scale (more symbolic than actual) indicated by Geoffrey of Monmouth and the medieval romancers—the myths and legends were to keep Arthur's name and the "glamor" of his Britannic realm necromantically alive. And that is indeed as fair a piece of magic as ever prophesied by any Brythonic poet-sage!

Thanks to recent archaeological investigation, no longer is it possible to maintain (after at least a disbelieving first half of the twentieth century) that "the original Arthur, if he lived at all, must have been a semi-barbaric Celtic chief" (Grebanier 1.207).

XIV. Back to Caerleon

Two years after Machen published for the first time his short fantasy "The Bowmen" in the London *Evening News* for September 29, 1914—thereby creating the twentieth-century legend of "the Angels of Mons"—a book appeared that contains an interesting citation apropos of Caerleon. This was *A Tennyson Dictionary*, compiled by Arthur E. Baker.

An ancient town in Monmouthshire on the river Usk. [. . .] This "city of Legions" with its golden domes and magnificent churches, and its gorgeous palace, with its giant tower

> from whose high crest, they say,
> Men saw the goodly hills of Somerset,
> And white sails flying on the yellow sea. [i.e., Severn Sea]

is supposed to have equalled Rome in splendor. It was one of the principal residences of king Arthur, where he lived in splendid state, surrounded by his knights, and where he held his court.

> For Arthur on the Whitsuntide before
> Held court at old Caerleon upon Usk.

King Arthur's ninth great battle against the Saxons was fought here. (87; the quotations are taken from Tennyson's *Idylls of the King*)

Now, on the face of it, the statement—"This 'City of Legions' . . . is supposed to have equalled Rome in splendor"—seems patently absurd, since it is a matter of plain historical fact that Rome was incomparably the largest and greatest city of classical antiquity. How could such a provincial *town* as Caerleon (no matter its own charisma and mystique) even be mentioned in the same breath as the archimperial *city* of "Mother Rome" upon the River Tiber? Nevertheless, this statement (which really stresses magnificence rather than size) reflects an older British tradition and is by no means without its basis in historical fact.

This tradition clearly dates back to the time of Arthur (as well as before and after), when Caerleon would have served quite logically as capital of Western Britain. By the time of Arthur's imperial coronation (c. 510 or 512) as High King of Britain and Armorica, Rome had endured two major sackings (one by the Goths under Alaric in 410 and the other by the Vandals under Gaiseric or Genseric in 455). In 476 another barbarian chieftain, Odoacer, deposed the "last" Roman Emperor of the West, Romulus Augustulus (an event often deemed "the Fall of Rome"). By 547 the great imperial city was actually deserted for a while. After Arthur's death in 537 or 542, Rome underwent a third and last major "sacking" of a most peculiar kind. Totila, king of the Ostrogoths, captured Rome in the middle of December 546 *and evacuated everyone out of it,* but perpetrated no material plundering. Thus, by late 546 and early 547 the city lay deserted and solitary: if one single event could be said to symbolize the death of the classical Rome of antiquity, this would be it. The city was still subjected to occasional plundering by barbarians later in the same period. By the time of Geoffrey of Monmouth, the ancient city of Rome was a vasty ruin, inhabited by herders and their flocks, and by a few great feudal families—a wreck that had foundered on the reefs and shoals of inimical Time.

Thus, allowing for some pardonable patriotic exaggeration on the part of British commentators, but keeping in mind the actual *physical* deterioration of Rome's great municipal architecture, it is possible to see how Caerleon by a curious fluke of historical accident could have been conceived as equalling Rome in splendor during Arthur's period. This tradition would have had even greater weight in the twelfth century (the time of Geoffrey of Monmouth and Gerald of Barry) when Caerleon still possessed an impressive array of ancient architecture, and whilst Rome had become an enormous and catastrophic wreck overgrown with weeds and thickets, and infested with desperadoes and bandits.

As we have previously established, the best candidate for Camelot as a genuine city remains Machen's own Caerleon. Within the old "Castra Legionis" proper, the former residence of the Roman legionary commander would have served quite well as one of King Arthur's own palaces. However, we cannot rule out the possibility of a special residence being built for the "Briton King"—in addition to Arthur's using the *domus legati* as well as any other especially fine residences already existing in the city proper.

During Arthur's period Caerleon would have presented a splendiferous appearance as a city. Both the *civitas* and the old "Castra Legionis" would have been girdled by walls at least 20 feet high with crenellated parapets and with attached turrets or towers at least every 150 feet. It is a distinct possibility that these walls were refurbished and then heightened further during Arthur's reign by means of a second smaller wall (also with turrets and crenellated parapets) superimposed upon the original Britanno-Roman defenses. Further stories may have been added to many of the original edifices in both city and camp at this time. This further building up (both walls and added stories) may have been of a mixed stone-and-timber construction or of a purely timbered style (more typically Brythonic). As capital of Western Britain and as a gathering place for the British refugees from eastern and southeastern England, Caerleon would have seen its population increase dramatically during the period 440/450-500/510 and then to a lesser extent during the period 510/512-550.

Southwest of the Roman fortress there yet lay the old walled parade ground (700 by 500 feet), one rare open area within the city proper that would have been available for new construction during the reigns of Ambrosius Aurelianus and Caesar Augustus Artorius. Here there may have arisen that special residence, the legendary "gorgeous palace" proper to King Arthur. If we postulate a typically Brythonic and purely timber-built edifice, it is not hard to see why no vestiges of it have survived the passage of time into the twentieth century.

What possible shape might such a royal palace as Arthur's have taken? This would probably reflected the architectural tradition (but magnified considerably, as would seem appropriate) of such wooden woodland citadels as Castle Dore in Cornwall, Caer Tintagel upon Tintagel Headland, Cadbury Castle near Queen's Camel in Somerset, and Caer Avalon Annwn within the island-vale of Avalon. This "Caer Imperatoris" (let us call it after the Welsh fashion) would probably have reflected as well certain details and elements from the Britanno-Roman architectural tradition. Thus we can postulate a great central towered hall rising donjon-like from the midst of subsidiary halls and towers, in turn environed by a series of inner courtyards and various outbuildings, and all set within an outer line of towered and/or turreted fortifications, superimposed upon the original boundaries of the old walled parade ground. We can also safely assume a highly sophisticated wooden architecture; it is much easier to be fanciful and elaborate in wood than in stone and cement. One of the likeliest places to look for some kind of example—which would give us at least some idea, some archetype, to image by—would probably be among the so-called stave churches found throughout Scandinavia; and such a specific example as the stave church at Heddal in Norway would serve as well as any. (The form of the stave churches is thought to preserve that of the pre-Christian Norse temples.) The postulation of such a typically Brythonic and purely timber-built edifice is a perfectly logical choice in view of the mixed Keltic and Roman culture characteristic of Arthurian times.

Close to the southern gateway symmetrically situated in the southern wall of the Roman fortress there still arose Caerleon's military amphitheatre, which would certainly have played an important part in large public gatherings during Arthur's period. It may have been domed or somehow roofed over at this time in a typically Brythonic and purely timbered fashion with some kind of carapace, even if only temporarily for Arthur's coronation. However, with or without roof or carapace, the amphitheatre would surely have been the logical choice for Arthur's imperial coronation since it could easily accommodate around 6,000 persons.

Sometime after his death Arthur's realm fragmented into a large number of small independent successor states. Quite apart from its traditional status as one of his former seats, and apart from its rank as the metropolitan see of Wales before the establishment of St. David's, it is a fact that Caerleon continued as a Welsh princely capital up to the time of the Norman Conquest of 1066 A.D. Subsequently it became a Marcher lordship but principally in Welsh hands until 1235; a sizable motte and a tower of its castle survive. During the Middle Ages and later, Caerleon became a borough, and enjoyed a considerable coastal trade, eventually destroyed by the development of the railways (characteristic of Victorian times) as well as that of the city of Newport, which lies 3 miles southwest of Caerleon.

Considerable expansion occurred in the Caerleon area following World War II, and on December 15, 1947, Arthur Machen himself died, at the age of eighty-four, as one of Caerleon's most illustrious natives.

The Welsh had long agone lost their dominion of Britain, and whilst the West Country (notably Wales and Cornwall) almost alone had preserved the remnants of Arthurian splendor, had not King Arthur himself become a dubitable myth, a mere legend concocted from some mystic Welshman's fertile imagination, and an insubstantial fable compounded in equal parts of empty air and restless wind? Why, who could place credence in those old stories, the artless testimony to the dreams of rude and barbaric ages?!

When Arthur Machen was born on March 3, 1863, Queen Victoria had already reigned on the throne of England since 1838, that is, for some twenty-six years. By this time Caerleon—"once a city, and the headquarters of a Roman legion"—had shrunken into "a forgotten village." Moreover, "the Augustan Legion and the clash of arms, and all the tremendous pomp that followed the eagles"—did not all these form part of a dim and fading past? The "quiet little town" lay in "the long, lovely valley" of the lower Usk "crossed in midvision by a mediaeval bridge of vaulted and buttressed stone." Here, of an evening, in the twilight following sunset, one could see "the broad river swimming to full tide" and "the pure white mist tracking the outline of the river like a shroud." Then "across the valley, and beyond, hill followed on hill as wave on wave": altogether then, "a vague and shadowy country" with "imaginations and fantasy of swelling hills and hanging woods, and half-shaped outlines of hills beyond." Now "here a faint blue pillar of smoke rose . . . from the chimney of an ancient grey farmhouse, there was a rugged height crowned with dark firs, and in the distance . . . the white streak of a road that climbed and vanished into some unimagined country. But the boundary of all was a great wall of mountain, vast in the west, and ending like a fortress, with a steep ascent and a domed tumulus clear against the sky."

This then was the Caerleon into which Machen was born, and this then was the countryside surrounding it at the time of his birth and later childhood. The great courtyard of the headquarters or *principia* of Caerleon's old Roman fortress lay then, as it still lies, beneath the parish church and churchyard of St. Cadoc's, which is thus located above the very center of the "Castra Legionis" and which stands also virtually at the heart of modern Caerleon. Machen was born here in a house owned by his grandmother (and not at the small parish of Llanddewi Fach—some five miles north of Caerleon—where his father presided as the resident clergyman). Most of the then "quiet little town" or "forgotten village" was thus contained within the area once bounded by the walls of the Roman fortress-camp.

Not far to the west of St. Cadoc's there had long agone stood the *domus legati* and in all likelihood one of the headquarters of King Arthur within the ancient "City of the Legions." Caerleon's present-day Legionary Museum is located not far away to the north or northeast of St. Cadoc's; this is one of the best institutions of its type in all modern Britain.

So to the town of Caerleon the present writer came early in the first week of April 1972 (on a Tuesday, to be exact, following the Monday spent at the ruins of Caer Nodentis in Lydney Park), together with two English friends Jack and Audrey Hesketh, during our pilgrimage to the specifically local Arthur Machen country as well as to the West Country at large. We had driven into the area from near Chepstow-on-Wye (immediately adjacent to Caerwent, the ancient "cantonal" capital and market-town of Venta Silurum) and had gone via the city of Newport, whose modern suburbs rise upon the hills environing Caerleon to the south; these suburbs encroach increasingly upon the elder community.

We visited a local pub, made a few inquiries under the guise of refreshing ourselves with the local ale and cider, and then continued on into Caerleon. First, we visited St. Cadoc's without disturbing the present occupants of the rectory and lingered for a brief while in the church, proffering our silent devoirs on behalf of Machen's spirit. From there we motored to the Legionary Museum where again we lingered for more than a little, imbibing as much historicity as we could in the short period at our disposal.

But the highlight of the visit came next, as we reconnoitered to the ancient military amphitheatre and part of the old fortress's southern (or actually southwestern) wall nearby. The amphitheatre survives amazingly intact, being (we would say) about one half its former size or height. To the three of us, upon that early afternoon, while a brisk wind was blowing out of the west and under cool gray skies, it seemed a haunted and haunting place, endowed still with strange occulted splendors left over from Arthurian and Late Roman times as well as from Machen's own immediate period, the Victorian Age.

Then Tennyson, the poet laureate of the British Empire, had located various portions in his series of epic-narratives *Idylls of the King* within this ancient "City of the Legions" where local traditions yet maintained a connection betwixt the amphitheatre and Arthur's regime. Once again, the elder mythopoetic Keltic magic welled up from dark depths, to inform and guide intuitively the vision of an imperial poet laureate on the one hand and on the other the vision of a young prose-poet who was himself Keltic, descended most particularly from the ancient Brythons, and actually born in this former seat of King Arthur's.

XV. An Arthur Machen Summary

Looking back from California to that visit in Wales, the present writer finds himself arrested again and again by certain facts of Machen's own mundane life (especially relative to certain facts or factors in his creative or *dream* life) and also, and above all, by the overall significance of the *aesthetic pattern* peculiar to Machen's life-period.[7]

We have already considered certain prime elements and factors from Machen's immediate (as well as extended) native environment: elements and factors that contributed tremendously to his personal and artistic development. But now let us look directly at certain salient facts of his biography.

He was born as the only child of a clergyman; he developed into a dreamy, introspective boy, a solitary, and a mystic; and he grew up very much attached to his native land of Gwent as well as to the Arthurian legendry indigenous to Caerleon. His father was descended from a long line of Welsh clergymen that can be traced back at least to the last quarter of the eighteenth century.

Machen had a sound classical education (Greek and Latin) both in school

---

7. This chapter is heavily indebted for many basic biographical and bibliographical data to David Ieuan's biography "Arthur Machen: 1863-1901" and "Arthur Machen 1901-1947," which appeared in the British periodical *Balthus*, Numbers 3 and 4, respectively (edited and published by Jon M. Harvey, Cardiff, Wales). The quotation from the speech of Chief Seattle in 1855 is taken from its redaction in the issue for July 15, 1975, of *East West Journal*. Chief Seattle, who was born in 1786, died on June 7 1866.

and then out on his own. His own later writing (essays or fiction or miscellanies) is rife with classical reminiscence. But he also had a knowledge (in both writing and speaking) of Welsh, and evidently something of the immemorial poetic usages native to the Brythonic bards.

His first period of exile from his beloved Wales occurred when he went away to school to pursue that training that would enable him to continue the unbroken ecclesiastical tradition of his father's family. He attended Hereford Cathedral School from January 1874 until April 1880 (with the exception of six months in 1876 when he remained in the Caerleon area). While still at school Machen had submitted a poem in blank verse based upon the Arthurian legends to the *Gentleman's Magazine*, but the periodical rejected it.

It is significant that Machen's first serious effort as a writer should concern the Arthurian legendry so dear to his childhood and adolescence, thus reflecting his reaction to the vestiges of Arthurian splendor still remaining in his native Caerleon.

The Reverend Jones-Machen had planned to send his only child to Oxford, but increasing poverty prevented this. Without such higher education both the clergy and the teaching profession were closed to his son Arthur Llewelyn.

At the instigation of his family Machen then made his first journey to London in June 1880, when he appeared before the examiners for entrance into the Royal College of Surgeons. Quite sensibly they did not accept him as a candidate.

After his return from London he wrote another long poem titled *Eleusinia* in a mixture of rhymed and blank verse; this concerned the pagan rites at Eleusis in ancient Greece. It was printed and published locally in a limited edition largely financed by his family. Later Machen suppressed this pamphlet.

His second period of exile (far more difficult than the first) occurred when he went to live in London (again at the instigation of his family) to pursue a career in journalism, or so they thought and hoped. This called for a profound readjustment on Machen 's part, as he instinctively preferred the superior physical quality of country living. London was then, as it still is to this day, "the City" par excellence.

Even stated generously, his early career there proved almost repulsively wretched, but it found exquisite artistic reflection in his later creative writing (especially the often highly autobiographical novel *The Hill of Dreams*). During this early London period (from the summer of 1881 into the late autumn of

1885), although he suffered often from acute loneliness and intense melancholia, he somehow got by: for a while as a clerk in a publishing house, then as a teacher (that is, as a private tutor), later as an assistant to a genealogist, and finally as some kind of freelance writer. His life appears to have been at times only slightly less dreadful than the London career of his alter ego Lucian Taylor in *The Hill of Dreams*.

Two excellent books emerged from this period, however. *The Anatomy of Tobacco* reflects Machen's dual passion for tobacco and the occasional pint of ale or beer; this book is an early masterpiece in what we may term the peculiarly Machenesque genre of the miscellany. He published it (significantly enough) under the pseudonym of "Leolinus Siluriensis." He was now twenty-one, and he had come of age in the same year (1884) as his first real book's publication. Machen then devoted most of 1885 and 1886 to the creation of his first bona fide and full-length piece of fiction, *The Chronicle of Clemendy*, a highly original imitation of certain fictional procedures and formulations as found in the *Gargantua and Pantagruel* of François Rabelais. The singularly varied and adroitly picaresque narrative in *The Chronicle of Clemendy* demonstrates the enchantment created for Machen by his native land of Gwent (in which, apart from one scene, the action of the book takes place).

In 1884 he had undertaken his first major translation for the publisher of *The Anatomy of Tobacco*, and he devoted much of that year to the project. This was a translation of *The Heptameron* from the French of Queen Marguerite de Navarre. In the late autumn of 1885 Machen returned from London to Caerleon and Llanddewi Fach; his mother was dying. His father, declared a bankrupt, became apathetic after his wife's death and progressively deteriorated. Machen stayed in Gwent until January 1887.

Then in that same month he returned to London, making the great city now his home. In August 1887 he married his first wife, Amelia Hogg. (She was to die in the summer of 1899.) Those twelve years were as happy for Machen as his first London period had been painful and lonely. A few weeks before his marriage his father had passed on. Arthur and Amelia then spent a little while in Caerleon and Llanddewi Fach, clearing up various family affairs. The couple then returned to their home in London. In 1887 and 1892 Machen received a number of legacies from some long-lived Scottish relatives on his mother's side of the family. This added income enabled the couple to live much more comfortably than what otherwise might have obtained. During the later 1880s Machen was working as a cataloguer of second-hand books, and for his then present employers he undertook his next major translating project.

He devoted his days during the greater part of 1888 and 1889 to translating the interminable *Memoirs* of Casanova (they fill twelve volumes in all); Machen's has become the classic English translation of this work. During the same period of time he devoted his evenings to yet another translation from the French, *The Way to Actain* (*Le Moyen de Parvenir*, literally *The Way to Succeed* or "get ahead") by Beroalde de Verville (an imitator of François Rabelais). All these translations were professional work (even if Machen's rate of pay might seem rather low to us today), but the last was printed privately. He put a great deal of time and effort into these translations.

In 1890 he wrote, or began the writing of, *The Three Impostors*; this did not see publication until 1895, In 1894, the year previous, he had published two of his most famous tales "The Great God Pan" and "The Inmost Light" in one book (with illustrations by the great English Decadent artist Aubrey Beardsley). Despite the fact that Machen was a serious creative writer of genuine integrity and even of real genius, none of these books already mentioned received any critical hurrahs from the contemporary English press.

Although he was officially a member of the Anglican Church, there is an undeniable Roman Catholic quality to much of Machen's writing; perhaps from this there may have stemmed much of the antipathy to his work demonstrated by the London-area and largely Protestant-dominated English press. Machen was both Welsh and (aesthetically) Catholic, and these factors could have contributed to an unsympathetic reaction on the part of his critics in the 1890s and early 1900s.

Following the publication of *The Three Impostors* in 1895, Machen gave definitive artistic expression in his magisterial novel *The Hill of Dreams* to the agony and pain he had undergone as a dedicated creative artist during his first London period. Now during the middle to later "Yellow 'Nineties" he recreated the aching loneliness and alienation of that earlier life; and at the same time he passed through the agony of recreating his own proper prose style, in order to do justice to this unique compendium of dream-life and reality combined. The book, surely Machen's masterpiece of full-length fiction, had to wait ten years for publication in book form, that is, until 1907. *The Hill of Dreams*, in a somewhat abbreviated version, had appeared serially in *Horlick's Magazine* during the last six months of 1904 under the title *The Garden of Avallaunius*.

Machen was later to write, and justly, in his autobiographical volume *Far Off Things* (1922) the following pivotal words: "I shall always esteem it as the greatest piece of fortune that has fallen to me, that I was born in that noble, fallen Caerleon-on-Usk, in the heart of Gwent. My greatest fortune, I mean, from that point of view which I now more especially have in mind, the career of letters. The older I grow the more firmly am I convinced that anything which I may have accomplished in literature is due to the fact that when my eyes were first opened in earliest childhood they had before them the vision of an enchanted land" (FOT 8).

In *The Hill of Dreams* Machen succeeded in retrieving not only something of his own immediate past but just as much (especially in the "Roman Chapter") a glorious period from the early history of Wales. Moreover, he succeeded in capturing, in significant token form, something of the tremendous yearning of the Welsh for their own magnificent past, as well as their almost religious attitude toward their own past and language and culture and musico-poetic arts.

This almost religious attitude of the Welsh toward the mythical and historical totality of their own way of life is not that dissimilar—in a general way—to the attitude displayed by Chief Seattle, the head of the Suquamish and Duwamish tribes, in his speech on the occasion of the founding in 1855 of the city that bears his name in the state of Washington. Here he speaks of their religion (and then elsewhere he prophesies with tremendous pathos of the inevitable passing of the Amerindian way of life): "Our religion is the traditions of our ancestors—the dreams of our old men, given them in the solemn hours of night by the Great Spirit, and the vision of our sachems, and is written in the heart of our people."

Following the completion of Machen's fictional magnum opus (whose creation took from late 1895 to the middle of 1897), he created his single outstanding piece of nonfiction (apart from his later volumes of autobiography), *Hieroglyphics: A Note upon Ecstasy in Literature*. In this treatise he developed and illustrated his theory of great literature as "ecstasy." Completed in the summer of 1899, this appeared in book form in 1902.

The Hill of Dreams and *Hieroglyphics* probably represent the crème de la crème of Machen's literary output, together with his autobiographical volumes. But they also represent something more than that. In the late 1800s and early 1900s, a momentous event was happening in Anglo-American letters. This was nothing less than the final flowering of Late Romantic, and peculiarly British, Kelticism. This particular final flowering—represented by such poets and authors as William Butler Yeats, Lord Dunsany, Padraic Colum, etc.—is symbolized perfectly in both *Hieroglyphics* and *The Hill of Dreams*.

The new generation of eager or clever young writers at this time was either hostile or indifferent to, or ignorant of, this event; or else they were totally blind to anything beyond their own new and narrow and uniquely modern anthropocentrism. The English Decadents (a group that definitely does not include Machen)—to judge, for example, by the remarks of Oscar Wilde on some of Swinburne's later poetry—were not hostile to this Keltic spirit but merely indifferent to certain larger aspects and considerations of this same spirit, particularly its vast epic-imaginative qualities. They were too busy being clever and "up-to-date" as well as involved in trivial aspects of "art for art's sake."

The death from cancer of his first wife Amelia in the summer of 1899 plunged Machen into a period of intense depression. The turn of the century found him seemingly unsuccessful as a professional writer as well as depressed and short of money. For a brief while he became an occultist. Together with such respectable figures as W. B. Yeats and George Moore, he joined the Hermetic Order of the Golden Dawn, more or less presided over by his great and good friend, the expatriate American A. E. Waite. Machen considered investigating Satanism, but fortunately he became infatuated instead with a young actress Pierpont Vivienne, whom he called his "Shepherdess." Although they were good friends, she did not return his love but married someone else instead (a musician).

However, by now Machen had already started a leave of absence (as it were) from his creative writing when in January 1901 he first went on the stage. He possessed as a mature man a deep sonorous voice à la Dylan Thomas (another and later Welshman), and this served him well as a Shakespearian actor when he joined Frank Benson's Shakespeare Company, mouthing the "tremendous" lines of Elizabethan rant, rhetoric, and poetry. Thus, he became an actor at thirty-nine and began a whole new life for himself, which lasted from 1901 to 1905, a remarkable achievement for a middle-aged man.

Moreover, he married—again in middle age—one of the actresses in the Benson Company, Dorothy Purefoy Huddleston, on June 25, 1903. From this union, his second marriage, there emerged two children, a boy and a girl. The year 1906 saw Machen return for a while to his creative writing when he published *The House of Souls*. Finally in 1907 he published *The Hill of Dreams*. That year also saw him on the stage for the last time as a regular trouper. Late 1907 marked his final and lasting return to writing of all kinds, and thus there began his last major period as a creative artist, renewed and replenished by his experience on the stage as well as by his second marriage.

For the next few years Machen wrote for various periodicals: the *Academy* (owned and edited by Lord Alfred Douglas), the *Neolith*, and *T.P.'s Weekly*. In

1906 and 1907 he had put together *The Secret Glory*, a patchwork of material accumulating over the last dozen years; it did not see publication until 1922. Then almost at the age of fifty he became a journalist, a profession he detested, writing for the (London) *Evening News*, beginning around 1911. The newspaper encouraged him to do his own creative writing, which they also published in addition to his purely journalistic pieces.

The year 1914 saw the "Great War"—or World War I—commence its destructive and stupid course. During these war years (ending 1918), a time of great physical and spiritual danger for many Europeans and Englishmen, Machen accomplished some of his finest fiction, in addition to perpetrating willy-nilly a myth for his fellow Britons with his tale "The Bowmen," first published in 1914. *The Angels of Mons: The Bowmen and Other Legends of the War* appeared in 1915 and proved to be Machen's greatest commercial success. *The Great Return* (1915), although a masterpiece of artistic reserve and balance, as well as his most important story of supernatural joy, proved to be one of his least successful publications from a purely popular viewpoint; cast in the form of a newspaper report, this tale narrates the manifestation of the Holy Grail in a lonely Welsh town by the sea. *The Terror*, first appeared in 1917, is one of his most potent stories of supernatural horror.

After nearly a decade as a regular contributor—he was almost sixty—Machen resigned in 1921 from the *Evening News*. The next five years were a time of great happiness for the veteran writer. He and his family had moved to a new house in London (at 12 Melina Place). Here he and his wife Purefoy developed a kind of salon on Saturday evenings, for punch, games, and good conversation. This became a kind of tradition with them for quite a while.

Meanwhile in America that publisher of unusually good taste, Alfred A. Knopf of New York City, had in the early 1920s begun publishing Machen's works in those handsome yellow editions that one can still see today in used bookstores as well as in private and public libraries. Machen had by now issued the three volumes of his unique autobiography (one of the finest things in his overall oeuvre): *Far Off Things* in 1922, *Things Near and Far* in 1923, and *The London Adventure* in 1924. The first two volumes in particular surely rank with the best he ever wrote.

For the first time in his life Machen was enjoying a considerable vogue, principally in the U.S., thanks to the Knopf editions and thanks to certain preeminent proselytizers. Among his more outstanding American enthusiasts active at this time (as well as later) were Vincent Starrett, Carl Van Vechten, Robert Hillyer, James Branch Cabell, H. P. Lovecraft, and Clark Ashton

Smith, but not (alas!) H. L. Mencken or Edmund Wilson, those two arbiters of literary "elegance."

Machen was at last rewarded somewhat for the long hours he had put into his translation of *The Memoirs of Casanova* when an agreement was negotiated for a Casanova Society edition of the memoirs in 1922. Martin Secker of London issued in nine volumes the "Caerleon Edition" of Machen's novels, tales, and memoirs in 1923.

Machen took advantage of this unexpected but certainly welcome vogue for his work by issuing in book form four miscellanies, a genre in which he was a natural and intuitive master: *Strange Roads* in 1923, *Dog and Duck* in 1924, and lastly *Notes and Queries* together with *Dreads and Drolls* in 1926. Other books of this same general time were *The Glorious Mystery*, *The Canning Wonder*, and *Precious Balms* (this last being a collection of all the adverse book reviews Machen had received since the 1890s).

His remaining books of creative fiction appeared over a period of twelve years: *The Shining Pyramid* in 1924, *The Green Round* in 1933, and then *The Cosy Room* and *The Children of the Pool* in 1936. *The Green Round*, his last novel, received its first American publication in 1968 by Arkham House; August Derleth, its owner-editor, had championed Machen's cause on many occasions.

In 1929 Arthur and Purefoy Machen retired from London to Old Amersham, Buckinghamshire, in the Chiltern Hills, northwest of London. Here, where Arthur and his first wife had lived for a few years in the early 1890s, the olden beechwood forests linger to this day from Britanno-Roman and pre-Roman times. By 570 A.D. London had been lost to the Romano-Britons but some real British-Keltic influence remained longer here in the Chilterns than in any other area of Eastern Britain. Indeed, the Chilterns by virtue of their forested heights and uplands (forests and hills were always favored areas for the original Brythons) had served in their aggregate as a kind of citadel or bulwark against the Saxons and other Germanic barbarians, thus to preserve the ancient "Augusta" or "Londinium" for a much longer period of time than what would have otherwise obtained. London had belonged to the Britons during the regime of King Arthur and immediately subsequent to his death.

So to this ancient stand of beechwood trees that had also functioned as an ancient stand of the Romano-Britons, Machen and his wife Purefoy retired to live in Old Amersham. His books had never earned him any real livelihood, and substantial recognition (even if only of a highly specialist kind) had not come to him until he was a comparatively older man. Writing had always been a torture to him: his own creative writing had proven a virtual torment to him for the most part; and journalism (usually writing trivial items for hire) proved an aesthetic horror for him, however manfully he did it and however much his income benefited from it at the time.

In the later decades of his life, as pleasant and enjoyable as his early London career had proven bitter and painful, Machen could have reflected that during his lifespan he had indeed become a variety of things just as a Jack-of-all-trades literary. Perhaps foremost as a writer of weird fiction (especially tales of supernatural horror and supernatural joy, and always of the secret ecstasy inherent in mortal existence). But he had started out as a none-too-successful poet in verse with the subsequently suppressed *Eleusinia*. Later he developed into a fascinating and often superb essayist, as well as a sovereign translator, particularly from the French (of two different centuries, the 1500s and the 1700s). Since he had a mystical outlook on life, he functioned in his writing as a literary mystic, a sort of Druidic poet in prose. He had been a serious critic of literature, but he became a professional journalist late in his life: his parents had originally sent him off to London to become just that at the very beginning of his long career. He developed into an autobiographer of especial excellence. Although he had never had a great commercial success (apart from *The Bowmen and Other Legends of the War* in 1915), he remained a great master of English prose, even though the ecstasy that burns at the heart of it is distinctly Welsh, that is to say, distinctly Brythonic. At his best he was an eminently successful poet in prose. Then, after all the difficulty and great lonely pain of his first major creative period (ending around the turn of the century), in the last decades of his life Machen became his own self-legend, with himself as his own best book, or work of art; or in the hermetic language of the Middle Ages that he loved so discerningly, his own alchemy and alchemist into a happier and more enlightened state. And it is distinctly significant that he deliberately killed himself (so to speak) as a writer in his early sixties. He still did some work, interesting and valuable as all his writings are, but not major in the sense of "The Great Return" or *The Hill of Dreams.*

In the very last decade of his life Machen received a number of signal honors, and we must say that they were certainly well deserved by this time. On March 3, 1937, that is, upon his seventy-fourth birthday, he sat at a luncheon in his honor put on in the city of Newport by his home county of Monmouthshire with many local dignitaries on hand. They presented Machen with a check for 20 guineas. In the autumn of 1937 the National Liberal Club in London held a dinner in his honor.

In 1939 World War II broke out. The war effort in Britain immediately commenced, and Machen made his own contribution by editing the book *A Handy Dickens*. He passed eighteen months in the selection of his favorite chapters from the works of Charles Dickens, and wrote an introduction for each chapter thus chosen. This personal anthology appeared just before Christmas 1941. In the spring of 1942 his great and good friend A. E. Waite died at the age of eighty-five; he and Machen had been close friends for fifty-five years.

As the war years dragged on, the financial condition of Arthur and Purefoy became increasingly straitened. Certain stalwart friends (a number of them quite influential) determined to rectify this once and for all. Inspired by Desmond MacCarthy and administered by Colin Summerfield, an appeal was made six months before Machen's eightieth birthday. This appeal appeared in the national press as a letter signed by twelve well-known literary figures: Max Beerbohm, Algernon Blackwood, Walter de la Mare, T. S. Eliot, John Masefield, Bernard Shaw, Arthur Quiller-Couch, Compton Mackenzie, Edward Marsh, A. E. W. Mason, Michael Sadlier, and Desmond MacCarthy. This appeal proved a remarkable success (particularly considering that it was wartime), and Machen's home county of Gwent or Monmouthshire organized a separate appeal that also proved successful. Meanwhile, Alfred A. Knopf in New York City organized yet another appeal that also yielded a considerable sum of money. The overall fund finally closed at well over £2,000.

On Machen's eightieth birthday on March 3, 1943, in a Hungarian restaurant in London, Desmond MacCarthy presented Arthur with a check for 1,200 guineas, the first installment of the fund. The archetypal Great Old Man of Letters held the seat of honor surrounded by a distinguished company indeed. This was probably the single greatest public moment of Machen's life. Neither Arthur nor Purefoy would want for money for the rest of their lives.

On March 30, the Palm Sunday of 1947, Purefoy died quite suddenly. After his wife's death Machen's health deteriorated, and his children established him at St. Joseph's, a nursing home operated by nuns in Beaconsfield, just south of Old Amersham. Not far from Beaconsfield the great Puritan poet John Milton had written *Paradise Regain'd*, the sequel to *Paradise Lost*. Machen firmly stated his desire to his daughter (Mrs. Janet Machen Davis), who had come to see him, to go live with her and her family at her home in Bristol, back in his beloved West Country, once his health improved enough to allow this. But this was not to be. In the early morning of December 15, 1947, Arthur Llewelyn Jones-Machen died in the presence of his daughter and Colin Summerfield.

In 1948 Alfred A Knopf published Machen's *Tales of Horror and the Supernatural*, selected and edited by Philip Van Doren Stern, who had written in the "Introduction" apropos of Machen's work as follows:

> A taste for his work has to be acquired; the writing is polished and elaborate, the thinking is subtle, and the imagery is rich with the glowing color that is to be found in medieval church glass. His style does not belong to our period of stripped diction and fast-moving prose; it stems instead from the latter part of the nineteenth century, and preserves some of the formality of that age when authors were learned people who had to undergo long apprenticeships to master their profession. (v–vi)

Also, as pointed out perceptively by Stern, Machen's art "is firmly based on the belief that the mystical interpretation of life is the only one worth holding. Machen is the artist of wonder, the seeker for something beyond life and outside time, the late-born disciple of Christianity who sees the physical world as the outer covering of a glowing inner core that may someday be revealed" (xi). During the last decades of Machen's life, H. P. Lovecraft, writing in his now classic study "Supernatural Horror in Literature," penned what must surely rank as some of the most judicious, perceptive, and eloquent praise in honor of his literary achievement.

> Of living creators of cosmic fear raised to its most artistic pitch, few if any can hope to equal the versatile Arthur Machen, author of some dozen tales long and short, in which the elements of hidden horror and brooding fright attain an almost incomparable substance and realistic acuteness. Mr. Machen, a general man of letters and master of an exquisitely lyrical and expressive prose style, has perhaps put more conscious effort into his picaresque *Chronicle of Clemendy*, his refreshing essays, his vivid autobiographical volumes, his fresh and spirited translations, and above all his memorable epic of the sensitive aesthetic mind, *The Hill of Dreams* [. . .] his powerful horror-material of the 'nineties and earlier nineteen-hundreds stands alone in its class, and marks a distinct epoch in the history of this literary form. (81)

But it should be pointed out that Lovecraft, writing most attractively about Caerleon-on-Usk and Machen's masterpiece, actually misrepresents *The Hill of Dreams*. Lovecraft cites the novel as one "in which the youthful hero responds to the magic of that ancient Welsh environment *which is the author's own*, and lives a dream-life in the Roman city of Isca Silurum, shrunk to the relic-strown village of Caerleon-on-Usk" (81; emphasis added). Lucian Taylor's dream-life in Isca Silurum is most vividly and amply described in Chapter IV—the so-called "Roman Chapter"—but it is true that its immediate artistic effect is adroitly adumbrated in the first three chapters, and then haunts the remainder of the book. Incidentally, the "Roman Chapter" can stand on its own in any anthology as a classic of English prose and must take rank with some of the noblest passages in English literature, including not only those of Thomas De Quincey (of whom Machen was a great admirer) but the last and most celebrated chapter (the fifth) of Sir Thomas Browne's *Hydriotaphia*, or *Urn-Buriall* (1658). Lovecraft gives the impression from his description (completely authentic otherwise) that the overall book is largely concerned with the hero's dream-life in the Late Roman town and fortress combined (which it is not): the "Roman Chapter" is only one chapter among a skillfully juxtaposed mosaic of seven chapters, even though its effect does haunt at least half the book (especially the beginning and the end), if not indeed most of the book.

Lovecraft had an instinctive understanding *in depth* of such a signally cosmic master artist as Machen, as (for example) when he writes: "Of utmost delicacy, the passing from mere horror into true mysticism, is *The Great Return*, a story of the Graal, also a product of the war period" (87). Then immediately he continues: "Too well known to need description here is the tale of 'The Bowmen'; which, taken for authentic narration, gave rise to the widespread legend of the 'Angels of Mons'—ghosts of the old English archers of Crécy and Agincourt who fought in 1914 beside the hard-pressed ranks of England's glorious 'Old Contemptibles'" (87).

But perhaps Lovecraft is at his most eloquent when he sums up some of the apparatus of Machen's interior fantasy life as a writer.

> Mr. Machen, with an impressionable Celtic heritage linked to keen youthful memories of the wild domed hills, archaic forests, and cryptical Roman ruins of the Gwent countryside, has developed an imaginative life of rare beauty, intensity, and historic background. He has absorbed the mediaeval mystery of dark woods and ancient customs, and is a champion of the Middle Ages in all things—including the Catholic faith. He has yielded, likewise, to the spell of the Britanno-Roman life which once surged over his native region; and finds strange magic in the fortified camps, tesselated pavements, fragments of statues, and kindred things which tell of the day when classicism reigned and Latin was the language of the country. (82)

And thus has Mr. Lovecraft opined, and justly, apropos of Mr. Machen.

There is something peculiar about the Keltic element in modern English that should be mentioned here. Although relatively few Keltic words remain directly in modern English, many writers have opined that, in place of an immediate transference of words into English, the Keltic spirit exercised a much more profound and subtle influence on later English literature. Matthew Arnold, for one, has maintained that this Keltic spirit represents a species of "natural magic"—a magic which has accounted for some of the abilities possessed by Spenser, Marlowe, Shakespeare, Keats, Coleridge, and other poets. And it is peculiar that although the work of Arthur Machen is the very essence—the *quintessence* (to use the alchemical diction of the Middle Ages)—of Late Romantic (British) Kelticism, it was almost completely misunderstood at the time by the contemporary press, especially in England. Its real and genuine significance has remained, for the most part, unknown or presumably too vague and "cloudy" to define aright. But this fact—that Machen's work embodies the quintessence of Late Romantic Kelticism—explains in large measure why so many historic layers, so many mystic auras, and so many spiritual or aesthetic splendors, are subsumed into Machen's viewpoint and his art.

As a writer in the highest sense Machen may be seen in various roles; and these would form some of them. As a Welsh "bard" in highly musical English prose (rather than verse), his own usage of poetic prose parallels that of the French Decadents and Symbolists, and anticipates the poetic prose once again so popular in written fantasy. As a "mythographer" or myth-maker, he continues both the Welsh and the classical (Greek and Latin) traditions of myth in an unique and autochthonous synthesis of his own. As a Druid or high priest of literature (conversant with strange medieval rigors and mortifications of the flesh, many in description and a selective number in practice), he skillfully mosaicks into the English of his narratives incantatory passages of truly "hermetic" meaning in Latin, Welsh, and Greek. Above all and always—and this is the collective art which permits all the other functions—as a paramount master of English prose, he stands beside Thomas De Quincey, Sir Thomas Browne, the Robert Burton who penned *The Anatomy of Melancholy*, the super-aesthete and pedagogue Walter Pater, and selective others.

Arthur called Machen was well named indeed: Arthur the Maker—yes, Arthur the Myth-Maker—as "fabulous" a figure in various recondite aspects as Merlin and Taliesen themselves, or as Geoffrey of Monmouth, from Machen's own native country of Gwent.

By being born in Caerleon-on-Usk, Machen inherited the various historic layers or traditions associated with that ancient town (as well as with southern Wales), and which he subsumed into his own unique genus of Kelticism: first, the lore relative to the pre-Keltic "Little People" (later transformed into "féerie" or Faerie); then the British-Keltic or Brythonic culture; the Britanno-Roman culture; the Dark Ages; the Middle Ages; the Renaissance; the early

Romantic period, middle Romantic or Victorian, and Late Romantic or Late Victorian; and then on into the 1920s, which were to witness the first major triumphs of the then new "modernism."

Like a last of the Romano-British bards displaced in both time (Victorian England, *not* Arthurian Britain or Late Roman Britain) and space (London, *not* Wales), Arthur Machen—by preserving, and by necromantically evoking, various ancient and then later historical "splendors"—became, in a deep, subtle, and innermost sense, truly "The Last of the Arthurians" himself. Alienated in his own time and space for much of his life (and we are speaking here in a mystical or spiritual sense), he was moreover descended from people, the Welsh, who had once maintained their dominion over the whole of Britain, who had become dispossessed of most of their ancient national patrimony, and who had thus been transformed themselves into "aliens" in most of their former realms. Nor could they forget this. However, they had endured, as Machen himself was to endure.

Toward the last of his first major creative period, "Leolinus Siluriensis" had achieved his own self-myth as a dedicated and painstaking "artist-martyr" when he had to become the Lucian Taylor of his own romance, *The Hill of Dreams*. But whereas Lucian dies of an accidental overdose of laudanum (perhaps symbolic of Machen writing "finish" to his early London career and all that it represented in terms of his earlier, less experienced, but certainly more purely idealistic self), Machen merely went on living in that determined and persevering way of his, and continued writing his books, articles, and reviews.

If the splendor that his work reflects in a symbolic or actual (historic) way could be summed up in one word or phrase, it might be either "Arthurian" or "Late Roman." And if we finally decided that it might be Arthurian, then it would be with the understanding that it subsumed within itself at least the various historic layers or traditions just previously adumbrated. His early training at Hereford Cathedral School, with which he was originally to continue that unbroken ecclesiastical tradition peculiar to his father's family, prepared him instead uniquely well indeed for his real career or destiny: that of creative literature of a completely individual class. By receiving his earliest and greatest influence from Caerleon and from the presumably "mythical" age of King Arthur—Arthur, "the Bright Light of the Dark Ages"—Machen thus became supremely well equipped to create his own expression of the Keltic spirit, a spirit at once mystic and magical.

Machen, it must be emphasized, evolved into his own kind of *modern* romancer. His powerful supernatural stories of the 1890s and early 1900s have elements akin to the "scientific romances" of the same period. For just one salient example, Machen's novella "The Great Return" is a *modern* story of the Holy Grail (a story that takes place completely in Wales, a fact that is noteworthy in that Machen's native country remained the single greatest sanctuary for the Arthurian traditions and magnificence) *with no mention of Glastonbury*. In his handling of such a well-known property of medieval romance, Machen is notable for the purity of his approach: the Grail is simply used as a kind of supernal catalyst for inducing a sense of deep and inner spiritual splendor in those who come into contact with it, a type of paradisaical serenity or sublimity, the "peaceable kingdom" restored.

Throughout Machen's oeuvre and balancing the great fears "captured" in his most powerful tales of horror and the supernatural, there is the curious and ironic emphasis on splendor and enlightenment (often purchased at great loss or expense within the given stories), as indicated by some of his titles and main images: "The Inmost Light," *The Secret Glory*, "The Shining Pyramid," *The Glorious Mystery*.

The Holy Grail in "The Great Return" is refulgent with strange transdimensional glories. Whilst originally in the medieval romances it was a symbol of "grace," in our own time it has developed into simply a symbol for that lost or Arthurian splendor so persistently associated with the San Graal in myth and legend. In Machen's work overall it is the cup of wonder and marvel overbrimming with great joy and great awe, with otherworldly magnificence, and with a lost and Atlantean exaltation.

Despite his birth in eminently "Arthurian" Caerleon, this is one of the few instances (virtually unique) within the canon of his oeuvre where Machen permits himself, as a mature artist, to use such a pre-eminently Arthurian property: significantly it is the San Graal, the symbol par excellence of Keltic mysticism.

Machen's own artistic preoccupation with the ultimate sunset of the Arthurian splendor (which in its own turn seems but a reflection or continuation of the still potent Late Roman Imperial magnificence) is indicated in the highly autobiographical pages of *The Hill of Dreams*, where he again shadows his own Caerleon under the name of "Caermaen," and is particularly highlighted at the beginning and the end of the novel by the tremendous image of the setting sun likened to the fire in a great brazen furnace. But the final statement of this image is projected within the open eyes of the writer Lucian Taylor who is dead at his writing table and thus literally "amort" with splendor. In some incredibly elusive way the artist's spirit has passed into the splendiferous world of his vision ... the dreamer has passed into his dream....

Just as he had given over the best part of his adolescent imagination to relating the various local Arthurian traditions and legends immediately to his native environment of Caerleon, so did Machen devote the best part of his first major creative period as a mature artist (from the early 1800s up to 1899) to the imaginative reconstruction of Late Roman life in Isca Silurum.

In his later novella "The Great Return" he was to use the Arthurian splendor to retrieve a paradisaical presence or immanence, a notably "Christian" endeavor on the part of the author, and very much in keeping with the overall tradition of the legend in question. But in his fictional magnum opus, *The Hill of Dreams*, Machen is above all notable for his use of the Arthurian splendor to recapture (paradoxically enough) a pagan glamor. Machen's heritage of Arthurian dream and wonder from old Caerleon becomes the specific window or focus through which he perceives the rich and variegated world of Roman British life in Isca of the Silurians.

In his introduction to the 1923 Alfred A. Knopf edition of *The Hill of Dreams*, the author gives us a fascinating description of the overall origin of his novel, as well as of the specific creation of the "Roman Chapter."

> The required notion came at last, not from within, ..., but from without. I am not quite sure, but almost sure, that the needed hint was discovered in an introduction to "Tristram Shandy" written by that most accomplished man of letters, Mr. Charles Whibley. Mr. Whibley, in classifying Sterne's masterpiece, noted that it might be called a picaresque of the mind, contrasting it with "Gil Blas" which is a picaresque of the body. This distinction had struck me very much when I read it; and now as I was puzzling my head to find a spring for the book that was to be written, Mr. Whibley's dictum occurred to me, and applying it to another eighteenth century masterpiece, I asked myself why I should not write a "Robinson Crusoe" of the soul. I resolved forthwith that I would do so; I would take the theme of solitude, loneliness, separation from mankind, but, in place of a desert island and a bodily separation, my hero should be isolated in London and find his chief loneliness in the midst of myriads of myriads of men. His should be a solitude of the spirit, and the ocean surrounding him and disassociating him from his kind should be a spiritual deep. And here I found myself, as I thought, on sure ground; for I had had some experience of such things. For two years I had endured terrors of loneliness in my little room in Carendon road, Notting Hill Gate, and so I was soundly instructed as to the matter of the work. (CF 2.522-23)

Machen had received the overall conception of his novel toward the end of October 1895, but it was not until early February 1896 that he began the actual writing. He encountered arduous difficulties and problems but persevered and resolved them, very much to his credit as a painstaking craftsman. He details further in his introduction something of the specific creation of the celebrated Chapter IV.

> Then I found somewhere or other, the recipe for the "Roman Chapter," an attempted recreation of the Roman British world of Isca Silurum, Caerleon-on-Usk, the town where I was born, and soaked myself so thoroughly in the vision of the old golden city—now a little desolate village—and listened so long in the deep green of Wentwood for the clangour of the marching Legion and for the noise of their trumpets that I grew quite "dithery" as they say in some parts of England. I would go out on my dim Bloomsbury strolls, deep in my dream, and would "come to myself" with a sudden shock in Lamb's Conduit Street or Mecklenburgh Square or in the solitudes of Great Coram Street, realizing certainly, that I was not, in actuality, in the Garden of Avallaunius or delaying in the Via Nympharum or on the Pons Saturni—it is called Pont Sadwrn to this day—but utterly at a loss to know exactly where I was or what I was doing, without the faintest notion of the various positions of north and south, east and west, and not at all clear as to how I was to get home to Gray's Inn and my lunch. And it was in this queer way that the fourth chapter was accomplished. I was somewhat proud of it, and went on gaily . . . (CF 2.525–26)

The composition of *The Hill of Dreams* required from first to last a period of eighteen months, from February 1896 to July 1897. It first appeared in book form in 1907, ten years after its completion.

The sentence that opens this magisterial romance of alienation is remarkable for its utter simplicity: "There was a glow in the sky as if great furnace doors were opened" (CF 2.9). Further on in Chapter I, Machen describes Lucian Taylor's progress away at school; this evidently reflects something of the author's own experience at Hereford Cathedral School.

> Lucian went slowly, but not discreditably, up the school, gaining prizes now and again, and falling in love more and more with useless reading and unlikely knowledge. He did his elegiacs and iambics well enough, but he preferred exercising himself in the rhymed Latin of the middle ages. He liked history, but he loved to meditate on a land laid waste, Britain deserted by the legions, the rare pavements riven by frost, *Celtic magic still brooding on the wild hills and in the black depths of the forest*, the rosy marbles stained with rain, and the walls growing grey. The masters did not encourage these researches; a pure enthu-

siasm, they felt, should be for cricket and football, the dilettanti might even play fives and read Shakespeare without blame, but healthy English boys should have nothing to do with decadent periods. (CF 2.12-13; emphasis added)

However, Machen reserves some of his most skillful writing, his finest descriptive powers, for the "Roman Chapter" wherein he adroitly juxtaposes and contrasts the modern and rather asinine Victorian life in Caerleon with the wonderfully sensuous and certainly sensual world of Isca. The author shadows Caerleon under the name of "Caermaen" and adumbrates his own self as Lucian or, in his Late Roman incarnation, as Avallaunius. The chapter's opening is memorable for its poetic and evocative description whose imaginative qualities would not have been lost on either H. P. Lovecraft or Clark Ashton Smith.

In the course of the week Lucian again visited Caermaen. He wished to view the amphitheatre more precisely, to note the exact position of the ancient walls, to gaze up the valley from certain points within the town, to imprint minutely and clearly on his mind the surge of the hills about the city, and the dark tapestry of the hanging woods. And he lingered in the museum where the relics of the Roman occupation had been stored; he was interested in the fragments of tessalated floors, in the glowing gold of drinking cups, the curious beads of fused and coloured glass, the carved amber-work, the scent-flagons that still retained the memory of unctuous odours, the necklaces, brooches, hairpins of gold and silver, and other intimate objects which had once belonged to Roman ladies. One of the glass flagons, buried in damp earth for many hundred years, had gathered in its dark grave all the splendours of the light, and now shone like an opal with a moonlight glamour and gleams of gold and pale sunset green, and imperial purple. Then there were the wine jars of red earthenware, the memorial stones from graves, and the heads of broken gods, with fragments of occult things used in the secret rites of Mithras. Lucian read on the labels where all these objects were found: in the churchyard, beneath the turf of the meadow, and in the old cemetery near the forest; and whenever it was possible he would make his way to the spot of discovery, and imagine the long darkness that had hidden gold and stone and amber. All these investigations were necessary for the scheme he had in view, so he became for some time quite a familiar figure in the dusty deserted streets and in the meadows by the river. (CF 2.71)

Then, further on, Machen elucidates the purpose behind his hero's numerous visits and investigations.

All these journeys of his to Caermaen and its neighbourhood had a peculiar object; he was gradually levelling to the dust the squalid kraals of modern times, and rebuilding the splendid and golden city of Siluria. All this mystic town was for the delight of his sweetheart and himself; for her the wonderful villas, the shady courts, the magic of tesselated pavements, and the hangings of rich stuffs with their intricate and glowing patterns. Lucian wandered all day through the shining streets, taking shelter sometimes in the gardens beneath the dense and gloomy ilex trees, and listening In the course of the week and trickle of the fountains. Sometimes he would look out of a window and watch the crowd and color of the market-place and now and again a ship came up the river bringing exquisite silks and the merchandise of unknown lands in the Far East. He had made a curious and accurate map of the town he proposed to inhabit, in which every villa was set down and named. He drew his lines to scale with the gravity of a surveyor, and studied the plan till he was able to find his way from house to house on the darkest summer night. On the southern slopes about the town [i.e., across the river] there were vineyards, always under a glowing sun, and sometimes he ventured to the furthest ridge of the forest, where the wild people still lingered, that he might catch the golden gleam of the city far away, as the light quivered and scintillated on the glittering tiles. And there were gardens outside the city gates where strange and brilliant flowers grew, filling the hot air with their odour, and scenting the breeze that blew along the streets. (CF 2.75)

Still further on, Machen gives us—from a vantage point high on the steep slope south of the town across the river—a wonderful "impressionistic" panorama of Isca Silurum as seen through the eyes of his hero Lucian still in his Late Roman incarnation as Avallaunius.

At other times it was his chief pleasure to spend a whole day in a vineyard planted on the steep slope beyond the bridge. A grey stone seat had been placed beneath a shady laurel, and here he often sat without motion or gesture for many hours. Below him the tawny river swept round the town in a half circle; he could see the swirl of the yellow water, its eddies and miniature whirlpools, as the tide poured up from the south. And beyond the river the strong circuit of the walls, and within, the city glittered like a charming piece of mosaic. He freed himself from the obtuse modern view of towns as places where human beings live and make money and rejoice or suffer, for from the standpoint of the moment such facts were wholly impertinent. He knew perfectly well that for his present purpose the tawny sheen and shimmer of the tide was the only fact of importance about the river, and so he regarded the city as a curious work in jewellery. Its radiant marble porticoes, the white walls of the villas, a dome of burning copper, the flash and scintillation of tiled roofs, the quiet red of brickwork, dark groves of ilex, and cypress, and laurel, glowing rose-gardens, and here and there the silver of a fountain, seemed arranged and contrasted with a wonderful art, and the town appeared a delicious ornament, every cube of colour owing its place to the thought and inspiration of the artificer. Lucian, as he gazed from his arbour amongst the trellised vines, lost none of the subtle pleasures of the sight; noting every *nuance* of colour, he let his eyes dwell for a moment on the scarlet flash of poppies, and then on a glazed roof which in the glance of the sun seemed to spout fire. A square of vines was like some rare green stone; the grapes were massed so richly amongst the vivid leaves, that even from far off there was a sense of irregular flecks and stains of purple running through the green. The laurel garths were like cool jade; the gardens, where red, yellow, blue and white gleamed together in a mist of heat, had the radiance of opal; the river was a band of dull gold. On every side, as if to enhance the preciousness of the city, the woods hung dark on the hills; above, the sky was violet, specked with minute feathery clouds, white as snowflakes. It reminded him of a beautiful bowl in his villa; the ground was of that same brilliant blue, and the artist had fused into the work when it was hot, particles of pure white glass.

For Lucian this was a spectacle that enchanted many hours; leaning on one hand, he would gaze at the city glowing in the sunlight till the purple shadows drew down the slopes and the long melodious trumpet sounded for the evening watch. Then, as he strolled beneath the trellises, he would see all the radiant facets glimmer out, and the city faded into haze, a white wall shining here and there, and the gardens veiled in a dim, rich glow. On such an evening he would go home with the sense that he had truly lived a day, having received for many hours the most acute impressions of beautiful colour. (CF 2.79-80)

Through his focus onto the pagan world of Isca Silurum, the true purpose of life—to wit, the simple acceptance and enjoyment of its wonder, mystery, and beauty—has become apparent to Lucian Taylor; and the "Roman Chapter" concludes with his full and expanded understanding of this revelation.

To Lucian, entranced in the garden of Avallaunius, it seemed very strange that he had once been so ignorant of all the exquisite meanings of life. Now, beneath the violet sky, looking through the brilliant trellis of the vines, he saw the picture; before, he had gazed in sad astonishment at the squalid rag [i.e., "the dull modern life"] which was wrapped about it. (CF 2.89)

The "Roman Chapter" records thus the best and brightest period in Lucian Taylor's life, his imaginative sojourn within the marbled confines of ancient and beautiful Isca (with all its transcendent emotions and sensations) when he had lived the life of a Late Roman aesthete. The seventh and ultimate chapter of *The Hill of Dreams* describes, on the other hand, his delirium and descent into death through an overdose of laudanum. Machen's narrative of his hero's final "trip" contains some of his most powerful and poignant passages of prose, culminating of course in Lucian's death, the final revelation.

> Without, the storm swelled to the roaring of an awful sea, the wind grew to a shrill long scream, the elm-tree was riven and split with the crash of a thunderclap. To Lucian the tumult and shock came as a gentle murmur, as if brake stirred before a sudden breeze in summer. And then a vast silence overwhelmed him.
>
> A few minutes later there was a shuffling of feet in the passage, and the door was softly opened. A woman came in, holding a light, and she peered curiously at the figure sitting quite still in the chair before the desk. [. . .] She put her hand to his heart, and looked up, and beckoned to some one who was waiting by the door.
>
> "Come in, Joe," she said. "It's just as I thought it would be: 'Death by misadventure';" and she held up a little empty bottle of dark blue glass that was standing on the desk. "He would take it, and I always knew he would take a drop too much one of these days." [. . .]
>
> The man took up the blazing paraffin lamp, and set it on the desk, beside the scattered heap of that terrible manuscript. The flaring light shone through the dead eyes into the dying brain, and there was a glow within, as if great furnace doors were opened. (CF 2.155, 156)

The Hill of Dreams closes with the same directness and simplicity with which it begins; indeed, with virtually the same words. The novel's final pages possess a rare pathos and grandeur, a genuine epic dignity as the narrative moves to its inexorable finish. Moreover, the tremendous image with which the story opens and then ends is not actually the setting sun but is instead the sunset's immediate aftermath, that is, the afterglow that just precedes the twilight and then the ultimate night.

Behind the definitive artistic expression contained within his *Robinson Crusoe* of the soul, there lay the bitter actuality of the agony and pain that Machen had undergone as a dedicated creative artist—as well as the aching loneliness, the intense melancholia, and the profound alienation which he had experienced simply as a person—during his first London period (from the summer of 1881 to the late autumn of 1885).

The reality of those two full years in particular, during which (as he later wrote) he "endured terrors of loneliness" at his then home (his little room) in Clarendon Road, Notting Hill Gate, London, formed the crucible in which Machen's character as well as his personality as a mature creative artist were fired and tested. But like the Welsh in general, he was to endure, and emerged from his ordeal as a better and a stronger person. He had survived the worst part of his self-imposed apprenticeship both as a person and a writer. All this then was part of the actuality of real experience which lay behind his fictional magnum opus, and which gives the novel its especial flavor of authenticity.

Machen then in his most characteristic creative writings is a peculiar mixture of hard-edged realist and poetic fantaisiste. Just as the critical respect and admiration for him as a man of letters has always been more pronounced in America than in England, his influence as a writer on other writers has apparently always proved greater in the U.S. than in the United Kingdom, and has always been limited to writers of a similar temperament as well as of similar tastes. The true connoisseur of Machen's works is your genuine lover of *mystery*—that is, mystery that remains fundamentally inviolate despite all hints and adumbrations—and is not necessarily by any means the same as the lover of conventional mystery tales, or detective stories, wherein the unknown is reduced at the end to something perfectly well known and even commonplace.

Machen exercised a profound and undeniable influence on both H. P. Lovecraft and Clark Ashton Smith, an influence not only deep-reaching but subtle and selective as well. Lovecraft, it will be remembered, was a lover of Latin and classicism in general, and Smith was no less a lover of the classical than Lovecraft but also, by process of strict historical evolution, a Late Romantic poet of the most pronounced kind. For such sensitive and unique artists as these, Arthur Machen would have provided a source of pure and undiluted ROMANticism.

Both Lovecraft and Smith learned from the elder writer, but whereas Lovecraft, as a "photographic realist" in his own most characteristic stories, would have studied more closely the realistic aspects of Machen's fiction, Smith would have studied more attentively the poetic or lyrical aspects of Machen's art. However, we can be sure that both Lovecraft and Smith would have equally appreciated these two major aspects of Machen's most idiosyncratic fiction.

In a number of profound and significant respects there is perhaps a greater kinship between Machen and Smith than between Machen and Lovecraft. Machen and Smith in regard to a given story of their own respective creation possessed an instinctively more lyrical or poetic approach than Lovecraft, although Machen is probably more obviously human and humane than Smith. However much Smith came to the writing of his own most characteristic prose fictions as a result of his own interior artistic evolution, it is curious and striking how the conclusion of The Hill of Dreams—which features the death of Lucian Taylor—anticipates many of Smith's own short stories, the majority of which always end with the death of their protagonists.

However, apart from such a selective albeit profound influence as that on Lovecraft and Smith, both Arthur Machen and The Hill of Dreams will probably remain *sui generis* and basically inimitable.

Postlude

No matter that most of the Late Romantic were to end their days—even as most of them had passed their lives—in obscurity or near-obscurity. They had accomplished a brave and courageous work in the very teeth of a cuttingly hostile counterreaction on the part of the modern anti-Romantic establishment (artists and critics alike). Especially had some of them developed further, and indeed achieved the preservation of, literary fantasy in the grand manner on into the twentieth century. And certainly few other Late Romantics had achieved as much as Arthur Llewelyn Jones-Machen, prose-poet par excellence.

Machen would surely have been beloved of *Elen*, the Welsh goddess of the sunset. And did he not indeed receive at least some token guerdon—toward the sunset of his own life—for labor lovingly designed and accomplished often in the face of singular bitterness and (on occasion) breadless days?

Machen is that particular poet of wonder and romance who sings the tremendous and kaleidoscopic glories invoked by the ultimate sunset of the Arthurian splendor. All through the best part of his first major creative period (specifically the "Yellow 'Nineties") he was transfixed and enraptured by that especial moment "like some eternal sunset brave with gold," to quote from "Fetlain's *Elegy for Vixeela*" by Clark Ashton Smith.

Off the west of Europe, and from the west of Britain, specifically from ancient Wales, "Leolinus Siluriensis"—virtually alone, unknown, and unhonored (at least in a comparatively larger sense)—was to preserve something of the ancient British-Keltic spirit, the elder Brythonic magic in a singularly pure and intrinsic form, into an alien age until such time as wonder and romance would find again a later cyclical and mystical rebirth.

In the far west of the United States of America, the Californians (native or adopted) were also to preserve something of this ancient epic-imaginative spirit, this Arthurian or Atlantean splendor of romanticism.

When the new romanticism surged up exuberantly in the late 1960s and early 1970s, the collective work of the Late Romantics had somehow survived to remain as a valuable heritage of beauty and inspiration for the practitioners of the new romanticism (as well as for the general public, of course), and from this new romanticism's immediate, hitherto largely unknown but recently discovered or re-discovered past. In that collective *living* museum which is the mind of the Western world, this heritage remains an unique and radiantly magical treasure somehow miraculously left over from an otherwise irrevocably lost Atlantis.

Works Cited

Ashe, Geoffrey. *King Arthur's Avalon.* New York: E. P. Dutton, 1958.

Baker, Arthur E. *A Tennyson Dictionary.* London: Routledge, 1916.

Cavendish, Richard, ed. *Man, Myth and Magic: An Illustrated Encyclopedia of the Supernatural.* New York: Marshall Cavendish, 1970. 24 vols.

Grebanier, Bernard D., et al. *English Literature and Its Backgrounds.* 1939. Rev. ed. New York: Holt, Rinehart & Winston, 1949. 2 vols.

Lovecraft, H. P. *The Annotated Supernatural Horror in Literature.* Ed. S. T. Joshi. New York: Hippocampus Press, 2nd ed. 2012.

Morris, John. *The Age of Arthur.* New York: Charles Scribner's Sons, 1973.

Stern, Philip Van Doren. "Introduction." In *Tales of Horror and the Supernatural* by Arthur Machen. New York: Alfred A. Knopf, 1948. v–xvi.

IV. Myths and Wonders

The Impossible History: Machen's "A Fragment of Life"

John Howard

> It was somewhere about the autumn of 1899 that I began to be conscious that the world was being presented to me at a new angle.—Arthur Machen (*TNF* 125)

Introduction: "Here in the world he changed his life"

Fine and enduring literature can rise out of the anguish and disruption of personal tragedy. Arthur Machen knew tragedy when his wife Amy died in the summer of 1899 after several years of painful illness. Then he discovered that experience can be transmuted through the written word. All through that desolate period Machen had continued to write. He completed *Hieroglyphics*, a remarkable book which although ostensibly setting out a theory of literature also stated in no uncertain terms Machen's attitude to the world, both visible and invisible. And as well as writing this "handbook for those who acclaim the imaginative in literature" (Valentine 67), Machen wrote that imaginative literature.

At the time Machen wrote very little about his wife's death, and his profound grief. As he subsequently further recorded, he had been left "in a state of very dreadful misery and desolation and dereliction of soul" (*TNF* 188). And yet, even as his life had fallen into fragments, he soon experienced the dawning of a new life. Many years later Machen described this with puzzlement in his memoir *Things Near and Far* (1923). For example, there were "the savours of the sanctuary that were perceived by me in all manner of grim London wastes and wanderings" (*TNF* 130). And there was the morning in November in which, while "walking up Rosebery Avenue with a friend," Machen had the sensation of "walking on air" (*TNF* 131). "There was no more grief . . . the great sorrows of life, these were seen to be but passing trifles of the moment, like the sorrow of a little child which is past and forgotten before its tears are dry" (*TNF* 141).

Three of Machen's most notable stories came from this grievous time. These were "The White People"; part of what, much later, was to be published as *The Secret Glory*; and "A Fragment of Life." This essay will discuss the last of these, of which Machen had completed the first chapter just as the "great sorrow which had long been threatened" fell upon him, leaving him alone (*TNF* 124).

These experiences were every bit as wondrous as something from one of his own stories happening to one of his own characters—and not least, to Edward Darnell of the then unfinished "A Fragment of Life." It had been Machen's intention in 1899 to write a single story "quite long and elaborate and magnificent." But it seems the story fractured or never cohered, and the separate, although not always distinct, pieces we know today were the result (Reynolds and Charlton 70).

Of those separate pieces, "A Fragment of Life" had its origin in an earlier story, "The Resurrection of the Dead," which had appeared in 1890, but the place of publication is unknown. But what had been lost was transformed. As Machen gradually came to life again he returned to his magnificent fragments and began to fashion one of them at least into the finest "fragment" of all, one in which husband and wife are not parted and would gradually leave the world behind them, receiving joy and wonder in exchange—and all chronicled as another sort of resurrection.

Arthur Machen married Dorothie Purefoy Hudleston (1878-1947) in June 1903. He completed "A Fragment of Life" in a version that he was willing to see published as a four-part serial in *Horlick's Magazine* the following year (February–May 1904). The author later declared that the fourth and final chapter of this original magazine publication was a "false ending" (*SL* 227) which he rewrote when the story was reprinted in *The House of Souls* (1906). It is this version with the revised Chapter 4 that has appeared in print ever since.

Perhaps Machen had felt that, as he wrote the story, circumstances were against him and the "false" ending was the best he could manage at the time. By the time he revised the final chapter, his circumstances were different and he could look again on how he wished to treat the theme of Edward and Mary Darnell and their "resurrection" from the death of a normal existence and their approach to true reality and, possibly, their ineffable passage through and into it. The fragments could be picked up and reassembled to some extent and, with the substitution of a new and "true" ending, restore something, in its final form, of the lost whole.

Machen's biographers Aidan Reynolds and William Charlton described "A Fragment of Life," "The White People," and the early draft sections of *The Secret Glory* as "fragments" (70). And they clearly are fragments, in the sense of being parts of a larger intended whole. But this is misleading, at least as far as "A Fragment of Life" is concerned. According to this view, it in fact consists of two stories which collide rather than cohere, and contrast so violently that any unity between them is strained, the result of haste and the author's inability to work with his chosen theme and material. Perhaps there is much justice in this view, but it is a superficial one: because "A Fragment of Life" does work as a self-contained and intelligible story. Its structure might not be straightforward and its manner smooth; and it might well contain enigmas wrapped in mysteries, with an obscure conclusion that could be the beginning of some other and greater story. But it is also complete in itself. The text still allows for endless speculation and interpretation, but there is no more text to be added, nor is any necessary.

Machen was concerned to "express the inexpressible, to rend the veil" (Sweetser 31). He had to do the first, which was by definition impossible, as well as the second, while putting the veil back together, making the torn parts into one piece again, so that there could a chance—no matter how small—of communicating the paradox, again and again for as long as it was necessary. Through hints and symbols Machen used all the art he could summon in order not to show the joins and his working. The result is that reading "A Fragment of Life" is to set out on a seemingly confused journey, with many digressions and irrelevances. But the reader ends up where the author wants him to be and can never quite work out how he was taken there, and precisely when and where he crosses the boundary.

"Something about fairyland": Chapters 1–3

"A Fragment of Life" is the story of Edward and Mary Darnell, and of how their marriage develops from conventionality to something of the deepest significance. From the opening sentence Machen establishes a mood of contrast. Edward Darnell wakes from a dream of misty rural paradise into the sunlit morning in his suburban London bedroom. He has left the world of dream for that of reality, and the contrast between the dream and reality could hardly be greater. Darnell and his wife Mary then spend the rest of the story finding out which world is the dream and which the reality. Although "A Fragment of Life" charts Edward Darnell's story rather than Mary's, they are of course intimately connected. There is never any sense that they would ever part, at least not until death.

The Darnells have been married for a year. Edward still "seriously and dutifully" kisses his wife at breakfast; they still "got on excellently" (CF 2.222). In the midst of their life together, where roles are clearly defined, Edward Darnell nevertheless slowly becomes aware that something is missing. He feels a growing dissatisfaction; appearances to the contrary, he is not fully in control and has the awareness that life is changing. He is sure that Mary would be an integral part of the new life and would play her role in his finding and entering into it. As in the dream, their new life is one to be entered into together as a couple. Not only does Darnell find the contrast of dream and reality losing their labels and fading into each other, he becomes more and more aware of the steps—sometimes literally—to take in order for the new reality, the "real" reality off the dream, to be reached, as they gradually move with the changes.

As the Darnells' story opens in our "real" world, the important decision dominating their conversation is what to do with £10 remaining from a generous wedding present of money given them by Mary's uncle and aunt, the Nixons. This first chapter contains much of the class and domestic comedy that is another of the contrasts in "A Fragment of Life." This comedy is not only that of the apparently placid life of the Darnells, their servant, and their relations with the local tradesmen; at times it is also more sharply focused.

Darnell's friend Wilson is portrayed as a worldly man who knows all the right people and all the right tricks and tips in order to get a good deal. But Machen makes it abundantly clear that Wilson's knowledge is of no real value whatsoever, and the things he takes seriously are of no importance or are wrong. Wilson is in fact a deluded fool, and only Machen and the reader can (presumably) see. Darnell has his suspicions of the worth of his friend's multifarious activities and views, and will eventually leave any respect for them behind. Wilson will not—and cannot. The reader has been taken into the world of George and Weedon Grossmith's comic novel *The Diary of a Nobody* (1892). On the surface someone who is a greater fool than Mr. Pooter is being lampooned. But it is intended that the reader feel for and respect Mr. Pooter, whereas Mr. Wilson is merely an irritating bore. We laugh against him rather than at him, and without sympathy. This comedy is heightened because it not only contrasts with Machen's serious message, but points towards it. What seems important is really of no importance, and we ignore the things of true importance at our peril, or at least, our impoverishment.

By the end of the day the Darnells still have not made any decision about how to use their £10. Further possibilities are suggested, and more thinking and "talking it over" will have to be done. This is the trap of the "real" material world, and it presents another contrast with the world of the dream. There, such things as worrying over bedroom furnishings, carpets, and kitchen ranges would surely assume its proper proportion or would not arise. Recollection of a recent discussion about a range causes Darnell to remember his journey home from work on that evening. He heard a nightingale, and "in spite of the fuming kilns under Acton, a delicate odour of the woods and summer fields was mysteriously in the air" (CF 2.239).

Borders are already beginning to fluctuate. The dream emerges from the twilight of approaching sleep, and day and dream merge. Machen's narrative up to this point has also subverted the reader's sense of time. It seems that the entirety of Chapter 1 has in fact taken place as the Darnells eat their breakfast, the morning after Edward Darnell awoke from his dream. "A Fragment of Life" is not told straightforwardly. There is little obvious linear chronology. Recollections and hints of past events are mingled with presentiments of the future and the outcome of decisions taken (or to be taken) by the Darnells, as well as earlier ones taken by others. As the chapter closes, Machen as voiceover narrator explains why dreams and realities are so intermixed and perplexing for the Darnells. He reveals the truth, illuminates the background: Edward has forgotten his legitimate inheritance and thinks he is really a City clerk living in Shepherd's Bush.

The second chapter returns to middle-class domesticity and the Darnells' discussion about their servant Alice and her "young man"—or, more precisely, his mother (and therefore Alice's potential mother-in-law). To begin with, the mother is shown, through what Alice has confided to Mrs. Darnell, to be a cantankerous, mean-spirited, and pretentious old woman. Then Mrs. Murry's attitude has suddenly changed, and she bestows maternal blessings on the prospective young couple. She seems to have come to appreciate the importance of her son in marrying a suitable woman—and the fact that in Alice he has found one. In this episode Machen highlights the capricious nature of families and relationships: the human element that seems to delight in spoiling things for other people, even if they are flesh and blood. And yet, there are also comedic aspects to the antics of the old woman and her son's growing yet still hesitant exasperation with her. Perhaps Machen intended the relationship between Alice and her suitor to parallel that of Edward and Mary Darnell, although at different stages in their lives together.

Problems made for Alice by her (prospective) family will be echoed in the dilemma the Darnells face when confronted with the conflicting accounts that Mary Darnell's uncle and aunt, the Nixons, give for the sudden breakdown in their apparently settled marriage. The contrast is with Edward Darnell's ancestry. While not particularly conventional, any revelations it promises would seem wholly positive, even if perplexing until better understood. Edward Darnell's background seems not to include the possibilities of trouble and scandal, but rather to hold the one chance they have for present and future bliss.

The younger couple's problems seem to have been caused by outside interference, and its abrupt cessation comes as a gift of grace, with no reason being given for it. The Darnells' problems come, by contrast, from within: their unvoiced dissatisfaction, and unwillingness, to accept their pleasant but ultimately false and valueless life. The Darnells' solution—their salvation—is also to come from within, as Edward begins seriously to recall his past and, in particular, the inheritance, both physical in terms of family books and documents and mental in terms of his openness to his ancestry and its implications. His new interests help to bring him closer to his wife. This is made plain throughout the narrative—even as Darnell himself cannot articulate it in words—and is symbolised by the dream he keeps on having to awake from. As he starts to open up to his wife, she wishes to know more and to understand—and to journey with him.

The previous week Mrs. Murry had been very nasty to Alice during a trip to Hampton Court and refused to be pleased by the attractions of the palace and park. Even though she now seems to have changed her mind about her son's prospective wife, praising her and hoping they get married, Darnell says that her dislike of Hampton Court "shews how bad she must be" (CF 2.250).

Darnell, by contrast, immediately recalls his very different experience the first time he saw Hampton Court, which leads him on to further reminiscence. He tells his wife for the first time about his wanderings in and around London as a young man. For financial reasons he decided not to go on a walking tour with a friend, but to make his own holiday—a tour of London. He did not buy a map, but gradually made one of his own for his "voyage of discovery" (CF 2.253). The young Darnell strolls through regions he had never known before, and it seems likely his readings in his father's "queer old book" had helped prepare him for the wonders he encountered (CF 2.251). Veils were surely opened, at least in his mind, and at least for a short while. A later attempted reading of a book on London took the heart out of the city, and he had to stop. And one morning he left his room at dawn and went–

straight off the map, it seems. He found the "Strange Road" and was glad (CF 2.256). Darnell started to add names and symbols to his map as they presented themselves to him (CF 2.258).

Machen transmutes London at the same time as he shows Darnell beginning to undergo a similar process—hence the mention of Alice's spoiled visit to Hampton Court helping to trigger a recollection of Darnell's own experience, and leading him further into more voyaging. Without ever quite realising it, the London clerk has been introduced to the true reality and can only treat it as if it existed in the ordinary world, just around the corner or waiting to be entered when the right preparations have been made. But the eyes of the soul do have to be ready for the veil to be drawn back and the truth revealed, to be grasped and entered into if the desire is there. The boundaries are elusive. Machen knew this, and it worked in his favour even as he lamented not being able to communicate his vision, because Darnell's journeys off the map were entirely extraordinary and could not be expressed in any familiar way. The reader perceives the problem and grants that it will be solved some other time. The reader needs to possess the heritage of a Darnell; and Machen's art, imperfect as he believed it to be, allows it to happen—at least for a while.

In another contrast of moods, Chapter 3 opens with Edward Darnell on his way home from the office wishing he could continue from where he and Mary had left off talking the previous evening. But the "real" world has broken in on them again. Mary tells her husband that her aunt Mrs. Nixon had asked to meet her in London, whereupon she poured out a tale of woe and deceit. She has become convinced that Mr. Nixon has embarked on an affair or taken up with Anarchists, as she describes to her niece a string of bizarre happenings and her husband's increasingly far-fetched explanations for them. Darnell thinks the old lady has gone mad, but also senses the absurdity in her rambling stories of Mr. Nixon's misdemeanours and his half-glimpsed companions. At one point he bursts out laughing, and soon Mary "also shook with merriment" (CF 2.263). As Mary continues to relate what her aunt told her, both feel some remorse at finding the old lady's predicament funny, but for Darnell the only explanation must still be that Mrs. Nixon has become mentally ill.

The contrast with the previous night is considerable. Mary Darnell comments on it. Then, her husband had described his marvellous wandering in London and away from it by the "Strange Road." Now, the stories of Nixon's "goings-on" that she has been repeating strike her as "queer" after all Edward Darnell's "beautiful things." But as he falls asleep Darnell links the two, commenting that in the walls of the great church he had seen there were "all kinds of strange grinning monsters, carved in stone" (CF 2.266).

Darnell is forcefully made aware of Mrs. Nixon's plight at first hand, when she pays a Sunday visit. Marian Nixon is a pathetic old lady, a complete contrast to how he had always imagined her—as the wife of a prosperous businessman who could easily afford to have made the Darnells a gift of £100. Mrs. Nixon asks to live with the Darnells, which would solve all their financial problems, but obviously cause others. After she has left, Darnell finds a leaflet she had dropped. Headed "THE NEW AND CHOSEN SEED OF ABRAHAM," the sensational prophecies it contains seems to confirm Darnell in his belief about his wife's aunt (CF 2.273).

But Darnell has been changing too. His quiet life with Mary seems to be threatened: "there seemed to be gathering on all sides grotesque and fantastic shapes, omens of confusion and disorder" (WP 2.275). Yet he finds himself not afraid, because of the "Daystar" that had risen in his heart. "Daystar" can refer to the sun, or to Mercury or Venus as the "morning star" rising in the dawn sky ahead of the sun. It is Christian imagery, to be found in the New Testament, for example: "We have also a more sure word of prophecy; whereunto ye do well that ye take heed, as unto a light that shineth in a dark place, until the day dawn, and the day star arise in your hearts" (2 Peter 1:19). The first stanza of Charles Wesley's hymn "Christ, whose glory fills the skies" includes the lines "Dayspring from on high, be near; / Daystar, in my heart appear" (Wesley 376). Although written by one of the founders of Methodism, the hymn found favour in Anglo-Catholic parishes and was included in *The English Hymnal*, the hymnbook most used in parishes in the movement. The sentiments of the hymn are those of the character and, very possibly, of Machen himself. Darnell would soon discover "a little church of another fashion" and assist at its "high and glorious" Sunday morning service (CF 2.288). The Daystar newly risen within him brought him to realise that despite appearances to the contrary, he lived each day in a "serene and secure world of brightness" which filled his heart with joy, so that when he woke in the morning "he was glad" (CF 2.276).

"A haze as of a dream": Chapter 4

The narrative initially keeps to the established time-period as it moves into the following week. Then it moves into a less defined period as the accurate recording of time passing seems to diminish in importance, or be much noticed, as Darnell comes to the realisation that "he was apart from other men, preparing himself for a great experiment" (CF 2.278).

The alarming events of the previous week are put to rest when Mr. Nixon pays an unannounced visit. The Darnells hear his side of the story as he tells them that his wife had gone mad and been committed to an asylum. He blames the "schism shop" she had been attending—the one run by the author of the prophetic paper she had left behind (CF 2.281). With his wife's side of the family in London now reconciled, Darnell's own ancestry can come to the fore.

Darnell decides to spend his holiday in going through the trunk of old family papers. He makes a spare room into his "study" and settles down seriously to explore his lineage and understand it better. Mary Darnell takes a keen interest: the deepening of their marriage is directly connected to the strange awe that she feels for her husband's heritage. Darnell's family is descended from ancient Welsh roots: now the "old blood [is] calling to the old land" as Darnell speculates about inheriting the old house and going to live there one day (CF 2.287). The attainment of the old house and land again symbolises a return to paradise, where "there was hidden a purpose, that they were to embark on a great and marvellous adventure" (CF 2.288).

By this point Machen must explicitly adopt the role of an impersonal commentator. As the Darnells' lives outwardly continue little changed, the inner transmutation proceeds. The "gross accidents" are being refined away. They stop attending their parish church in favour of a different one, and Darnell makes Machen's own discovery and lifelong preoccupation that the world is a sacrament. They enter a New Life, in which London has become Bagdad, but must be further transmuted so that it becomes Syon, "City of the Cup" (CF 2.290).

This shift in narrative procedure, jerking it out of a third-person narrative into what could seem a hasty and clumsy conclusion, has the effect of fragmenting the story as if there had been no alternative. Machen admits this in the text: "It would be impossible to carry on the history of Edward Darnell and of Mary his wife to a greater length . . . but this is a work which no chronicler has cared to describe with any amplitude of detail" (CF 2.293). But his solution is in fact anything but hasty and clumsy. That accusation can be made with justice against the first and "false" ending—and Machen realised its crudities and unsuitability. Yet again Machen found his story in danger of falling apart in his hands as he overreached himself; but in the revised chapter he strains as ever to express that which cannot be expressed, and even if the result was still far from successful in his eyes, Machen harnessed this inherent inability to point towards what he wants to say. This is appropriate in a story of yearning and transmutation.

The transformation of the Darnells' lives is recounted with a breathless intensity. The theme is "In Exitu Israel": "When Israel came out of Egypt" (Psalm 114). This is the great song of a people's joyous release from slavery that Machen would have known in the Book of Common Prayer version. And it is the title Darnell gives to the little book of "queer verse" and "notes and exclamations" that he makes (CF 2.293). And it is in this book that Darnell declares that "all legends . . . every Scripture is telling a story about ME."[1] The City clerk is everyman, in potential. And so, even as it is impossible to be given any definite information from the book, it seems that at its very end Darnell has closed the circle of "A Fragment of Life" as he awakes from a dream and achieves with Mary the dream of the opening words.

Conclusion: "I saw my Treasure found at last"

In their biography of Machen, Reynolds and Charlton describe "A Fragment of Life" as "very fragmentary indeed" (77). Of course, as they point out, this was because Machen abandoned the story at the time of his first wife's death in 1899. But while it is undeniable that "A Fragment of Life" does not proceed in a smooth and well-plotted manner, its "fragmentary" nature perhaps paradoxically does show what Machen actually achieved with this part of his great work that fell to pieces in his hands. Through chronicling the apparently mundane lives of the Darnells and their relatives and acquaintances, he expresses his own horror of mundane suburban life and devotes himself to showing how those condemned to it can strive to escape it.

In an apparently disjointed and rambling story Machen illustrates the dislocations and contradictions of real life, together with much dark comedy. Machen undermines realism for his own ends: to show that the mundane actually masks reality—or what should be true reality. And it is when the covering slips—as Machen must allow it to do—that the paradox is invoked. The disjointed aspect masks a seamless quality: the transition from "reality" to Reality. It is not possible to place the exact point of transition definitively. It is a process that overwhelms fragments even as it acknowledges them; it binds them together, even if uneasily, into a whole.

At the lowest point of his life Arthur Machen had found himself with the

---

1. *The White People and Other Weird Stories*, edited by S. T. Joshi (London: Penguin, 2011), 366n24 (editor's translation of Machen's Latin).

fragments of a great work. Despite loss and a genuine experience of darkness and despair, he found deliverance through his Christian faith and in his second marriage. Although not as originally intended, with "A Fragment of Life" Machen did succeed. The fragments were gathered together and a magnificent single story did emerge after all.

Works Cited

Reynolds, Aidan, and William Charlton. *Arthur Machen: A Short Account of His Life and Work*. 1963. Oxford: Caermaen, 1988.

Sweetser, Wesley D. *Arthur Machen*. New York: Twayne, 1964.

Valentine, Mark. *Arthur Machen*. Bridgend, Wales: Seren, 1995.

Wesley, Charles. "Christ, whose glory fills the skies." Hymn no. 258 in *The English Hymnal*, ed. W. J. Birkbeck et al. London: Oxford University Press, 1906.

Three Great Hoaxes of the War

Aleister Crowley

Blessed are they that have not seen and yet have believed.

On three notable occasions, since the war began, the credulity of the English people has passed all belief. The student of religious origins has probably noted that the hoaxes on all three occasions follow the generally accepted lines of demarcation, namely; legend, prophecy, and miracle.

It is now no secret that the famous legend of the "Russian Soldiers," that wonderful story of a million and a half Russian troops (with horses and artillery) smuggled through England in the dead of the night, was put about by the secret service to try to check the panic caused by the collapse at Mons. It was quite useless to point out to the English people that Archangel is served by a single line of rail, and that to ship even 10,000 troops would have strained the resources of the line for an entire summer. It was useless to ask why, having got all these troops on transports, the English did not sail them quietly down to the place where they were wanted, but went to the enormous and senseless trouble of disembarking them in England and embarking them again.

It was useless to make calculations; to show that as an English railway coach holds fifty men, and ten coaches make a pretty long train, it would have needed 3,000 trains to "flash by, with drawn blinds" for the men alone, and that the disguising of the horses, artillery, champagne and other necessary appurtenances of a Grand Ducal Russian army must have been a task worthy of Sherlock Holmes at his best.

One was always countered by the reply: "But Admiral X, or Captain Y, or Lord Z, or my Uncle Harry (as the case might be) saw them with his own eyes." The best of the joke was that the papers never printed a word of it, though the story was the sole topic of discussion for weeks. The idea was to keep the whole thing a secret from the Germans! Ultimately long after the yarn had been exploded—even among the semi-educated—*The Evening News* featured it as a "Strange Rumour" and one that might well be believed.

So much for legend: now for prophecy! The clairvoyants, astrologers, and psychics in England were of course besieged from the beginning. Everyone who was reputed to be able to "look into the seeds of time and see which grain will grow and which will not" was immediately paid to do so.

But the clairvoyants were confronted with this difficulty: current prophecy must always be conceded as rather a matter of faith. But if there could be found a prophecy, many years old, which had foretold the details of the war, foretold them accurately, then it would be safe to assume that the prophet who had foretold the beginning might foretell the end. This demand soon created the supply: several prophecies were discovered—Madame de Thèbes and others—but they were all lacking in satisfactory details and antiquity, until the great and glorious find—the find of the Abbot Johannes.

The Sar Péladan, a moderately good *littérateur* and a really fine critic (you can read all about him in Nordau's *Degeneration*), has, in his time, contributed much to the gaiety of the French people. Years ago, someone remarked to him in a cafe that his name was rather like that of the Assyrian, Beladan. Péladan jumped at the idea and said that he was Beladan, in a new incarnation; after that he gave himself the title of Sar. He even conferred similar glories on his associates; hence his friends, who became Mérodach-Jauneau, Belshazzar-Dupont, and so on! Also he had announced himself to he a Rosicrucian—anything romantic and mysterious helps to work a clever trick—and published a book on the doctrines of that august Fraternity called *Le vice suprême*, rather as if a learned Presbyterian divine were to preach on "Why We Believe in the Mass."

The worthy Péladan was therefore not taken very seriously by his contemporaries in France; but England nowadays will stand for anything, even cubists and futurists and vorticists. So the English lent a willing ear to the masterpiece of Péladan. It appeared that the Sar—so he said—in going through some old papers of his father's, some ten years previously, had found a Latin prophecy of the Abbot Johannes. (There were two or three of these Abbots about 1600, but none of them were particularly prophetic.) Péladan had made a translation, but did not, of course, produce the original for the inspection of experts. The prophecy is in the best allegorical style; all about a cock, and a lion, and an eagle, and a bear. The Kaiser is described unmistakably, owing to his withered arm, and the details of the war, down to the battle of the Marne, are given with an accuracy which reflects extraordinary credit on the seership of Johannes. After this point, however, he becomes a little indefinite and less careful of detail.

The present writer warned the Editor of *The Occult Review* that anything emanating from Péladan could only be a jest, but was rebutted by the evidence of an alderman from Harrogate, who was said to have seen the original. "An alderman from Harrogate" only made it worse!

However, the story "got over" and went the rounds of the press, and was swallowed by everybody. It did not last very long, though, for that part of the prophecy dealing with events subsequent to the Marne, though vague, was not vague enough to prevent even the most faithful believers from perceiving that it was totally wrong.

But all this palls before the superb story of "The Bowmen." There is nothing to beat it in all the annals of mythopoeia.

There is a writer in England who is not very well known over here, but who is certainly among the first half-dozen living English authors. He is saturated with the love of mediævalism and sacramentalism. His name is Arthur Machen. Falling upon evil times, he has had to write for *The Evening News*. In the course of this unhappy occupation, he read the famous *Weekly Dispatch* account of the retreat from Mons, which account was true, and caused the prosecution of the publishers. This was on Sunday morning, and he went to church later, and thought of the battle instead of the sermon. By and by he wrote a story on it called "The Bowmen." In a few words, this was his yarn:

Five hundred British soldiers, the remains of a regiment, were covering the retreat from Mons. Disorganized and desperate, they saw annihilation approaching them in the shape of ten thousand pursuing cavalry. One of the men, who had been educated in Latin and the like, in the stress of emotion, found his mind wander back to a vegetarian restaurant in London where the plates had had on them a design of St. George and the motto "*Adsit Anglis Sanctus Georgius.*" With involuntary piety he uttered this motto. A shudder passed through him; the noise of battle was soothed to a murmur in his ears; instead, he heard a great roar as of thousands of soldiers shouting the ancient battle-cries that rang out at Crécy and Poitiers and Agincourt! He also saw before him a long line of shining shapes, "drawing their yew bows to their ears, and stroking their ell-long shafts against the Germans."

It was then observed by all that the enemy was being swept away, not in single units but in battalions. In fact, they were slain to a man; and the British rear guard strolled off quietly in the wake of their army.

It is to be noted that the author very artistically refrained from trying to lend verisimilitude to an otherwise bald and unconvincing narrative by stating that the burying-parties found arrows in the dead Germans. He thought it too much mustard!

Well, he printed the story on September 29, 1914, and thought that that would be the end of it. But no! A few days later *The Occult Review* and *Light* wrote to ask for his "authorities!" He replied that the old musty English ale at the "Spotted Dog" in Bouverie Street might know; if not, nobody did.

In a month or so, several parish magazines asked leave to reprint it; and *would* he write a preface giving the name of the soldier, and so on? He replied, "Reprint away; but as for the soldier, his name is Thomas Atkins of the Horse-Marines." The editor of one magazine replied (it was April, 1915, by now): "Pardon me, sir, if I appear to contradict you; but I know positively that the facts of the story are true; all you have done is to throw it into a literary form."

So they reprinted the story. But that was only the beginning of it. Variants began to appear. The soldier was an officer, and the picture of St. George a canvas instead of a plate. The dead Germans, too, were now found with arrow wounds—the very detail that Machen had rejected as too absurd. Then again in some accounts a cloud appears between the armies to conceal the British. This is obviously an echo from Exodus. Sometimes the cloud disclosed shining shapes which frightened the chargers of the Uhlans. But April was to wane before the great transfiguration.

In May, Mr. A. P. Sinnett (the man who first wrote of the Blavatsky teacup fables) had an article in *The Occult Review* saying: "Those who could see said that they saw 'a row of shining beings' between the two armies."

Now Machen did say "a long row of shining shapes." In this phase one may find the *raison d'être* of the last stage of the myth. Angels are still popular in England; fairies are dead, and saints are held a trifle Popish; St. George is only a name except to mediævalists like Mr. Machen. So he drops out of the story. "The Bowmen" became *The Angels of Mons* and the story fairly took the bit between its teeth, and bolted. It was quoted in *Truth*, in *The New Church Weekly*, in *John Bull*, in *The Daily Chronicle*, in *The Pall Mall Gazette*, and in every case it was treated as a serious story.

Bishop Welldon, Bishop Taylor Smith (the Chaplain-General), Dr. Horton, Sir J. C. Rickett—all of them serious divines in England—preached about it. Canon Hensley Henson said he did not believe it, but we must remember that he has quite often been near trouble for holding heterodox opinions!

The *Evening News* has been bombarded with letters on the subject; even the Psychical Research Society has got into one of its usual muddles over it. In a word, despite Machen's repeated explanations and denials, the silly fancy is taken everywhere for established fact.

The only attempt to give details of the yarn from the front has been that of Miss Phyllis Campbell, who is very young and very beautiful, but who, if she had been wiser, would have given, as her authorities, soldiers who had figured on the Roll of Honour. That would have sounded better than "a soldier," or than "a wounded man of the Lancashires," or "an R.F.A. hero," or "a nurse."

England believes it all, and, as faith can move mountains, perhaps it can help the Allies to force the Rhine!

The Canning Enigma: Some Observations on Arthur Machen's *The Canning Wonder*

Jeremy Cantwell

Of all Machen's primary published work, *The Canning Wonder* (1925) arguably seems to have received the least critical attention. It is of course mentioned, albeit fleetingly, in the standard biographies and bibliographies, and there are several oblique references to it in Machen's own published correspondence. But to this writer's knowledge, little seems to exist in the way of criticism and commentary, and the title appears to have become something of a "lost" Machen, its physical scarcity matched only by the comparative lack of attention it receives in relation to the rest of his published output.

Perhaps this is not unsurprising, for it must be said at the outset that *The Canning Wonder* is not one of Machen's most distinctive works. It is not a Machen title one would recommend to the uninitiated, nor is it one that immediately leaps to the minds of those who are. It is possibly one of the few books by Arthur Machen that even enthusiasts themselves have cast aside before completing, or perhaps never got around to reading. It is not truly representative of Machen's literary style, possessing neither the inspired, intoxicating qualities that fired his best fiction nor the subtle arabesque of his journalistic work. In many respects, *The Canning Wonder* is not really a Machen title at all.

The work nonetheless remains an important, although hardly seminal, Machen text, being written and published at a critical period of his life and career. In 1925 Arthur Machen was in his early sixties. His creative ability, by his own admission and by his exacting standards, was diminishing. In a letter to Colin Summerford in August 1924, and talking of his *London Adventure* (published that same year), he had complained of his "failed powers" (*SL* 97). He was also financially distressed, royalties from his previous work being negligible or nonexistent. In such a conspiracy of circumstance, there was no alternative other than to keep writing in order to maintain a living. But Machen knew that he could not, at least at this time, create another fictional masterpiece, and it was to his old instincts as a reporter and journalist that he once more turned in an effort to eke out what was becoming a precarious financial existence. *The Canning Wonder* was written and published at the very cusp of this uncomfortable and insecure interlude in Machen's career.

For those unfamiliar with the title, *The Canning Wonder* is a literary reconstruction of events surrounding an eighteenth-century trial, for perjury, of Elizabeth Canning, "a young girl of the rosy and chubby kind," who on New Year's Day 1753 failed to return home from an afternoon spent with her uncle and aunt in East Smithfield in the City of London. Despite frantic searches and appeals, nothing was heard or seen of Canning until, quite out of the blue, she arrived back at her mother's home almost one month to the day that she had originally disappeared. Bloody, dishevelled, dirty, fevered, and malnourished, she claimed that she had been abducted by brigands whilst on her way home that New Year's night and forcibly taken to the dwelling house of "Mother" Susannah Wells—a brothel in Enfield, Middlesex, a good few miles from the City. Here she was held hostage after refusing to "go the way" of the other women of the house. So as to prevent her escaping, Canning claimed that her stays were cut, and that she was then imprisoned in a hayloft at the house until she managed to escape on January 29.

On January 31, after obtaining mayoral warrant, a semi-official search party, with Canning in tow, went out to Mother Wells's house. Here, after much confusion and procedural indiscretion, Canning identified one Mary Squires, a gypsy, as the person who had cut and stolen her stays. Squires was arrested, along with Wells (as principal accomplice) and other members of the house. A trial was convened some weeks later in February, at which Canning duly attested, and at which Squires and Wells were both found guilty by the jury of theft and abduction, a capital crime at the time. The pair were sentenced to hang.

The trial of these women was a farce, as it emerged both during and immediately after the proceedings that Canning had, with the connivance of others, at the very least fabricated evidence and at the most invented the entire circumstances of her disappearance. Even by summary eighteenth-century judicial standards it became evident that the convictions were unsound, and the then Lord Mayor of London, Sir Crisp Gascoyne (the first Lord Mayor to reside at the Mansion House), was moved to initiate an inquiry. As a consequence of this, later that same year, 1753, Canning was put on trial at the Old Bailey for wilful and corrupt perjury. She was found guilty and sentenced to seven years' transportation to the Plantations (USA). Squires and Wells were completely exonerated. Canning, subsequently, married in the USA and died there some twenty years later.

This brief account paraphrases matters in the extreme; suffice it to say that the entire affair was a tangle of complicity, duplicity, and downright culpability on the part of Canning and her sympathisers. The proceedings were equally shambolic. *The Canning Wonder* is essentially a documentary reconstruction of the circumstances of the case, with the trial of Canning its centrepiece. In setting out this record, Machen spares no detail. The labyrinthine procedural twists and turns, the nuances of the court protocol, and the lengthy, interminable cross-examination of witnesses—all is reconstructed chapter and verse, as reportage.

There is little doubt that Machen had access to original documentation and accounts of the indictments and court proceedings. However, there are no acknowledgements in the book to this effect, nor references in the text. It is likely that he sourced the information from the surviving court manuscripts and also from contemporary eighteenth-century broadsheets, but whether all the extracts Machen quotes as verbatim from the recorder's pen are authentic or not is a matter for conjecture. He does in passing ask the reader at one point to observe, in relating a quote from prosecuting counsel, "the odd grammar of the age," but this may amount to nothing more than a literary device of his own to add verisimilitude.

The documented account is laborious, Machen relentlessly tracking the proceedings step by step. Much of it is, frankly, tedious. There are very few moments in the book where the reader might be relieved by an insightful comment or leap of abstraction on the author's part. Machen assumes the mantle of documentarist and remains objective throughout, pausing here and there for reflection but allowing no digression and precious little speculation—even though the material facts of the case cry out for it. The narrative itself, although clear and concise, is—uncharacteristically for a work by Machen—contrived and occasionally turgid. Where, ordinarily, we would expect him to infuse even the most mundane of observations with a hint of "far off things," in *The Canning Wonder* Machen gives us only cold, clinical reportage.

Cause célèbre the case may have been in 1753, but the real enigma—the tantalising question of what actually happened to Elizabeth Canning between January 1 and January 29—is hardly touched upon. True, Machen does indulge in a paragraph or two of speculation in the preface—to the effect that Canning was at another brothel, of her own free will, and that the Enfield scenario had been invented by an associate of Canning's who wanted revenge on Mother Wells—but he nonetheless admits that this does not help explain why Canning arrived home ill-nourished, bloody, and dishevelled. Elsewhere in the text, and perhaps in an effort to lend some mystique to the factual treatment, Machen disingenuously emphasises an inconsequential part of the proceedings in which Canning's mother told the court she had consulted an astrologer during her daughter's disappearance, in the hope of divining her whereabouts. In fact, this "cunning man" was unable to bring any intelligence to the circumstances, the incident having no material bearing on the matter whatsoever.

The irony is that the Canning case could have provided all the elements needed for a fine Machen foray into historic and subterranean London, the unseen and the unknown. But the rigid documentary formula and the decision to concentrate on the material aspects of the case render the work devoid of atmosphere. The evocative backdrop of Hanoverian London (surely frequented by a man with ginger bulbous side-whiskers and a woman with flaming red hair!), the stink, the mob, and the grubby lace finery, all so redolent of the period, is entirely absent. It is additionally the London of Henry Fielding, the novelist and magistrate before whom Elizabeth Canning originally made depositions. It was Fielding, together with his brother John, who around the time of the Canning events organised the semi-official police force in London (popularly referred to as "Fielding's Gang") and which gave rise to vigilante groups of individuals taking the "law" into their own hands. These gangs were not dissimilar to the party that went out to Enfield on January 31 to intimidate the occupants at the House of Mother Wells.

The precise circumstances leading to the writing and publication of *The Canning Wonder* are obscure, but the indisputable facts are that Machen was, by 1925, at the mercy of a denuded market for his work. Financially impecunious and working for hire, he had to come up with something regardless. Additionally, the American publisher Alfred A. Knopf, who at around this time had established with Machen what was to all intents and purposes a position of first refusal for his work, was doubtless keen to see a new title under his imprint. No matter how personally reluctant Machen may have been to promote it, there was nonetheless an imperative (if a diminishing one) to consolidate the small but influential reputation he already had achieved in the US.

Whether Machen conceived the idea for the Canning project or whether it was suggested to him is a moot point, but it is almost certainly the case that the book's UK publishers, Chatto & Windus, commissioned it. There would appear to be no surviving records at the Chatto & Windus archive that might clarify this or the nature of the arrangement. The files reveal that the contract for the book was dated 3 April 1925 and was standard. L. Tilden-Smith, who on this occasion acted as Machen's agent, submitted the completed draft to the publishers on 15 July 1925. At that time, the volume was provisionally entitled *The Trial of Elizabeth Canning*, an accurate enough description of the content, and certainly more representative than the one finally adopted. However, Chatto & Windus, presumably concerned that the title would be unlikely to inspire the marketplace, did not like it. Hence the change, whether by itself or by Machen, to the published title.

The Canning Wonder was published in the UK on 28 October 1925, perhaps to Machen's own surprise, for only a few days before he was writing to Summerford that if the publisher intended an October release, it probably would not publish until February next (*SL* 102). The volume appeared as a trade edition of 1,250 copies, and also in a deluxe edition of 120 signed and numbered copies. The trade edition retailed at 10/6 and the limited edition at £2.2.0. The publishing ledger denotes that 130 deluxe editions were in fact produced, the extra ten presumably either retained for private or repository purposes, or perhaps destined for the US. The title was to be published in the US by Alfred A. Knopf in 1926.

Both editions were illustrated, containing eight black-and-white plates, five of them being contemporary broadsheet prints from the period, depicting Canning and other events associated with the proceedings. These include one of Elizabeth Canning at the house of Mother Wells, crudely drawn "from the life" by one A. Herbert "on London Bridge" and originally published in March 1753 "according to Act of Parliament." Another, of Elizabeth Canning receiving sentence at the Old Bailey and printed in 1754 "pursuant to the Statute the Eighth of George the Second," was additionally used as the cover illustration of the book's fine dust wrapper.

The Canning Wonder was subsequently abridged and rewritten by Machen for serialisation in *T.P.'s and Cassell's Weekly*, appearing in the editions for 26 June and 3 July 1926. The article is essentially a précis of the affair as recounted in the book. But interestingly, Machen brings a more enigmatic dimension to the article than he allows in the book itself. One of the central planks of evidence in the Canning prosecution was that the principal defendant, the gypsy Mary Squires, could not have been at the House of Mother Wells at the time in question. As an itinerant, she was travelling in the west of England and was in Dorset at the time of Canning's disappearance. This was corroborated through a number of independent witnesses ("country folk") who gave evidence at the Old Bailey. Machen does indeed go into this in the book, and with all the documentary dispassion that so characterises it. But, intriguingly, he gives these same events an entirely different emphasis in the *T.P.'s and Cassell's Weekly* article, effectively using the final part of the serialisation to eulogise the village, highway, and tavern life of the time—much more familiar Machen territory. He ends the article with a spirited celebration of times past: "The clock is put back; dead England of George the Second's day is alive again; one hears clearly across the bridge of years the scrape and shriek of Melchisdech's fiddle and the beat of the gypsies' feet upon the tavern floor." Within a single paragraph, Machen evokes an atmosphere that entirely eludes the book itself.

That Machen largely chose to eschew the unexplained events that lay at the core of the Canning business is the real enigma of *The Canning Wonder*. It would surely have been a combination of the mysterious circumstances of Canning's disappearance and the reek of old London that originally inspired his enthusiasm for the story. Machen's interest in criminology notwithstanding, he could have chosen from dozens of more interesting cases had he simply wanted to document a *cause célèbre* trial. The book is consequently something of a minor puzzle, for Machen saliently orientates the account around the known facts of the case, despite the fact that it is the uncertain and the unknown (zones in which he excelled) that provide the pivotal point of departure for the subsequent events. Without a development of these ingredients there is really not much of interest that can be made of the Canning events, for the trial itself is unremarkable outside of its sociological context.

Perhaps the adverse circumstances in which the author found himself, and in particular the inability to re-summon those creative energies that had informed so much of his previous work, constrained him from doing anything more than re-creating established facts and fashioning *The Canning Wonder* as a documentary work. Machen's facility for elevating a subject from the mundane to the enigmatic—traditionally his forte—was certainly eluding him at the time. Whether or not Chatto & Windus expected a slightly more Machenesque work can only be guessed at, but the change of title could suggest that it indeed hoped for something more.

All Machen's principal biographers are agreed that the book is overlong and repetitive. To this extent, Machen was doubtless conceding (in part or in full) to the publisher's brief and delivering the number of words asked of him. The rigid literary style and relative lack of content further betrays the fact that for the writer, the commission was a bread-and-butter affair, a work commitment that had to be done to order, against a deadline. It was to all intents and purposes a journalistic assignment, and not a project that Machen embraced heart and soul.

If *The Canning Wonder* disappoints from a literary perspective, it nonetheless remains one of Machen's more unusual and collectible works. A copy of the signed, limited deluxe edition is a rare find indeed. The trade edition is almost as elusive, and even scarcer to find complete with dust wrapper. It is an essential volume for the Machen collector. But whether it is an essential component of the overall Machen canon is, perhaps, open to question.

Sadly, and for all the promise of the title, there is little wonder to be found in Machen's account of the Canning affair, in spite of the enigma that lies at its heart. Had circumstances been more conducive, and had the author's real genius been to hand, it is tempting to think that *The Canning Wonder* might have been a very different book. In a letter to Oliver Stonor the year following its publication Machen wrote: "When the creative power is gone, we have to fall back on sincerity, and try what we can make of that" (quoted in Dobson 13). Perhaps we should view *The Canning Wonder* accordingly.

Works Cited

Dobson, Roger. "Introduction" to *A Few Letters from Arthur Machen*. Warrall: Aylesford Press, 1993. 7–14.

Machen, Arthur. *The Canning Wonder*. London: Chatto & Windus, 1925.

Reynolds, Aidan, and Charlton, William. *Arthur Machen: A Short Account of His Life and Work*. London: Richards Press, 1963.

Sweetser, Wesley D. *Arthur Machen*. New York: Twayne, 1964.

Valentine, Mark. *Arthur Machen*. Bridgend, Wales: Seren, 1995.

(With thanks to Michael Bott, University of Reading Library, and Ray Russell.)

"All Manner of Mysteries": Encounters with the Numinous in *The Cosy Room and Other Stories*

James Machin

"There are things of 1890 in it: save us all!" (quoted in Dobson xvi). So Machen remarked of this collection to the novelist Oliver Stonor in 1935, the year before its publication. Machen also expressed his gratitude that John Gawsworth (the pseudonym of Terrence Fytton Armstrong, 1912-1970) had made the effort to excavate the constituent parts of *The Cosy Room and Other Stories* from such a variety of recondite sources, salvaging many of them from being lost among the periodical archive. Gawsworth, in his early twenties at the time, had taken upon himself the task of rousing many writers who had made a name for themselves in the 1890s from sinking into obscure dotage, including Machen, M. P. Shiel, and others. Lawrence Durrell said of Gawsworth that he was "one of nature's lobbyists" and that there were "several writers who owe him thanks for a pension in their old age." This included Machen:

> [Gawsworth kept] a hawk-like eye on a number of his elders, just to make sure that they were not starving. I remember him disappearing for a week-end to visit Arthur Machen in Buckinghamshire whom he suspected of being too proud to ask for help at a time when he (John) knew full well that the old writer was in grave financial difficulties. He just wanted to make quite sure before going down to terrorize those people at the Royal Society of Literature. (21)

However, a possibly less-welcome corollary of this practical help was that Gawsworth also insisted that his assumed charges did not resign themselves complacently to the solaces of an unproductive old age. Although Machen at times resented being thus shaken up by Gawsworth—as though he were Smallweed in *Bleak House*—he also seemed for the most part to have appreciated Gawsworth's efforts in ensuring that his legacy was not entirely a victim of its incommensurability with the prevailing literary tastes of the early twentieth century.

Gawsworth had previously worked with the publisher Rich & Cowan on a collection of short fiction titled *Full Score: Twenty-Five Tales* in 1933. The volume included work by both Machen and Shiel, alongside younger voices such as H. E. Bates, Rhys Davies, and Caradoc Evans. With *The Cosy Room and Other Stories*, Gawsworth undertook an expansive survey of Machen's corpus beginning with three magazine stories from 1890 (so causing the above-noted consternation from Machen): "A Double Return," "A Wonderful Woman," and "The Lost Club"—all originally published when Machen was still in his twenties. They are undoubtedly slight pieces, but nevertheless worthwhile and interesting ones. The risqué nature of the first two anticipates the *Yellow Book* by several years, as indeed did the short-lived journal in which "A Wonderful Woman" and "The Lost Club" appeared. The *Whirlwind*—which styled itself as a "lively and eccentric newspaper"—included contributions from Stéphane Mallarmé, James Abbott McNeill Whistler, and Walter Sickert, and such decadent company made it an ideal venue in which Machen could unveil the first, brief iteration of "The Great God Pan" (also in 1890), as well as the two stories included here.

They also drew Machen to the attention of Oscar Wilde. Wilde complimented Machen on "A Double Return," which he approved of as having "fluttered the dovecotes" (Gawsworth 104). In his biography of Machen, Gawsworth records that the story had "annoyed and enraged" (103) the readership of the *St. James's Gazette* to the extent that its editor declined to accept any more submissions from Machen. "The Lost Club," with its clear debt to "The Suicide Club," marks the beginning of one of the prevailing features of Machen's output for the first half of the 1890s: that of playing the sedulous ape to Robert Louis Stevenson. Machen not only imitated Stevenson stylistically, but also—with *The Three Impostors*—appropriated Stevenson's strategy, employed in his portmanteau works *The New Arabian Nights* and *More New Arabian Nights: The Dynamiter*, of using a frame narrative to tie together existing short stories, many originally written for the periodicals market. Despite Machen's reservations, all three of these early tales are still immensely entertaining diversions, and also already gesture towards some thematic concerns which would typify Machen's fiction for the rest of his life: the mystery of London, occluded ritual, and the related notion that the material world is merely a contingent and degraded representation of an ineffable reality.

These three conceits are demonstrated in an exemplary way, and with careful economy, in "The Holy Things" (CF 2.182-84). The protagonist, sitting in a quiet corner of Holborn—"racked with perplexities and doubts, with the sense that all was without meaning or purpose, a tangle of senseless joys and empty sorrows"—gradually becomes aware of a miraculous transmutation of his environment and his place within it. The "odd intonation" of a passing coster's proclamations reminds him of a Gregorian chant. The "jangling insistent" bell of a cyclist and a nearby idler lighting his tobacco similarly evoke peals from a church tower and smoke rising from a censer. Soon the transmutation of the drab London street scene into a spiritually redemptive liturgy is complete.

Although published in 1908, "The Holy Things" was written several years earlier. The 1895 trial of Oscar Wilde ("the disaster" as Machen called it) precipitated a climate of hostility to "unhealthy" art such that publishing risqué material became a commercial liability. The *succès de scandale* was no longer viable and the whiff of controversy associated with Machen's "The Great God Pan"—not only its content but also the decadent reputation of its publisher, John Lane—meant that Machen, after an initially promising career, struggled to place work from that point on. He did not stop trying, however, and *The Cosy Room* includes no fewer than nine stories written (rather than published) in the late 1890s. "The Holy Things," "Psychology," and "Nature" first saw the light of day in the *Academy* in 1908, appearing as a triptych titled simply "Notes." These, together with "Torture," "Witchcraft," "The Turanians," "The Rose Garden," "The Ceremony," and "Midsummer," were all eventually anthologized as *Ornaments in Jade* in 1924. These prose poems are superlative examples of fin-de-siècle delicacy and poise, although Machen also resists the extravagances and indulgences of decadent style: they are spare and precise distillations of mood and incident, where the misleading serenity of the surfaces conceals the fact that Machen is subtly pressing readers into making disquieting speculations of their own about what might actually might be occurring.

"The Hidden Mystery" also first appeared in the pages of a 1908 edition of the *Academy*, then operating under the somewhat controversial editorship of Lord Alfred Douglas (Wilde's "Bosie"). Machen was a prolific contributor, his high church inclinations giving him an entente with Douglas's recent conversion to Roman Catholicism. As well as fiction, Machen contributed numerous essays to the *Academy*, usually straightforward, scholastic exercises in theology, literature, and other diverse subjects. "The Hidden Mystery," however, is a fictional narrative cleverly disguised as such an essay. Machen claims to be providing a commentary on an article by one Ambrose Meyrick, allegedly published in another unspecified journal, but what seems to be a discourse on aesthetics subtly transmutes into an alchemical treatise. Machen concludes his experiment with the troubling suggestion that when read in tandem with another work by Meyrick (the "Rosa Mundi"), "most unpleasant conclusions" are to be drawn. The original readership, taking the article at face value, were presumably baffled, disturbed, or some combination thereof. In fact, the piece was originally written as one of two concluding chapters of *The Secret Glory* (Ambrose Meyrick being the protagonist of that novel) that were not included in the version published in 1922. These "missing" chapters were eventually published by Tartarus in 1991, which also published a complete version of the novel in 2015.

From here the collection skips forward a decade or two. Much of the remainder of the Gawsworth's selection is made up of work commissioned in the 1920s and early 1930s by Lady Cynthia Asquith for the highly-regarded anthologies she edited and contributed to in that period. Anthologies such as *The Ghost Book* (1926) and *Shudders* (1929) saw Machen rubbing shoulders with the likes of D. H. Lawrence, Elizabeth Bowen, and L. P. Hartley, as well as fellow weird-fiction specialists like Algernon Blackwood. Lawrence, whose celebrated tale "The Rocking-Horse Winner" was commissioned by Asquith for *The Ghost Book*, occasionally used the glamorous and erudite editor as the basis for some of his characters, including, it is rumoured, Lady Chatterley. Well-connected, and with much literary talent at her disposal, it says much for Asquith's understanding of the genre that she regularly called upon Machen to contribute to her ghost story anthologies, for which she stipulated that all contributing authors must be "still living and modern in technique."

Machen retooled "The Munitions of War" for Asquith from an earlier account of an incident encountered when on a journalistic assignment in Bristol. Gawsworth pairs the piece with another supernaturally-tinged wartime tale, "Drake's Drum." Both are variations on a theme that Machen explored with notable impact in his 1914 tale "The Bowmen," a fiction that famously elided into the "facts" of the Angels of Mons legend: the intervention of nebulous supernatural forces on behalf of the British to bolster the war effort. Most of Machen's output during the Great War could be fairly classed as propaganda, and his non-fiction *War and the Christian Faith* (1918) is explicitly so. A notable exception is perhaps the wartime serial *The Terror* (1917), in which it is implied that the supernatural intervention is to sabotage the machinery of war itself. Machen's High Tory hawkishness, although of course completely unremarkable for the time, is now occasionally a source of surprise and discomfort for those who would prefer to position him as a subversive outsider, and retroactively appropriate him for the counterculture. Inconveniently, his sympathies were always with the establishment and the political right—he even declared for Franco during a 1937 survey of writers and poets' reactions to the Spanish civil war, undertaken by W. H. Auden and others. Arguably this was more a reflection of his religious convictions than his political sympathies, but nevertheless Machen was one of only five respondents to do so (another was Evelyn Waugh). Even among this minority, Machen is startlingly unequivocal in his support of a man Aleister Crowley unhesitatingly describes in the same document as a "common murderer and pirate" (n.p.).

Although "Awaking" was written for Asquith's annual volume of children's fiction, *The Children's Cargo* (1930), this did not deter Gawsworth from including it in *The Cosy Room*. Unlike Blackwood (who also appeared in *The Children's Cargo*), Machen rarely made forays into writing for a younger audience. "Awaking" and "Johnny Double," from another Asquith anthology, 1928's *The Treasure Cave*, perhaps represent the sum total of his work in the genre. With 'The White People' Machen had certainly demonstrated a keen facility for recreating the voice and thought processes of youth, but—as in "The Ceremony" and "The Turanians"—he usually employed it to the ends of contriving a disjunction between an apparently naive and partially-related anecdote, and the reader's growing suspicion that what is being obliquely related is something really quite sinister. "Awaking," although by no means a typical children's story, is rather more straightforward in communicating what Machen always regarded as the blight of modernity on human life and its degradation of the imagination with the quotidian. This theme is picked up again by Machen in "A New Christmas Carol," a Dickens-inspired satire again lambasting what Machen considered to be the spiritual vacuity of the modern world. Machen was never at his best when writing in this vein, and his lack of lightness of touch is perhaps increasingly evident the more time passes.

Machen's career as a journalist occasionally brought him into the purlieus of the criminal world. His interest in this area resulted most substantially in a book-length study of the historical case of the alleged kidnapping of Elizabeth Canning (*The Canning Wonder*, 1925), also alluded to here in "The Islington Mystery." Stylistically, this account of the likely murder of a taxidermist's wife by her husband would not be out of place in Borges's *A Universal History of Infamy*, and similarly obscures the line between imaginative speculation and fact. Machen offers additionally some reflexive rumination on the inevitability of sooner or later encountering an insurmountable barrier in the pursuit of truth, that mystery at the centre of all things. The inexplicable glossolalia experienced by the Reverend Thomas Beynon in "The Gift of Tongues" is one such mystery, which Machen hints has wider ramifications for the small Welsh community in which it occurs. "The Cosy Room," another Asquith commission (from *Shudders* [1929]), is another crime story of a sort, but focuses on the psychological strain placed on the perpetrator, conveying, in a manner of which Hitchcock might have approved, the claustrophobic paranoia of the wanted man. Structured like a Venus flytrap inexorably closing around its victim, Machen conveys vividly the unsupportable strain placed upon the sanity of someone who may temporarily be able to elude their pursuers, but can never escape consciousness of their own guilt.

"Opening the Door" (originally published in Asquith's *When Churchyards Yawn* in 1931) has thematic resonances with Machen's late novel, *The Green Round* (1933), concerning as it does the inexplicable events experienced by an aging, reclusive scholar. Much like the protagonist of *The Green Round*, in "Opening the Door" the Reverend Secretan Jones is left in a state of perplexity rather than terror. The experience—in this case a 'missing time' episode suggestive of fairy folklore—leaves him profoundly disoriented, at the limits of his ability to parse what has happened to him. Typically of Machen's later writing, there is a sense of resignation to this bewilderment: rather than tilting at the mysteries of existence, Machen suggests through his narratives that it is the mystery that matters, not the essentially unknowable quiddity of things in themselves.

Depending on one's tolerance for such material, "The Compliments of the Season" is either a charming festive fable or an example of Machen veering uncomfortably close to twee. Machen's apologetics for religion are typically far from apologetic in tone, and this is no exception, being rather an attack on two of his bugbears: rationalism and materialism. As in "Opening the Door," the key point being made is the one that was so fundamental to Machen's worldview that he had it chiselled into his gravestone: *Omnia exeunt in mysterium*. According to Machen, a failure to grasp this insight—an insight unavailable to those blinkered enough to recourse to rational argument—is a failure to understand the nature of existence itself.

And here, appropriately, we come to the final tale of the collection, "N." This was the only original contribution to *The Cosy Room*, and if we are grateful to Gawsworth for nothing else, we should be grateful to him for provoking Machen into its creation. "N"—written when Machen was 72 (the manuscript is dated 13 December 1935)—is a distillation of many ideas he had previously explored, but they are perhaps more perfectly expressed in this tale than in any other. Once again, the narrative is presented indirectly, anecdotally; it is an assembly of first-, second- and third-hand testimony. It is left up to the reader to piece together these strange fragments; tantalizing pieces of an unsolvable puzzle. Another of Machen's otherworldly clerics is central to the narrative, this time the Reverend Hampole, author of the 1853 work, *A London Walk: Meditations in the streets of the Metropolis* (one of Machen's false documents, a conceit of which he was fond—see "The Hidden Mystery" and "The White People" for other examples). Machen had originally introduced his readers to both in *The Green Round*, and Hampole's meditations on wandering London and his sensitivity to a spagyric truth lurking behind the mundane world are of course fully commensurate with Machen's own intentionally aimless explorations of the capital in search of similar revelations. "N" is certainly written in the same journalistic, anecdotal style that distinguishes much of his later writing, and is off-putting to some of his commentators. Here, however, the hazing of the reader with disparate glimpses of an only obliquely delineated whole is executed with really extraordinary legerdemain, resulting in a seamless unity of effect. It is, in short, a masterpiece.

The fact that many of the stories included in *The Cosy Room* are, with some notable exceptions, not the work for which Machen is generally celebrated may suggest that Gawsworth haphazardly cobbled together a curate's egg from leftovers. Is there, however, any over-riding theme or rationale behind its assembly? The most immediately apparent quality shared by these stories is that they all steer relatively clear of the overtly horrific or gruesome (if one discounts the truly grotesque implications of "Torture"). There are none of the immediate terrors of "The Great God Pan" and *The Three Impostors* lurking within the pages.

Most Machen enthusiasts first encounter his writing through his classic weird tales of the 1890s, a body of work that has been regularly plundered for genre anthologies ever since. The reader is dazzled by their pyrotechnic displays of outré late-Victorian horror, and fascinated to discover therein much of the source material for H. P. Lovecraft's seminal contributions to *Weird Tales* in the early twentieth century. This aspect of Machen's writing has a continuing influence on the genre and wider culture to this day, through the work of Stephen King, Ramsey Campbell, John Carpenter, Guillermo del Toro, and many more. Machen may now be a far less ubiquitous presence than Lovecraft, but he is certainly a distinct one. The unfortunate corollary of approaching Machen through his influence on subsequent weird and horror fiction is that there is often a sense of disappointment when one moves on to his later, less-celebrated, writing and finds it so different in tone: the Stevensonian exuberance of the strange, exotic 1890s replaced by a journalistic, anecdotal, all-too recognisably twentieth-century voice.

Such disappointment is unavoidable when the expectations are simply the wrong ones, and this has perhaps contributed to the prevailing view that after his early achievements Machen was an increasingly spent force—a view reinforced by Machen's habit of ostentatiously disparaging his own work at every opportunity. Gawsworth's endeavours as a curator here, however, present us with a very different perspective. Arguably, and assuming this alternative reading of Machen's trajectory, one could argue that "N" is Machen's riposte, almost at the end of his career, to one of its opening salvos, "The Great God Pan": both stories rely on a fragmentary, nonlinear structure, with multiple characters offering oblique perspectives on a central, unresolved mystery. However, where the latter plunges the alarmed reader into a netherworld of weird gruesomeness, in the former Machen uses accomplished sleight of hand to instead leave the reader with a genuine sense of quiet revelation. Machen once famously complained that his "failure" as a writer was one of translating "awe, at worst awfulness, into evil" (FOT 123). "N" is, however, the very refinement he sought for, the literary equivalent of an alchemical transmutation of evil into awe.

For the most part, *The Cosy Room and Other Stories* represents some of Machen's best efforts in pursuing these gentler but no less potent encounters with the numinous. In "The Hidden Mystery," Machen records Meyrick urging that "all manner of mysteries, splendours, beauties, delights may be—nay are—present to us, before our eyes," with the qualification that "the Object or Objects which we see and apprehend after a certain sort are strangely withheld from us" (857). This is the conundrum repeatedly—entertainingly, compellingly—presented to us within the pages of this collection.

Works Cited

Authors Take Sides on the Spanish Civil War. London: Left Review, 1937.

Dobson, Roger. "Notes on the Text." In John Gawsworth. *The Life of Arthur Machen.* Ed. Roger Dobson. Leyburn: Tartarus Press, 2005.

Durrell, Lawrence. *Spirit of Place: Letters and Essays on Travel.* Ed. Alan G. Thomas. New York: E. P. Dutton, 1969.

Machen, Arthur. "The Hidden Mystery." *Academy* 74, No. 1883 (6 June 1908): 856-58.

Some Thoughts on "N"

Thomas Kent Miller

Machen's work abounds in ideas of unseen worlds pressing in on ours.–John Howard ("Interpenetrations" 43)

[W]riting [for Machen] was the only thing in life worth doing.–Aidan Reynolds and William Charlton (39)

Roads to Perichoresis

Arthur Machen's work is, nearly all of it, alchemical; that is, by some divine magic, he made mere words and sentences seem far more than the sum of their parts; when he strung together any eight words, they would always sound more charming than the same eight words strung together by any other author.

Being at once Celtic and intensely thoughtful, he often focused on the nature of existence. He early on forged his values and beliefs on this subject, and they filled his writings. Across the decades he wrote endless variations on these convictions—though, in their essence, his published thoughts fell into two distinct camps, the differences between them often escaping notice because they sounded so similar.

For example, in 1906, in the introduction to his seminal compilation of some of his best works up to that time, Machen told his readers in the clearest possible terms that "almost every page [of *The House of Souls*] contains a hint . . . of a belief in a world that is not that of ordinary, everyday experience, that in a measure transcends the experience of Bethel and the Bank" (xii). And to illustrate that point, he served up "The Great God Pan," "The White People", and the others that time has now sanctified.

Yet in 1924, in his third autobiography, as Machen scholar John Howard has pointed out, Machen makes an unequivocal statement (prompted by the principal metaphor of a Henry James story): "Here then is the pattern in my carpet, the sense of the eternal mysteries, the eternal beauty hidden beneath the crust of commonplace things; hidden and yet burning and glowing continually if you care to look with purged eyes" (*The London Adventure* 75).

I would argue that the quotations above, though they sound much the same, are fundamentally different. The first, I submit, assumes the existence of conjoined realities and of the avenues between them; the second refers to a vivid, even transcendental, but not entirely uncommon state of mind.

To illustrate further, in 1936 Machen declared (albeit through a character's conviction at the end of one of his last stories, "N"): "I believe that there is a perichoresis, an interpenetration" (CF 3.344)–which is a state of being, not a state of mind. However, in the same story, he has another character reflect:

> Has it ever been your fortune ... to rise in the earliest dawning of a summer day, ere yet the radiant beams of the sun have done more than touch with light the domes and spires of the great city? ... If this has been your lot, have you not observed that magic powers have apparently been at work? The accustomed scene has lost its familiar appearance. The houses which you have passed daily ... now seem as if you beheld them for the first time. They have suffered a mysterious change, into something rich and strange [and] now "stand in glory, shine like stars, apparelled in a light serene." They have become magical habitations, supernal dwellings, more desirable to the eye than the fabled pleasure dome of the Eastern potentate, or the bejewelled hall built by the Genie for Aladdin in the Arabian tale. (CF 3.265)

This latter passage, in my view, is an example of that subtle and transitory enhancement in perception that many of us have experienced, and which can be precipitated by anything from various kinds of intoxicants and hallucinogens to being vouchsafed exceedingly good news.

In other words, over the decades Machen's mystical pronouncements seemed to vacillate between cheerful metaphors on the one hand and virtual acceptance of rips in the universe on the other—though the language and vocabulary were sufficiently similar to obviate the differences without especial scrutiny. Was this conscious obfuscation or was he himself unsure? How does the reader decide which had more validity for Machen—the "belief in a world" or the "pattern in the carpet"?

I am of the opinion that Arthur Machen gravitated more to the belief in the reality of connected dimensions, insofar as this seemed to be, over a fifty-year literary period, his predominant theme ("the intermingling of this world and another of far vaster significance," as Machen biographer Mark Valentine puts it [126]). From first to last he succeeded in imbuing nearly all his fiction (and much nonfiction) with successive variations of that one theme—a belief that he in all likelihood absorbed by virtue of his youth and upbringing in the folklore- and myth-immersed border region of Gwent. Howard, paraphrasing critic Joseph Wood Krutch, says that "Machen had only one main plot in his fiction, that of 'rending the veil'" ("Interpenetrations" 44).

I suspect it is probable that Machen wrote the short story "N" in 1935 quite consciously as a final punctuation point to his long literary career. It was the only new original story that he added to the collection *The Cosy Room and Other Stories,* compiled by John Gawsworth from Cynthia Asquith's anthologies and odds and ends from across Machen's career. If Machen was feeling his mortality at the time, since he was in his seventies, it may have been on his mind that Gawsworth's effort could well be his swan song, and that if he had any last words to say or convey regarding ecstasy and humanity's place in the universe, the time was then or never. (In such a frame of mind, of course, he may not have considered just then that there were more stories to come, and fairly quickly at that, which would result in *The Children of the Pool*.)

If this conjecture is correct, then it would be a serious matter indeed that the antepenultimate sentence in what he may have thought was his very last story was, "I believe that there is a perichoresis, an interpenetration."

Of course, to take this argument to the next logical level, it would be useful to know what he meant by "perichoresis," a word hardly in common currency either in 1936 or 2012. In fact, we find that even that great arbiter of nearly all things in the English language, the *Oxford English Dictionary,* comes up wanting. My 2002 printing of the second edition of the *OED* is not much help at all, saying only: "perichoresis . . . *Theol.* [Gr. . . . Going round, rotation] = CIRCUMINCESSION, q.v." Then the entry for *circumincession* tells us merely: "[A]s employed by Damascenus (8th c.) in his explication of the text 'I am in the Father, and the Father in Me', it became a standard term of scholastic theology."

In fact, we find that most dictionaries do not even include the word perichoresis, and those that do define it strictly in the Christian sense of the penetration and interconnectivity of the three divine persons of the Trinity. But is that what Machen meant for us to take away from the word? Probably not. So far as I can tell, from the *OED* and other standard reference works, one would never know that the word had any other meanings. However, through a little bit more digging I found that perichoresis was also employed in specialised occult circles, such as the Order of the Golden Dawn (with which, of course, Machen had been affiliated for a time), to mean the interpenetration of dimensions or of the connecting principle between matter and spirit.

I mention all this simply to illustrate that a fair amount of effort is required of the average reader to get to the root of what Machen might have been trying to say in one of the very last sentences of one of his very last stories—even when it appeared that he had resolved at that point at long last to spell out the essence of his world principle in some detail in the guise of fiction.

Thus we are not all surprised by horror writer Peter Atkins's opinion:

> [Machen] has little patience with the undereducated. He assumes of his readership the same classical learning that he himself possessed and thus his writings abound with Greek and Latin quotations which he rarely bothers to translate or explain and references to philosophical theorems with which the modern reader, unschooled in classical logic and renaissance theology, might be far from familiar. (68)

John Howard, who has clearly stayed the course, explains, "'Perichoresis' in Greek literally means the area or space around about: in this case perhaps the boundary between the worlds, between reality and illusion, or two orders of both" ("Interpenetrations" 41).

When one considers that this notion of perichoresis/interpenetration/boundaries is at the heart of not only most of Machen's stories but most of those in particular that have gone on to influence so indisputably the development of the supernatural horror or weird genre to this day, there may well be much truth in Howard's conclusion that "the theme of 'boundaries' is central to Machen's work," to the degree that it can be considered "Arthur Machen's lasting contribution to literature" ("Interpenetrations" 39).

Yet by the same token, it may be just as valid to reflect on the possibility, as Machen scholar Wesley D. Sweetser has, that Machen's stories "are in their entirety exceedingly repetitious in theme [which] thus . . . limited his chances of survival as an author" (131).

"*Opening the Door*"

> Gates and doors are important symbols, for they often mark the threshold between one world and another.—Stephen Peithnan in an annotation to "William Wilson" from *The Annotated Tales of Edgar Allan Poe* (81)

I will focus on three of Arthur Machen's "later" tales, because they are manifestly connected and together cast an unusually bright beam on this self-imposed literary crusade at just the moment when his career felt as if it were winding down. (Howard suggests that Machen may have on some level been "engaged in nothing less than an alternative religion" ["A World of Great Majesty" 41] through much of his career.)

"Opening the Door," written for Cynthia Asquith's anthology *When Churchyards Yawn* (1931), is one of few stories by Machen that avoids "beating around the bush" with regard to perichoresis and interpenetration. That is to say, while "The Great God Pan," "The White People," "The Great Return," "Out of the Earth," and all the rest present us with incidents illuminating the *results* of interpenetration, the concept is almost always presented glancingly, indirectly, so that Machen stops short of stating out loud what has just happened, and we are left to infer the author's intentions.

For example, in "The Great God Pan" we observe an experimental surgical procedure and later we are told that years afterward London is beset by the horrifying influence of a trans-species woman. We are left to our own devices—myriad hints notwithstanding—to conclude that by means of the surgery a boundary was somehow crossed (in which direction is not clear), and the woman operated on was somehow impregnated by a nature god. In other cases (e.g., *The Green Round*, "Out of the Earth"), we learn of terrible beings who are seen by some and not by others, by which circumstance we are expected to conclude that a supernatural veil has briefly lifted.

"Opening the Door" may be the first of Machen's stories that illustrates the theme in concrete terms. The Reverend Secretan Jones opens a door and somehow experiences "interpenetration." There is no surgery, no powders, no apparitions, no paintings, no crystals, nor any of the other devices Machen used to symbolise the transition between this world and the "world that is not that of ordinary, of everyday experience."

A man opens a door.

Period.

Of course, a door is probably the simplest archetype or metaphor for the presumed interconnection of here and there—that is, of ingress and egress through or across boundaries, as Howard puts it. But not only that; there is also the salient fact that Machen chose to name the story's protagonist "Jones"—so thought-provoking when we remember that he himself was born Arthur Jones. Moreover, this is the first of his later 1930s-period pseudo-journalistic stories in which he incorporates himself as a journalist (his common wartime device, unused for fifteen years) and in which he troubles to identify the Reverend Jones as a distant cousin. It is almost as though he is giving us a picture of himself conversing with himself, doppelgänger-like, as a further device to emphasise his preeminent theme in the baldest terms.

The Green Round

> ... to turn a corner, or take a way hitherto neglected, might unlock the doors of a new region; and he was reminded of ... the story of a man who, passing along some street that he has trodden a hundred times, sees a door before unnoticed, and opening it enters a world of marvel and strange experience, that has been unsuspected but close at hand all his days.–Arthur Machen, *The Green Round* (68)

Of *The Green Round*, Machen himself said, "It is sad stuff; & necessity is its only excuse" (*Arthur Machen and Montgomery Evans* 55), a sentiment in which most Machen commentators concur. The novel seems closely to have followed the composition of "Opening the Door," and the plotting or writing of the two may have even overlapped. It is in the novel that Machen introduces both the Reverend Thomas Hampole and this cleric's memoir *A London Walk: Meditations in the Streets of the Metropolis*, copious passages of which fill *The Green Round*. The book sounds suspiciously similar both in title and topic to Machen's autobiography *The London Adventure*. Considering all this, it is likely that the Reverend Secretan Jones and the Reverend Thomas Hampole were both modelled on the scholarly aspect of Machen himself, and as such were not only in themselves twins of a sort (again, doppelgängers) but also reflections of Machen, and that they both uttered views that Machen tended to take seriously. However, as *The Green Round* did not quite work as a novel, Reverend Hampole's debut was correspondingly diminished. Though the extracts from Hampole's memoir are interesting, their integration into *The Green Round* seem more in the line of padding then necessary elements, either of plot or colour.

"N"–The Story

> My earliest recollections of a school-life, are connected with a large, rambling, Elizabethan house, in a misty-looking village of England, where were a vast number of gigantic and gnarled trees, and where all the houses were excessively ancient. In truth, it was a dream-like and spirit-soothing place, that venerable old town.–Edgar Allan Poe, "William Wilson" 81)

Reverend Thomas Hampole and his memoir were used to much better effect three years later in the story "N."

Howard wrote that "It is in the late story 'N' ... that [Machen's] idea of interpenetration and perichoresis is most strikingly developed" ("Interpenetrations" 44). While "Opening the Door" uncharacteristically and finally gets to the point and depicts the main principle of Machen's worldview in concrete terms, it is only in "N" that a spotlight is focused (however briefly) on that which is beyond the door—the unearthly, peerless region that is always hinted at and is so central to so much of Arthur Machen's writing. Machen twice opens the door a crack in the story. The first time, the character Perrott tells two friends of an observation his cousin made about passing through Stoke Newington. As such, it should be noted that this statement can be considered hearsay (that is, once removed from an eyewitness account) and necessarily tainted by its careless brushing against the ordinary (e.g., England, Kew Gardens, summer houses, China):

> [I]t was like finding yourself in another country. Such trees, that must have been brought from the end of the world: there were none like them in England, though one or two reminded him of trees in Kew Gardens; deep hollows with streams running from the rocks; lawns all purple and gold with flowers, and golden lilies too, towering up into the trees, and mixing with the crimson of the flowers that hung from the boughs. And here and there, there were little summer-houses and temples, shining white in the sun, like a view in China. (CF 3.328)

Interestingly, some passages from Hampole's volume, *A London Walk*, presented first in *The Green Round,* reappear in "N" with some text replaced with ellipses, but Machen's genius in this shorter work is that the new passages from Hampole are presented not even as Hampole's text proper, but as no more nor less than an elaborate endnote, and it is in that mere note that Machen probably best articulates his vision of that other world he never tired of suggesting to his readers. Hampole is asked to look out a window by a peculiar character. He does so, and afterwards describes the experience:

> For a moment, my heart stood still, and I gasped for breath. Before me, in place of the familiar structures, there was disclosed a panorama of unearthly, of astounding beauty. In deep dells, bowered by overhanging trees, there bloomed flowers such as only dreams can shew; such deep purples that yet seemed to glow like precious stones with a hidden but ever-present radiance, roses whose hues outshone any that are to be seen in our gardens, tall lilies alive with light, and blossoms that were as beaten gold. I saw well-shaded walks that went down to green hollows bordered with thyme; and here and there the grassy eminence above, and the bubbling well below, were crowned with architecture of fantastic and unaccustomed beauty, which seemed to speak of fairyland itself. I might almost say that my soul was ravished by the spectacle displayed before me. I was possessed by a degree of rapture and delight such as I had never experienced. A sense of beatitude pervaded my

whole being; my bliss was such as cannot be expressed by words. I uttered an inarticulate cry of joy and wonder. (CF 3.334-35)

If "N" were in fact Arthur Machen's conscious summation of his favourite topic of conjoined realities towards the end of his literary career, I suggest that it also be a vital and seminal work, perhaps a keystone, in the understanding of Machen's worldview and on how that view consequently has been featured in the development of supernatural fiction for more than a century. In "N," he lays out his vision most succinctly and creates a kind of roadmap with which to navigate his literary apparatus of suggestions, implications, inferences, hints, and sly winks that were so fundamental to all those stories that he knew fully well by then, by 1935, were already considered his classics.

When sitting down to write "N," he likely chose Stoke Newington as the setting because of its real-life historical connections to Edgar Allan Poe and the Manor House School that Poe describes so well in "William Wilson," a story that Machen presents as a sort of Rosetta Stone to reflect light on his own tale. In fact, it would not be far-fetched to imagine that "N" is a kind of sequel to Poe's story inasmuch as "N" owes much to "William Wilson," not only in setting but in tone. Poe wrote:

> But the house!—how quaint an old building was this!—to me how veritably a palace of enchantment! There was really no end to its windings—to its incomprehensible subdivisions. It was difficult, at any given time, to say with certainty upon which of its two stories one happened to be. From each room to every other there were sure to be found three or four steps either in ascent or descent. Then the lateral branches were innumerable—inconceivable—and so returning in upon themselves, that our most exact ideas in regard to the whole mansion were not very far different from those with which we pondered upon infinity. (82)

Can there be a better architectural analogue for the mystical realities that Machen conveys in much of his fiction, and in particular "N"?

"N"–The Title

Undoubtedly, "N" is something of a mystery story. It unfolds subtly in the manner of "Novel of the Black Seal," "The Red Hand," and *The Terror,* slowly building up particulars that lead to the denouement. Little by little we hear about situations and circumstances that belie common sense. For example, there is the matter of a man (a devotee of Poe) who seeks out "again and again" the Manor House School with less than satisfying results, as though he had "gone into the mist" (paralleling Machen's own futile attempts "for years" to pinpoint the school); there is the statement of Perrott's cousin describing a fairyland park in the Stoke Newington neighbourhood that a former resident finds ridiculous and untenable; there is the broaching of the topics of the malleable universe of Behmen and Law and those supernal experiences of the Reverend Hampole; and so forth, up to Arnold's conclusion about the perichoresic nature of all these experiences.

And, then, of course, there is the very title of the story, which is imbued with so much mystery. The title "N" is at odds with title conventions of the entire Machen corpus. Typically, his titles are straightforward, regardless of the subtlety and charm of language with which he crafted his stories. After all, "The Great God Pan," "The White People," "Change," "The Inmost Light," even "The Secret Glory" do in fact reflect something that is manifestly in the story. But the title of "N" is most uncharacteristic because it is not in the least obvious what it means or refers to. Why would Arthur Machen chose such an obtuse and puzzling title that seems completely at odds with his many straightforward titles? Why would he choose a title that we all have had to guess and conjecture about with difficulty for decades?

It is almost as though he hoped to draw attention to the story by giving it a unique title.

Of course, there are some who consider the meaning of the title almost self-evident. For example, Donald R. Burleson gives some consideration to "the most obvious meaning of the title, i.e., if one regards 'N' (standing alone, in capital form, without a period following) as a compass point: North . . . . The titular 'N', by the most facile explanation, reflects the fact that the events of the story revolve around the Stoke Newington area north of London proper (a region and a direction treated rather mystically in the tale)."

Indeed, during a digital tête-à-tête among Machen enthusiasts, a favourite view was indeed that "N" stands for the London postcode district N, or North London, the district in which Stoke Newington falls. A variation of this suggests that "N" for North is offered as a symbol for unknown and unmapped territory.

Taken together, these are reasonable conclusions, especially since the word "North" appears in the story eight times; I include all those instances here in their entirety, rather than summarise them, because it is my contention that Machen said in this particularly important story precisely what he intended to say, weighing every word even as Edgar Allan Poe advised:

Perrott began it, by tracing a curious passage he had once made *north*ward, dodging by the Globe and the Olympic theatres into the dark labyrinth of Clare Market. . . . And thence, *north*ward and eastward, up the Gray's Inn Road, crossing the King's Cross Road, and going up the hill.

"And here,' said Arnold, "we begin to touch on the conjectured. We have left the known world behind us." (CF 3.326)

> Harliss said he had been brought up in *North* London, but much farther *north*—Stoke Newington way. (CF 3.326)

Indeed, they had felt for some time that they had gone too far away from their known world, and from the friendly tavern fires of the Strand, into the wild no man's land of the *north*. To Harliss, of course, those regions had once been familiar, common, and uninteresting: he could not revisit them in talk with any glow of feeling. The other two held them unfriendly and remote; as if one were to discourse of Arctic explorations, and lands of everlasting darkness. (CF 3.329)

. . . but there was something in the tale of this suburban park that remained with Arnold and beset him, and sent him at last to the remote *north* of the story. (CF 3.330)

A college friend of mine, whom I will call the Reverend Mr. S——, was, I was aware, a curate in a suburb of the *north* of London, S.N. I wrote to him, and afterwards called at his lodgings at his invitation. (CF 3.331-32)

. . . there still remains in many places, and above all in the remoter *north*ern suburbs, an old fixed element [i.e., "talkative old men"] which can go back in memory sometimes for a hundred, even a hundred and fifty years. (CF 3.338)

Thus we have a strong contender for Machen's purpose for choosing "N" as a title; but a contender does not equal a solution. And while the compass point may be obvious to Burleson, such an interpretation is by no means necessarily apparent to others. After all, South can be just as strong a symbol of the unknown: ask Poe; ask, too, Jules Verne, Lovecraft, Shackleton, Amundsen, and Scott. Numerous similar examples can be easily presented to affirm the historical and archetypal mysteries of the West and East.

Doubtless there is no end to the possibilities that the title "N" can conjure. Here are some more to consider.

Burleson himself gives weight, in the spirit of literary deconstruction, to the notion of "en [which] is a printer's measure, suggesting the spacing or differentiation that lies at the linguistic heart of texts." Then, too, there has been discussion of the mathematical term referring to infinity or an indefinite number—the nth degree; of the possibility that "N" is a deliberate allusion to

"Nemo" (Latin for "no one"), a key character in Charles Dickens's *Bleak House*; of the fact that in English law "N" was used to indicate a person whose name was unknown; of, perhaps, Machen alluding to the duplicitous "N" (Ambrose Meyrick) to whom he devoted 2,700 words in *The Secret Glory*; or, perhaps, even of Machen eschewing giving the story a real title and topping it with "N," which would mean "no title." Then again, the title "N" may be intentionally ambiguous, reflecting the shadowy, indistinct edges of virtually all elements of the story. Yet if Machen was in the mood just then, as I am supposing, to bequeath onto posterity his final words on the subject of borders and interpenetration, and given his propensity for otherwise straightforward titles, then I think a specific meaning—but a *secret* one—would have been more to his purpose.

With such an intent in mind, I lean toward another explanation, one presented by Machen specialist Godfrey Brangham: "The letter N starts the second half of the alphabet. Canon's Park in the story is present in two states, reality and wonder. Perhaps the first half of the alphabet (A-M) represents reality and of course Machen's initials, whilst the letter N begins the second half of the alphabet equating with the 'unreal'?" (n.p.). How simple! Rather like the purloined letter hiding in plain sight! However, I think we can take Brangham's notion one step farther. We know that Machen had an affinity to Latin and Greek and other aspects of a classical education. Certainly an alphabet that goes from "A to Z" would not have the allure for him as one that goes from "Alpha to Omega." Thus I suggest "N" refers to the first letter in the second half of the *Greek* alphabet and represents the door through which one must pass to view the "world that is not that of ordinary, everyday experience, that in a measure transcends the experience of Bethel and the Bank." Either way, the symbolic result is that, in order to pass through to the other side, one must pass through the door N.

Still, we do not know how it came about that Machen chose that particular title. Did he know from the start what the title would be? Did the story and title merely pop into his head fully developed?

I have recently discovered an interesting circumstance (I do not think it is strong enough to be considered a coincidence) that may shed light on this mystery within a mystery. We know that "N" was published in *The Cosy Room* and that Machen was not especially keen on that book; nevertheless, he respected John Gawsworth's efforts of locating, compiling, and championing so many long-forgotten stories. The one new story he added to the collection was the story that we now know as "N," the last story to be included in a volume that he may have felt was his final contribution to the realm of literature. Despite his habit of deprecating his own work, there can be little doubt he held that particular story in high esteem.

Then let's pretend for a moment that an original title of the story was more like his descriptive practice in other titles, perhaps something like "The Urban Oasis" or "Another Paradise Lost" or "Scenes from Himalaya House" or something of the sort. And then one day–27 January 1936 to be exact–he is writing a letter to his longtime correspondent Montgomery Evans. In that letter he refers to the artist whom Evans had commissioned to create a likeness of Machen: "Nevinson has done you a fine portrait. . . . The sittings (2) were quite painless: say, cheerful. N. is excellent company" (*Arthur Machen and Montgomery Evans* 86). Now note that three short paragraphs later, Machen writes, "I have just corrected the proofs of the short story collection I spoke of: 'The Cosy Room.' After going through it, I want [*note the present tense*] to amend the Curate's Egg story: 'Parts of it are horrible'" (87).

In other words, Arthur Machen was just then (in "real time" as we would say now) checking the proofs of *The Cosy Room*. What if he suddenly and randomly noticed his own abbreviation of Nevinson's name–"N."–and was struck by its potential as a symbol? Perhaps, seeing the N, his imagination ran rampant and a whole universe of possibilities ran through his mind, one in particular striking him as utterly apropos of the reason he wrote the story in the first place. He might have then marked the proofs, first by striking out the original title and replacing it with "N," but then he smiles to himself and thinks what fun it would be to include some red herrings. And so he adds a few "Norths" and tweaks a few sentences to send readers off on a false scent.

Then he is quite content, thinking to himself that he has crafted a neat little story that not only defines the literary intent of his career, but also serves as a literal key to his œuvre–but a key that in itself is a bit of a puzzle.

Of course, this is the purest sort of speculation, but there is the undoubted happenstance that in this one letter he references "N." and also says a few words later that he is then and there checking the proofs of *The Cosy Room*, in which "N" would be published for the first time.

All things considered, therefore, it is all the more odd to me that the story is one of his least noticed, apparently unanthologized during the three-quarters of a century between its original 1936 publication in *The Cosy Room* until recently.

"Opening the Door" Redux

Finally, if four years earlier, in 1931, Machen believed that his contribution to Cynthia Asquith's anthologies would be his final story, with no further prospects in sight—which historically would in fact have been the case if it had not been for Ernest Benn's unexpected request for *The Green Round* and Gawsworth's assembling *The Cosy Room*—then all the very same emotions, thought processes, creative impulses, behaviours, and decisions that I have supposed made up the composition of "N" could well have come into play four years *earlier* as he was writing "Opening the Door," which would account for that story's intimate connection to "N." It would also mean that Machen was *then* consciously writing "Opening the Door" as the summation of his views on perichoresis and interpenetration with the intention of *its* being, as I put it earlier, "the final punctuation point to his long literary career." The imminent 1936 publication of *The Cosy Room*—which included "Opening the Door"—then gave him the opportunity to revisit his favourite topic, and thus we have "N," which Valentine extols as having "all the elusive dimension of 'Opening the Door', but an even greater grace in the telling" (127).

Works Cited

Atkins, Peter. "Preface" to "Opening the Door" by Arthur Machen. In *My Favorite Horror Story*, ed. Mike Baker and Martin H. Greenberg. New York: DAW Books, 2000.

Brangham, Geoffrey. Personal communication, 8 June 2011.

Burleson, Donald R. "Arthur Machen's 'N' as Allegory of Reading." *Studies in Weird Fiction* No. 7 (Spring 1990): 8–11.

Howard, John. "Interpenetrations: Boundary Imagery in the Works of Arthur Machen." In *Machenalia, Volume 2*, ed. Ray Russell. Lewes, UK: Tartarus Press, 1990. 39–45.

———. "A World of Great Majesty." *Avallaunius* No. 17 (Winter 1997): 41–47.

Machen, Arthur. *Arthur Machen and Montgomery Evans: Letters of a Literary Friendship*. Ed. Sue Strong Hassler and Donald M. Hassler. Kent, Ohio: Kent State University Press, 1994.

———. "The Grande Trouvaille (A Legend of Pentonville)." In John Gawsworth. *The Life of Arthur Machen*. Ed. Roger Dobson. Leyburn, UK: Tartarus Press, 2005.

———. *The London Adventure*. London: Martin Secker, 1924.

———. "Note." In *The House of Souls*. London: E. Grant Richards, 1906.

———. "Opening the Door." In *My Favorite Horror Story*, ed. Mike Baker and Martin H. Greenberg. New York: DAW Books, 2000.

Poe, Edgar Allan. *The Annotated Tales of Edgar Allan Poe*. Ed. Stephen Peithman. Garden City, NY: Doubleday, 1981.

Reynolds, Aidan, and William Charlton. *Arthur Machen*. 1963. Oxford: Caermaen Books, 1988.

Sweetser, Wesley D. *Arthur Machen*. New York: Twayne, 1964.

Valentine, Mark. *Arthur Machen*. Bridgend, Wales: Seren, 1995.

"It Is Getting Very Late & Dark": Machen's Last Fiction

Mark Valentine

Arthur Machen was seventy-three years old when he wrote the six stories in *The Children of the Pool* in the spring of 1936. They were to prove his last work of fiction. He was living in semi-retirement in Lynwood, a house in the High Street of the Buckinghamshire town of Old Amersham, in the Chiltern Hills, with his wife Purefoy. The revival of interest in his work in the 1920s, led by American champions such as Vincent Starrett, Paul Jordan-Smith, and James Branch Cabell, which had resulted in new editions of many of his books, had by now lost its first fierce fire.

But he was by no means wholly forgotten, and at Amersham he still received a stream of visitors who admired his writing and enjoyed his company, and old friends from his various careers in literature, the theatre, and journalism. These included Frank Baker, later to delight readers with *Miss Hargreaves* (1940), his story of a poet invented by two bored young men on holiday, who then turns up at their hometown; and Oliver Stonor, already a novelist and man of letters, who had published at Machen's recommendation a version of the seventeenth-century French canon Beroalde de Verville's *Le Moyen de Parvenir* (as *The Way to Succeed*, 1930)—a work Machen himself had also translated and which he described as a "cathedral constructed entirely of gargoyles" (*TNF* 90).

Edwin Greenwood, actor, filmmaker, scriptwriter, and the author of lively, irreverent detective novels, was another regular visitor; as was Colin Summerford, former monk, once proprietor of the liturgical publishers Cope & Fenwick, and his partner Sidney Duncan. Machen's niece Sylvia Townsend Warner, herself making her way in literature, and already the acclaimed author of *Lolly Willowes* (1926), her novel of an independent woman finding her identity through witchcraft, was also often seen at Lynwood.

An excellent evocation of Machen in Amersham at about this time appeared in that mysterious book *Peterley Harvest* (1960) by "David Peterley." It is written pseudonymously in the form of a semi-fictional journal, but Janet Machen, his daughter, confirmed that this part of the book recalled a real occasion. The journal entry is dated 23 September 1935. The narrator visits Machen in the company of Sylvia Townsend Warner, and they make their way

> upstairs to Machen's sitting-room for the first libation of his secret punch which he pours into a goblet from a huge earthenware pitcher. It is at first taste the most innocent seeming, the least apparently alcoholic, the mildest of beverages—left over, surely, from a Church bazaar.... You drink more deeply. The round countenance of Machen smiles and he says disarmingly, "A private blend of my own," and refills your glass ... you will not rejoin yourself and the ordinary world for twenty four hours. (139-40)

Peterley gives a physical description of his host: "He is fashioned on the lines of the oblate spheroid and would look like a Confucian sage if he did not look exactly like a Welsh wizard, which he is. The smile and white locks of Lloyd George are a mediocre imitation: for the politician is wholly of the present world, but Machen quite beyond it" (140). The two discuss Mithraism and the persistence of folk memories. Peterley's visit is at the time of the town's noisy and rather riotous annual street fair, and he writes: "When I reached the little upper room and saw our host pouring his punch, I had the impression of a necromancer who had conjured up the unnatural scene outside; and thought that at any moment he might put down his jug and leaning out of the window utter the cabalistic word at which the noise and the carnival would become moonlight in an empty street" (141). He concludes: "He seemed a literary creation by Machen. The man is the quintessence of his works" (141).

The lethal effect of Machen's ladles of his famous punch becomes clear when the narrator wakes up in unexpected company in London the next day, with little idea how he got there. "Machen's party," he wrote "seemed a shadowy fantastic rite performed in the light of torches to the clash of cymbals and the shouts of Bacchantes, a long way off in time and space" (Peterley 144).

Machen enjoyed offering generous hospitality to his visitors, even though, after writing for over fifty years, he was not particularly well off: indeed he was, as he said himself, "a man of very narrow means" (*SL* 245). He therefore continued to look for opportunities to have old or new work published. A few years later, in 1943, an appeal fund organised by Colin Summerford and signed by many literary luminaries, such as John Masefield, T. S. Eliot, Walter de la Mare, and Siegfried Sassoon, raised a substantial enough sum to allow the Machens to live in a measure of comfort in their final years.

But in the period before then, Machen was also assisted by the poet, bibliographer, anthologist, and busy bibliophile John Gawsworth (the pen name of Terence Ian Fytton Armstrong, 1912-1970). Gawsworth, though then still in his early twenties, seemed to have an uncanny knack of persuading publishers to agree to his many projects. It would be fair to say that he "collected" writers, especially neglected ones, as well as their books, and he gave practical help to quite a number when their reputations and earnings were low. He became a particular and persistent champion of Machen, and at this time was also writing a biography of him, which foundered when Rich & Cowan, the publisher who paid for it, went bankrupt. It was not published until 2005, as *The Life of Arthur Machen*, edited by Roger Dobson, and issued by Tartarus Press.

In Machen's case, Gawsworth had already persuaded Rich & Cowan to issue a selection mostly of his earlier work, *The Cosy Room and Other Stories*, in 1936. Though this included one newly written piece, the fine enigmatic story "N," Machen was embarrassed by this need to resurrect work he did not think much of, telling his old friend the occult scholar A. E. Waite in a letter of 11 April 1936 that Gawsworth "dug and scraped in old literary dustbins, got the stuff typed, discovered the agent, who found the publisher" (*SL* 56). He was blunter in writing to Colin Summerford about the book on 3 March 1936, his birthday: "There are things in it, dating from 1890, that make me sick to look at" (*SL* 148).

Nevertheless, it was because of this publication that he wrote *The Children of the Pool and Other Stories*. "Spurred by this fine example of Armstrong's [Gawsworth], I have entered into a contract with Hutchinson to produce, by the end of July, a collection of short stories amounting to 50,000 words. I have already done 10,000 of them. I am sure that, in the words of Dryden (more or less) you will not, from the dregs of Art, think to receive what the first sprightly running could not give" (*SL* 148-49).

Machen's typically modest comment about the new book was of course made before he had written most of it, and his later estimation, as we shall see, was rather more positive. He had recently provided an introduction to a lively study from the same imprint, *Witches and Warlocks* (1935) by Philip Sergeant, who had been a pupil of his when he briefly made a living from tutoring in his early days in London. Possibly this had led to the agreement to take new fiction from him.

Perhaps because commentators have taken Machen's early estimate of these stories at his own value, there has not been very much discussion of them. Of course, they are bound to seem twilight work, writings of the dusk after Machen's much-praised story collection *The House of Souls* (1906) or his masterpiece, the spiritual autobiography *The Hill of Dreams* (1907). It is probably fair to say they do not aspire to the same lyrical beauty and incantatory prose as these works, and naturally do not have the fervour and fierceness of this younger fiction. But even so, the stories in *The Children of the Pool* have different qualities of their own and show a writer still alert to the singular, fascinated by the strange, drawn to by the byways of folklore and myth, and to the furthest reaches of that unknown world, the human mind. They are worth our attention.

All his life Machen held to the idea that the visible world is only a façade, a symbol of a far greater and stranger world beyond. That accounted, he thought, for the sense of mystery that some places possess: at these, the veil is thinner and it is possible to glimpse a different domain. He had recently explored this in the story "N," in which one of his characters wanders into a marvellous garden in Stoke Newington. But when he tells his friends of this they are certain there is not, nor ever was, any such pleasaunce in the London suburb. It becomes apparent it is no earthly realm: "I believe there is a perichoresis, an interpenetration," his narrator proposes. "It is possible, indeed, that we three are now sitting among desolate rocks, by bitter streams. . . . And with what companions?" (CF 3.344)

A similar theme, though with a more implied wandering into another world, is found in another 'Thirties story by Machen, "Opening the Door," in which the liturgical scholar Secretan Jones walks through his garden gate and disappears for several days. On his return he cannot tell of what he has seen, but he is clearly affected by it. Before he disappears in the Black Mountains, never to be seen again, he sends a letter to the narrator containing the single line "*Est enim magnum chaos*" (CF 230), which we might translate as "For there is a great void" or "a great gulf."

Machen himself had known experiences which seemed to hint at an intermingling of this world and another during the period 1899–1901, in the aftermath of the death of his first wife, Amy. As John Gawsworth recounted in his biography:

> Simply, he realised that incredible things were happening, that symbolical signs were being manifested to him, signs which he could not make out. What could a man do but distrust his senses when great gusts of incense were blow into his nostrils, and the odours of rare gums fumed about him, in Holborn, in Claremont Square, in Clerkenwell. . . . And again, on a bright

keen morning in November, when walking up Rosebery Avenue to become aware suddenly of a strange but delicious sensation . . . of "walking on air", with the pavement resilient, the impact of the feet upon it buoyant . . . (151)

These mystic experiences culminated in a vision in his rooms in Gray's Inn when, as he wrote in *Things Near and Far* (1923), the second of his three autobiographies, "the wall trembled and the pictures on the wall shook and shivered before my eyes, as if a sudden wind had blown into the room," though the day was still (*TNF* 131). He tried again to explain what he meant: the wall and the pictures "trembled, dilated, became misty in their outlines; seemed on the point of disappearing altogether, and then shuddered and contracted back again into their proper form and solidity" (*TNF* 132). Following this experience he entered "a peace of the spirit that was quite ineffable . . . a rapture of delight" (*CF* 3.281) in which everything he touched "carried with it, mysteriously and wonderfully, the message of a secret and interior joy" (*TNF* 137, 138).

This vision is clearly recalled in the first story in *The Children of the Pool*, "The Exalted Omega." The protagonist lives, like Machen, in rooms in Gray's Inn Square and is in dejection, remembering happier days. In his case, it is not the walls and pictures that shimmer, but the table, chairs, and bookcases that seem not quite fixed in their place. But thereafter the story takes a darker turn as his character hears harsh voices and the mutterings of a plot. Machen takes the opportunity to reflect upon Spiritualism. He had previously reflected on the banality of the messages supposedly received from the beyond and written quite pungently of the credulity of those involved in the movement, including Sir Arthur Conan Doyle. In this story he also makes clear that many of its manifestations are parlour tricks or frauds. But, unlike many other stern critics, he is willing to concede that even amongst the charlatans there are some incidents that remain inexplicable, and some did indeed seem to have unusual powers. Those powers—of prophecy, and of picking up on things happening at a distance, in a different time and place—are what drive the story, which in fact turns out to include a carefully contrived and structured murder plot.

That element of the story, artful though it is, is not, however, its main allure. The reader today is more likely to relish the sense of strange conspiracy Machen weaves, and the story of the lonely bookman Mansel who makes the mark in his books that gives the story its title—a glyph like a crowned trident, the Omega Exalted. How we should like to find copies of his books with that sigil on the front endpapers, perhaps in the successors to the "threepenny and sixpenny boxes" in the "smaller shops and poor neighbourhoods" where Machen says his volumes probably ended up. And perhaps even the very book he names among Mansel's library, the otherwise unknown *Secret Counsels of a Certain Exile*. And yet—perhaps not. It might not be wise. For Machen leaves satisfyingly dark precisely what part the mark played in the sinister outcome of his story.

The title story also has its setting in an old haunt of Machen's, but this time in the country of his youth, in the Welsh borderlands. He rejoices again in the deep lanes, secret valleys, and little wandering streams of Gwent. Machen explores the links between landscape and mood, and the black, stagnant pool of the title proves to be a potent symbol for the unconscious. The victim in the story, harried as he thinks by a girl crying out his past misdeeds, is suffering from the creations of his own tormented mind. Using the same term he had invoked in "Opening the Door," Machen comments that "In him, as in many men, there was a great gulf fixed between the hidden and the open consciousness . . ." But this psychological explanation is not all that is at work. The dank pool itself played its part: the old stories about its progeny, the children, must have had some origin.

In this element of the story, Machen was no doubt drawing upon authentic folklore he had heard. His country was blessed with many hundreds of holy wells, associated with the saints and miracles of healing. But there were also tales of the reverse of these—dark waters with an unholier reputation. Francis Jones, in his study *The Holy Wells of Wales* (1954), gives a striking example: "When Ffynnon Chwerthin in boggy land near Llanberis (Caern[arvonshire]) is approached the ground tremor causes the well to bubble or to 'laugh'. People attributed this to witches and their servitors, the 'old black men' (*hen fechgyn duon*), and avoided it as a sinister well" (129). He also recounts a peculiar game played by children in the Taf valley on the Pembrokeshire-Carmarthenshire border, called "Bwci'r ffynnon"("goblin of the well"), a hiding and chasing game in which children pretended to take away limbs and features from a child with covered eyes, who counted to fifty. When the total was reached, the child had to seek out those who had taken away his body.

"The Bright Boy" is a story that begins in an atmosphere of genteel decay, such as Machen had himself known when his father, the last of a line of priests and scholars, fell into poverty. The decline of old towns and country seats, and of obscure colleges, is sketched in at the beginning of the tale. Machen proceeds with a deft touch to hint at the lives of those not destined for great office or wealth, minor characters indeed, like the old actor in the story, based no doubt on many Machen had met in his own acting days, who is "reliable in the smaller Shakespearean parts" (CF 3.389). Here we see a different, more reflective Machen exhibiting a gentle interest in the broad stream of humanity, rather than the singular connoisseurs and flâneurs of his outré tales of the 'Nineties.

But the main scene of the story is set in Machen's Gwent—indeed, in a place he had used before. The White House, as he names it here, "terraced on a hill-side, high above a grey and silver river winding in esses through a lonely, lovely valley" (CF 3.400) is Bertholly, a remote manor whose pale walls he could see from his childhood home in the rectory at Llandewi, near Caerleon. He made it the scene of the sinister experiment in his occult romance "The Great God Pan" (1894). The solution to the mystery of the child prodigy that the tutor in "The Bright Boy" is engaged to teach is ingenious, perhaps rather too much so, and takes us again into the realms of twisted psychology.

In his memoirs, Machen writes evocatively of his days as a lonely, bookish young man in rural Gwent in the 1870s and '80s. They tell us much of the country, the families, the conventions and the eccentricities of this lost domain. The old armigerous squires in their low-beamed stone houses, who are full of character and uncertain temperament, preservers of obscure feuds and ancient loyalties, are respectfully portrayed. Machen forgives them their peppery remarks upon his wayward choice of writing as a career: and he is at pains to show that amongst all this bluster there were also signs of high courtesy and unexpected generosity. It is just these last qualities that he celebrates in "The Tree of Life." We think we are witnessing the increasingly peculiar orders given by a young gentleman of this sort of lineage to his steward, but soon discover that all is not as it seems. The story is a gentle tribute to the finer qualities of the families of his country, in some ways the slightest of the six gathered here, but with its own subtle strangeness.

"The Tree of Life" is a kabbalistic term for a diagram of the spiritual spheres. This concept is not in fact explored in the story of that title. But Machen certainly had in mind a kabbalistic theme in his next story "Out of the Picture," as is clear from a query he put to Waite in the letter quoted earlier: "And since we are discoursing of interior things," he wrote, "tell me if I am right in declaring that the Serpent did not ascend beyond Daath (the logical understanding) in the Tree of Life? And furthermore; that being so, we may speak of the world of Kether, & the works of it as uncorrupted? Or, in terms of literature, may it justly be said that Pope's Character of Addison is of

Daath, while Coleridge's Kubla Khan is of Kether?" (SL 56).

He added: "All this, let me tell you, relates to a mystical painter of mine in a 50,000 word collection of stories, commissioned by your pal Hutchinson" (SL 56-57). The publisher was Waite's "pal" because he had agreed to publish the occult scholar's extensive autobiography: Machen jokingly suggested to Waite that "Walter" Hutchinson, the head of the firm, was often found sobbing over his tea as he contemplated a further large batch of the memoirs.

In "Out of the Picture," Machen uses similar phrasing to that in his letter to Waite and explains what this means in the mystical tradition: that humanity's highest faculties were not tainted by sin, by the Fall. He is also using kabbalistic terms to support his long-held distinction between "literature," characterised by a sense of ecstasy, and other, supposedly more "realistic" writing, which he regarded as something lower, less inspired. The story also includes a passage referring once more to a variation on his own experience in his Gray's Inn rooms, and still trying to find the words to convey this: "A mystic once told me that after he had finished his meditation and gone out into the street, he had seen the grey bulk of the houses opposite suddenly melt, evaporate, go up like smoke, leaving void nothingness in their place" (CF 3.433).

M'Calmont, the artist in the story, argues that the finest music achieves a pure form and wonders if art can do the same. As if conscious that these discussions might seem somewhat esoteric and abstruse, Machen soon introduces a more tangible, physical horror into his story. His tale is a variation on the idea that a painting could contain a dark, supernatural secret within it, most notably explored by Oscar Wilde in *The Picture of Dorian Gray* (1891): Machen met and dined with Wilde several times in the period after this book appeared. In Machen's hands the theme is notable for the scenes set in the lonely, obscure back streets of London where the artist has his studio, and the work is a very effective drama of mounting dread.

We might wonder whether Machen had in mind an actual artist in his creation of M'Calmont. There are aspects of this character that seem to suggest Austin Osman Spare (1886-1956), the London artist who was immersed in kabbalistic magic and his own original system of sorcery. It is not known that Machen ever met Spare, but he did know well Spare's former partner in the journal *Form* (1916-17), Francis Marsden, the pseudonym of Frederick Carter. He had been introduced to him by John Gawsworth, met him several times for pub conversations, admired Carter's story "Gold Like Glass," which the poet and editor had anthologised, and wrote an introduction to Carter's book of mystical art, *The Dragon of the Alchemists* (1926). It seems at least possible he had heard of the remarkable character and art of Spare from Carter.

In the final story in this volume, "Change," the setting is Pembrokeshire, which Machen had also used in a novel written in this period, *The Green Round* (1933). He and his family had taken annual holidays in this region, around the town of Tenby and the coastal village of Penally, and Machen explored the neighbouring country and discovered something of its folklore. And in this story he revisits another strong element of his past writings, when he was the chronicler of the Little People, the subterranean survivals of an ancient race, in stories such as "Novel of the Black Seal" and "The Shining Pyramid."

Starting with the mild picture of families on holiday and children playing on the beach, he soon brings us, with all his old gusto, into scenes where this darker world impinges on our own, in a macabre account of that most ancient tradition, of the changeling: the child taken by fairies, who leave one of their own in its place. In his last significant work of fiction, Machen demonstrates he has lost none of his power to convey the utterly outlandish and sinister. The final words of the story, of his book, and of his long career in the fiction of the supernatural, sum up his conviction that we live in a world that, if it sometimes offers us great wonders, is also fraught with spiritual peril: "the darkness is undying" (CF 3.467).

Arthur Machen's considered verdict on this book was given in a letter to A. E. Waite of 16 November 1936: "I believe you are right in thinking that there are hints or indications of new paths in 'The Children of the Pool':—but it is getting very late & dark for treading of strange ways" (SL 59). He was always a modest man, reluctant to acclaim his own work, but between the lines of this comment it is possible to see a quiet pride that he was still able to advance original ideas and pursue curious, unexpected paths of thought.

Works Cited

Gawsworth, John. *The Life of Arthur Machen*. Ed. Roger Dobson. Leyburn, UK: Tartarus Press, 2005.

Jones, Francis. *The Holy Wells of Wales*. Cardiff: University of Wales Press. 1954.

Peterley, David. *Peterley Harvest*. Ed. Richard Pennington. London: Hutchinson, 1960.

Bibliography

A. Primary

i. Fiction and Poetry

The Bowmen and Other Legends of the War. London: Simpkin, Marshall, Hamilton, Kent & Co., 1915.

The Children of the Pool and Other Stories. London: Hutchinson, 1936.

The Chronicle of Clemendy. Carbonnek [i.e., London]: Privately printed for the Society of Pantagruelists [i.e., Arthur Machen and Harry Spurr], 1888.

Collected Fiction. Edited by S. T. Joshi. New York: Hippocampus Press, 2019. 3 vols.

The Cosy Room and Other Stories. London: Rich & Cowan, 1936.

Eleusinia. By "A Former Member of H.C.S." [i.e., Hereford Cathedral School]. Hereford: Privately printed for the author, 1881. New edition with commentary edited by Jon Preece. Newport, Gwent: The Friends of Arthur Machen, 2013.

The Great God Pan and Other Horror Stories. Edited by Aaron Worth. Oxford: Oxford University Press, 2018.

The Great God Pan and The Inmost Light. London: John Lane, 1894.

The Great Return. London: Faith Press, 1915.

The Green Round. London: Ernest Benn, 1933.

The Hill of Dreams. London: Grant Richards, 1907.

Holy Terrors: Short Stories. Harmondsworth, UK: Penguin, 1946.

The House of Souls. London: Grant Richards, 1906.

The Grande Trouvaille: A Legend of Pentonville. London: First Edition Bookshop, 1923.

Ornaments in Jade. New York: Alfred A. Knopf, 1924.

Ritual and Other Stories. Lewes, UK: Tartarus Press, 1992.

The Secret Glory. London: Martin Secker, 1922. Full edition with two omitted chapters, Lewes, UK: Tartarus Press, 1998.

The Shining Pyramid. London: Martin Secker, 1925.

Tales of Horror and the Supernatural. Introduced by Philip Van Doren Stern. New York: Alfred A. Knopf, 1948. London: Richards Press, 1949.

The Terror: A Fantasy. London: Duckworth, 1917.

The Three Impostors. London: John Lane; Boston: Roberts Brothers, 1895.

The White People and Other Weird Stories. Edited by S. T. Joshi. New York: Penguin, 2011.

ii. Nonfiction

The Anatomy of Tobacco. By "Leolinus Siluriensis." London: George Redway, 1884.

The Canning Wonder. London: Chatto & Windus, 1925.

Dr. Stiggins: His Views and Principles. London: Francis Griffiths, 1906.

Dog and Duck. New York: Alfred A. Knopf, 1924.

Dreads and Drolls. London: Martin Secker, 1926.

The Eighteen Nineties Notebook. Leyburn, UK: The Friends of Arthur Machen/Tartarus Press, 2016.

The Glorious Mystery. Edited by Vincent Starrett. Chicago: Covici-McGee, 1924.

Hieroglyphics. London: Grant Richards, 1902. Rpt. London: Martin Secker, 1926.

Notes and Queries. London: Spurr & Swift, 1926.

Precious Balms. London: Spurr & Swift, 1924.

The Secret of the Sangraal and Other Writings. Horam, UK: Tartarus Press, 1995.

The Shining Pyramid. Edited by Vincent Starrett. Chicago: Covici-McGee, 1923.

Strange Roads; With the Gods in Spring. London: Classic Press, 1923.

War and the Christian Faith. London: Skeffington, 1918.

iii. Autobiographies

The Autobiography of Arthur Machen. Introduced by Morchard Bishop. London: Richards Press, 1951. [Includes *Far Off Things* and *Things Near and Far.*]

Far Off Things. London: Martin Secker, 1922 (rpt. 1926).

The London Adventure; or, The Art of Wandering. London: Martin Secker, 1924.

Things Near and Far. London: Martin Secker, 1923.

iv. Letters

A Few Letters from Arthur Machen [to Munson Havens]. Cleveland: Rowfant Club, 1932.

Arthur Machen and Montgomery Evans: Letters of a Literary Friendship, 1923–1947. Edited by Sue Strong Hassler and Donald M. Hassler. Kent, OH: Kent State University Press, 1994.

Selected Letters: The Private Writings of the Master of the Macabre, Arthur Machen. Edited by Roger Dobson, Godfrey Brangham, and R. A. Gilbert. Wellingborough, UK: Aquarian, 1988.

v. Translations

Fantastic Tales; or, The Way to Attain [by Beroalde de Verville]. Carbonnek [i.e., London]: Privately printed, 1889.

The Heptameron; or, Tales and Novels of Marguerite Queen of Navarre. London: Privately printed, 1886.

The Memoirs of Jacques Casanova. London: Privately printed, 1894. 12 vols.

B. Secondary

i. Bibliographies

Danielson, Henry. *Arthur Machen: A Bibliography*. London: Henry Danielson, 1923.

Goldstone, Adrian, and Wesley D. Sweetser. *A Bibliography of Arthur Machen.* Austin: University of Texas Press, 1965. New York: Haskell House, 1973.

ii. Biographies and Memoirs

Baker, Frank. *I Follow But Myself.* London: Peter Davies, 1968.

Cumberland, Gerald. *Written in Friendship.* London: Grant Richards, 1923.

Gawsworth, John. *The Life of Arthur Machen.* Edited by Roger Dobson. Leyburn, UK: Tartarus Press for The Friends of Arthur Machen in association with Reino de Redonda, 2005.

Hogan, J. P. *Hair under a Hat.* London: Chaterson, 1949.

Jepson, Edgar. *Memoirs of an Edwardian and Neo-Georgian.* London: Richards Press, 1937.

Lejeune, Anthony. "An Old Man and a Boy: Memories of Arthur Machen." *Listener* 55 (29 March 1956): 315, 318-19. *Aylesford Review* 2 (Winter 1959-60): 315-20 (as "Memories of Machen"; as by C. A. Lejeune and Anthony Lejeune).

Peterley, David. *Peterley Harvest.* Ed. Richard Pennington. London: Hutchinson, 1960.

Reynolds, Aidan, and William Charlton. *Arthur Machen: A Short Account of His Life and Work.* London: Richards Press, 1963.

Stonor, Oliver. *The Table Talk of Arthur Machen.* Unpublished.

Valentine, Mark. *Arthur Machen.* Bridgend, Wales: Seren, 1995.

Waite, Arthur Edward. *Shadows of Life and Thought.* London: Selwyn & Blount, 1938.

iii. Critical and Other Studies

Cavaliero, Glen. *The Supernatural and English Fiction.* Oxford: Oxford University Press, 1995.

Eckersley, Adrian. "A Theme in the Early Works of Arthur Machen: Degeneration." *English Literature in Transition* 35 (1992): 277-87.

Ellis, Stewart M. *Mainly Victorian.* London: Hutchinson, 1925.

Eng, Steve. "M. P. Shiel and Arthur Machen." In *Shiel in Diverse Hands: A Collection of Essays.* Cleveland: Reynolds Morse Foundation, 1983. 233-47.

Geckle, William. *Arthur Machen: Weaver of Fantasy.* New York: Round Table Press, 1949.

Goodricke-Clarke, Nicholas. "The Enchanted City: Arthur Machen and Locality: Scenes from His Early London Years (1880-85)." *Durham University Journal* 87 (July 1995): 301-13.

Jordan-Smith, Paul. "Black Magic: An Impression of Arthur Machen." In *On Strange Altars.* New York: Albert & Charles Boni, 1924. 214-35.

Joshi, S. T. "Arthur Machen: The Mystery of the Universe." In *The Weird Tale.* Austin: University of Texas Press, 1990.

Klein, T. E. D. "Arthur Machen: *The House of Souls.*" In *Horror: 100 Best Books,* ed. Stephen Jones and Kim Newman. London: Xanadu, 1988; New York: Carroll & Graf, 1988. 64-67.

Lovecraft, H. P. "Supernatural Horror in Literature." *Recluse* (1927): 23–59 (esp. 51–54). In *The Annotated Supernatural Horror in Literature*. Edited by S. T. Joshi. 2nd ed. New York: Hippocampus Press, 2012.

Matteson, Robert S. "Arthur Machen: A Vision of an Enchanted Land." *Personalist* 46 (1965): 253–68.

Michael, D. P. M. *The Life and Works of Arthur Machen*. Aberystwyth: University of Wales, 1941.

Owens, Jill Tedford. "Arthur Machen's Supernaturalism: The Decadent Variety." *University of Mississippi Studies in English* NS 8 (1990): 117–26.

Penzoldt, Peter. *The Supernatural in Fiction*. London: Peter Nevill, 1952; Atlantic Highlands, NJ: Humanities Press, 1965.

Rickett, Arthur. "A Yellow Creeper." In *Lost Chords: Some Emotions without Morals*. London: A. D. Innes, 1895.

Russell, R. B. *The Anatomy of Taverns*. Hunters Bar, UK: Tartarus Press, rev. ed. 1990.

Russell, R. B., ed. *Machenalia*. Lewes, UK: Tartarus Press, 1990. 2 vols.

Sewell, Brocard, ed. *Arthur Machen*. Llandeilo, Wales: St. Albert's Press, 1960.

Simons, John. "Horror in the 1890s: The Case of Arthur Machen." In *Creepers: British Horror and Fantasy in the Twentieth Century*, ed. Clie Bloom. London: Pluto Press, 1993. 35–46.

Starrett, Vincent. *Arthur Machen: A Novelist of Ecstasy and Sin*. Chicago: Walter M. Hill, 1918.

Sweetser, Wesley D. *Arthur Machen*. New York: Twayne, 1964.

Underhill, Evelyn. *Mysticism: A Study in the Nature and Development of Man's Spiritual Consciousness*. London : Methuen, 1911.

Van Patten, Nathan. *There Are Some Who Mourn*. [Canton, OH]: Privately printed, 1948.

Wagenknecht, Edward. "Arthur Machen." In *Seven Masters of Supernatural Fiction*. Westport, CT: Greenwood Press, 1991. 95–120.

Wandrei, Donald. "Arthur Machen and *The Hill of Dreams*." *Minnesota Quarterly* 3, No. 3 (Spring 1926): 19–24. *Studies in Weird Fiction* No. 15 (Summer 1994): 27–30.

Acknowledgments

The editors are very grateful to S. T. Joshi and Derrick Hussey for asking them to edit this book, and for courteous and invaluable help throughout. Ray Russell, Mark Valentine's co-editor for many years of *Faunus*, the journal of The Friends of Arthur Machen, was prompt and unstinting with his support: and, with Rosalie Parker, their Tartarus Press has kept many Machen titles in print in fine editions. His interest in Machen was sustained and immeasurably enhanced by many discussions and expeditions in the company of my late and much-missed old friend Roger Dobson. His literary colleague and valued friend John Howard has also shared many Machen interests over the years. Stephen Cashmore kindly gave timely technical help. William Breeze and David Tibet were also swift to help. Every Machen publisher, commentator, or reader approached has offered cheerful help and advice. Mark's wife Jo has shared the progress of this book with encouragement and kindness. Finally, Timothy Jarvis would like to thank James Machin for assistance in tracking down Machen esoterica.

The editors and publisher are grateful to the following parties for permission to print or reprint the following essays in this volume (those articles for which permission is not indicated are believed to be in the public domain):

S. T. Joshi, "Arthur Machen: The Evils of Materialism," in *Unutterable Horror: A History of Supernatural Fiction* (Hornsea, UK: PS Publishing, 2012). Reprinted by permission of the author.

Geoffrey H. Wells, "Arthur Machen: The Pagan; His Work and Personality," *Cassell's Weekly* (17 October 1928).

Vincent Starrett, Extract from *Arthur Machen: A Novelist of Ecstasy and Sin* (Chicago: Walter M. Hill, 1918).

Arthur Machen, "About My Books," from *Arthur Machen: A Bibliography* by Henry Danielson (London: Henry Danielson, 1923).

Godfrey Brangham, "The City, the Vision and Arthur Machen." Original to this volume. Printed by permission of the author.

Roger Dobson, "The Book in Yellow: How Dorian Inspired Lucian," *Faunus* No. 16 (Summer 2007). Reprinted by permission of the editor, representing the author's estate.

Arthur Rickett, "A Yellow Creeper," in *Lost Chords: Some Emotions without Morals* (London: A. D. Innes, 1895).

James Machin, "Arthur Machen and Decadence: the Flower-Tunicked Priest of New Grub Street." Original to this volume, although it contains some material adapted from the author's book *Weird Fiction in Britain, 1880–1939* (Palgrave Macmillan, 2018). Printed by permission of the author and the publisher.

Roger Dobson, "New Arabian Frights: Unholy Trinities and the Masks of Helen," *Faunus* No. 19 (Summer 2009). Reprinted by permission of the editor, representing the author's estate.

Jon Preece, "A Glow in the Sky: Some Observations on Machen's Style." Original to this volume. Printed by permission of the author.

John Howard, "The Secret and the Secrets: A Look at Machen's *Hieroglyphics*," *Faunus* No. 5 (Spring 2000). Reprinted by permission of the author.

Marco Pasi, "Arthur Machen's Panic Fears: Western Esotericism and the Irruption of Negative Epistemology," *Aries: Journal for the Study of Western Esotericism* 7, No. 1 (2007). Printed by permission of the author and the original publisher, Brill.

Karen Kohoutek, "A Fit Symbol for His Meaning: Arthur Machen and the Inexpressible." Original to this volume. Printed by permission of the author.

Graham Cooling, "The Revenge of Vulcan," *Faunus* No. 3 (Spring 1999). Reprinted by permission of the author.

Ron Weighell, "Perfume of the Trellised Vine," *Faunus* No. 7 (Autumn 2001). Reprinted by permission of the author.

Peter Bell, "Of Sacred Groves and Ancient Mysteries: Parallel Themes in the Writings of Arthur Machen and John Buchan," *Faunus* No. 21 (Summer 2010). Reprinted by permission of the author.

Emily Foster, "Beyond the Veil of Reality: Mysticism in Arthur Machen's 'The White People.'" Original to this volume. Printed by permission of the author.

Iain Smith, "Sanctity Plus Sorcery: The Curious Christianity of Arthur Machen." Original to this volume. Printed by permission of the author.

Geoffrey Reiter, "'The Abyss of All Being': 'The Great God Pan' and the Death of Metaphysics" has appeared in earlier versions as "'Man Is Made a Mystery': The Evolution of Arthur Machen's Religious Thought," Ph.D. diss.: Baylor University, 2010, and as "'The Abyss of All Being': Metaphysical Poets and the Death of Metaphysics in Arthur Machen's 'The Great God Pan,'" The Journal of Faith and the Academy Conference, Faulkner University, 8 February 2013. Revised version original to this volume. Printed by permission of the author.

Donald Sidney-Fryer, "Arthur Machen and King Arthur, Sovereigns of Dream: A Personal Interpretation," *Nyctalops* Nos. 11/12 (April 1976): 89–122. Reprinted by permission of the author.

John Howard, "The Impossible History: Machen's 'A Fragment of Life'," *Faunus* No. 35 (Spring 2017). Reprinted by permission of the author.

Jeremy Cantwell, "The Canning Enigma: Some Observations on Arthur Machen's *The Canning Wonder*," *Faunus* No. 5 (Spring 2000). Reprinted by permission of the author.

Aleister Crowley, "Three Great Hoaxes of the War," *Vanity Fair* [New York] (January 1916). Reproduced by the kind permission of the O.T.O.

James Machin, "'All Manner of Mysteries': Encounters with the Numinous in *The Cosy Room and Other Stories*," introduction to *The Cosy Room and Other Stories* (Lewes, UK: Tartarus Press, 2017). Reprinted by permission of the author. With thanks to Tartarus Press.

Thomas Kent Miller, "Some Thoughts on 'N,'" *Faunus* No. 26 (Autumn 2012). Reprinted by permission of the author.

Mark Valentine, "'It Is Getting Very Late & Dark': Machen's Last Fiction," introduction to *The Children of the Pool* (Leyburn, UK: Tartarus Press, 2015). Reprinted by permission of the author. With thanks to Tartarus Press.

Index

À Rebours (Huysman) 77, 78
Academy 34, 214, 311, 361
"Adventure of the Copper Beeches, The" (Doyle) 63
"Adventure of the Missing Brother" (Machen) 110
"Afternoon, An" (Buchan) 183
Against Nature (Huysmans) 78
Age of Arthur, The (Morris) 268
Aiwass 174
Alexander, George 56
Allingham, William 190
All the Year Round 92, 190
Anatomy of Taverns, The (Russell) 67
Anatomy of Tobacco, The (Machen) 15, 28, 41–42, 308
Angels of Mons 23–24, 75, 215, 247, 300, 317, 348, 362
Angels of Mons: The Bowmen and Other Legends of the War, The (Machen) 23, 24, 31, 312, 314
Annotated Tales of Edgar Allan Poe, The (Poe) 370
Aphrodite (Louÿs) 96
Arabian Nights 19, 28
Arkham House 25, 313
Armstrong, Terence Ian Fytton. *See* Gawsworth, John
Arnold, Matthew 318
"Arrest of Oscar Wilde at the Cadogan Hotel, The" (Betjeman) 78
Arthur, King 239–329
Arthurian Mythos 239–329
Arthur Machen (Sweetser) 79
Arthur Machen: A Bibliography (Danielson) 103
"Arthur Machen: A Novelist of Ecstasy and Sin" (Starrett) 89

Ashe, Geoffrey 275, 278n4, 289, 296, 299
Asquith, Lady Cynthia 25, 362, 363, 364, 369, 371, 379
"At the Article of Death" (Buchan) 186
Athanasius, St. 219
Athenaeum 89, 96
Atkins, Peter 370
Attar, Fariduddin 214
Auden, W. H. 363
"Auguries of Innocence" (Blake) 165
Aurelianus, Ambrosius 267, 297
Austen, Jane 23, 132, 133
"Awaking" (Machen) 363

Bagh-I-Muattar; or, Scented Garden of Abdullah the Satirist of Shiraz (Crowley) 175
Baker, Arthur E. 300
Baker, Frank 381
Baldick, Robert 78
Balthus 306n7
Balzac, Honoré de 43
Bards of Cornwall 294
Bataille, Dr. 146n10
Bates, H. E. 360
Baudelaire, Charles 35, 65, 86, 89, 90
Beardsley, Aubrey 77, 186, 309
"Beneath the Barley" (Machen) 185
Benham, Patrick 217
Benn, Ernest 379
Bennett, Arnold 89
Benson, Sir Frank 57
Betjeman, John 72, 78
Bibliography of Arthur Machen (Goldstone–Sweetser) 132
Bierce, Ambrose 240
Birds, The (film) 217

Blackwood, Algernon 16, 21, 362, 363
Blake, William 61, 165
Blavatsky, Madame 152
Bleak House (Dickens) 377
Bookman 214
Book of Common Prayer 342
Book of Law, The (Crowley-Aiwass) 174
Bourget, Paul 86
"Bowmen, The" (Machen) 23, 24, 28, 54, 75, 215, 247, 300, 312, 317, 347-49, 362
Bowmen and Other Legends of the War, The (Machen). *See Angels of Mons, The*
Bradley, F. H. 231
Brangham, Godfrey 377
"Branwen Daughter of Llyr" 215
"Bright Boy, The" (Machen) 25, 386-87
Brontë, Emily 119
Brook, Peter 117
Browne, Sir Thomas 46, 317
Buchan, Anna Masterton 186
Buchan, John 181-96
Bulwer-Lytton, Edward 150-51, 152
Burgess, Anthony 118
Burke, Edmund 162, 167-69
Burleson, Donald R. 375, 376
Burton, Sir Richard 174, 178

Cabell, James Branch 174, 381
Cadbury Castle 275-78, 282, 283, 284, 303
Caerleon-on-Usk 15, 27, 28, 52, 60, 199, 241, 242, 244-49, 258, 259-65, 268, 270, 271, 275, 277, 283, 296, 300-306, 308, 310, 316, 318, 322, 323
Caer Nodentis (Temple of Nodens) 251-59, 274, 290, 291
Caesar, Julius 260, 289, 290, 291
"Call of Cthulhu, The" (Lovecraft) 151, 152
Canning, Elizabeth 352-57, 363
Canning Wonder, The (Machen) 351-57, 363

"Captain of Salvation, A" (Buchan) 186
Carlyle, Thomas 125
Carter, Frederick 388, 389
Casanova, Giacomo 15, 28, 46, 161, 309, 313
Cassian, John 149-50
Catechetical School of Alexandria 219
Cavaliero, Glen 80, 222
Cavendish, Richard 243, 275n3, 278n4, 288n6
Caxton, William 299
Century 55
"Ceremony, The" (Machen) 361, 363
Cervantes, Miguel de 28, 37, 39, 132
Chambers's Journal 92
"Change" (Machen) 25, 389
Chapman's Magazine 52
Charlemagne 245
Charlton, William 218, 224n1, 227, 335, 342
"Charm of Old Churches, The" (Machen) 218
Chartier, Émile-Auguste 62
Chatto and Windus 47, 354-55, 356
Chemical Marriage of Christian Rosycross, The 44
Children's Cargo, The 363
Children of the Pool, The (Machen) 25, 214, 217, 313, 369, 381, 383, 384, 385, 389
"Child That Went with the Fairies, The" (Le Fanu) 190
Chrétien de Troyes 275
Chronicle of Clemendy, The (Machen) 15, 28, 31, 40, 43, 113n6, 114, 115, 119, 120, 308, 316
Collected Machen (Machen) 218
"Compliments of the Season, The" (Machen) 364
Confessions of a Literary Man, The (Machen) 60. *See also Far Off Things*
Connell, F. Norreys 96
Constantine the Great (Emperor of Rome) 255, 297
Contes Drolatiques (Balzac) 43
Cornhill 92

Cosy Room and Other Stories, The (Machen) 25, 217, 313, 359-66, 369, 377-79, 383
Couch, Sir A. T. Quiller 49
Cowley, Abraham 230
Crackanthorpe, Hubert 92
Crashaw, Richard 230-31
Crawford, F. Marion 240
Critique of Judgment (Kant) 162
Crollius, Oswald 165
Crombie, R. Ogilvie 145
Crowley, Aleister 144, 155, 173-75, 177, 178, 179, 180, 363
Cumberland, Gerald 67, 68

Dancing Faun, The (Farr) 187
Dancing Floor, The (Buchan) 189
Danielson, Henry 103
Davis, Janet Machen 315
De Bello Gallico (Caesar) 289, 290
de la Mare, Walter 382
Debussy, Claude 122, 126
Decadent movement 77, 85-100, 311, 318
Decadent Movement in Literature, The (Symons) 87
Decline and Fall of the Roman Empire, The (Gibbon) 121
Decline of the West, The (Spengler) 154
"Decorative Imagination, The" (Machen) 18
Degeneration (Nordau) 154, 205, 346
del Toro, Guillermo 223
Derleth, August 313
Devil-Worship in France (Waite) 147n10
Diable au XIX siècle (Bataille) 146n10
Diana Vaughan and the Question of Modern Palladism (Waite) 147n10
Diary of a Nobody, The (Grossmith-Grossmith) 336
Dickens, Charles 30, 37, 38, 119, 123, 132, 133, 161, 315, 377
"Disintegration Machine, The" (Doyle) 106
Dobson, Roger 129, 383
Dog and Duck (Machen) 313

"Don Quijote de la Mancha" (Machen) 42
Don Quixote (Cervantes) 37, 42, 132
Doors of Perception, The (Huxley) 64
"Dotage" (Herbert) 225, 229, 230
"A Double Return" (Machen) 360
Douglas, Lord Alfred 311, 361
Douglas, Norman 176
Doyle, Richard 190
Doyle, Sir Arthur Conan 63, 93, 106, 385
Dragon of the Alchemists, The (Carter) 389
"Drake's Drum" (Machen) 362
Dreads and Drolls (Machen) 313
Dr. Stiggins: His Views and Principles (Machen) 36-37, 50
Duncan, Sidney 381
"Dunwich Horror, The" (Lovecraft) 17, 236
Durrell, Lawrence 359
Dynamiter, The (Stevenson-Stevenson) 18, 47, 90, 103-15, 360

East West Journal 306
"Ecclesia Anglicana" (Machen) 214
Eckersley, Adrian 205, 227, 229
Education Act of 1870 88
Edward I (King of England) 282, 299
Eisteddfod, The 294
Eleusinia (Machen) 41, 185, 210, 307, 314
Eliot, George 23, 118, 132, 133
Eliot, T. S. 230, 382
Elizabeth I (Queen of England) 246, 250, 294
Ellmann, Richard 78
"Encounter on the Pavement, The" (Machen) 65
English Hymnal, The 340
Essential Sufism (Fadiman-Frager) 214
Evans, Montgomery 378
Evening News. See [London] *Evening News*
"Exalted Omega, The" (Machen) 25, 385

Fadiman, James 214

Faerie Queene, The (Spenser) 241, 298, 299
Fairyland (Doyle) 190
Fantastic Tales (Verville) 40, 44-45, 76
Far from the Madding Crowd (Hardy) 118
"Far Islands, The" (Buchan) 196
Far Off Things (Machen) 15, 27, 29, 60, 62, 122, 199, 202, 222, 309, 312
Farr, Florence 187
Ferguson, Christine 231
"Fetlain's *Elegy for Vixeela*" (Smith) 328
Fielding, Henry 354
Fielding, John 354
fin-de-siècle 11, 68, 86, 111, 186, 225, 227, 228, 361
Findhorn Community 145
Flameng, Léopold 42
"Flaming Heart, The" (Crashaw) 231
"Folklore and Legends of the North" (Machen) 17
Fool and His Heart, A (Connell) 96
Forest of Nodens 249-51
Form 388
Fortunate Lovers, The (Marguerite de Navarre) 43
"Fountainblue" (Buchan) 183, 196
Fowles, John 101, 112n5
Frager, Robert 214
"Fragment of Life, A" (Machen) 19, 21, 22-23, 28, 50, 51, 69, 183, 213, 333-43
Frazer, Sir James George 189
Freeman, Mary E. Wilkins 132-33
Freeman, Nicholas 201
French Lieutenant's Woman, The (Fowles) 101, 112n5
French, Nora May 240
"From Beyond" (Lovecraft) 217
Full Score (Gawsworth) 360

Garden of Avallaunius, The (Machen) 51, 52, 309. See also Hill of Dreams, The
Gargantua and Pantagruel (Rabelais) 37, 38, 39, 308
Gascoyne, Sir Crisp 352

Gawsworth, John 64, 185, 359-60, 362-66, 369, 377, 379, 383, 384-85, 388
Gentleman's Magazine 307
Geoffrey of Monmouth 241, 244-49, 264, 265, 270, 272, 273, 275, 282, 295, 297, 298, 300, 302, 318
Geraldus Cambrensis 282
Ghost Book, The (Asquith) 362
Gibbon, Edward 121, 124
"Gift of Tongues, The" (Machen) 364
Gissing, George 89, 90
Glastonbury 278-83, 299
Glastonbury Abbey 278, 279, 281, 293, 299-300
Glorious Mystery, The (Machen) 313, 320
Golden Bough, The (Frazer) 189
Golden Twigs (Crowley) 177
"Gold Like Grass" (Carter) 388
Goldstone, Adrian H. 132
Gothic Body, The (Hurley) 228
Grahame, Kenneth 187, 188
Grande Trouvaille, The (Machen) 66
Grant, Kenneth 175
"Great God Pan, The" (Machen) 15-16, 22, 33-34, 45, 50, 51, 68, 76, 91, 95, 104, 105, 111-12, 144-49, 151, 162, 164-66, 171, 179, 184, 186-87, 188-89, 192, 210-12, 221-36, 309, 360, 361, 366, 367, 371, 387; sexuality in 16-17, 22, 187
Great God Pan and The Inmost Light, The (Machen) 28, 90-92, 95, 115, 162, 182
"Great Return, The" (Machen) 24, 40, 215-16, 265, 320, 321
Great Return, The (Machen) 29, 54-55, 312, 317
"Great Terror, The" (Machen) 25. See also Terror, The
Green, Roger Lancelyn 90, 91
"Green Glen, The" (Buchan) 187-88
Green Round, The (Machen) 25, 217, 313, 364, 365, 371, 372, 373, 379, 389
Greenwood, Edwin 381
Greig, James C. C. 182, 185

Grey Weather: Moorland Tales of My Own People (Buchan) 182, 183–85, 186, 189, 190
Grossmith, George 336
Grossmith, Weedon 336
"Grove of Ashtaroth, The" (Buchan) 189–90
Gurdjieff, G. I. 152–53, 154

Hair under a Hat (Hogan) 62
Hamilton, William 177
Hamlet (Shakespeare) 235
A Handy Dickens (Dickens) 315
Hardy, Thomas 118
Harland, Henry 93, 186
Henry VII (King of England) 246, 299
Henry VIII (King of England) 282
Heptameron (Marguerite de Navarre) 15, 28, 40, 42, 43, 308
"Herd of Standlan, The" (Buchan) 184
Hereford Cathedral School 28, 41, 171, 185, 210, 307, 319, 322
Herbert, A. 355
Herbert, George 225–26, 229, 230–31
Herbert, Henry 57
Hermetic Order of the Golden Dawn 141–44, 178, 201, 212, 216, 224n1, 311, 369
"Hérodiade" (Mallarmé) 77
Herodotus 24, 42
Hesketh, Audrey 243, 253, 305
Hesketh, Jack 243, 251, 253, 305
Hesse, Hermann 241–42
"Hidden Mystery, The" (Machen) 361, 365, 366
Hill of Dreams, The (Machen) 15, 18, 21, 23, 29, 34–36, 39, 51, 52–54, 70, 75, 76–79, 80, 86, 95–96, 101n1, 124, 142n5, 171–72, 175, 176, 183, 188, 213, 241–42, 259n2, 307, 308, 309, 310, 311, 316, 319–26, 328
Histories (Herodotus) 24
Hieroglyphics: A Note upon Ecstasy in Literature (Machen) 23, 30, 36, 37, 39, 48–49, 51, 111, 112n3, 129–35, 161, 174, 213, 221, 310, 333

Historia Regum Britanniae (Geoffrey of Monmouth) 241, 244, 247, 264, 275, 298
Hitchcock, Alfred 217
Hodgson, William Hope 228
Hogan, J. P. 62
Hogg, Amelia 75, 142, 212, 224n1, 308, 311, 333, 384
Hollow Hills, The (Stewart) 270
Holy Grail 24, 29, 32, 51, 55, 66, 209, 215, 216, 279, 296, 320
"Holy Things, The" (Machen) 69, 213, 360, 361
Holy Wells of Wales, The (Jones) 386
Horlick's Magazine 51, 309, 334
House of Souls, The (Machen) 23, 28, 32, 33, 39, 40, 45, 50–52, 79, 103, 173, 311, 334, 367, 384
House of the Hidden Light, The (Machen-Waite) 174
Howard, John 130, 367, 369, 370, 372
Hudleston, Dorothy Purefoy 201, 311, 312, 313, 315, 334, 381
Hughes, Ted 117, 118
Hurley, Kelly 228
Hutton, Ronald 144–45
Huxley, Aldous 64
Huxley, Thomas Henry 228
Huysmans, Joris-Karl 35, 77, 78
Hydriotaphia (Browne) 317
"Hymn to Pan" (Crowley) 179

Idylls of the King (Tennyson) 55, 301, 306
Ieuan, David 306n7
"Incident of the Private Bar" (Machen) 112
"Inmost Light, The" (Machen) 17, 33, 39, 50, 51, 61, 64, 71, 76, 103n2, 104, 162, 163–66, 210, 212, 229, 309, 320
Isca Silurum 15, 52, 78, 250, 259n2, 260, 261, 263, 264, 270, 316, 321, 322, 323
Islam 213–14
Island Night's Entertainment (Stevenson) 182

"Islington Mystery, The" (Machen) 363

Jackson, Holbrook 85, 86
James, Henry 112n4
James, M. R. 93, 102, 113
James I (King of England) 246
Jennings, Hargrave 42
John Bull 179
John Buchan: The Presbyterian Cavalier (Lownie) 182
"Johnny Double" (Machen) 363
Johnson, Samuel 230
Jones, Francis 386
Jones, John Edward 307, 308, 386
Jordan-Smith, Paul 381
Joseph of Arimathea 279
Joshi, S. T. 103, 131, 200, 222
"Journey of Little Profit, A" (Buchan) 186
"Joy of London, The" (Machen) 167
Judaism 219
Jurgen (Cabell) 174

Kabbalah 214, 387, 388
Kant, Immanuel 162
Kapstein, Matthew T. 140n2
Keats, John 162
Kelticism 272, 288, 310, 318
Keynote Series 45, 68, 85, 90, 92, 93, 94, 186, 187, 189
Key to the Tarot (Waite) 101n1
Kilcher, Andreas 139
King Arthur's Avalon (Ashe) 296
Kipling, Rudyard 24
Klingopulos, G. D. 119
Knight, Richard Payne 47, 177
Knopf, Alfred A. 125, 312, 315, 316, 321, 354, 355
Konx Om Pax (Crowley) 178, 180
Krutch, Joseph Wood 369

Lady's Pictorial 68
La Gallienne, Richard 186
Lancelot (de Troyes) 275
Lane, John 78, 85, 91, 92, 93, 95, 182, 183, 186, 187, 189, 361
Langley, Hugh 96
Lawrence, D. H. 362

Le Fanu, J. Sheridan 190
Leland, John 275
Leo III (pope) 245
Leslie-McCarthy, Sage 227
Lewis, C. S. 209, 228
Liber Aleph: The Book of Wisdom or Folly (Crowley) 174
Liber Liberi vel Lapidis Lazuli (Crowley) 175
Life 51
Life and Opinions of Tristram Shandy, The (Sterne) 52
Life of Arthur Machen, The (Gawsworth) 64, 383
Light 348
Lippincott's Monthly Magazine 76, 77, 87
Literature 48, 51
Literature of Occultism and Archaeology, The 42
little people 17, 18, 20, 21, 25, 47, 190, 191, 193, 194, 195, 318, 389
Lives of the English Poets (Johnson) 230
Livre, Le 31
"A Lodging for the Night" (Stevenson) 90
Lolly Willowes (Warner) 381
London Adventure, The (Machen) 65, 103, 131, 312, 351, 367-68, 372
[London] *Evening News* 23, 24, 25, 39, 54, 55, 56, 60, 75, 86, 215, 216, 300, 312, 346, 347, 348
"Lost Club, The" (Machen) 76, 104, 105, 360
"Lost Legion, The" (Kipling) 24
Lovecraft, H. P. 17, 21, 22, 92, 102, 103, 151-52, 155, 217, 236, 316, 317, 327, 365
Lownie, Andrew 182
Louÿs, Pierre 96
"A Lucid Interval" (Buchan) 187
Lumen de Lumine (Vaughan) 228
Lyonnesse 285-88

Mabinogion 215
MacCarthy, Desmond 315
MacDonald, George 103
Machen, Arthur: as actor, 48, 49, 56, 57, 58, 75, 213, 311, 387; on Bud-

dhism, 53; childhood of, 27, 62, 199, 203, 247, 306, 307; and Christianity, 22, 134, 155, 179, 186, 201, 209-19, 223, 229, 340, 369; death of, 304, 315; on drinking, 38; and ecstasy in literature, 23, 30, 35, 37, 38, 129-35, 213, 216, 222, 223, 369; as journalist, 23, 49, 57, 68, 217, 307, 312, 314, 353-357, 363; later years of, 313, 381-389; and London, 15, 19, 28, 63, 67, 68, 167, 307-9, 326; and materialism, 15-26, 206, 223, 227, 231-32, 364; and modernity, 21, 67, 68, 155-56 181-82, 363; on music, 163; and mysticism, 134, 162, 199-206, 213, 214, 218, 225, 385; and the occult, 42, 44, 45, 46, 51, 63, 142-45, 146-47, 150, 173-80, 192-93, 210, 212, 311, 346-48, 369; and rationalism, 21, 24, 134, 364; on spiritualism, 385; on writing, 161, 163, 164

MacLeod, Fiona (pseud. of William Sharp) 186, 190
MacLeod, Kirsten 87, 88, 92
Macmillan's Magazine 182
Maggot, A (Fowles) 101n1
Magick in Theory and Practice (Crowley) 174
Magus, The (Fowles) 101n1
Malamud, Bernard 118
Mallarmé, Stéphane 77
Malory, Sir Thomas 275, 299-300
Man, Myth, and Magic (Cavendish) 243, 275n3, 278n4, 288n6
Marguerite de Navarre 15, 28, 40, 42, 43, 308
Marius the Epicurean (Pater) 80
Marriage of Heaven and Hell, The (Blake) 61
Marsden, Francis. *See* Frederick Carter
Masefield, John 382
Matthews, Brander 89
Mead, G. R. S. 179

Memoirs of Jacques Casanova, The (Casanova [tr. Machen]) 28, 46, 309, 313
"Men of the Uplands" (Buchan) 184
Merivale, Patricia 145, 236
"Midsummer" (Machen) 125, 213, 361
Milton, John 315
Miss Hargreaves (Baker) 381
Montesquieu, Charles-Louis de Secondat, Baron de la Brède et de 86
Moon Endureth, The (Buchan) 182, 187, 189, 190
"Moor Song, The" (Buchan) 190
Moore, George 311
Morris, John 268
Morte d'Arthur, Le (Malory) 275, 299-300
"Moth and the Flame, The" (Attar) 214
"Moth and the Flame, The" (Machen) 214
Moyen de Parvenir, Le (Verville) 28, 44-45, 309, 381
"Munitions of War" (Machen) 362
Murray, Margaret A. 18
Mysticism (Underhill) 201

"N" (Machen) 25, 69, 217, 218, 364, 365, 366, 367-79, 383, 384
National Liberal Club 314
National Review 93
"Nature" (Machen) 361
"Nature and the Art of Words" (Buchan) 181, 185
Navarette, Susan J. 227, 228
Neolith 311
New Arabian Nights, The (Stevenson) 18, 47, 64, 90, 104, 360
"New Christmas Carol, A" (Machen) 363
New Grub Street (Gissing) 89, 90
Nietzsche, Friedrich 144
Nollekens, Joseph 176
"No Man's Land" (Buchan) 189, 190-96
Nordau, Max 154, 205, 346
Notes and Queries (Machen) 313
Novel Now, The (Burgess) 118

408   THE SECRET CEREMONIES

"Novel of the Black Seal" (Machen) 18, 20, 47, 70, 110, 112, 182, 188, 190, 191, 193, 247-48, 389
"Novel of the Dark Valley" (Machen) 20, 105-6, 109
"Novel of the Iron Maid" (Machen) 18, 20
"Novel of the White Powder" (Machen) 18, 20, 47, 107, 177, 182, 187

Observer 214
Obsolescence of the Oracles, The (Plutarch) 144n8
Occult Review 347, 348
"On the Physical Basis of Life" (Huxley) 228
"Opening the Door" (Machen) 364, 370-71, 372, 379, 384, 386
Orghast (Hughes) 117, 118
Ornaments in Jade (Machen) 21, 75, 95, 125, 213, 361
"Outgoing of the Tide, The" (Buchan) 195
"Out of the Picture" (Machen) 25, 214, 387, 388
Owen, Alex 155
Owens, Jill Tedford 223, 236

Pagan Papers (Grahame) 187
Pall Mall Gazette 87
Palmer, Christopher 218
Pan Group 176-77, 178
Paradise Lost (Milton) 315
Paradise Regain'd (Milton) 315
"Parasite, The" (Doyle) 93
Pater, Walter 80, 86, 185
Peithnan, Stephen 370
Péladan, Joséphin 346-47
Peterley, David 67, 382
Peterley Harvest (Peterley) 67, 382
Peter Whiffle (Van Vechten) 67
Phantastes (MacDonald) 103
Philo of Alexandria 213
Philosophical Enquiry into the Origin of Our Ideas of the Sublime and Beautiful, A (Burke) 162
Pickwick Papers, The (Dickens) 30, 37, 38, 132

Picture of Dorian Gray, The (Wilde) 76-79, 87, 186, 388
Pilot 49
Place of Enchantment, The (Owen) 155
Plato 211, 213, 286
Plato and Platonism (Pater) 185
Pliny the Elder 290
Plutarch 144n8
Poe, Edgar Allan 35, 37, 66, 89-90, 370, 372, 374, 375-76
Poller, Jake 227, 228
Precious Balms (Machen) 313
Presence of Light, The (Kapstein) 140n2
Priapeia, The 178
Private Life of Sherlock Holmes, The (Starrett) 106
Procopius 195
Proust, Marcel 123
"Psychology" (Machen) 361

Quilter, Harry 92n2, 93, 112n3

Rabelais, François 28, 37, 38, 39, 43, 114, 132, 308
Radcliffe, Ann 102
Radford, C. A. Ralegh 282
Radio Times 85
"Rajah's Diamond, The" (Stevenson) 104
"Red Hand, The" (Machen) 21, 24, 28, 50, 52, 70-71, 176
Redway, George 42, 63, 177, 210
Republic (Plato) 211
"Resurrection of the Dead, The" (Machen) 51, 334
Reynolds, Aidan 218, 224n1, 227, 228, 335, 342
Richard III (King of England) 299
Richards, Grant 45, 54, 110
"Rime of True Thomas, The" (Buchan). See "Moor Song, The"
Robert Elsmere (Ward) 112
Robinson, A. Mary F. 43
"Rocking-Horse Winner, The" (Lawrence) 362
Rolle of Hampole, Richard 218
Romantics 121, 145, 240-42, 328-29

Romanz de Brut, Li (Wace) 241
"Rose Garden, The" (Machen) 213, 361
Rosicrucians, The (Jennings) 42
Runagates Club, The (Buchan) 182, 187
"Rus in Urbe" (Machen) 183
Russell, R. B. 67

St. James's Chronicle 46
St. James's Gazette 183, 360
Sassoon, Siegfried 382
Saturday Review 89
"Satyrs Gathering" (Spare) 179
Seattle, Chief 306n7, 310
Secker, Martin 60, 313
Secret Glory, The (Machen) 23, 28, 29, 56-60, 75, 103, 132, 175, 214, 312, 334, 335, 362, 377
Secret History (Procopius) 195
Secret of the Sangraal, The (Machen) 132, 168, 215
Sergeant, Philip 383
Scholar-Gipsies (Buchan) 182-83, 184, 185, 187
Schwob, Marcel 90
Shadows of Death (Stenbock) 87
Shakespeare, William 235
Sharp, William. *See* Macleod, Fiona
Shea, J. Vernon 22
Shiel, M. P. 93, 360
"Shining Pyramid, The" (Machen) 17, 18, 70, 190, 192, 193, 313, 320, 389
Shudders (Asquith) 362, 364
Sick Heart River (Buchan) 183
Sinnett, A. P. 348
Siren Land (Douglas) 176
Smith, Clark Ashton 21, 240, 327, 328
Smithers, L. C. 178
Smith's Classical Dictionary 41
Sophocles 38
"Soldiers' Rest, The" (Machen) 23
"Some Remarks on Ghost Stories" (James) 102
"Somerset's Adventure: The Superfluous Mansion" (Stevenson) 107
Spanish Civil War 155, 363

Spare, Austin Osman 178-79, 388, 389
Spengler, Oswald 154
Spenser, Edmund 241, 298, 299
Spurr, Harry 44
Squires, Mary 352, 355
Starrett, Vincent 44, 89, 106, 201, 247, 381
Stenbock, Count Eric 87
Steps to the Temple (Crashaw) 231
Sterling, George 240
Sterne, Laurence 52, 321
Stern, Philip Van Doren 316
Stevenson, Bob 107
Stevenson, Fanny van de Grift 18, 47, 90, 103-15, 360
Stevenson, Robert Louis 18, 32, 37, 47, 52, 64, 90, 92, 103-15, 118, 182, 187, 360
Stewart, Mary 270
Steppenwolf (Hesse) 242
Stonehenge 289, 291
Stonor, Oliver 76, 357, 359, 381
"Story of the Destroying Angel" (Stevenson-Stevenson) 104, 105, 106, 109
"Story of the Fair Cuban" (Stevenson-Stevenson) 104, 108
Strange Case of Dr. Jekyll and Mr. Hyde, The (Stevenson) 32, 37, 107, 187
Strange Roads (Machen) 313
Stuckrad, Kocku von 140
Study in Scarlet, A (Doyle) 106
"Suicide Club, The" (Stevenson) 105, 107, 360
Summerford, Colin 315, 351, 355, 381, 382, 383
"Summer Weather" (Buchan) 184
Supernatural and English Fiction, The (Cavaliero) 80
"Supernatural Horror in Literature" (Lovecraft) 102, 103, 316
Supernatural Tales (Buchan) 182
Swearingen, Roger G. 104
Sweetser, Wesley D. 79, 132, 221, 222, 370
Swete, Lyall 49
Symons, Arthur 87, 91

T.P.'s and Cassell's Weekly 311, 355, 356
"Table-Talk of Arthur Machen, The" (Stonor) 76
Tales of Horror and the Supernatural (Machen) 316
Taxil, Leo 146n10
Temple, The (Vaughan) 231
Temple Bar 90
"Tendebant Manus" (Buchan) 187
Tennyson, Alfred, Lord 55, 86, 301, 306
Tennyson Dictionary, A (Baker) 300
Teresa of Ávila, St. 213, 231
Terror, The (Machen) 24, 25, 40, 55–56, 217, 312, 362
Thackeray, William Makepeace 30, 37, 132, 133
Theosophical Society 152, 179
Thesaurus Incantatus: The Enchanted Treasure (Machen) 44
Things Near and Far (Machen) 29, 63, 64, 75, 76, 212, 224n1, 312, 333, 385
Thomson, John Cockburn 233
Thomson, Katherine 233
Three Impostors; or, The Transmutations, The (Machen) 18–20, 28, 46–48, 50, 52, 65–66, 75, 79, 90, 91, 93, 94, 101, 102, 104, 110–14, 167, 178, 182, 187, 210, 212, 224, 247, 309, 360
Tides Ebb Out to the Night, The (Langley) 96
Tilden-Smith, L. 355
Time Machine, The (Wells) 190
Times, The 48, 49
Times Literary Supplement 55
Tintagel 283–85
Tolkien, J. R. R. 209
"Torture" (Machen) 361, 365
Toulet, P. J. 45, 76, 223, 228
Treasure Cave, The (Asquith) 363
Treasure Island (Stevenson) 109
"Tree of Life, The" (Machen) 25, 214, 387
Tristam Shandy (Sterne) 321
"Triumph of Love, The" (Machen) 113n6
"True to Life" (Machen) 132

"Turanians, The" (Machen) 361, 363
Turner, Alfred 56, 60
Turn of the Screw, The (James) 112n4
Tyndale, William 121

Underhill, Evelyn 201, 202
Unicorn 8, 54
Unknown World 190
"Upon Nothing" (Villiers) 232
"Urban Greenery" (Buchan) 183
Uzanne, Octave 31, 46

Vanity Fair (Thackeray) 30, 37, 132
Valentine, Mark 145, 184, 187, 368
Van Vechten, Carl 67, 247
Vaughan, Henry 229, 230–31
Vaughan, Thomas 147, 227–29
veil, beyond the 29, 69, 122, 139, 140, 166, 201, 203, 211, 221, 225, 335, 339, 369, 384
Verville, Béroalde de 28, 44–45, 309, 381
Victoria (Queen of England) 304
Victorians, The (Wilson) 87
Views from the Real World (Gurdjieff) 153
Villiers, George 232, 233
Vita Merlini (Monmouth) 282, 295
Vivienne, Pierpont 311
Vizetelly, Henry 42, 91

Wace 241
Waite, A. E. 51, 66, 101n1, 142, 143, 147n10, 174, 190, 214, 215, 311, 315, 383, 387, 388, 389
Walford, Edward 47
Wandragesilaus, St. 218
War and the Christian Faith (Machen) 24, 56, 216, 219, 362
Ward, Mrs. Humphrey 111–12
Warner, Sylvia Townsend 10, 381, 382
Warre, Edmond 58–59
"Watcher by the Threshold, The" (Buchan) 187
Watcher by the Threshold and Other Tales, The (Buchan) 182, 183, 189, 190, 195
Weekly Dispatch 347

Weird Tale, The (Joshi) 103, 131
Weird Tales 365
Welcome Guest 92, 122
Wells, H. G. 94, 190
Wells, Susannah 352, 354
Wesley, Charles 340
Western Esotericism (Stuckrad) 140n1
Westminster Gazette 68
When Churchyards Yawn (Asquith) 364, 371
Whibley, Charles 52, 321
Whirlwind 360
"White People, The" (Machen) 16, 18, 21-22, 28, 33, 50, 51, 75, 111, 123, 124, 129, 174, 178, 199-206, 212, 223, 334, 335, 363, 365, 371
White People and Other Weird Stories, The (Machen) 223, 342
Wilde, Oscar 75, 76-79, 89, 186, 311, 360, 388; trial of, 87, 94, 95-97, 361
William the Conqueror (King of England) 246, 250
"William Wilson" (Poe) 66, 370, 372, 374
"Willows, The" (Blackwood) 21
Wilmot, John 232
Wilson, A. N. 87-88

Wilson, Christopher 67
"Wind in the Portico, The" (Buchan) 187, 188-89, 196
"Witchcraft" (Machen) 361
Witch-Cult in Western Europe, The (Murray) 18
Witches and Warlocks (Sergeant) 383
Witch Wood (Buchan) 195
Wits and Beaux of Society, The (Thomson-Thomson) 233
"Wonderful Woman, A" (Machen) 104, 120, 123, 126, 360
"World of Great Majesty, A" (Howard) 130
World 51
"World, The" (Vaughan) 229
World War I 24, 154, 187, 215, 216, 247, 312, 345, 362
World War II 216, 218, 314
Written in Friendship (Cumberland) 67

Yeats, W. B. 186, 311
Yellow Book 78, 85, 93, 96, 186

Zanoni (Bulwer-Lytton) 150-51
"Zero's Tale of the Explosive Bomb" (Stevenson-Stevenson) 104, 108